WHO'S
WHO
ON RADIO

Compiled by
SHEILA TRACY

World's Work Ltd · Kingswood

Acknowledgements

My grateful thanks to the following people who have given me immeasurable help in the compilation of this book.
Michael Barton, Controller BBC Local Radio; Brian Sloman and David Keighley of BBC Local Radio Publicity; Greg Truscott; and Amanda Easterbrook, my research assistant. And of course, all those people who were good enough to answer my endless list of questions without whom there would have been no Who's Who on Radio.

MUSICIANS 155

Independent Local Radio Stations

North Sound	Aberdeen	Centre Radio	Leicester
West Sound	Ayr	Radio City	Liverpool
BRMB Radio	Birmingham	Capital Radio	London
Two Counties Radio	Bournemouth	LBC	London
Pennine Radio	Bradford	Piccadilly Radio	Manchester
Southern Sound	Brighton	Metro Radio	Newcastle-upon-Tyne
Radio West	Bristol	Downtown Radio	Newtownards, Belfast
Cardiff Broadcasting	Cardiff	Radio Trent	Nottingham
Mercia Sound	Coventry	Hereward Radio	Peterborough
Radio Tay	Dundee	Plymouth Sound	Plymouth
Chiltern Radio	Dunstable	Radio Victory	Portsmouth
Radio Forth	Edinburgh	Red Rose Radio	Preston
Devonair Radio	Exeter	Radio 210	Reading
Radio Clyde	Glasgow	Radio Hallam	Sheffield
Severn Sound	Gloucester	Essex Radio	Southend-on-Sea
County Sound	Guildford	Radio Tees	Stockton-on-Tees
Moray Firth Radio	Inverness	Swansea Sound	Swansea
Radio Orwell	Ipswich	Wiltshire Radio	Swindon
Saxon Radio	Ipswich	Beacon Radio	Wolverhampton
Radio Aire	Leeds	Radio Wyvern	Worcester

BBC Local Radio Stations

Radio Brighton	Radio Lancashire	Radio Northampton
Radio Bristol	Radio Leeds	Radio Nottingham
Radio Cambridgeshire	Radio Leicester	Radio Oxford
Radio Cleveland	Radio Lincolnshire	Radio Sheffield
Radio Cornwall	Radio London	Radio Solent
Radio Cumbria	Radio Manchester	Radio Stoke on Trent
Radio Derby	Radio Medway	Radio WM (West Midlands)
Radio Devon	Radio Merseyside	Radio Guernsey
Radio Furness (Radio Cumbria)	Radio Newcastle	Radio Jersey
Radio Humberside	Radio Norfolk	

Foreword

'Little Miss Bouncer
Loved an announcer,
Down at the BBC. . .'

The Flotsam and Jetsam song from the golden days of radio, which those of you who know it will recall, ends with Little Miss Bouncer getting a letter from the wife of the announcer down at the BBC! But it was not quite so flattering a remark that prompted me to compile this book of vital statistics of radio personalities: 'Oh, you're a lot older than you sound,' said one of my 'fans' after I had sent him a photograph. I suppose everyone builds up a mental picture of the face behind the voice on the radio and when you dip into this book you'll discover just how right, or how wrong, you have been!

So, come with me behind the broadcasting scene to meet not only the DJs, but also the reporters, the commentators, the correspondents, the newsreaders and the music makers. I've divided the book into two sections, the speakers and those who provide the 'live' music on radio. As well as the BBC Network, it covers the local radio stations, both BBC and Independent and Radio Luxembourg, so wherever you live in the UK, your favourite broadcasters will almost certainly be included . . . how they started in radio, what other jobs they have done, which schools they attended, a never-to-be-forgotten moment in their careers, whether they are married and have any children.

I would like to thank everyone included for their co-operation. The response I got was tremendously encouraging and only two local radio stations, (Plymouth Sound and Beacon Radio) felt they didn't want to contribute. It's good to know that after more than three decades of regular television transmissions, radio is alive and well in the 80s and I hope this book will provide some of the facts, figures and faces that you who listen to the radio would like to know.

To all the present day Little Miss Bouncers (or Master Bouncers) this book is affectionately dedicated.

SHEILA TRACY 1983

1

CHRIS ALDRED
'You'll only get bored lying in the sun. . .'
BORN: 16th April 1942 in Chislehurst, Kent.
Father an Army officer. EDUCATED: Various
convents and forces schools abroad (14
altogether), finally at Bath High School. FIRST
JOB: Student teacher at Grittleton School,
Badminton. Has also been an actress in 'Rep'
and a clerical officer with the Ministry of
Defence. FIRST BROADCAST: May 1975 for BFBS
in Malta. 'While I was in Malta with my "RAF
Aircrew" husband, a friend said "come along
to the BFBS station and help out, you'll only get
bored lying all day in the sun!"'
Shows for BFBS in Malta included the
Lunchtime Show, the *Five O'clock Run* and
Late Bird. Two years later her husband was
posted back to the UK and she joined BBC
Radio 2 as a newsreader/announcer. Is one of
the regular presenters of *You and the Night and
the Music*.

■ Most exciting moment of career: *'Presenting
You and the Night and the Music* on July 29th,
1981, The Royal Wedding and *my* own
wedding anniversary and ending up with a
Champagne Breakfast in the canteen.'
■ A moment to remember: 'My very first "live"
interview was with the King's Singers and, as
they did a lot of touring, I thought it would be of
interest to my audience of service personnel to
ask them if they ever took their wives with
them. There was a terrible silence as they
looked askance at each other. Eventually one of
them managed some kind of answer.
Afterwards they told me that one marriage was
over, one on the rocks and another etc, etc. I
can't remember all the details now, but I'll
never ask that question again.' ■ Likes
swimming, reading, upholstery and collecting
antiques. Dislikes travelling in coaches,
smoking and full ashtrays. ■ Married to John
Aldred, has three daughters and lives in West
Sussex.

IAN ALDRED
*'Played his very first record on Radio 3 at the
wrong speed. . .'*
BORN: 1949 in Manchester. EDUCATED:
Greenock Academy. FIRST JOB: Insurance
trainee. Also worked as a sales rep. FIRST
BROADCAST: 1978. Is a newsreader/announcer
for BBC Radio Scotland and has introduced
many 'live' orchestral concerts on BBC 1,
BBC 2, Radios 3 and 4 and Radio Scotland.

■ Most exciting moment of career: 'Presenting
"live" the opening concert of the 1982
Edinburgh International Festival.'
■ A moment to remember: 'On a visit to Radio
3 in London, I played my very first record at the
wrong speed. Quite a lot of listeners noticed!'
Dislikes car wipers scraping across a dry
windscreen. ■ Lives in Edinburgh.

DAVID ALLAN
'Make mine country style'.
BORN: 7th August 1940 in Bury, Lancashire.
Father a dentist. EDUCATED: Bury Grammar
School. FIRST JOB: Assistant Stage Manager at
Manchester Library Theatre. Went on to act
and stage manage for various repertory theatres
ranging from Harrogate and Windsor to
Guildford and Canterbury, (thereby hangs a
tale!). Last job in the theatre was as Stage
Manager for the West End production of *Funny
Girl* starring Barbra Streisand in 1966. FIRST

BROADCAST: June 1966 from Radio 390, a pirate station in the Thames estuary, achieved by sheer persistence, and it did help being able to supply the Programme Controller of Radio 390 with tickets for *Funny Girl*.
Has become well known for his country music programmes: *Country Club, Countrystyle, Country Greats in Concert* for BBC Radio 2. *Country Folk* for BFBS and *Countrystyle* for the BBC World Service.
Can easily be persuaded to depart from the country scene to 'dep' for Messrs Wogan, Hamilton and Moore on Radio 2. His voice is also heard several times a week announcing for BBC Television.

■ Most exciting moment of career: Taking over the Terry Wogan Show for a month on Radio 2.
■ A moment to remember: Having done an action-packed breakfast show on Radio 390 for almost four hours, being told at the end that the transmitter hadn't been switched on, so the show had been heard by no one! ■ Likes photography and wine tasting; Dislikes getting up early and heavy metal music. ■ Married to Meg; has two sons, Simon and Robin and lives in Buckinghamshire.

LIZ ALLEN
'Thank you for your application to be a disc jockey...'
BORN: 13th September in Halifax, Yorkshire. EDUCATED: Princess Mary High School, Halifax. University of Leeds (B.A.Hons). FIRST JOB: Secretary to BBC Radio Drama Producer Alfred Bradley. Has been a member of Cunard's cruise staff on both the QE2 and the *Countess* on transatlantic crossings and Caribbean cruises: 'a bit like a Redcoat only in evening dress'. Has worked as a TV extra and as a freelance journalist. Has had one novel published and is working on a second. FIRST BROADCAST: 'As a small barking dog and a distant hooting owl in a couple of radio plays! But my first proper broadcast was in September 1975 on Radio Pennine's opening night, presenting their *Late Night Show*, the most

terrifying moment of my life so far. I had written to Pennine whilst a drama production secretary, after the franchise had been granted but before the station was fully staffed, asking if they had any vacancies as a producer. They wrote back saying "thank you for your application to be a disc jockey, please come to an audition". So I went.' While with Pennine Radio she presented *Artweek*, the *Rock Show* and the *Album Review Show*. She then joined BBC Radio Leeds as the co-presenter and radio-car roving reporter of the *Saturday Show*. And after a few months, in the spring of 1979, joined BBC Radio 2 as a newsreader/announcer. Is one of the regular presenters of *You and the Night and the Music*.

■ Most exciting moment of career: 'Presenting my first programme on a national network.' ■ Likes photography, freelance magazine journalism, songwriting and pottering in the garden. Dislikes pretentious people, coffee and Danish Blue cheese.
■ Married to a BBC engineer and lives in Buckinghamshire.

RICHARD ALLINSON
'Made it straight from university...'
BORN: 12th October 1958. Father a marketing consultant. EDUCATED: Lancaster University B.A.(Hons) in Economics and Law. FIRST JOB: Working for Capital Radio. FIRST BROADCAST: On Capital Radio in 1980, having joined straight from University where he had been involved in University radio for three years. He presents the *Weekday Early Show* and also a one hour magazine on Sundays called *Sunday Supplement*. Has filled in on the *Lunchtime* and *Breakfast Shows* for Nicky Horne and Graham Dene, and presented a special six-week series called *Small Beginnings*, tracing the rise to stardom of Kate Bush, the Boomtown Rats etc.

■ Most exciting moment of career: 'Joining Capital, I was scared stiff! Watching the Help a London Child total reach £90,000 while I was on air with Roger Scott and opening the 1981 Capital Jazz Festival at Knebworth Park with 20,000 people!' ■ A moment to remember: Reading a quote from Capital Radio's 1983 Diary: 'Richard Allinson is every would-be DJ's hero. He's made it straight from being a University DJ. The "demo" tape he sent in was considered one of the very best Capital had heard in years.' (Capital's words, not mine!) [OK Richard, I believe you, 'though there's many that wouldn't!] ■ Likes tennis, running, photography and anything to do with cars. Dislikes queues, being late, Ford Capri's [can't offer you a lift then!] and records that jump, plus 4am. ■ Is a bachelor, doesn't think he's got any children and lives in West London.

He is the author of several books and articles on modern history, international relations and current affairs. FIRST BROADCAST: An Interval talk on Radio 3 in 1978. Since then he has written and presented The Profession of Intelligence (documentary series in history of British Intelligence); More Than A Game? (social history of football); Christmas 1941, 1942 and 1943 on Radio 4; An Exalted and Exceptional Destiny (career of De Gaulle); The Night of the Miracle (Hitler's rise to power) and File on Four. All of which resulted in six appearances on Pick of the Week! Television credits include Timewatch BBC 2 and Today's History Channel 4.

LIZ AMBLER
'With BBC Radio Leeds from the "off"...'
BORN: 6th April 1947. EDUCATED: Bradford Girls Grammar School. FIRST JOB: Junior secretary with the BBC. FIRST BROADCAST: June 1968 in the very first programme on BBC Radio Leeds. Since then has presented most of Radio Leeds programmes apart from sport. Presents the mid-morning show West Riding.

■ Most exciting moment of career: 'Doing a "live" commentary for combined N.E. local radio on the Pope's visit to York, from a 40-foot-high hydraulic platform.' Dislikes jargon. ■ Married to Chris Ambler, has three daughters and lives in West Yorkshire.

CHRISTOPHER ANDREW
'Wearing the right kind of blazer...'
BORN: 23rd July 1941 in Bourne, Lincolnshire. Father an accountant. EDUCATED: Norwich School. Corpus Christi College, Cambridge. B.A. (First Class Hons. History) 1962; M.A, Ph.D. 1963. FIRST JOB: University Lecturer. Senior Tutor at Corpus Christi College, Cambridge, he is the Editor of 'The Historical Journal' and adviser Commons Select Committee on Education, Science and the Arts.

■ Most exciting moment of career: 'Getting a job at Cambridge University. My most exciting moment in the BBC was probably finding a 1942 radio talk in the archives by a Soviet journalist, later discovered to be Blunt's KGB control. It contains the remarkable statement: "Of course the Soviet Intelligence Service is one of the best in the world." (a joke at the expense of the BBC which must have amused the KGB no end.) ■ A moment to remember: 'During the Commons' fuss over Fagin's visit to the Royal Bedchamber and breaches of Buckingham Palace security in the summer of 1982, I visited the House of Commons to interview several well known politicians. I was allowed in without producing any evidence of identity or being asked to open a very large brief case capable of containing enough explosive to finish the job Guy Fawkes began. I asked Roy Hattersley, the Shadow Home Secretary, why. He replied: "Security round this building is almost based on the assumption that when the IRA come they will speak with thick Cork accents, have dirty fingernails, red faces, thick boots and drive a 1958 Ford. You, on the other hand, are wearing a Cambridge blazer."' ■ Likes living in Cambridge and getting away from Cambridge. Dislikes long committee meetings. ■ Married to Jenny Garratt, has one son, Charles and two daughters, Emma and Lisa.

DICKIE ARBITER
'From Africa to AM. . .'

BORN: 25th September 1940 in London.
EDUCATED: Preparatory School, Wokingham,
Berkshire. College in London. FIRST JOB: Acting
and stage managing in what was the Federation
of Rhodesia and Nyasaland, South Africa and
later in the UK. FIRST BROADCAST: 1959, a
Youth Programme with the Federal
Broadcasting Corporation. 'I was in an amateur
stage production and was asked by the
manager of the regional radio station if I would
be interested in auditioning as a freelance
contributor. Television and radio news
reporting followed in what was then Rhodesia,
now Zimbabwe. On returning to the UK, he
joined LBC in London presenting *Weekend AM*
and also news reading for Independent Radio
News. Is the organizer and presenter of Special
Events and Outside Broadcasts for LBC News
Radio and Court Correspondent for IRN.

■ Most exciting moment of career: 'Organizing
the coverage and commentating on the Royal
Wedding in July 1981.' ■ A moment to
remember: 'A quarter of the way through the
breakfast show, *Weekend AM*, when my voice
began to disappear. I battled on and managed
to finish the three-hour stint which included a
number of "live" interviews in the studio as
well as reading "on-hour" Network News
bulletins.' ■ Likes horse riding, tennis and
reading. Dislikes moaners. Is divorced, and has
one child.

DAVID ARSCOTT
'First novel out in 1983. . .'

BORN: 9th December 1942 in London.
EDUCATED: Hertford College Oxford. FIRST JOB:
With the 'Investor's Chronicle' in London. Was
financial journalist with the 'London Evening
Standard' followed by a spell in South America
working as a journalist on the 'Daily Journal' of
Caracas, Venezuela. Has edited for a house
magazine in Somerset and reported for a local
evening newspaper while preparing for

University as a mature student. FIRST
BROADCAST: October 1974, having applied for
a job with local radio on coming down from
University. Produces and presents BBC Radio
Brighton's *Sussex Scene* each weekday
covering current affairs and all aspects of life in
Sussex.

■ Most exciting moment of career: Has his first
novel coming out in 1983 – that could well be
it. ■ Married to Pauline, has four children and
lives in Sussex.

MICHAEL ASPEL
'Handled Miss World superbly . . .'

BORN: 12th January 1933 in London.
EDUCATED: Emanuel School, London. FIRST
JOB: A tea-boy in a publishing house. Has also
tried his hand as a labourer, a gardener, a
salesman and a radio actor. FIRST BROADCAST:
A 1954 *Children's Hour* play from Cardiff.
Having been involved in amateur dramatics, he
knocked on the door of a well-known actress,
got the name of a producer, asked for an
audition and was on the air within a few weeks.
[So, that's how it's done!] From radio acting he
became a television announcer in the West
Region which led to him becoming a BBC
Television newsreader, perhaps one of the best
they have ever had. A wide variety of television
shows followed . . . a long spell as the compère
of the BBC's *Crackerjack; Ask Aspel*, a sort of
forerunner of *Jim'll Fix It*. He was also the
compère for Miss World for several years,
which he handled quite superbly and which

nobody else has managed to come within an ace of, before or since. He crossed over to the 'other side' in Sept 1974 joining Capital Radio for whom he now presents a daily show. On television, he presents the *Six O'clock Show* for London Weekend TV and *Give Us a Clue* for Thames TV.

■ Most exciting moment of career: Having a drink in the BBC Club with the Mayor of Toytown. ■ A moment to remember: 'I was once attacked by a sex mad St. Bernard on a "live" television programme. We became good friends'. [And I remember the time when we were working on *A Spoonful of Sugar*, a sort of *Jim'll Fix it* in hospitals! We were in deepest Shropshire, and as we weren't expected to finish filming until late, we had all been booked into an hotel. But things went well and by 4pm we were through. I announced I was going home. 'You're going to phone your old man first?' said Michael. 'No, I'll give him a surprise' I said. I shall never forget the look on his face!] ■ Likes writing, the cinema, reading, travel catalogues and good food guides. Dislikes machinery. ■ Married to actress Elizabeth Power, has one child, plus four from previous marriages and lives in Surrey.

RICHARD AUSTIN
'Chorister at Winchester Cathedral. . .'
BORN: 22nd May 1948 in Windsor, Berkshire. Father a chartered accountant. EDUCATED: Winchester Cathedral Choir School. Ardingly College, Sussex. Bede College, Durham. The Open University. FIRST JOB: Teacher. Joined the BBC as a radio producer in Further Education. Also worked as an instructor in the BBC's Local Radio Training Unit. FIRST BROADCAST: As a chorister in 1958! As a student broadcaster in 1968 and in 1970 on the staff of BBC Radio Durham. Is the presenter/producer of *A.M.*, BBC Radio Cumbria's breakfast show.

■ A moment to remember: 'Producing a "live" two-hour programme from the 3,000-foot

summit of Skiddaw in the Lake District on August Bank Holiday 1981. During a Mountain Rescue demonstration, the down draught from an RAF Sea King helicopter blew away the studio tent and also caused the pack ponies, carrying all the Outside Broadcast gear to the top of the mountain, to bolt. However, the programme stayed on the air!' ■ Married to Margaret and has two sons.

JACK BAKER
'Studio striptease. . .'
BORN: 16th June 1947 in Oldham, Lancashire. Father a master baker. EDUCATED: Stockport Grammar School. Pembroke College Cambridge. Manchester Polytechnic. FIRST JOB: Administrative assistant at the Textile Institute in Manchester. Then went on to sell encyclopaedias; became a promoter of little theatre projects and discos; lecturer in English and Media Studies and Drama; a petrol pump attendant; a landscape gardener; an advertising executive and a club DJ which led to. . . FIRST BROADCAST: Radio Manchester in 1973 as part of the *New Voices* audition series for club DJs. He then applied to virtually the last station in the first wave of Independent Local Radio stations, Pennine Radio. The station didn't want DJs but 'Presenters', so he was hired as Julius K. Scragg. Presented the *Games Show* on Pennine Radio which in 1981 was nominated the Best Light Entertainment programme in local radio. Is now a producer at BBC Radio Sheffield, presenting the *Afternoon Shows* from Monday to Thursday, *The Sixties Club* (pop in the 60s) and the *Quiz Show* on Sundays.

■ Most exciting moment of career: 'When during the summer run of the *Games Show* I persuaded over 300 students to turn up in fancy dress outside Pennine Radio at 3 o'clock in the morning.' ■ A moment to remember: 'During the 1977 charity auction on Pennine Radio (where the DJs did various stunts and sold various items like colour TVs and washing machines to the highest bidder, to raise

6

money). I came up with the unique idea of doing a sponsored 'strip-tease' on the radio. We asked the listeners to pledge money – £10 per shoe. £15 per sock – right up to £200 for my underpants. Within 20 minutes, we'd raised over £1,000 and I was stark naked, with the entire staff of the radio station crowding into master control to see what they could see. The Managing Director took a full-frontal photo of me (with a carefully positioned 12" single to hide my bits and pieces), and the next thing I knew was that the "Daily Star" carried the photograph together with the story of how we'd raised all this money, under the caption "Superman He Ain't, but he's got a heart of gold". I didn't know whether to be pleased or annoyed at their description of my rather weedy frame!' ■ Likes radio, computing, music and writing. Dislikes incompetence, caffeinated coffee, and prejudice. ■ Married to Angela, has one child and lives in South Yorkshire.

PETE BAKER
'Shorts in summer, scarf in winter. . .'
BORN: 1st June 1955 in London. EDUCATED: Farnborough Grammar School. Bath University (electronics and radio). FIRST JOB: University Radio in Bath/BBC World Service. He was on what is known as a 'Sandwich' course at University: six months there followed by six months at Bush House for the World Service. He sneaked into the studios one weekend and recorded a 'demo' tape which got him a job with Piccadilly Radio just one month later. While at Piccadilly Radio has presented everything from *Nitebeat* to the kid's show *Tripe and Onions*, to *Rock Relay* to the *Hit 30 Show* etc. Is head of music at Piccadilly and presents their *261-AM* show Monday to Friday.

■ Most exciting moment of career: Interviewing the stars – Abba, Genesis, Blondie – and 'I love my yearly month-long visits to 03 International, a Viennese Station where I do the *Breakfast Show* in English although the technicians only speak German. (I'm learning).' ■ A moment

to remember: 'Sitting in the studio at Piccadilly Radio dressed in shorts in the summer and a scarf in the winter. Not that the temperature ever varies, it just puts me in the right mood'. ■ Likes writing music (has his own studio with three synthesizers), reading and outdoor sports. Dislikes smoke and loud noise. Discos/Niteclubs/pubs and bad music. ■ Married to Sally, has two kittens and lives in Trafford, Manchester.

RICHARD BAKER
'The out-of-work actor who took a job as an announcer. . .'
BORN: 15th June 1925 in Willesden, London. Father a plasterer. EDUCATED: Kilburn Grammar School. Peterhouse, Cambridge. FIRST JOB: 1948 as an actor in Birmingham Rep. The following year he became a schoolmaster at Wilson's School, Camberwell, London. FIRST BROADCAST: A speech of Aeneas from Shakespeare's *Troilus and Cressida* in Italian for the BBC's Italian service, when at Cambridge. 'In 1950 as an out-of-work actor, I wrote to the BBC and they offered me a job as an announcer. I thought I would do it for six months, and I have stayed ever since!' He started as an announcer for the BBC Third Programme 1950–53. In 1954 he became a newsreader for BBC Radio and in 1957 became the first newsreader on television, a job he was to hold for over a quarter of a century! He was named TV Newscaster of the Year by the Radio Industries Club in 1972, 74 and 79. But apart from being a well known face on the screen, he has built up an enormous following on radio over the years with such programmes as *These You Have Loved* and *Bakers Dozen*. Has been presenting *Start the Week with Richard Baker* since 1970 and *Bakers Dozen* since 1976. He has written several books including 'Here is the News', 'The Magic of Music', 'Richard Baker's Music Guide' and 'Mozart'. Was awarded the OBE in 1976 and also holds the Royal Navy Reserve decoration, RD.

■ Most exciting moment of career: (My radio

career) 'Introducing *Start the Week* from HMS Hermes at sea off Iceland.' ■ A moment to remember: 'In my early newsreading days on Radio, I was on the early morning shift and sleeping in a certain office where there was a clock which ticked every thirty seconds. At about 1am I at last managed to stop it. The next morning I got up at about 5.30, but the clocks in the corridor said 1am. So did the clock in the canteen, so did the clock in the studio. I had stopped every single clock in Broadcasting House and they had been searching all night for the culprit.' ■ Likes sailing and walking. Dislikes pomposity. ■ Married to Margaret, has two sons, Andrew and James, and lives in Hertfordshire.

RICHARD ANTHONY BAKER
'Changing sides. . .'

BORN: 2nd September 1946 in Leigh-on-Sea, Essex. Father Will Keogh, the comedian. EDUCATED: Westcliff High School for Boys. FIRST JOB: Reporter on the 'Southend Standard'. Has also played the tuba in traditional jazz bands. From working on newspapers he joined the BBC External Services News department at Bush House. FIRST BROADCAST: *Spin Off*, a Radiophonic Workshop series which he presented on BBC Radio London. Since then he has written and presented several series of programmes for Radio 2, including *Top of the Bill, Anything for a Laugh* and *The Comediennes*; and a series for Radio 3, *Altogether Now*. He has also produced *Six Continents* for Radio 3 and *International Assignment* for Radio 4. From spending many years behind the microphone for the BBC, he is now proving he has the ideas and the personality to be in front of the microphone and is using his middle name in order to avoid confusion with his famous namesake!

■ Likes history.   ■ Lives in Essex.

KENT BARKER
'Gate crashed a Hollywood reception. . .'

BORN: 14th June 1953 in London. Father a theatre/film critic on the 'Evening News'. EDUCATED: Felsted School, Essex. The Choate School, Connecticut, USA. Crown Woods, London. FIRST JOB: Mechanic on pre-war Austin Sevens. Has worked as a delivery driver for an off-licence; a door to door salesman and has worked in the movie industry in Hollywood . . . well really cleaning out cinemas at night! FIRST BROADCAST: On a college radio station in Los Angeles where he had a regular weekly show, but guaranteed no listeners. 'I used to offer money to people to phone in but no one ever did.' He became a professional broadcaster by borrowing a tape recorder, gate-crashing a reception for *That's Entertainment*, and selling an interview with Gene Kelly and Liza Minnelli to Capital Radio. On his return to the UK, he pestered editors and producers and wrote to every local radio station in the country, before landing a job as a reporter for Radio Tees. He then joined a freelance agency, North East News, and from there came south as a reporter for the *World at One* and *PM*. As a BBC Radio News reporter he is heard on all the news and current affairs programmes.

■ Most exciting moment of career: 'Parachuting with thirty MPs and trying to record a commentary at the same time.' [I think he means Military Police, or do we have thirty brave Members of Parliament?] ■ Likes renovating old houses. Dislikes renovating old houses. ■ Lives in London.

PETER BARKER
'As a chorister his voice training started at eight years old. . .'

BORN: In Nottinghamshire. EDUCATED: Southwell Cathedral Choir School. FIRST JOB: Actor. FIRST BROADCAST: 1962. He became a BBC Radio announcer when announcers worked across all the networks, Home, Light

and Third. When Radios 1,2,3 and 4 came into being he chose Radio 3 and is a Radio 3 newsreader/announcer.

■ Married to Eileen, has two daughters and lives in London.

SUSIE BARNES
'I'm a BBC Baby...'

BORN: Billingborough, Lincolnshire. Father a builder. EDUCATED: Kesteven & Sleaford High School for Girls. City of London College. FIRST JOB: A BBC secretary. 'I'm a BBC Baby'. She joined straight from college and after a spell in administration, became a production secretary in Talks and Current Affairs, then Popular Music and Light Entertainment, working on the final series of *Round the Horne.* FIRST BROADCAST: Reading listeners' letters on *Woman's Hour.* Radio 1 shows have included *Wheels* and *Staying Alive.* Has presented music shows on Radio 2 and on Radio London has worked on the breakfast show *Rush Hour* as well as magazine and phone-in programmes. Is the Action Girl on the *Tony Blackburn Show* on Radio London.

■ Most exciting moment: 'Several . . . having lunch with Cary Grant; flying Concorde; driving round Brand's Hatch with Stirling Moss and passing my driving test, after a series on Radio 1 on learning to drive.' ■ Likes going to the cinema, reading and following Queen's Park Rangers FC. Adores travelling abroad. ■ Lives in London.

NICK BARRACLOUGH
'Professional musician to DJ...'

BORN: 22nd May 1951 in Cambridge. Father a teacher. EDUCATED: Cambridgeshire High School for Boys. FIRST JOB: Office boy at University College (now Wolfson College), Cambridge. Has been singer and guitarist with several groups including Baby Whale and Telephone Bill and the Smooth Operators. FIRST BROADCAST: In 1974, playing banjo for Pete Sayers in *Folk on Two.* Has made many television and radio appearances as a musician. His television credits as a presenter include The Cambridge Folk Festival for BBC 2. Presents the weekday afternoon magazine programme, the Saturday morning record show and a weekly specialist music programme for BBC Radio Cambridge.

■ Most exciting moment of career: 'Standing on a small platform with a cameraman on a 50-foot hoist at the Cambridge Folk Festival, trying to look relaxed.' ■ Likes playing the guitar, now he is no longer a professional musician, and playing with his 1962 Mercedes. Dislikes impoliteness. ■ Married to Anne Livingstone Baker and lives in Cambridgeshire.

SIMON BATES
'Instant hair-do for the cameras...'

BORN: In Birmingham. EDUCATED: Grammar School, Newport, Salop. FIRST JOB: Artificial Insemination of animals. FIRST BROADCAST: 1966 on a radio station in San Francisco. He joined the BBC in 1973 as a Radio 2 announcer/newsreader. He went freelance in 1977 when he joined Radio 1 and has had a daily show ever since. Television credits include *Top of the Pops* and *Food and Drink*. Has written a novel under a pseudonym which he won't reveal as he wants people to take it seriously!

■ Most exciting moment of career: 'Being kissed on the cheek by Monica Sims.'
■ A moment to remember:' During a television O.B on Epsom Downs, 30 seconds to go to transmission with my hair blowing all over the place in the wind, I grabbed a can of hair spray and gave a quick squirt. There was only one thing wrong, it wasn't hair spray – it was shaving foam!' ■ Likes horses, the cinema and books. ■ Dislikes people who wear cravats, double breasted blazers with yachting motifs and shout 'play that thing' in jazz pubs on Sunday afternoons. ■ Married to Carolyn, has one daughter, Nicola and lives in Surrey.

MICHAEL BATH
'Uncovered a housing scandal. . .'
BORN: 21st April 1945 in Gillingham, Kent.
EDUCATED: Gillingham Grammar School. Manchester University (drama department). FIRST JOB: English and Drama teacher in South London secondary schools. Was a reporter on the 'Western Daily Press' in Bristol. News producer for Bristol Channel cable television station. Editor 'Preview' magazine, Bristol. Editor 'New Theatre' magazine. FIRST BROADCAST: October 1958 being interviewed on children's playwriting competition television programme *Write it Yourself*, after winning three times. 'In 1970 I suggested to BBC Bristol that I talk about my thesis on the history of the city's Little Theatre. It was broadcast as a six-part dramatized serial.' From Radio Bristol he moved to BBC Radio Medway where he presented the award winning edition of *Newstide*. Other programmes for Radio Medway include *Midway* and *Mid-Kent Mirror*. He is a news producer for Radio Medway.

■ Most exciting moment of career: 'Uncovering a housing scandal in Bristol in 1975.' ■ Likes the theatre and book-collecting. ■ Married to Lynette Cronin, has one child and lives in Kent.

DAVID BELLAN
'A strong personal interest in the arts. . .'
For two years ran an English Radio Station covering the Middle East from Jeddah in Saudi Arabia. On his return to the UK presented and contributed to many programmes, mainly for the BBC, including *Today, Start the Week, Nightride.* Joined Radio 2 as a newsreader/announcer in 1974 and presented their twice weekly film magazine *Star Sound* for many years. World Service programmes include *The Lively Arts*, and *Science in Action*. Because of a strong personal interest in the arts, especially dance, he has been making increasing contributions on that theme to such programmes as Radio 2's *Round Midnight* and *Outlook* on the World Service.

■ Likes playing the piano, cooking and travel.

JON BENYON
'BFBS to local Radio. . .'
BORN: 22nd February 1950 in Swansea, South Wales. Father a steelworker. EDUCATED: Hazel Leys School, Corby; Kettering Tech; London University. FIRST JOB: At the Ministry of Defence, Warminster, Wiltshire. Has also been a teacher for the Inner London Education Authority. FIRST BROADCAST: British Forces

Broadcasting Service in Germany. Whilst teaching with the ILEA, he had provided taped programmes for the Education Department at BBC Radio London and it was through this that he obtained a post with BFBS in Germany. While with them he presented *Family Favourites*. Back home as a fully fledged broadcaster, he presented *Home Run* and *If You Don't Get up You'll Miss It* for BBC Wales. He now presents *Start the Day*, the early show on BBC Radio Northampton.

■ Most exciting moment of career: Presenting a *Down Your Way* programme from the military train from West Berlin to West Germany and presenting the very first programme to be broadcast on Radio Northampton.
■ A moment to remember: Recording a conversation with the then Prime Minister Harold Wilson during a tour of Number 10 Downing Street. ■ Likes horses, fast cars and painting. Dislikes getting up early in the morning. ■ Is a bachelor and lives in Northamptonshire.

MICHAEL BERKELEY
'Next, a piece by the old man. . .'
BORN: 29th May 1948 in London. Father, the composer Lennox Berkeley. EDUCATED: Westminster Cathedral Choir School. The Oratory School. The Royal Academy of Music. FIRST JOB: Organist in a pop group called Seeds of Discord. Has also worked as a journalist, a dishwasher, a farmer and a phlebotomist. FIRST BROADCAST: A music talk on the BBC World Service in 1969. As a result of having several interviews with musicians published in the 'Observer' and the 'Listener', was invited to contribute to *Record Review* on Radio 3. Was a Radio 3 announcer from 1974–79 before becoming a freelance composer and broadcaster contributing to such programmes as *Kaleidoscope*, and *Mid Week*. Is one of the regular presenters of *Mainly For Pleasure* on Radio 3. He composed the music for *Vision of Piers Ploughman* series and *The Romance of the Rose.*

■ Most exciting moment of career: 'The Robert Mayer Centenary Concert from the Royal Festival Hall when I had to ad lib "live" for fifteen minutes; also introducing a "live" satellite relay of *La Traviata* from the Met on television and Radio 3.' ■ A moment to remember: 'The problem of how to go about introducing my father's music as a Radio 3 announcer – "Next, a piece by the old man!"' ■ Likes squash, reading, walking and farming. ■ Married to Deborah Rogers and lives in London.

COLIN BERRY
'Sometimes referred to as Wallace Beery. . .'
BORN: 29th January 1946 in Welwyn Garden City, Hertfordshire. Father a company director. EDUCATED: Wembley Grammar School. FIRST JOB: Slotting commercial air time for Granada Television in 1963. Has also sold commercial air time for Westward TV; was concerned with administration of Radio Caroline; a short spell in music publishing. FIRST BROADCAST: 1965 on Radio Caroline (South) newsreading and presenting sponsored programmes. 'I had always wanted to be a broadcaster and I auditioned for Radio Caroline while working in their admin department. Within a couple of weeks I was sent to the ship to take over the news bulletins when a presenter was taken ill.' In 1971 he became an announcer for HTV in Cardiff and the following year joined the BBC to work on programme promotions for Radio 1. In 1973 he joined Radio 2 as a newsreader/announcer and has presented just about every DJ slot on the network as well as such programmes as *Two's Best*, *Radio 2 Top Tunes*, *Band Parade*, *Europe 70/80* series, *Gala Night*, *The Happy Hour*. He has deputized for Terry Wogan, Jimmy Young and many others. He is a regular spokesman/chairman of juries for *A Song for Europe* and the Eurovision Song Contest. Presents *Golden Days*, a weekly series for BFBS and for Radio 2, is the chairman of European Pop Jury and one of the regular presenters of *You and the Night and the Music.*

■ Most exciting moment of career: 'October 1980 co-presenting *Top of the Pops* with Peter Powell on BBC 1, the same week as I was deputizing for Terry Wogan on Radio 2. Also, appearing as one of six mystery guests on Bruce Forsyth's *Generation Game* in the early 70s.' ■ Likes motoring, walking and a good pint of real ale. Dislikes traffic jams, bad timekeepers and pressurized beer. ■ Married to Sandra and lives in Hertfordshire.

MICHAEL BILLINGTON
'One really felt one was going to the source...'
BORN: 16th November 1939 in Leamington Spa, Warwickshire. Father a hospital finance officer. EDUCATED: Warwick School. St. Catherine's College, Oxford. FIRST JOB: Trainee journalist on the 'Liverpool Post and Echo' (1961–62). Was film critic of the 'Illustrated London News' and the 'Birmingham Post' for 14 years. Writes on arts subjects for the 'New York Times' and the 'Australian'. Has been drama critic of the 'Guardian' since 1971. Has written three books including 'The Modern Actor' (1973) and 'The Guiness Book of Theatre Facts and Feats'. (1982). FIRST BROADCAST: May 1965 Review of a Charles Wood play *Meals on Wheels* for Radio 3's *Arts Commentary*. 'I had written letters to producers of radio arts programmes. I had an instant reply from Philip French who read some of my published reviews and took a gamble on me. From then on I did a number of reviews for him and gradually moved into the business of presenting.' Radio programmes include *Options* and *Scan* for Radio 4, *Theatre Call* for the BBC World Service. Occasional appearances on *Woman's Hour, Stop the Week, Start the Week, Round Midnight* (Radio 2) etc. Presents *Kaleidoscope* on Radio 4, *Critics Forum* on Radio 3 and *Meridian* on the World Service.

■ Most exciting moment of career: 'Interviewing Lord Olivier for *Kaleidoscope* in

1982. After an amiable, discursive lunch at Broadcasting House, we turned on the microphone and out came his sharp, clear, affectionate reminiscences of Ralph Richardson (the programme was an 80th birthday tribute) and of his own astonishing career. One really felt one was going to the source'. ■ A moment to remember: 'Like interviewing Gore Vidal who, as the producer changed tapes, asked me how Rachel was. I said, well, as far as I knew but I wasn't actually married to her. Gore then insisted that he had dinner with us a few months previously. I gently explained that I was not Kevin Billington (who is married to Rachel) but Michael Billington. Unfazed, he looked me up and down and said, "Ah, I thought you'd filled out a bit."' ■ Likes cricket, travel and work. Dislikes swimming, DIY and people who walk or cycle listening to head sets. ■ Married to Jeanine Bradlaugh, has one child and lives in London.

THERESE BIRCH
'Night Extra on LBC...'
BORN: 15th April 1954 in Surrey. EDUCATED: St. Maurs Convent, Weybridge. FIRST JOB: Reporter on the 'Surrey Herald'. FIRST BROADCAST: Reading a children's story on LBC. Since then has presented Granada TV's *Saturday Morning TV Show* and *Making the Most of* for Channel 4. Broadcasts mostly on LBC, presenting Children's, and Magazine programmes also phone-ins. Produces and presents *Night Extra* on LBC.

■ Likes music and horse riding.

TONY BLACKBURN
'Started with the pirates...'
BORN: 29th January 1943 in Guildford Surrey. Father a doctor. EDUCATED: Millfield School, Street, Somerset. FIRST JOB: Guitarist and singer with the Ian Ralfini Orchestra at the Bournemouth Pavilion. FIRST BROADCAST: August 1964 on Radio Caroline South, after

answering an advertisement in the 'New Musical Express'. Presented their *Big Line Up* and their *Breakfast Show*. Moved to another pirate station Radio London (not the current BBC station!) and presented their *Breakfast Show*. He then did some shows for Radio Luxembourg and also the *Midday Show* for the old BBC Light Programme. Opened up Radio 1 in 1967 with the *Breakfast Show*. Later moved to the 9–12 spot and the 2.30 to 5.30 spot on Radio 1. Presented *Junior Choice* on Radio 2. Now has a daily show on BBC Radio London from 9am to 12 and on Radio 1, the *Tony Blackburn Saturday* and *Sunday Shows* from 8am to 10am.

■ Most exciting moment of career: Joining Radio Caroline and opening up BBC Radio 1. ■ Likes collecting films on video. Dislikes red tape. ■ Was married to actress Tessa Wyatt, now divorced, has one son Simon.

ALVIN BLOSSOM
'He'll be with you at Alvin Blossom time...'
BORN: 'I really can't remember, I was only tiny at the time.' EDUCATED: St. Bede's Grammar School and Bradford Technical College. FIRST JOB: Working in a local bakery on a Saturday, packing crumpets (honestly!) After leaving school he worked as a wages clerk in a mill. Then came night school, business studies and eventually a post as Divisional Financial Accountant of Initial Services in Bradford. FIRST BROADCAST: On hospital radio at the General

Infirmary, Leeds. Getting into the 'big time' involved lots of 'Don't ring us, we'll ring you', but eventually four trial shows materialized on Radio Hallam. He was short-listed but was told he didn't have enough experience. But it was BBC Radio Leeds who gave him the chance to learn, the first year behind the scenes, then trails, the odd Bank Holiday show and eventually producing a teenage show. 'Getting my teeth into the teenage magazine show was marvellous experience.' Now produces and presents *On Your Way* on BBC Radio Leeds, Monday to Friday . . . 'Hard work but good fun!' Has been described as Local Radio's zaniest presenter.

■ Most exciting moment of career: 'Two really, fronting five audience shows for teenagers with very open, frank conversations with MPs, DHSS, MSC, sports people on the panel; and landing the afternoon spot on Radio Leeds.' ■ A moment to remember: 'Well, being a very shy sort of guy, I tend to lean heavily on "others" when broadcasting. Take "Arthur Car Park" (I wish you would), he butts in through the tannoy system with monotonous regularity complaining about the temperature outside etc. "Rene in reception" (they're married by the way) does the same, not to mention Geoff Tallboy the manager. There are exceptions. Croyther (he's my butler) brings in refreshments, plays piano and guitar for the "viewers" (I prefer to cal them viewers) and doesn't mind too much if I tell him off. It's all very friendly . . . and rather different'. ■ Likes books, films, travelling, my house, and fresh air. Dislikes naggers and braggers. ■ Married to 'Pardon?'. ■ Lives in West Yorkshire.

CHRIS BLOUNT
'First to be heard on Radio Cornwall...'
BORN: 17th July 1943 in Newquay, Cornwall. Father a Post Office official. EDUCATED: Pendennis School, Newquay. Plympton Grammar School. FIRST JOB: A technical operator for the BBC at Bush House. He worked his way up in the BBC moving from

Bush House to Television Centre as a cameraman. Then to BBC Television in Plymouth as a floor manager. FIRST BROADCAST: 1969 on *Today in the South West* reporting on pilot gigs at Newquay. Moved to BBC Radio Oxford in 1972 as a producer/presenter. Returned to Plymouth two years later to produce *Morning Sou' West* and during the next six years made it the West Country's most popular morning radio show. He has now moved further south-west to Truro to present *Coast to Coast* on one of the newest local radio stations, Radio Cornwall.

■ Most exciting moment of career: 'Being the first voice to be heard on BBC Radio Cornwall at 0625 on 17th January 1983, arriving at the studio building, on the banks at Phoenix Wharf, by boat.' ■ A moment to remember: 'A *Morning Sou' West* April 1st spoof production in which the presenter and other contributors were supposedly driving from Plymouth to Looe via Tavistock, Launceston and Liskeard in a radio car. Along the way they "met" people (who had been pre-recorded in the correct location). Presenter & Co were actually broadcasting throughout from our car park and supposedly ended up on the beach at Looe where Tony Soper had discovered some amazing fossils which were being carried from afar by birds (also pre-recorded). There were dozens of irate calls from listeners who had come out to meet us along the way!' ■ Likes model railways, boating and walking. Dislikes over-zealous and exaggerated news reporting. ■ Married to Kay, has three children and lives in Cornwall.

announcer, then Head of Presentation for the British Forces Network in Hamburg. After demobilization, he joined the BBC. From Home Service newsreader to Radio 2 presenter, he has been associated with a wide variety of programmes over the years. *Variety Bandbox, Family Favourites, Hancock's Half Hour, Navy Lark, Star Sound, Marching and Waltzing, Band Parade, Glamorous Nights, International Festival of Light Music, National Brass Band Championships* and the programme he is probably best known for, *Friday Night is Music Night.*

■ Most exciting moment of career: 'Making a high speed dash during a holiday in Portugal to the Festival Hall in London for *Stars of Friday Night is Music Night*, and being back on the beach again next morning!' ■ A moment to remember 'En route to Bournemouth for a "live" Concert Orchestra show, a dreadful thought dawned on me near Winchester. A quick look in the luggage boot confirmed my worst suspicions – no dinner jacket and trousers. The Concert Orchestra manager came to my rescue, but a portly 5'8" suit on a 6'1" compère caused ribaldry from the orchestra, and I am sure, a few raised eyebrows among the audience at the Winter Gardens. The draught around my ankles was shocking!' ■ Likes motorcycling, touring and practising the trumpet. Dislikes maintaining the motorcycle, traffic jams and cleaning the trumpet. ■ Married to Nan, has two daughters, Carolyn and Susan and twin grandsons, James and Matthew. ■ Lives in London.

ROBIN BOYLE
'Friday Night is Music Night . . . even in Portugal.'
BORN: Folkestone, Kent. Father in the Royal Air Force. EDUCATED: Various grammar schools. FIRST JOB: Industrial heating engineer. Then joined the army, Royal Armoured Corps (Inns of Court Regt. and Royal Dragoons). FIRST BROADCAST: 1945 when he became an

TONY BRANDON
'A Carroll Levis discovery. . .'
BORN: 12th December 1933 in Portland, Dorset. EDUCATED: Portsmouth Grammar School. FIRST JOB: Cub reporter on 'Portsmouth Evening News'. While 'resting' in the early days of his stage career he worked as a waiter in a coffee-bar and a mini-cab driver. FIRST BROADCAST: February 1952 in the Carroll Levis

Show on the BBC Light Programme. This resulted in him being offered his first professional engagement with the touring *Carroll Levis Discovery Show.*

He joined Radio 1 in 1967 presenting *Midday Spin* and *Radio One Club.* The following year he was given a daily show on Radio 1. The cross-over to Radio 2 came in 1971 where he presented many different shows over the next five years including a late night chat show, *Tony Brandon Meets the Saturday People.* He has also starred in two situation comedy series on Radio 2, *The Family Brandon* and more recently *Wally Who.* Presents and writes *Acker's 'Alf 'Our* featuring Acker Bilk and regularly presents the weekend *Early Show* on Radio 2. He still treads the boards whenever possible, having made his debut as Pantomime Dame at the Yvonne Arnaud Theatre, Guildford 1982/83 and appearing at Lewisham with Basil Brush and Lulu 1983/84.

■ Most exciting moment of career: 'Passing the Carroll Levis audition at the Theatre Royal, Portsmouth, which gave me my start in show business.' ■ A moment to remember: 'I always remember with affection my "digs" in Sheffield. On my very first visit the landlady pointed out very early on that as it was a very old house, the toilet was down the garden. Moreover, the most convenient route was through the kitchen. Eventually the call of nature came and I tentatively knocked on the kitchen door and entered. To my astonishment the kitchen bore a very close resemblance to a doctor's waiting room during a flu epidemic. Not only were both the landlady and her husband there, but Granny and Grandad, the landlady's daughter and her boy friend, plus a seemingly endless selection of grandchildren as well. Across the crowded room and above the general hubbub the landlady shouted at the very top of her voice; "Do you want to go the the toilet?" "Yes please," I said visibly wilting with embarrassment. And then came the immortal words that have haunted me ever since: "Amy!" said the landlady, shouting even louder than before, "fetch Mr Brandon the key, and paper off loaf."!' ■ Likes curry, old cars (owns a 1954 Austin Somerset with under 22,000 miles on the clock), peaceful surroundings, wine making, gardening (in small doses) and an almost limitless range of music. Dislikes parties of any kind, flying and being alone. ■ Married to Jill and lives in Surrey.

PIET BRINTON
'That's quite a mouthful isn't it. . .'
BORN: 7th April 1946 in West Bromwich. Father an interior designer. EDUCATED: Yes! Wolverhampton Grammar Technical School. Wolverhampton College of Art and Design. FIRST JOB: Graphic designer. Has also worked as a forestry nurseryman for the Earl of Bradford, and as a self-employed sign-writer. Has sung with Bob Harris's Whistlestop Roadshow and now sings with the group Elite. FIRST BROADCAST: November 1980 on the children's programme *Playday* on BBC Radio Wales. Working as a solo singer and writer for both radio and television brought him the opportunities to work as a presenter. Television credits include *The Old Grey Whistle Test.* He has done many programmes for BBC Radio Wales including *Beside the Sea, Working it Out, Open Secrets.* He now presents *Playday* and *Sou'Wester* for BBC Radio Wales.

■ Most exciting moment of career: Interviewing the Swansea Sky Diving team in mid-air. (Several members were later tragically killed in Germany.) ■ A moment to remember: 'We all have memories of classic mistakes and I think my biggest boo-boo was when I was required to interview a lady representing a group who supply mothers' milk to babies who have no supply from their own mothers. (Something like the blood transfusion service.) My words went something like, "Mrs. . ., your organization is called the Express Breast Milk Bank, that's quite a mouthful isn't it?"!' ■ Likes music, MG sports car *c.* 1968. Dislikes being patronizing to the people I meet and interview! ■ Married to Carol, has one daughter, Becky, and lives in Pembrokeshire.

BENNY BROWN
'I've always lived, eaten and breathed commercial radio. . .'
BORN: 1949 in Texas, USA. Father, Judge Advocate for US Army. EDUCATED: In South

Carolina and the University of Kansas (radio and television). FIRST JOB: In radio from the start. He first became interested when he was fifteen and a radio DJ made an appearance at his High School dance, spinning the discs. 'It was an instant glamour trip. I saw the world of the DJ for the first time and decided there and then, it was for me.' Has worked on radio stations all over the States. He served in the Vietnam War as a tank commander until wounded in action. He joined Radio Luxembourg in 1980 and in 1981/82 won Billboard's International Air Personality of the Year Award. Has also worked for the American Forces Network in Germany and while with them started his *Benny Brown Road Show* which he takes all over Europe housed in a six-ton Mercedes truck.

■ Likes flying 'elaborate' kites. Dislikes the growing lack of creativity in American Radio. ■ Married to Marlies, has one son, Markus and lives in Betrange, just outside Luxembourg.

KEN BRUCE
'A Suspendergram delivered "on air".. .'
BORN: 2nd February 1951 in Glasgow. Father a manufacturer's agent. EDUCATED: Hutchesons' Boys Grammar School, Glasgow. FIRST JOB: Apprentice chartered accountant (a very bad one). Has also been a car washer, a painter of tennis club railings and an office manager.

FIRST BROADCAST: 'A badly read 10 o'clock news bulletin on Radio 4 Scotland.' Having gained experience on hospital broadcasting in Glasgow, he heard about a vacancy for an announcer at BBC Scotland, applied and was given a three-month contract. Has presented many programmes for Radio Scotland including *Night Beat*, the *SRO Road Show* and *Ken Bruce's Saturday*. Has also presented the *Early Show, Friday Night is Music Night* and *Radio 2 Ballroom* for BBC Radio 2. Has his own daily afternoon show on Radio Scotland and a Sunday morning programme called *Beat the Band*.

■ A moment to remember: 'Having a "Suspendergram" delivered by a nubile young lady wearing the aforementioned articles but little else. This being carried out in the course of a "live" radio programme and under the gaze of BBC film cameras, which had gained entry to my studio under false pretences.' ■ Likes grovelling for work. Dislikes unpunctuality. ■ Married to Fiona, has two sons and lives in Scotland.

BRUNO
'His job spot a huge success.. .'
BORN: Trevor Neil Brookes on 24th April 1959 in Newcastle-under-Lyme. Father Chairman of Kelly's Organization Exclusive Restaurants. EDUCATED: Wolstanto Prep School. Bradwell and Seabridge High Schools. FIRST JOB: DJ in clubs from the age of 14. By the time he had left school he was promoting teenage dance halls and car washing! He worked as a club DJ for ten years including a spell afloat on the *Canberra* on a cruise to America. In 1975 he sent a 'demo' tape to the then Programme Organizer at Radio Stoke, Geoff Lawrence who wrote back and told him he was nasal, an average DJ with no new ideas and spoke in a monotone! FIRST BROADCAST: In 1977 he was invited to guest on a teenage programme reviewing records. He put the idea of a 'Job Spot' for teenagers to the producer. He liked it and gave him two minutes' air time a week.

Within eight weeks he had taken over the 50-minute show, re-titled as Bruno's 4–35 Express. A mixture of pop music and reports on any jobs available for teenagers. It was a huge success, was extended and became Bruno's 2–50 Express. He has sat in for Mike Read on Radio 1 and joined in the *DLT Show* from Earls Court. He now presents the weekday afternoon show on BBC Radio Stoke as well as the *Saturday Show*.

■ Most exciting moment of career: Being chosen to stand in for Mike Read and landing the afternoon show on Radio Stoke resulting in a rise in the audience ratings from 0.9 to 4.1. ■ Likes fishing and knocking houses about. Dislikes cars that don't work, ironing boards that don't stand up, runny eggs, crab sauces and farmyard smells. ■ Has a very understanding and good looking girlfriend called Anthea and lives in Staffordshire.

PAUL BURNETT
'A case of mistaken identity. . .'

BORN: 26th November 1943 in Manchester. Father and mother, Paul and Alice Burnett, were a variety act. EDUCATED: Twelve different schools, travelling the length and breadth of Britain with his parents. FIRST JOB: Salesman in a shop in Darlington at the age of fifteen. He then joined the RAF and started broadcasting while in Aden. FIRST BROADCAST: In mid 60s on Aden Forces Broadcasting Association. He spent two years with AFBA before buying himself out of the RAF to join Radio 270, the pirate station off Scarborough, 'or Bridlington, depending on the wind!' From Radio 270, he went to the Isle of Man with the first of the commercial radio stations, Manx Radio and in 1967 joined Radio Luxembourg where he presented their Top Twenty for the next six years. In March 1974 he took over the Sunday morning show on Radio 1 and the following year started a six-year stint on the Monday to Friday lunchtime show. 1983 saw a change of networks for Paul as he crossed over to Radio 2

to present the weekend *Early Show* and to 'dep' for David Hamilton. He was also one of the DJs to cover the 1983 London Marathon for Radio 2. Has presented the Top Twenty on the World Service since 1979.

■ Most exciting moment of career: 'Introducing the Miss World contest on BBC 1 in 1978.' ■ A moment to remember: 'I have the rare distinction of being the only Pirate Radio DJ to throw up half-way through a commercial. I'm not the world's best sailor and I had to describe the delights of sizzling Danish bacon. I tried to reach the cough key, but never made it! There was also the time when I emerged from Broadcasting House to be greeted by some nutty dame, a well aimed can of yellow paint and the words, "Take that Mr Hamilton!" She then had the cheek to ask me to play a record for her!' ■ Likes people with a sense of humour and a good night out with friends. Dislikes 'cant', hypocrisy and people who say something because it's the trendy thing to say. ■ Married to Nicole, has two sons, Darren and Philip and a Red Setter called Roxy. ■ Lives in Berkshire.

PAULINE BUSHNELL
'I am a very private person. . .'

BORN: Staffordshire. EDUCATED: Leeds University (B.A.Hons. English). Spent four years in Canada. Joined the BBC in 1973 writing trails for Radio 4. FIRST BROADCAST: 1974 as a Radio 4 announcer. Is a Radio 4 newsreader/announcer.

■ Lives in London.

ALMA CADZOW
'Doing a "Morecambe and Wise" at a concert. . .'

BORN: 4th October 1940 in Glasgow. Father a production manager in marine engineering. EDUCATED: Hillhead High School. Glasgow University. FIRST JOB: BBC Studio Manager in

London. Has also worked as a hotel receptionist, a supply teacher and as a library assistant in the Gorbals Library in Glasgow for a few weeks. FIRST BROADCAST: Reading 'Wee Willie Winkie' on *Home this Afternoon* in 1969. From working as a studio manager in London she moved to Radio 2 as a newsreader/announcer. Is now a presenter/continuity announcer for BBC Radio Scotland. Programmes include *Leisure Trail, Summer Sportsound*, the *Ken Bruce Show, Children in Need Appeal, Radio Portraits* and she also presents classical music programmes on Radio Scotland.

■ Most exciting moment of career: 'Announcing a "live" concert with the BBC Scottish Symphony Orchestra for the first time; and *trying* to interview Liz Fraser and Dora Bryan for the *Ken Bruce Show*!' ■ A moment to remember: 'Doing a "Morecambe and Wise" at a public concert, when I announced the soloist and turned to welcome him from stage left. He came on from stage right!' ■ Likes reading, walking, horse riding and singing. Dislikes BBC coffee. ■ Lives in Stirlingshire.

ANDY CAMERON
'Are you Andy Cameron? . . .'
BORN: 13th October 1940 in London. Father a London cabbie. EDUCATED: Rutherglen Academy. FIRST JOB: Structural plater. Has also

been a bus driver, a sales supervisor and a machine operator in a car plant. FIRST BROADCAST: 1978 on BBC Radio Scotland. Has presented their *Sunday Joint* and now presents the *Andy Cameron Show* every Sunday on Radio Scotland.

■ Most exciting moment of career: 'Appearing in front of the Duke of Cornwall. (Definitely the best pub in Edinburgh.)' ■ A moment to remember: 'A wee lady stopped me outside the BBC one day and asked "Are you Andy Cameron?", "Yes", I replied. "Well", says she, "could you get me Tom Ferries' autograph?"' ■ Likes watching football, especially Rangers. Dislikes adoring women (they're always trying to touch me!) ■ Married to Norma, has five children and lives in Glasgow.

DOUGLAS CAMERON
'Followed in Bill Simpson's footsteps. . .'
BORN: 29th October 1933 in Newcastle-upon-Tyne. Father a railwayman. EDUCATED: Edinburgh Academy. FIRST JOB: Chartered accountant. FIRST BROADCAST: September 1961 *Scotsport* on Scottish Television. After doing part-time sports reporting he successfully auditioned for a newscasting and interviewing job on Scottish Television in 1962, following in Bill Simpson's footsteps, who had left in order to star in the television series, *Dr. Finlay's Casebook.* Has presented Schools programmes for ITN and Adult Education programmes for BBC Television. Worked for BBC Radio in the South-East and then became a member of the *Today* team on BBC Radio 4. In 1974 joined LBC, and is the co-presenter with Bob Holness of their top-rating breakfast show *AM* for which he has won the Variety Club's Independent Radio Personality of the Year Award.

■ Most exciting moment of career: 'Being told I had got the STV job in 1962.' ■ A moment to remember: 'I was on continuity announcing for Scottish Television when the studio phone rang. I reached out with my right hand to pick up the receiver, without moving out of vision, and failed to locate it. (It was a call from our control room, telling me the next programme would be 30 seconds late. The phone continued to ring, and finally I had to move my whole body out of the picture, to look for it. By following the wire, I found it in a drawer in the studio desk and finally got the message. I then apologized profusely to the watching millions. STV received over four thousand letters, half saying what an idiot I was, the others saying they'd not enjoyed anything quite so much on television before.' ■ Likes playing squash and tennis and watching all other sports. Dislikes people who pretend to be what they are not. ■ Married to Marjorie, has two children and lives in Middlesex.

NOEL CANNON
'Told that broadcasting would be therapeutic...'

BORN: 20th January 1934 in Brooklyn, New York, USA. Father a private investigator.
EDUCATED: Public School 26 Brooklyn. Mitchell County Primary School. Bowman Grey High School, Bakersville, N. Carolina.
FIRST JOB: 'Folding dried washing in a Laundromat (took it because I was bored with having nothing to do).' He joined the US Army and fought in Korea. After his discharge he took a job as a baggage loader for National Airlines, rising to Operations and Dispatch officer and then to Station Manager, a process involving five separate airlines and 22 years. FIRST BROADCAST: 1954 on station WSA at Salisbury Veteran Administration Hospital, Salisbury, N. Carolina. 'Becoming a broadcaster was part of a therapy process prescribed by a Doctor Paden E. Woodruff. I had been a P.O.W. in Korea and was taciturn and withdrawn. Doctor Woodruff believed that broadcasting, albeit by a telephone type of system, would be therapeutic.' He came to the UK in 1962. Since 1974 has been presenting *Cannon's Country* on BBC Radio Scotland, also *Cannon's Country*

Music which became *Nashville Express*; and *Breaker 8–10*, a CB based programme. Latest project is a gospel music format called *Brush Arbor Meeting*.

■ Most exciting moment of career: 'Recording interviews back stage at the Grand Ole Opry in Nashville and being accepted by the personalities involved as more than just another radio interviewer.' ■ A moment to remember: 'Once when I was doing a special show which revolved around Hank Snow, I found reference books conflicted on his date of birth, so I telephoned him in Nashville and recorded the conversation, then built the show around it; also when back stage at the Opry I managed an interview with 'Spider' Wilson who was lead guitarist with the Opry houseband for over 25 years. The information he gave me about the old and new Oprys was fantastic, then the bag containing the tapes, not only of Spider Wilson but also Jim Ed Brown, Jimmy C. Newman and Roy Acuff jammed in the airport Xray machine and were wiped clean.' ■ Likes just 'collapsing' after compiling, timing and scripting 3 shows of varying length. Dislikes artists or DJs who 'talk down' to either listeners or fans. ■ Has four children and lives in Aberdeenshire.

DAVID CAPPER
'I think steam radio is supreme...'

BORN: 19th November 1932 in Belfast, Northern Ireland. Father a company director.
EDUCATED: Campbell College, Belfast. FIRST JOB: Reporter on the 'Newtownards Chronicle'. Has also worked as a Customs brokerage clerk, a delivery driver for the Dodge Motor Co. in Detroit, a cook on a Pacific fishing boat, a dustbin lorry worker and has owned and operated his own fishing boat on Frazer River, British Columbia. FIRST BROADCAST: A court report on CKWX Radio, Vancouver in 1955. 'I was in Vancouver, BC, to cover the 1954 British Empire Games, working for the ''Vancouver Herald''. After the Games ended

I tried for a job in newspapers, but no joy, so I joined a commercial radio station as a News Sub and went on to do occasional broadcasts. On my return to Northern Ireland I became editor of two weekly newspapers and then joined the BBC.' He read local and national news bulletins on television in Northern Ireland until 1980 when he was appointed Northern Ireland Regional Correspondent for BBC Radio News. He is also Irish Affairs Correspondent which means he covers the whole of Ireland, both North and South. He contributes regularly to *Today, World at One, PM, Newsbeat, International Assignment, From Our Own Correspondent* and various World Service programmes.

■ Most exciting moment of career: 'It's difficult to pick out one highlight. I have covered all the big events in N.Ireland since the troubles began in 1969. Paisley parading the Third Force in 1981 kept me working for 40 hours without a break; and I spent six weeks in Buenos Aires as a member of the BBC team covering the Falklands dispute.' ■ A moment to remember: 'As the holder of various sprint records for evading irate Loyalists/Republicans/police etc: who remain intent on physically forcing their various viewpoints on me, I was once chased the length of a small town by Paisley supporters and was just regaining my breath when the cops baton charged me and I had to race off again. A bit unfair that!' ■ 'I think steam radio is supreme and will still be going strong when telly, like the horseless carriage, is but a faded memory!' ■ Likes golf, DIY, and industrial archaeology research. Dislikes smokers.
■ Married to Sandy, has three children by a previous marriage and lives in County Down.

DESMOND CARRINGTON
'Not of sufficient promise. . .'
BORN: 23rd May 1926 in Bromley, Kent. Father a builder. EDUCATED: Bromley County Grammar School. FIRST JOB: Office boy for Macmillan's the publishers, for 18/- a week. His first job as an actor was in *Goodbye Mr Chips* at the Theatre Royal, Nottingham. He then joined the army, serving in the Royal West Kent Regiment. FIRST BROADCAST: 1946, opening up Rangoon Radio after the Japanese had left. In the army he was seconded to Forces Broadcasting, Radio SEAC in Ceylon along with David Jacobs and Macdonald Hobley. After his demob he knocked on the door of the BBC, and was told 'We regret your audition was not of sufficient promise to afford us the opportunity of employing you in our programmes from London in the near future.' Within a few months, he was in the BBC Rep! He was also presenting programmes for Radio Luxembourg which continued throughout the 50s. He became a household name as Doctor Anderson in television's long running hospital drama, *Emergency Ward 10* and then spent nine years as the presenter of the Daz commercials. Radio programmes include *Movie-Go-Round, Housewives' Choice* and *Album Time*. Presents many programmes for Radio 2 including Radio 2's *All Time Greats*.

■ Most exciting moment of career: 'Stepping onto the stage of the London Palladium to do an act with the puppet Topo Gigio on *Sunday Night at the London Palladium* in 1965.'
■ A moment to remember: 'One of the problems of apearing in Ward 10, was having to memorize some appallingly difficult and long medical terms. Then I had the bright idea of writing them on the inside of the sink as we were always scrubbing up for operations on the shows. During rehearsal, it worked fine, as there was no running water in the sinks. When it came to the "live" transmission I watched in horror as my "medical terms" were washed away as I started to scrub up. There was nothing for it but to improvise.' ■ Likes cooking, if somebody else does the washing up. Dislikes wire coat-hangers.
■ Is a bachelor and lives in Kent.

MAGNUS CARTER
'The roof fell in on me. . .'
BORN: 29th March 1948 in Sunderland. Father a solicitor. EDUCATED: Bede Grammar School for Boys, Sunderland. FIRST JOB: Junior reporter with freelance news agency in Sunderland. Worked on newspapers and then after a two year spell in theatre administration, joined Radio Forth in Edinburgh, first as a reporter then duty editor and finally senior news producer. Then joined the BBC. FIRST BROADCAST: As a last minute stand-in

presenting a Radio Clyde classical music show. Programmes include *Forth Report* on Radio Forth. BBC Scotland's *Good Morning Scotland* and *Rhythm 'n News*. In 1979 moved to LBC and presents the weekend *AM* show.

■ Most exciting moment of career: 'Reporting a warehouse fire "live" on air when the roof fell in on me.' ■ Likes birdwatching and real ale. Dislikes London traffic.
■ Lives in Hertfordshire.

RICHARD CARTRIDGE
'It's a great mistake to assume people know who you are. . .'
BORN: 20th November 1948 in Poole Dorset. Father a shipwright. EDUCATED: Poole and Brockenhurst Grammar Schools. FIRST JOB: Drummer in a Rock 'n Roll group. Other jobs include being an electronics engineer and a layabout! FIRST BROADCAST: June 1978. 'A friend and I used to make up tapes for our local Hospital Broadcasting Association. One of them was heard by a producer at BBC Radio Solent and I was asked to present a country music show for them. A year later I applied for a job at Radio Solent and, much to my surprise, got it. I now present every conceivable type of programme from gardening to religion, including *Happening Now*, a magazine programme with a little of everything.'

■ Most exciting moment of career: 'Pass'.
■ A moment to remember: 'Unless you're a

household name, I've always thought that it's a great mistake to assume that anybody knows who you are and what you do. We local mega-stars are always getting letters like this: "Dear X, all of us here are regular listeners to your daily programme and think you're far better than Tony Wogan. Please will you open our fête on June 2nd etc." So there you are, scissors in hand, ready to cut the ribbon and the local curate says a 'few words'. "Ladies and Gentlemen, we're delighted to have with us this afternoon, that well known local celebrity, popular broadcaster and a frightfully nice chap . . . Roger Partwright!"' ■ Likes music. ('I still play drums and guitar mainly for my own amazement'). Dislikes 'People who tell me I sound a lot shorter'. ■ Married to Carol, has two sons, Robert and James and lives in Hampshire.

DAVE CASH
'I love every minute of it. . .'
BORN: 18th July 1942 in Edgware Middlesex. Father almost a doctor. EDUCATED: R.H.S.Holbrook. King Edward, Vancouver. FIRST JOB: The coffee-boy at CFUW Vancouver.
FIRST BROADCAST: In 1963 for CFUW Vancouver. He progressed from coffee-boy to broadcaster by 'keeping trying'. Had his own show on CFUW and on return to the UK did the *Breakfast Show* on BBC Radio London. Has worked on BBC Radio 1 and 2 and also for Radio Luxembourg. Is currently with Capital Radio presenting a daily show.

■ Most exciting moment of career: 'The next programme. In the beginning it seemed the most natural thing for me to be in radio. It still does; I love every minute of it'. ■ Likes swimming and football. Dislikes Arsenal FC. ■ Has four children and lives in London and Avon.

HARRIET CASS
'From BBC secretary to BBC newsreader. . .'
BORN: 4th February 1952 in London. Father a
Civil Servant. EDUCATED: Queen's College,
Harley Street, London. FIRST JOB: BBC
Secretary. FIRST BROADCAST: In 1974, reading
letters in *You and Yours* on Radio 4. Has
contributed to *Start the Week*, *It's Your Line*
and presented *From Our Own Correspondent*,
all on Radio 4.
Is a Radio 4 newsreader/announcer.

■ Likes reading, narrow boats and
handicrafts. ■ Married to BBC journalist
Victor Osborne, and lives in London.

JEAN CHALLIS
'Look Daddy, is that the Queen. . .'
BORN: 22nd May 1934 in Cheadle Hulme,
Cheshire. Father a theatrical manager.
EDUCATED: Manchester Warehousemen and
Clerk's Grammar School. Kesteven Training
College. Rose Bruford College of Speech and
Drama. FIRST JOB: As an actress in repertory at
Tynemouth. Six years in various reps with very
little 'resting', followed. Appeared in the West
End musical *Canterbury Tales*. FIRST
BROADCAST: June 1962 with BFBS in Cyprus as
a continuity announcer. 'I had been asked to
join BFBS in Cologne in the late 50s and
eventually accepted the invitation.' In Cyprus
she presented *Family Favourites* for the first
time, little thinking that ten years later she

would be handling the London end of the
programme. Back in the UK, was the first
woman to be appointed to the announcing
team for Radios 1 and 2 in 1974. She then
presented *Family Favourites* on Radio 2 for four
years. Is now a Radio 2 newsreader/announcer
but still does the occasional acting part on
television.

■ A moment to remember: 'I was doing an OB
commentary for BFBS on the Queen's birthday
parade and was suitably dressed for the
occasion in hat and gloves etc, when a small
boy looked up at me on the balcony where I
was standing and cried loudly, "Daddy, is that
the Queen?".' ■ Likes the theatre, music hall,
driving, watching cricket and reading. Dislikes
housework and not working. ■ Has one son,
Ian and lives in Surrey.

ROB CHANDLER
*'They enjoyed taking me to bed with
them. . .'*
BORN: 17th February 1959 in Ipswich Suffolk.
Father a centre lathe turner. EDUCATED: Nacton
Heath School. Suffolk College. FIRST JOB:
Office boy with the Co-op. Moved on to
become a senior clerk for the Ipswich Co-op
coal department and has also been a car
salesman. FIRST BROADCAST: In August 1979 on
Radio Orwell. 'I'd run a mobile disco for years
and decided to send a "demo" tape in to the
station. They liked what they heard and took
me on as a freelance. For two years I presented
just about every show at every time of the day.
I was finally offered a full time job presenting
the *Late Show*, and now it's the *Breakfast Show*
on Radio Orwell and Saxon Radio (twinned
stations).'

■ Most exciting moment of career: 'First ever
programme on the air, then being offered the
Breakfast Show.' ■ A moment to remember:
'My fiancée used to get worried when I
received letters from ladies saying they enjoyed
taking me to bed with them when I was

presenting the *Late Show*. Unfortunately things haven't improved a great deal on the *Breakfast Show* – they now express their pleasure at waking up with me!' ■ Likes playing football and tennis, following Ipswich Town FC and Ipswich Speedway, films, photography and amateur dramatics. Dislikes smoking, violence, and bad drivers. ■ Lives in Suffolk.

CHARLIE CHESTER
'Cheerful as ever'.

BORN: 26th April 1914 in Eastbourne. Father an artist. EDUCATED: Eastbourne and LCC School at Clapham in London. FIRST JOB: Errand boy for a grocer, progressing to messenger for an embroidery firm, but had his sights firmly fixed on a show biz career when he formed his own accordian band at the age of 17. FIRST BROADCAST: August/September 1937 he thinks. (It was a long time ago!) Having won numerous talent competitions he took the plunge, turned pro and was offered his first broadcasting dates by producer Ernest Longstaffe. One of the country's best loved comedians, his many radio shows recall the heyday of BBC Radio . . . *Stand Easy, Keep Smiling, Variety Fanfare, Come to Charlie, A Proper Charlie, Worker's Playtime, Mid-day Music Hall.* In recent years he has concentrated more on presenting radio programmes, brightening up many a dull Sunday afternoon with his *Sunday Soapbox* on Radio 2, which has a huge following. He also presents *Listen to the Band* on Radio 2.

■ Most exciting moment of career: When *Stand Easy* became the first programme to beat *Itma's* listening figures. ■ A moment to remember: 'During my broadcasts, having four paralysed children walk for me, one of whom walked in on my *This is Your Life*.' ■ Likes painting portraits and landscapes. Dislikes the loss of old world courtesy and consideration. ■ Married to Dorita, has one son, Peter and lives in Kent.

ALAN CHRISTOPHER
'A step I shall never regret. . .'

BORN: 16th September 1941 in Mountain Ash, Mid-Glamorgan. Father a BR carriage and wagon examiner. EDUCATED: Mountain Ash Grammar School. University of Bristol. FIRST JOB: Trainee hospital administrator. Was a Classics teacher from 1966–73 and an administrative officer (Examinations Board) 1973–80. FIRST BROADCAST: A five minute news bulletin on BBC Radio Wales. 'I answered an advertisement for a Presentation Announcer, a step I shall never regret.' As a BBC Wales newsreader/presenter, he reads news on radio and is responsible for continuity on both radio and television. For 12 months he presented a weekly show *Play It Again Al* and now presents a programme of *Listener's Musical Memories* and *Nocturne*, a personal selection of the classics. Has introduced many concerts on Radio 3 and Radio Wales.

■ Most exciting moment of career: 'Introducing two Promenade Concerts "live" from the Royal Albert Hall on Radio 3 in September 1982. The BBC Welsh Symphony Orchestra was performing on both occasions.' ■ Likes walking, music of all sorts, studying politics and politicians and socializing. Dislikes sport, pretension, heavy lorries and planners. ■ Is a bachelor (alas!) and lives in Mid-Glamorgan.

PETER CHURCHILL
'The excitement of getting my cue will never wear off. . .'

BORN: 9th September 1933 in Borehamwood, Hertfordshire. Father a maintenance foreman in a local factory. EDUCATED: Queen Elizabeth's Grammar School, Barnet, Hertfordshire. FIRST JOB: Apprentice jockey with the late Tom Masson in Lewes, Sussex. Was a flat-race jockey in France. Has also been a show-jumping coach and rider. Has written twelve books on equitation, show jumping and horse racing. Show jumping correspondent to

'Horse and Hound' since 1974. FIRST
BROADCAST: *Riding with Radio Leicester* in
1974. Brought about by banging on doors and
pestering people! Wrote and narrated several
series of programmes for BBC Radio Leicester.
*The Story of Foxhunting, The Story of the
Horse, Horse's Tales.* Was the guest
commentator for ABC TV for the Festival of
Sydney International Show Jumping
Championships of Australia. Joined BBC Radio
Sport in 1977 and for ten months of the year
travels all over the world covering international
show jumping.

■ Most exciting moment of career: 'Every time I
hear the cue "Now show jumping etc, etc."
The excitement of that will never wear
off.' ■ A moment to remember: 'We were
getting ready one night at the Olympia
International Championships for the late *Sports
Desk* at 2302. The annual show is a brilliant
mixture of top-class show jumping and family
Christmas entertainment. My producer said to
me "Give it plenty of colour and Christmas
atmosphere". But a few minutes before we
were due to go on the air everything suddenly
went wrong and we lost contact with the studio
at Broadcasting House. Frantic phone calls
were made, back-up arrangements were
planned and the atmosphere in the
commentary box was getting just a little tense,
in fact it was good old-fashioned blind panic!
Then just as suddenly the lines came up again
and I heard the newsreader say ". . . and for all
the details we join Peter Churchill." And I
opened up, "Good evening and welcome to
Olympia, where we have a brilliant mixture of
world class sporting action with more than a
generous helping of Christmas FEAR!" What I
meant to say was Christmas Fayre, but my
sub-conscious took over and told the
truth.' ■ Likes 'my work and my family'.
Dislikes snobs. ■ Married to Penelope Rohan,
has four daughters and lives in Lincolnshire.

MARY CLARK
'A consuming interest in consumer affairs'.
BORN: 7th April 1940 in Caerphilly, South
Wales. Father a doctor. EDUCATED: Howell's
School Llandaff, Cardiff. University of London
(external student). FIRST JOB: Junior reporter on
'Penarth Times', South Wales. Has lectured in
law at the College of Business Studies in
Belfast. Was a member of the National
Consumer Council 1978 to 1981. Member of
Economic and Social Committee of EEC 1978
to 1982. Became chairman of Supplementary
Benefits and National Insurance Tribunals in
1982. FIRST BROADCAST: In 1975, as a lecturer
in law specializing in sale of goods, hire
purchase etc, was asked to take part in a
phone-in on Radio Ulster. Since then has
presented *Consumer Desk* and *Talk it Through*
for Radio Ulster and *You and Your Rights* for
Northern Ireland TV. Has contributed to
Woman's Hour and *You and Yours* on Radio 4.

■ Most exciting moment of career: Being
appointed as one of 24 UK members of
Economic and Social Committee of EEC in
1978. ■ A moment to remember: Winning
second place in 1982 Argos Awards for
Consumer Journalists with a programme about
fire hazard of children's chairs made of
polyurethane foam which resulted in the law
being changed. ■ Likes playing the piano
(badly!). Dislikes lack of punctuality in other
people. ■ Married to Basil Glass, a Belfast
solicitor and politician, and has two sons.

DAVID CLAYTON
'More than one string to his bow. . .'
BORN: 19th November 1952 in Marske,
Yorkshire (now County Cleveland). Father a
sales representative. EDUCATED: Great
Yarmouth Grammar School. FIRST JOB: Articled
clerk to an accountant. Later became the
manager of a Hi-Fi department and then a
partner in an entertainment agency (which he
still is). FIRST BROADCAST: In November 1974
on hospital radio. Made his first contribution to

BBC radio in 1978 on a Radio 4 regional 'opt-out' programme. Frequent contributions to local radio programmes led to him being offered his own show. Has presented *Country and Western Specials, Holiday Specials*, the *Weekday Breakfast Show*, all on BBC Radio Norfolk. Television shows include BBC East *Young People's Programme*, BBC East News and he has also been a continuity announcer for Anglia TV. Is now the producer and presenter of BBC Radio Norfolk's *Sunday Morning Show* and also occasionally presents for BBC East Television.

■ Most exciting moment of career: 'Seeing 5,000 people turn up to an Outside Broadcast of an Old Car Rally organized by my *Sunday Show*.' ■ A moment to remember: 'The day I wrote to Bob Wellings in 1965 to ask how I could become a television cameraman as I wanted to become a broadcaster!' ■ Likes work. Dislikes broken promises, burnt toast and lukewarm milk. ■ Married to Jennie, has two children and lives in Norfolk.

PETER CLAYTON
'I've been troubling people's ears ever since 1962. . .'
BORN: 25th June 1927 in London. Father a railway clerk. EDUCATED: Just about and mainly under the influence of a brilliant headmaster, E.H. Goddard of Aske's School, London. FIRST JOB: 'Making porridge in the Highlands before working for seven years in public libraries. I've

also edited a record catalogue in Gaelic which I didn't understand and written weird sleeve-notes which nobody else could.' FIRST BROADCAST: 1962. 'Teddy Warwick, then a young producer, invited me to audition for a slot in his new jazz magazine programme the *Jazz Scene*. I've been troubling people's ears ever since.' Has presented Radio 2's *Round Midnight* on many occasions and presents *Sounds of Jazz* on Radio 1, *Jazz Record Requests* on Radio 3 and *Album Time* on Radio 2.

■ A moment to remember: 'I once ghosted the autobiography of a very famous English popular singer. A few years later television did a programme about "ghost" writers and somebody said "Do you think (the above lady singer) had any help with her book?" To which Robert Robinson replied "No, I think the only help she had was somebody to sharpen her pencils." I couldn't resist dropping him a note, "No, Bob, I wrote the book, she sharpened the pencils!"' ■ Likes 'surviving'. Dislikes anything called 'Middle of the Road'. ■ Married to 'one lady for ever such a long time', has one daughter and lives in Kent.

RICHARD CLEGG
'Wrote all the usual letters of application. . .'
BORN: 14th July 1946 in Essex. Father a solicitor. EDUCATED: St. Peter's School, York. University of Leeds. FIRST JOB: Solicitor's articled clerk. FIRST BROADCAST: April 1974 from BFBS in Cyprus, an interview, the first of many. The following month presented his first record programme *Old Hits and New Misses*. Having been a founder member of Leeds University Union Television and Audio Production Society, *Network 4* in 1966, he wrote all the usual letters of application and was accepted by BFBS as one of the first six broadcasting trainees in their history. In Cyprus he presented all types of shows for BFBS plus doing literally hundreds of interviews. He joined BBC Radio 2 in 1977. Is a Radio 2

newsreader/announcer and one of the regular presenters of *You and the Night and the Music*.

■ Most exciting moment of career: 'July 1975 when a colleague and I were responsible for the coverage on BFBS Cyprus of the Apollo-Soyuz test project which involved direct liaison with the Russian and American space teams. After the mission we interviewed two of the astronauts. The whole thing took up about three hours of air time.' ■ Likes jazz and big band music and the history of the RAF. Dislikes increasing Americanization of the English language. ■ Married to Sue, has one son and lives in Buckinghamshire.

GORDON CLOUGH
'Chucked in at the deep end. . .'

BORN: 26th August 1934 in Salford, Lancashire. EDUCATED: Bolton School. Magdalen College, Oxford (William Doncaster Scholar) B.A. French and Russian. FIRST JOB: Studio Manager for the BBC External Services 1958–60. He then became a Senior Programme Assistant in the Russian Service which led to the post of Russian Programme Organizer. From the Russian Service he moved to Radio News Features as Senior Duty Editor. FIRST BROADCAST: *Top of the Form c.* 1950! In 1960 he gave a talk in Russian and presented his first *World at One* on May 1st 1967, the 50th anniversary of the Russian Revolution. 'When I applied to the BBC for a job, I really wanted to be a Drama producer, but it didn't work out that way. The first day I presented the *World at One*, Bill Hardcastle had been taken ill and I was chucked in at the deep end.' Has produced and presented sundry documentaries for Radio 4 and the World Service. Is the questionmaster and question-setter of *Round Britain Quiz* and *Round Europe Quiz*. Is one of the regular presenters of the *World at One, PM* and the *World This Weekend*. Has translated many books, mostly from French and Russian.' Several of the Russian ones have been by dissident authors which could be the reason

that the USSR won't grant me a visa any more. After all 'Izvestia' did once name me as a British spymaster, running agents in the Soviet Union by means of pop records played on the Russian Service. Not true, but a good tale.'

■ Most exciting moment of career: 'Being able to tell Judith Todd that her father, Garfield Todd, had been freed from detention in Rhodesia. Perhaps not terribly exciting but nice to be a bringer of good news for a change.'
■ A moment to remember: 'There is one incident in my career as a producer which I would prefer to forget, but since it will be forever remembered by everyone involved, notably Robert Williams, it had better be me who recalls it. Some time in the early 70s, I was editing the *PM* programme and Bob was presenting. Due to the failure of circuits to materialize, of radio cars to transmit, of meetings to end, of press conferences to start, I found myself with an acute shortage of material with about half the programme still to come. Drawers and filing cabinets were scoured for pre-recorded items which had been rejected by other, better endowed programmes, while Bob struggled on manfully reading PA tape, describing the studio furniture and chatting about the weather. We finally staggered off the air. No listener, apparently, noticed anything amiss, but it had been a sweaty time. Bob stamped off into the night to drown his sorrows with the panel studio manager. As he later married her, I think I am perhaps forgiven.' ■ Likes doing crosswords during editorial meetings. Dislikes people who don't answer questions and bad service in restaurants. ■ Married to Carolyn Stafford, has four children and lives in London.

EDWARD COLE
'The final announcement on Radio 390. . .'

BORN: 20th April 1939 in London. EDUCATED: Highgate School, London. FIRST JOB: Law student. FIRST BROADCAST: November 1965 on the pirate radio station Radio 390. 'When it was announced that Radio 390, a new pirate with a sweet music format, was opening, I applied for a job as a DJ and was auditioned by Mike Raven. I ended up as chief announcer and made the final announcement when 390 closed down in the summer of 1967.' In the mid 70s he joined BBC Radio 4 as a newsreader/announcer and since then has produced and presented many programmes for the network including *The Wickedest Wink in the World*, the story of Marie Lloyd, in October 1982. Has also been a regular presenter of *Up to the Hour* on Radio 4, and compiler and presenter of the network's late night sweet music programme *The Unforgettables*.

■ Likes skiing, travel, history of popular music and the cinema. Dislikes pot plants and smokers. ■ Is a bachelor and lives in London.

JOHN COLE
'The BBC's Political Editor. . .'

BORN: 23rd November 1927 in Belfast, Northern Ireland. Father an electrical contractor. EDUCATED: Belfast Royal Academy. London University. FIRST JOB: Reporter on the 'Belfast Telegraph.' Has also been Labour Correspondent, News Editor and Deputy Editor of the 'Guardian'; and Deputy Editor of the 'Observer'. FIRST BROADCAST: 1958. Was Appointed the BBC's Political Editor in November 1981 and contributes to all news and current affairs programmes for both radio and television.

■ Married to Madge, has four children and lives in Surrey.

IAN COLLINGTON
'His Mrs Average Briton, not quite so average. . .'

BORN: 28th June 1944 in Leicester. Father an architect. EDUCATED: Not more than basically necessary at Woodbank Preparatory School, Leicester and Githlaxton College, Leicestershire. Then the University of Life (BBC

internal degree!) FIRST JOB: Student porter with British Rail (resigned after three weeks), then got a real job as a BBC sound engineer. 'Having built a portable tape machine and interviewed Ella Fitzgerald and Dave Brubeck while still at school, it proved to be compensation for my inability to grasp the basic elements of science 'A' levels. FIRST BROADCAST: Interview with Jonathan King on the BBC's *Calling Antarctica*. Has announced on a BBC Relay station in Africa and advised on setting up of a new radio station in West Africa. Has produced the *Money Programme* and *24 Hours* for BBC Television and current affairs programmes for the World Service. Presents and produces the daily show *Collington Plus* on BBC Radio Brighton.

■ Most exciting moment of career: 'Producing all night coverage of two lunar landings for the World Service – to be told afterwards by NASA that we did a far better job than the Voice of America who were actually in on the action.' ■ A moment to remember: 'On the *Money Programme* I came up with the idea of job-evaluating a housewife. We devised a system for points scored, according to how many hours she put in as nanny, cook, cleaner, teacher etc:, then turned the points into earnings. At 1983 rates she proved to be worth around £10,000 per annum. We let the media have the story in advance and they lapped it up. Suddenly my randomly chosen housewife became Mrs Average Briton. There were even quotes from her husband, which were in fact fabricated, as no journalist ever talked to him. If they had, they would have discovered that they had made Mrs Average Briton out of the English wife of a West Indian!' ■ Likes video, glass collecting, computers, amateur radio and lapidary. Dislikes pretentious media people, pompous presenters, over-cooked beef and computerized letters. ■ Married to Scilla, housewife. [I hope you pay her £10,000 per annum], has three children and lives in Sussex.

CHARLES COLVILE

'My first cricket commentary and I didn't want to hand back. . .'

BORN: 29th March 1955 in Rochester, Kent. Father a Naval Officer. EDUCATED: Westminster School. FIRST JOB: A prep school teacher. Then joined the BBC as a finance clerk. FIRST BROADCAST: 24th April 1976. 'Working in the BBC's finance department, I started broadcasting part time on Saturday afternoons for Radio 4's *PM* programme as a sports correspondent. From there I moved to BBC Radio Oxford and then became a Radio 4 newsreader/announcer.' Has been on attachment to the Sports Unit and has presented *Test Match Special* and contributed to all the sports programmes on the BBC Radio networks.

■ Most exciting moment of career: 'Making my début as a cricket commentator when the lines went down during *Test Match Special*. I described the action from the television picture and they had great difficulty in getting me to hand back when all was mended!'
■ A moment to remember: 'My favourite personal fluff in a news bulletin when I managed to maroon a Russian submarine on rocks 'six miles south-east of Swindon'. It should have been Sweden of course!'   ■ Likes playing sport, especially cricket. Dislikes working overnights, mince pies, and my car breaking down.   ■ Married to Alison and lives in Wimbledon.

ALISTAIR COOKE

'A weekly Letter from America since 1946. . .'

BORN: 20th November 1908 in Manchester. Father an insurance agent. EDUCATED: Blackpool Grammar School. Jesus College, Cambridge. Yale and Harvard. FIRST JOB: BBC film critic 1934–37. 'Coming to the end of my two-year fellowship at Harvard, I saw a headline in a Boston paper "BBC Fires P.M's Son". . . Oliver Baldwin was out as film critic. I sent a cable of application, was told 200 people were in for the job, but if I cared to come for an interview . . . My fellowship fund sent me to London (by ship!), I appeared at Broadcasting House, did a six-minute specimen talk, was summoned by the Director of Talks, who after meeting me, turned to his assistant and said "the job is filled". The DT was Charles Siepmann. He is now my oldest friend.' FIRST BROADCAST: October 5th, 1934 in Studio 3D at Broadcasting House. Was the London correspondent for NBC 1936–37. He emigrated to America in 1937 and became a US citizen in 1941. Was Chief American Correspondent of the 'Guardian' 1948–72. He wrote and narrated *America: A Personal History of the United States,* which was shown on BBC Television in 1972 and won several awards including 4 Emmys, a Peabody Award and the Benjamin Franklin Medal of the Royal Society of Arts. Has been the host of Masterpiece Theatre on America's Public Broadcasting System since 1971. Has been broadcasting his weekly *Letter From America* since March 1946, making it one of the longest running radio programmes in the world. He also presents on Radio 4, a series of programmes on *American Jazz and Popular Music*. In 1973 he was made an honorary KBE.

■ Most exciting moment of career: 'There have been many, but my most exhausting assignment was broadcasting five or six times a day to the United States for the National Broadcasting Company, during the abdication crisis in 1936. I wrote 450,000 words in ten days – a record.'   ■ A moment to remember: 'Waking up one Saturday morning as BBC-New York telephoned to say 'Where are you? You are on the air to London in ten minutes.' I always taped my talk on Fridays and had just returned from a stretch with President Kennedy and the White House press corps in Palm Beach. I asked for another circuit at 2pm and sat down and banged out a talk in one hour and fifteen minutes – my record. This was a frequent nightmare come true, but it was one of my best talks and is published in my second

Volume of Letters, called *Talk About America.'* ■ Likes golf, music, photography, travel and reading about medicine. Dislikes parties, lunch, Muzak, Hard Rock, Broadway and Leftist intellectuals etc. ■ Married to Jane White, the portrait painter, has one son and one daughter and lives in Suffolk, New York.

MICHAEL COOKE
'Advised to broadcast, not lecture. . .'

BORN: 23rd April 1936 in Rotherham, Yorkshire. Father a steelworker. EDUCATED: Rotherham Grammar School. Didsbury College, Bristol. Bristol University. FIRST JOB: Clerk for the British Wagon Co. Has also been a lecturer in English, Liberal Studies and Drama. FIRST BROADCAST: An education programme on BBC Radio Sheffield in 1968, having been invited by the then Station Manager, Michael Barton (later to become Controller Local Radio), who thought he should be broadcasting not lecturing. Has worked regularly for Radio Sheffield ever since doing the *Breakfast Show*, pop shows, chat shows, sports commentaries and feature documentaries. Has contributed to network programmes including the *World at One, Today, Sunday*, all on Radio 4. Has deputized for Ed Stewart on Radio 2. Is a television sports presenter and has his own show, the *Michael Cooke Show*, on Radio Sheffield.

■ Most exciting moment of career: 'The day I was presenting the *World at One*, deputizing for William Hardcastle during the winter of 1973/74 when at the height of the miner's strike and power cuts, the Queen declared a State of National Emergency. There was just a quarter of an hour to go to the programme and we scrapped the lot and arranged a new one. I hardly knew what was happening for the entire programme, but boy, was it exciting!' ■ Likes sport and the theatre (currently Dramatic Director of the Rotherham Repertory Company). ■ Has one daughter and lives in South Yorkshire.

JEFF COOPER
'I was out of work and had to do something. . .'

BORN: 5th April 1952 in Bournemouth, Dorset. Father a department store manager. EDUCATED: Downer Grammar School, Edgware, Middx. Harrow College. FIRST JOB: BBC clerk. Was also a 'tape jockey' for Radio Veronica a Dutch offshore station where programmes were pre-recorded. (He stayed three days!) FIRST BROADCAST: Piccadilly Radio, Manchester, the 5.30am news, then hourly on their first day of transmissions, 2nd April 1974. 'I was out of work, had to do something and they offered me a job.' Since then has presented Piccadilly's *Breakfast Show; Rock Show*. Radio Trent's *Rock Show;* Radio Clyde's *Morning Show; Afternoon Show* and *Midnight Rock*. Manx Radio's *Morning Phone-in;* BBC Radio Manchester's *Morning Magazine*. Radio 2's *Music Through Midnight* and the *Early Show*. Is producer/presenter/Head of Music for BBC Radio Manchester, presenting a daily show and also a Rock Show.

■ Likes photography, music, railways. Dislikes smoking, Margaret Thatcher, Tory Party, people who don't complain loudly enough. ■ Lives in Greater Manchester.

LOUISE COOPER
'Rattled teacups on Waggoners Walk. . .'

BORN: 1st March 1950 in Manchester. Father a hairdresser. EDUCATED: Convent school and

Bristol University (B.A. English Lit.) FIRST JOB: Studio Manager for BBC Radio. But has also been a waitress, postman, printer, market stallholder, dressmaker and researcher. FIRST BROADCAST: In *Shop Around*, a consumer affairs programme on a community radio station in Milton Keynes (CRMK). Gained all her front-of-mike experience on community radio but in her days as a SM has rattled tea cups on *Waggoners Walk*, eaten sandwiches on *Late Night Extra*, and backroomed endless *Open Houses* and *World at Ones* (in the William Hardcastle days). Now presents *Hometime*, the drive-time show on BBC Radio Northampton.

■ Most exciting moment of career: Still waiting for it! ■ A moment to remember: 'Sharing Hometime with BUNNY, a rabbit of the squeaky variety who says "Happy Birthday" to young children and any crazy adult who requests it. BUNNY is much loved and revered by the other presenters on Radio Northampton.' ■ Dslikes writing letters. ■ Married to a television producer, has two children and lives in Milton Keynes, Buckinghamshire.

DAVID COSS
'Not alone in the commentary box. . .'
BORN: 17th June 1940 in London. Father a factory worker. EDUCATED: Ealing Grammar School. FIRST JOB: Insurance clerk. Moved into journalism and first reporting job was with the 'Iron and Coal Trades Review', followed by local papers in Slough and Windsor and provincial evenings and dailies in Wolverhampton and Liverpool. Finally became political Correspondent with the 'Daily Mail'. 'I got into broadcasting with some difficulty! Moving from being Political Correspondent of the "Daily Mail" to the "BBC's local radio unit at Westminster." Is now one of the BBC's political correspondents and as such contributes to all current affairs programmes and news bulletins. He launched the Radio 4

programme *Inside Parliament* which deals with the Select Committees.'

■ A moment to remember: 'When the broadcasting of Parliament began, I was the first regular commentator on the proceedings for local radio from a custom built commentary box in the Commons chamber. After one week, my fellow commentator, Chris Lowe, and I came up in lumps, which we diagnosed as flea bites. It was assumed the pests came not from our nearest neighbours, the MPs, but from the police sniffer dogs which patrol the building. The fleas had apparently been thriving in the cosy commentary box – until the extermination squad moved in. The inconvenience earned me my only mention in a BBC annual report!' ■ Likes reading, sketching, swimming and cycling. ■ Married to Anna, has one son and one daughter and lives in Surrey.

JAY CRAWFORD
'My boss thought I'd look good on radio. . .'
BORN: 25th November 1954 in East Lothian. Father a shopkeeper. EDUCATED: North Berwick High School. FIRST JOB: Uncivil servant in London! has also worked as a photographer. FIRST BROADCAST: 22nd January 1975 on *Edinburgh Rock* on Radio Forth. 'My boss thought I'd look good on radio, so I answered a Radio Forth "ad". Since then has presented their Top 40, *Soul Show*, the weekend morning and afternoon shows and *Drive Time*. Now presents the Monday to Friday *Lunchtime Show* and the Saturday *Breakfast Show*. Is also Head of Music for Forth Radio and does presentation for STV.

■ Most exciting moment of career: Interviewing Paul McCartney and touring the US with Nazareth. ■ 'I spent my first couple of years in radio trying to build a reputation which I spent a couple of years trying to live up to and the last couple of years trying to play down!' ■ Likes football, good wine, good company. Dislikes extremes and the English F.A. ■ Married to Jacqueline, has one son and lives in Edinburgh.

MORGAN CROSS
'First winner of Local Radio Personality of the Year award...'

BORN: 27th November 1933, in Leicester. Father a company director. EDUCATED: Portland House School, Leicester and Wyggeston Grammar School, Leicester. FIRST JOB: Trainee in the textile industry. Went on to a variety of other jobs mainly in the sales area. FIRST BROADCAST: December 1967. 'It all came about by accident. I went to look around a local radio station, was given a tape recorder and have never stopped since'. Has done most types of general programmes on local radio; has contributed to World Service programmes, *Woman's Hour, You and Yours, Newsbeat* etc. First television series for BBC 1 called *What a Picture.* Currently hosts BBC Radio Leicester's *Cross Talk* each weekday morning, a 3-hour phone-in/topicality/music show which he also produces.

■ Most exciting moment of career: 'Winning the very first National Local Radio Personality of the Year award in 1980.' ■ A moment to remember: 'The day HRH The Prince of Wales started asking me questions about the BBC's finances while I was holding a "live" mike.' ■ Likes watching most sports, playing snooker and chatting. Dislikes bores and bananas. ■ Married to Nancy, has three children and lives in Leicestershire.

BILL CROZIER
'The voice from Cologne...'

BORN: 11th July 1924 in Thornton Heath, Surrey. Father a coal merchant. EDUCATED: St. Giles' School, Addington. FIRST JOB: A garage hand. Also worked as a nursery gardener, a footman and a semi-pro band leader. FIRST BROADCAST: May 1948, by accident! Became a household name introducing *Two Way Family Favourites* from Cologne January 1958 to May 1965. Other programmes have included *Those Were the Days* (1967–74); *Music Through Midnight; After Seven. They Made a Million;*

Just Jazz; Spent six years at Radio Hallam along with Keith Skues, Roger Moffatt and Johnny Moran (1974–80) Is now a freelance presenter, researcher and producer, having produced the *Jimmy Young Show, Roundabout, Breakfast Special* and the *Gloria Hunniford Show.* Is heard on Radio 2 as a regular contributor to *You and the Night and the Music.* Has written his autobiography '"Sorry" Mike'.

■ Most exciting moment of career: Presenting *Two Way Family Favourites* for the first time and meeting Her Majesty the Queen in Konigswinter. ■ Likes: Broadcasting. Dislikes those who are less than gracious, and bad losers. ■ Married to Joan, has three children by his first wife Ruby, and lives in Surrey.

JON CURLE
'One pound a week in rep...'

BORN: 9th April nineteenumptything . . . in Gravesend, Kent. Father a foreman in a cable works. EDUCATED: Local Grammar School, but more importantly two years National Service. FIRST JOB: 'When my parents decided I should teach as a career, I dropped out of school to join the local repertory company at £1 per week. Acting, scene painting, prompting, handling light cues, often wrongly. One actress in a production reached out to switch on a standard lamp and I plunged the stage into gloom.' Also worked as a waiter ('I could never remember the orders, it was a wonder I got any tips.') Packing books and records for a book club. ('Tedium, but the tea was nice.') FIRST BROADCAST: Features for Arthur Swinson in the old Northern Home Service, while still a drama student. He continued as an actor until Peter Fettes, the BBC's Head of Staff Training had the idea of inviting a handful of radio actors to train as summer relief announcers. Jon was chosen and is the last survivor from the four who were weeded out from the original selection in the summer of 1959. Since then his voice has been heard on such programmes as *The Men from the Ministry, Friday Night is Music Night, Matinee Musical, The Best of Broadway, Mainly for Pleasure, Sounds Familiar* and *Whacko*. Is a Radio 3 newsreader/announcer.

■ Most exciting moment of career: 'Being asked to appear on the panel of *Sounds Familiar*, the series which I had been announcing.'
■ A moment to remember: 'During the radio series *Whacko*, I turned up at rehearsal wearing purple socks. Jimmy Edwards eyed them gleefully and said "Now I know what I'm going to talk about in the warm-up!" Aghast at the prospect and as I had a friend coming to the show, immediately I dragged him into the back row at the Paris studio and asked him to change socks! The exchange was effected, but by that time Jim had forgotten the original idea, so I spent the rest of the evening in borrowed socks.' ■ Likes good eating, the cinema, theatre, travel and lazing. Dislikes blancmange, English chocolate, pseuds, heavy metal music, string vests and answering letters. ■ Married to the job and lives in Kent.

ROGER CURRELL
'In at the deep end with a "live" report. . .'
BORN: 15th September 1947 in New Barnet, Hertfordshire. Father a lorry driver. EDUCATED: Queen Elizabeth Grammar School, Barnet. FIRST JOB: Trainee reporter on the 'Stevenage News'. Other newspapers followed; reporter on 'Welwyn Times', moving to Sports Editor. Reporter on the 'Evening Echo', St Albans. FIRST BROADCAST: 1972 for BBC Radio

Nottingham 'In at the deep end with a "live" report from the radio car of a council meeting, when the experienced reporter who I was supposed to shadow, didn't turn up.' From Radio Nottingham, he moved to BBC Radio Sheffield and then joined BBC Radio News as a reporter based in London.

■ Likes jazz, chess, and horse racing.
■ Married to Frances Foat, has three children and lives in London.

BRIAN CURTOIS
'They locked the studio door for the first time ever. . .'
BORN: 30th December 1936 in Southend-on-Sea, Essex. EDUCATED: Dulwich College. FIRST JOB: Reporter on the 'Ilford Recorder'. Has also worked on the 'Nottingham Evening News' and for the Press Association. FIRST BROADCAST: May 1964, having applied to the BBC for a job as a news reporter. Is now the BBC's Chief Political Correspondent and can be heard on all the news and current affairs programmes both on radio and television.

■ Most exciting moment of career: 'Doing the "live" commentary from the House of Commons in the spring of 1979 on the Vote of Confidence debate. The Government's defeat meant a General Election.' ■ A moment to remember: 'Discovering one night at 8.55pm that the door to our television studio at Westminster had been locked for the first time ever! Result – no Curtois on the 9 o'clock news. The report had to be read by the newsreader.' ■ Likes music, the theatre, watching cricket and rugby, and walking. ■ Married to Brenda, has two children and lives in Essex.

GARY DAVIES
'I bombarded Piccadilly Radio with demo tapes. . .'
BORN: 13th December in Manchester. FIRST

JOB: Worked in sales promotions for a mail order company. Also managed a discotheque in Manchester 'Placemate 7'. FIRST BROADCAST: November 1979. 'I bombarded Piccadilly Radio with demo tapes for 2 years until the only way they could stop me was to give me a job!' Has now moved to BBC Radio 1 and presents the 10pm to midnight slot on Saturdays.

■ Most exciting moment of career: Being accepted by Radio 1 and appearing on *Top of the Pops*. ■ Likes squash, tennis, water skiing, TV, eating out, Dislikes noisy eaters and yogurt. ■ A bachelor and lives in Cheshire and London.

GERRY DAVIS
'They ask me what I do for a "real" job. . .'
BORN: 7th October 1935 in Glasgow. EDUCATED: Shawlands Academy. Royal College of Science and Technology, Glasgow. FIRST JOB: Apprentice at ICI. Has also been a stage hand, an actor and a pharmacist! FIRST BROADCAST: On a school trip to Paris. 'I graduated from pharmacy to the theatre, from theatre to television continuity announcing and finally to radio.' Is a freelance broadcaster on Radio Scotland and presented their tea-time news magazine Northbeat 1971–75. Now presents Big Bands and Popular Music of 20s to 60s. Also contributes to news, current affairs, and documentaries on Radio Scotland.

■ Most exciting moment of career: 'My next job'. ■ A moment to remember: 'When people ask me, as they frequently do, what I do for a "real" job.' ■ Likes work. Dislikes people who don't care. ■ Lives in Aberdeen.

JULIE DAWN
'Ciao'.
EDUCATED: Universita di Venezia, Italy. Burlington College London. FIRST JOB: Singing with the Eric Winstone Quartette. Well known vocalist of the 50s and 60s who's talent took her to most of the top West End night spots such as Quaglino's, Hatchetts, Embassy Club, Savoy Hotel, Celebrity Restaurant. FIRST BROADCAST: With the Billy Ternent Orchestra after being heard by a BBC official while singing at Quaglino's who suggested she audition for the BBC. Became a regular broadcaster with Cyril Stapleton and the BBC Showband. Has sung on many BBC programmes including *Sing it Again, Nightride* and *Music Through Midnight*, but nowadays is best known for her 'Penfriend' spots on Radio 2's *You and the Night and the Music*.

■ Most exciting moment of career: 'Meeting Charlie Chaplin with his wife Oona whilst singing at the Celebrity Restaurant. He asked me to sing one of his songs and I sang "Smile". Also, having my own get together in the BBC Concert Hall in 1981 with my "penfriends" coming from all over the UK.' ■ Likes art in general and painting in oils and water colours. Dislikes pomposity. ■ Lives in London.

ALAN DEDICOAT
'Walking with intent at 5 in the morning. . .'
BORN: 1st December 1954 in Hollywood Nr Birmingham. Father a newsagent. EDUCATED: King Edward's Camp Hill School, Birmingham. University of Birmingham. FIRST JOB: Executive officer in the Civil Service. FIRST BROADCAST: *Home James*, drive-time show for BBC Radio Birmingham 1980. Joined Radio Birmingham as a station assistant after having gained

experience working in hospital radio. Has since been involved with most of the main weekday programmes on Radio WM (as it's now known) and the morning show *The 206 Team*. Is presenter and producer of the breakfast show *Morning West Midlands*.

■ Most exciting moment of career: 'Reporting airborne, from the open cockpit of a 1943 airplane – breezy!' ■ A moment to remember: 'Living within walking distance of Pebble Mill Broadcasting Centre, I have been stopped four times by the police for "walking with intent" at five in the morning!' ■ Likes reading, photography and video. Dislikes chilli. ■ Lives in the West Midlands.

FRANK DELANEY
'A man of few words'!

BORN: 24th October 1942 in Tipperary, Eire. EDUCATED: 'Yes'! FIRST JOB: Bank clerk. OTHER JOBS: Few enough. Got into broadcasting eventually, the big day being June 10th 1966. [What he did on that momentous occasion will forever remain a mystery!] Presents *Bookshelf* on Radio 4.

■ Likes squash, work and talk. Dislikes so many things, they are too numerous to mention. [Filling out forms I think]. ■ Lives in London.

ALAN DELL
'A 1983 Grammy award...'

BORN: March 20th in Capetown, South Africa.

EDUCATED: Kearnsey College, Natal. FIRST JOB: 'I joined the South African Broadcasting Corporation as a little clerk in the record library. I hadn't been there five minutes when I saw some 78s of Count Basie. I asked if they had ever done a programme with them and they said "Jazz?, we don't do jazz"! So, I wrote a programme and asked the Programme Manager if I could broadcast it and he said "Yes".' FIRST BROADCAST: The above took place sometime in the 40s. In 1952, having risen to producer/announcer, he took a years leave to go to America to study acoustics. On his way back to South Africa he came to Britain and decided to stay. The BBC gave him four late-night programmes with Eve Boswell. 'Following that, the producer, John Hooper, said "How would you like to introduce the Ted Heath Band?" I said, "You're joking, me, from the sticks!" But he wasn't joking and for eight months I introduced the *Late Night Swing Session* from the Aeolian Hall. What a kick off.' He was a staff producer with the BBC for two years in the 60s and then returned to being a freelance presenter with such programmes as *Session at 6* which incorporated a Big Band section. *Date With a Disc* followed and out of that came the *Dance Band Days* and the *Big Band Sound* which has been running on Radio 2 since 1969. He also presents *Sounds Easy* and introduces many Big Band concerts for Radio 2 including the Festival of Light Music from the Royal Festival Hall. In 1983 was awarded a Grammy for the complete recording sessions of Frank Sinatra and Tommy Dorsey which were released in the United States 10 years after being released in the UK.

■ Most exciting moment of career: 'Meeting Marilyn Monroe!' ■ A moment to remember: 'The announcer's studio at SABC overlooked the concert hall with large windows. Introducing a symphony concert, I had just announced a piano concerto with Claudio Arrau, and thinking I had plenty of time, departed for the loo. Suddenly voices yelled down the corridor, Alan! I thought, what the hell, they've got a whole bloody concerto. I ran back and they'd just played the first movement and there I was "undone" before the public gaze and they were all looking up at me as I stood there revealed, saying "that was the first movement, etc. . ."' ■ Likes photography and making programmes in his own studio at home. Dislikes pretentious music. ■ Married to Barbara, has two sons, Peter and Robert and lives in Kent.

Cambridge. FIRST JOB: Secretary for the World Wildlife Fund in London. Has also worked for UNESCO in Paris. FIRST BROADCAST: 1978, a report for the BBC World Service on the Trafalgar Square Whale Rally with an interview with Sir Peter Scott. Programmes include *Living World*, *Woman's Hour*, the *Food Programme*, *Groundswell*, *File on 4*, *Today*, all on Radio 4. *Outlook*, *Farming World*, *Nature Notebook* on BBC World Service and many contributions as a freelance reporter and interviewer to programmes on BBC Radio Oxford.

GRAHAM DENE
'A twenty-one gun salute to remember. . .'
BORN: 7th April 1949 near London Zoo. Father in wholesale costume jewellery trade. EDUCATED: Mill Hill School. FIRST JOB: Clerk in the BBC's Audience Research Department. FIRST BROADCAST: In 1968 on Hospital Radio Five, St. Mary's, Harrow Road, London. Neil Spence (formerly Dave Dennis of the Pirate Ship Radio London) introduced him to UBN (United Biscuits Network) 1970–74 and from there he moved to Radio City in Liverpool for a year before joining Capital Radio in London. Has presented lunchtime and late night shows on Capital and now presents the *Breakfast Show*.

■ Most exciting moment of career: Compèring a show at the London Palladium. ■ A moment to remember: (or rather to forget!) 'The morning of the Queen's birthday when I announced that in Hyde Park there would be a 21 gun salute by the Royal ARSE Hortillery.' ■ Likes vocal harmonizing and sport, especially soccer. Is a member of the Show Biz Eleven. Dislikes his alarm clock. ■ Is a bachelor and lives in Hertfordshire.

JENNY DEVITT
'I don't want to be taken to court. . .'
BORN: 24th December 1948 in Bangor, North Wales. Father a forestry expert. EDUCATED: Schools in Zimbabwe. Sunny Hill, Bruton, Somerset. The French Lycée. Girton College,

■ Most exciting moment of career: 'Most of it!' ■ Likes lots of things. Dislikes . . . 'I don't want to be taken to court!' ■ Lives in Oxfordshire.

STEVE DEWITT
'Come fly with me. . .'
BORN: June 21st, 1956 in Nottingham. Father a photographer. EDUCATED: Dynevor Senior Comprehensive, Swansea, Glamorgan. FIRST JOB: Auto electrician. Has also been a TV extra and walk-on. Has appeared in pantomime in Porthcawl and Swansea and has been area secretary for British Airways Jet Club. FIRST BROADCAST: September 1977 in a soul programme for Swansea Sound. 'I was spotted in a night club and asked to come to the studio to make a tape by the then Head of Presentation.' [What were you *doing* in the night club Steve?] Has presented all the daily shows on Swansea Sound as well as anything

from brass bands to current affairs. Presents and produces the Swansea Sound *Breakfast Show*.

■ Most exciting moment of career: Presenting a programme from RAF BRAWDY and spending an hour in a Hawk during a sortie. Also broadcasting on radio stations in Los Angeles and Las Vegas. ■ 'It's hard work getting up at 4am every morning but it's very rewarding to be able to make people happy and earn a living at the same time.' ■ Likes flying (holds a pilot's licence). Dislikes the price of aviation fuel. ■ Married to Eryl, has one son, Jonathan, and lives in West Glamorgan.

PETER DICKSON
'A degree in Psychology...'

BORN: 23rd June 1957 in Belfast, Northern Ireland. Father manager in the stock control department of Harland and Wolff. EDUCATED: Belfast Royal Academy. Queen's University, Belfast. (B.A. Hons Psychology.) FIRST JOB: Announcer BBC Radio Ulster. FIRST BROADCAST: *Midnight News* on Radio Ulster in 1975. 'Whilst at University, I applied for a voice test at BBC Belfast and I was accepted. My first job was to read the midnight news and the shipping forecast on Radio Ulster. I then went on to do television news and entered the job full time in 1979'. He has also acted in the BBC's *Play for Today*. Reported for *Newsbeat* and for *Walter's Weekly* on Radio 1. Has introduced *Good Morning Ulster* and *PM Ulster*, also *Network UK* for the World Service. Television credits include a *Song for Europe*. His voice is often heard on BBC 1 and BBC 2 television trails. He is a Radio 2 newsreader/announcer.

■ A moment to remember: 'An unfortunate mispronunciation of the town Hackballscross during a BBC television news bulletin in Northern Ireland in 1977!' ■ Likes swimming, eating out, wine, films, flying, travel. Dislikes bad service, video games and jingoism.
■ Married to Barbara McCormick and lives in Hertfordshire.

RICHARD DIGANCE
'Folk singer/DJ...'

BORN: 24th February 1949 in London. Father a lorry driver for Ford's at Dagenham. EDUCATED: Strathclyde University, Glasgow. Reid Kerr College, Paisley. FIRST JOB: Engineering draughtsman. FIRST BROADCAST: As a folk singer on BBC Radio 1. In 1976 his LP *How the West was Lost* was named the Melody Maker Album of the Year, and this led to many radio broadcasts. Has contributed to such programmes as *Start the Week* on Radio 4 and *Stop the World* and the series *Animal Alphabet* with Hannah Gordon and Peter Goodwright on Radio 2. He joined Capital Radio in 1979 presenting *Midnight Special* on Fridays and *Richard Digance and Friends*, but is still heard singing on *Stop the World*.

■ Most exciting moment of career: 'My first cheque from the BBC!' ■ Likes chess, fishing, snooker and dabbling in a recording studio. ■ Married to Debbie and lives in Essex.

PETER DONALDSON
'Alias Donald Peterson...'

BORN: 23rd August 1945 in Egypt. Father a teacher in the Intelligence Corps. EDUCATED: Schools in Cyprus and Suffolk. FIRST JOB: Actor with the National Youth Theatre. He then became a stage hand at Sadlers Wells, a property master at the Globe Theatre, an ASM/actor with the New Shakespeare

Company, Regent's Park and an actor with the Royal Shakespeare Company. Made his first broadcast as an announcer when he joined BBC Radio 2 on 6th April 1970. He transferred to Radio 4 in 1973. Is a Radio 4 newsreader/announcer.

■ A moment to remember: The morning he introduced *Up to the Hour* on Radio 4 as Donald Peterson! ■ Married to Aileen, has a daughter and two sons and lives in Sussex.

DOUGIE DONNELLY

'Scottish Radio and Television Personality 1982...'

BORN: 7th June 1953 in Glasgow. Father a contracts manager. EDUCATED: Hamilton Academy. University of Strathclyde. FIRST JOB: Entertainment agent! FIRST BROADCAST: December 1974 on Radio Clyde. While at University he had interviewed Andy Park, the Programme Controller of Radio Clyde, for Student Television and as a result was asked to submit an audition tape. He got his first television show by meeting a BBC producer while speaking at a dinner and now has his own show, *Friday Night with Dougie Donnelly*, on BBC TV Scotland. He has presented most of the daytime shows on Radio Clyde and now presents their *Mid Morning Show*.

■ Most exciting moment of career: 'Being awarded both "Radio Personality of the Year" and "Television Personality of the Year" at the Scottish Broadcasting Awards Dinner 1982; the first time anyone has ever won both'. ■ Likes sport, music, eating, drinking and travelling. Dislikes the cold and bad drivers. ■ Married to Linda, has one daughter, Kim and lives in Glasgow.

ED DOOLAN

'Always wanted to be a broadcaster...'

BORN: 20th July 1941 in Sydney Australia.

Father an accountant. EDUCATED: All Saints College, Bathurst, New South Wales. Randwick High School, Sydney. Alexander Mackie Teacher's Training College Sydney. FIRST JOB: Part time, on the cigarette counter in Woolworths. Full time, Checking Clerk in Western Assurance Co. Sydney. Spent eight years as a teacher in Sydney, Edinburgh and Highgate School, London. Always wanted to be a broadcaster and spent years hanging around the Macquarie Broadcasting audience shows in the 50s and 60s but his parents insisted on him becoming a teacher. FIRST BROADCAST: *Hitch-hikers in Germany*, a 15-minute documentary for Deutsche Welle in September 1970. 'Some friends who had contacts in Cologne, told me they needed an English voice on German Overseas Radio. Mine was near enough.' While in Cologne, he presented Afrika-Englisch Current Affairs for Deutsche Welle and Deutschlandfunk English transmissions to Britain. Also presented *Top Marks School Quiz* for BFBS. Moved to the UK to join BRMB Radio where he hosted numerous programmes before joining BBC Radio WM in 1982. Currently producing and presenting *Ed Doolan on WM*, Monday to Friday and *Ed Doolan on Sunday*.

■ Most exciting moment of career: 'To be invited by the greatest broadcasting organization in the world, the BBC, to join them with my own show in July 1982.' ■ A moment to remember: 'Arranged children's phone-in on "Raising Rabbits" (1975) A winner on the last day of the school holidays. Guest arrives, a little old lady. I didn't need to read book but had it on file. Hadn't actually even looked at cover properly. No problem. The confidence of inexperience. We go "live" with Little Old Lady. Calls flood in. It is then I pull out the book. "Raising Rabbits for Home Meat Production!"' ■ Likes anything connected with the media – is a workaholic. Dislikes phonies, resentment and spiders. ■ Has two Siamese cats and lives in the West Midlands.

JOHN DUNN

'Acquired a taste for radio in Germany. . .'

BORN: 4th March 1934 in Glasgow. Father an electrical engineer. EDUCATED: Christ Church Cathedral Choir School, Oxford. The Kings School, Canterbury. FIRST JOB: Of any consequence was a Studio Manager with the BBC but first money earned was 18/6 a week as a National Service Airman in the RAF. Filled in 18 months with odd jobs; porter at Euston station, car wash on the night shift, machine shop of Bristol Aeroplane Co, Will's Tobacco Co. Was also awarded a certificate of Competence to operate a Gaggia Espresso coffee machine! (Very useful for coffee bars). FIRST BROADCAST: Acting in a play in Germany during National Service. 'Having acquired a taste for radio in Germany, I applied to Forces Broadcasting for a job. They said I lacked experience and perhaps the BBC was the place to acquire it.' Like many a BBC Studio Manager, John moved into presentation and newsreading, working on all the domestic networks as well as the World Service. When the Home, Light and Third became Radios 1,2,3 and 4, announcers who had been working for all three networks had to choose and John chose Radio 2. He presented *Breakfast Special* from 1966–73 and also presented *Late Night Extra* for a year. Was on the BBC staff for many years, but eventually went freelance and now has his own daily magazine programme on Radio 2.

■ Most exciting moment of career: Introducing his own show from a) a hot air balloon; b) from a Nimrod aircraft on submarine patrol; c) from the middle of the English Channel in a Force 9 gale. But as far as ambition achieved – reading the 9 O'clock News on the old Home Service. ■ A moment to remember: 'Oversleeping on the night shift. I shot down to the continuity studio in pyjamas (not even a dressing-gown or slippers). Stayed until the end of the shift, 9.30am, and then strolled out unthinking into the lift. There was nobody around and the building seemed deserted, until the lift stopped at ground floor, when what seemed like the entire BBC, including the DG, came in to join me in my state of undress!' ■ Likes skiing, although it's more of an obsession really. ■ Married to Margaret, has two daughters and lives in Surrey.

DON DURBRIDGE

'Affectionately known as Deanna Durbin. . .'

BORN: January 13th, 1939 in Glasgow. Father in the Army (Died in a Japanese POW camp in 1945). EDUCATED: Henry Thornton Grammar School, Clapham, London. FIRST JOB: Junior clerk with the Jack Hylton Entertainment Organization. Also worked as a reporter on various local newspapers in London, before joining the 'Sunday Citizen' as a reporter. FIRST BROADCAST: October 1955 *The Younger Generation* on BBC Light Programme. 'I answered an "ad" in "Radio Times" for teenagers interested in broadcasting for *Younger Generation*. I auditioned and did over 200 programmes before National Service.' Has been heard regularly on Radio 2 on such programmes as *Family Favourites,* the *Early Show, Late Show, Band Parade, Friday Night is Music Night, Sport on Two* and has often sat in for Terry Wogan, John Dunn, Charlie Chester and Ed Stewart. Since 1978 has presented a daily show on BBC Radio Medway and a weekly Radio 2 'Breakthrough' feature. Does boxing and soccer commentaries for BFBS.

■ Most exciting moment of career: 'The Munich Olympics in 1972, specifically covering the siege of the Israeli quarters following the massacre and the subsequent shoot out. Sport it wasn't, exciting it was.' ■ Likes everything to do with entertainment and sport. Dislikes people with no sense of humour or fun. ■ Lives in Kent.

JOHN EBDON

'Something of a Radio 4 institution'.

BORN: 22nd December 1923 in London. Father

an Army officer. EDUCATED: Royal Academy of Dramatic Art and London University. FIRST JOB: As an actor under contract to Tennants, but during the Second World War in the RAF, his sight was badly affected by a blast and he was warned that returning to the literally 'bright lights' of the theatre could do irreparable damage. A brief spell at the Old Vic convinced him. He then went to Kenya buying and selling hides and skins and mastering Swahili in between deals. In 1960 answered an advertisement for the position of narrator at the London Planetarium and got the job. He became its Director in 1968 'by outliving my friends and outwitting my enemies'. FIRST BROADCAST: December 1961 when he presented the first of his 'Archive' programmes on Radio 4 after BBC producer Denys Guerault had heard him at the London Planetarium and liked his voice and his sense of humour. It was the first in a series of programmes that has been running ever since. He also presents *Near Myths* on Radio 4. Has appeared on *Any Questions* and hundreds of other Radio programmes too numerous to list!

■ Most exciting moment of career: My first broadcast. ■ A moment to remember: A funeral in Hove; 'for four years I had corresponded with an elderly woman who had written to me from a nursing home, thanking me for making her laugh on Monday mornings on Radio 4. I wrote back regularly once a week, in the knowledge she was living on borrowed time. But in her last letter she told me that when I received it, she would just have died. She thanked me for friendship and warmth and above all, as she put it, for keeping her going. I was immensely moved. Suddenly one realizes the amount of power you have as a broadcaster, to do either good or hurt. It's a very salutary feeling.' ■ Likes walking, following rugby and cricket, food and wine, astronomy. Dislikes bad manners, tripe and onions, cheap scent and slovenly speech. ■ Has three children and one grandson and lives in Middlesex.

NOEL EDMONDS
'The one who took over from the one everybody liked. . .'

BORN: 22nd December 1948 in Ilford, Essex. Father a headmaster. EDUCATED: Glade Primary School. Brentwood Public School. FIRST JOB: As a newsreader on Radio Luxembourg in 1968, having sent tapes to all the pirate stations. FIRST BROADCAST: On Radio 1 was on 21st July 1969, the day men stepped on the moon! He started by doing trailers and compilations but got his first break when Kenny Everett was ill and he stepped in at short notice on Everett's Saturday morning show. He then took over Johnny Walker's Saturday afternoon programme and when Kenny Everett was given the sack, Noel took his place saying, 'I doubt whether many people will take to me because I'm the one who's taken over from the one everybody liked.' He needn't have worried! He did the *Breakfast Show* on Radio 1 for many years and then moved to television where he has been as big a success as he was and still is on radio. 'I still think radio is the most exciting medium because it gives the presenter the opportunity to make what you can of the programme.' As well as presenting numerous programmes on Radio 1, he has presented *Midweek* on Radio 4 and at the time of going to press another Radio 4 programme is in the pipeline. Television credits include *Come Dancing, Top of the Pops, The Multi Coloured Swop Shop* which he presented for 6 years and *The Time of Your Life.*

■ Most exciting moment of career: 'Interviewing Prince Charles at Windsor Castle at the launch of his Jubilee Appeal in 1977, when his first words to me as I was half-way through my bow, were: "You're much smaller than you appear on television."!' ■ A moment to remember: 'It was my very first news bulletin on Radio Luxembourg. There I was, a spotty twenty-year-old among all these big stars like Paul Burnett and Tony Prince and I was very nervous. One of the stories was about a typhoid epidemic in Italy which had hospitalized 700 people and this is what I had to read: "Health officials think the epidemic was caused by an ice cream salesman washing his utensils in the Po" – I just broke up – the kind of thing that short careers are made of. I got a letter from the Managing Director saying that if it happened again, my stay with them would be short!' ■ Likes 'my Great Dane, Hovis – she's the most beautiful dog in the world', and helicopters. Dislikes anchovies, 'and I'm not too keen on politicians.' ■ Is single and available, if you don't mind a one-eared goat called Vincent, 10 sheep and two cows, one called Ermintrude! Lives in Buckinghamshire.

birds as well as a host of other animals and insects.

■ Most exciting moment of career: 'When I was featured in a film about my life called *The Man Who Talks to Animals*, and appearing on the BBC Television series *The Old Boy Network*.' ■ A moment to remember: 'I think my most thrilling moment in radio was in the days of Savoy Hill when Stuart Hibberd, radio's first announcer, congratulated me upon the excellence of my bird ornithology. He also said "It's the first time I have listened to someone imitating a nightingale who sounded like a real nightingale".' ■ Likes working as a naturalist. Dislikes hunting. ■ Married to Cicely, has two sons and five grandchildren and lives in Suffolk.

PERCY EDWARDS
'Psyche to Alien. . .'

BORN: 1st June in Fore Street, Ipswich, Suffolk. Father a tailor. EDUCATED: Central School, Ipswich. FIRST JOB: Training as a chef at Phillips & Piper, Ipswich. Also worked as an agricultural engineer with Ransomes, Sims & Jeffries, Ipswich. FIRST BROADCAST: 1929 in Vaudeville at BBC Savoy Hill, having auditioned for John Sharman. Has appeared in just about every Light Entertainment radio programme that one can name! – *Ray's A Laugh, Educating Archie, Variety Bandbox* – but made his name as the dog Psyche in *A Life of Bliss*. Has also appeared on *Woman's Hour, Children's Hour, Waggoner's Walk, The Archers, Variety Playhouse, Afternoon Theatre* etc. Contributes a weekly feature to Radio 2's *You and the Night and the Music*. Provides all the birds and animal sounds for just about every radio station in the country. Also works extensively in films. He was responsible for all the animal noises in *Plague Dogs* and played the monster in *Alien* [sound only of course!] His latest film is *Dark Crystal* made by the team who created the Muppets, in which he is the voice of Fizzgig, plus all the various swamp creatures that make an appearance in the film. Is able to imitate the voices of over 500 wild

TOM EDWARDS
'Found it great to broadcast from dry land. . .'

BORN: 20th March 1945 in Norwich, Norfolk. Father managing director of a wholesale company. EDUCATED: Avenue Road and Langley schools, Norwich. Norwich City Technical College. FIRST JOB: A stock taker in the family business. Also worked as a Blue Coat at Pontins, a switchboard operator and a clerk in the City. FIRST BROADCAST: *About Anglia* for Anglia Television in 1962. 'I auditioned for a presenter's job for a pop music show at Border TV in Carlisle in 1963 and from then on I've been lucky!' Television credits include *Look East, Nationwide, Pebble Mill, Cross Channel* and *Come Dancing*. Was a Radio 2 announcer for several years and then became a freelance presenting such shows as *Night Ride, Radio One Club, What's New*, and the Weekend *Early Show* on Radio 2. Presents *Radio Two Ballroom* and also announces for Thames TV in London.

■ Most exciting moment of career: 'Broadcasting from the BBC on dry land after being sick at sea with the Pirate stations for three years! Meeting Bette Davis and every time

I face a television camera or radio mike.'
■ A moment to remember: 'Ad-libbing to a camera "live" for four minutes during a breakdown. To this day will never know what I said but hopefully it did make some sense'. ■ Likes the theatre, old movies, Italian food, holidays in the sun and sleeping. Dislikes people who are late, snobs, winter, Income Tax, hangovers and dentists. ■ Is a bachelor and lives in London.

KENNY EVERETT   MAURICE COLE
'It's all done in the best possible taste...'
BORN: 25th December 1944 in Seaforth, Liverpool. Father a tug-boat captain.
EDUCATED: St Bede's Secondary Modern and St. Peter Claver College. FIRST JOB: Scraping gunk off sausage roll trays in Liverpool bakery. Later worked in an advertising agency and the advertising department of The Journal of Commerce and Shipping Telegraph. FIRST BROADCAST: On the pirate station Radio London sometime in the early sixties, having sent tapes to various radio stations. His zany type of presentation got him his own show on BBC Radio 1. It also got him the sack after he made a crack on the air about the wife of the then Minister of Transport bribing the driving examiner so she'd pass her test! The Beeb took him back but it wasn't long before he was asked to join Capital Radio. Then came his highly successful *Video Show* on television which eventually led to another offer from the BBC resulting in the *Kenny Everett Show* on BBC1, and a radio show on Radio 2. 'Waffling on the wireless is a nerve wracking business. Even before going on Radio 2, the most sedate, not to say asleep, radio station in the world, my little frame fills with panic . . . Radio let's me build wonderful pictures, and even though I may be looking and feeling like a hung-over water buffalo, all I have to do is sound sparky and I can get away with it.'

■ Most exciting moment of career: 'It's all been fun.' ■ A moment to remember: 'While doing the *Kenny and Cash Show* with Dave Cash on

Capital Radio, our programme Controller, Aidan Day, was in the studio with us one morning, browsing through the papers trying to find silly bits for us to read. Unaware that the microphone was on, he said "Ooh look, here's a jolly bit", to which I replied on air as well as to him, "Give it here then" and snatched it from his hand. The next thing millions of Londoners heard was Capital's Head of Everything That Is shout "Oh f--- off Everett!" I punched a button to play a record and three seconds later Aidan had turned the colour of beetroot, but as he was the boss nobody could say anything.' ■ Likes going to the cinema and eating wonderful food. ■ Married to Lee and lives in London.

JOHN EVINGTON
'In the right place at the right time. . .'
BORN: 28th November 1958 in Bramhall, Cheshire. Father a sales manager with Dunlop.
EDUCATED: Bramhall, Retford, Notts. Sandbach, Cheshire. Crewe 6th form college. Portsmouth Polytechnic. FIRST JOB: Technical Operator with Piccadilly Radio. FIRST BROADCAST: 'November 1978 on Piccadilly Radio, due to perseverance and luck, ie, being in the right place at the right time (plus a certain amount of talent!)' Presented Piccadilly's *Rock Show* for 18 months and also did the overnight shows before moving to Centre Radio to present the *Breakfast Show* Monday to Friday. Is now Centre Radio's Playlist Co-ordinator and presenter of the lunchtime programme.

■ Most exciting moment of career: 'First ever broadcast – chaotic but very exciting!'
■ A moment to remember: 'Once when presenting a "live" rock show an enormous sheet of metal fell off the desk. Not knowing what the dickens was going on, I quickly announced the next record, "A piece of HEAVY Metal from. . ." At the time I didn't realize how appropriate that expression was!' ■ Likes radio and real ale. Dislikes eating and having nothing to do (this rarely happens). ■ Lives in Leicestershire.

PADDY FEENY
'Top of the Form'

BORN: 25th April 1931 in Liverpool. Father a sales manager. EDUCATED: Ampleforth College, Yorkshire. FIRST JOB: Film projectionist moving quickly up the show biz ladder to become a stage electrician, scene shifter, stage manager and an extremely bad actor! FIRST BROADCAST: (as an extremely bad actor) playing the part of a lawyer in a radio play called *Duel of Honour* for the BBC in Birmingham in 1952, having passed a BBC audition [he can't have been that bad] After a spell in repertory, marriage and the need of a steady job brought a change of direction and he joined the BBC's European Services as a studio manager. Best known as one of the question masters on *Top of the Form* on Radio 4, and on television, along with *Young Scientists of the Year*. Other radio programmes include *Dial a Scientist*, *Children's Favourites* and many social documentaries for the old Third programme. Presents a Saturday afternoon sports programme for the World Service and a weekly programme on village-level developments in the Tropics.

■ Most exciting moment of career: 'Talking to a young Rastafarian mother in Antigua who said that what she'd heard on my development programme had really helped her to bring up her child in a healthy way.' ■ A moment to remember: 'I got a message from Barbados asking me to send greetings to listeners to "Voice of Barbados" on one of my Saturday afternoon sports programmes on the World Service. I duly sent the greetings and the next day received a telex saying "Thank you for the greeting, Voice of Barbados has now stopped taking your programme." That's the effect I have on listeners!' ■ Likes playing bowls. Dislikes buying clothes, having his photo taken and unneccessary noise. ■ Married to Patricia Brewer, has two children and lives in Sussex.

NIGEL FELL
'Doesn't like his boss finding out what he's up to. . .'

BORN: A long time ago in the South. Father a BBC studio manager. EDUCATED: St. Hilda's School Horbury, Yorkshire. Southend-on-Sea High School. The Open University. FIRST JOB: Washer-up in a coffee bar. FIRST BROADCAST: The *Anti City Show* on Radio City 1965. Has presented various programmes for BBC Radio Leeds; *Sweet and Low, Big Band Bash, Fells Folley, One Fell Swoop* and every election programme since 1969. Is the co-presenter of *West Riding* on BBC Radio Leeds, Monday to Friday.

■ Most exciting moment of career: 'Numerous occasions on which I've nearly got the sack.' ■ A moment to remember: 'Several. I was once accused by an important council official of committing a breach of the Highways Act when I told listeners that if they couldn't afford tickets for a pop concert, they'd be able to hear just as much by standing in the middle of the road outside; and the occasion when we lost the line to the Radio Leeds transmitter. Never at a loss we broadcast from the field where the transmitter was situated using OB equipment. It would have been fine if there had not been a horse in the same field, which showed it's interest by eating our scripts. Radio mikes hate me. I had to undertake an army assault course three times because my radio mike wouldn't work. Neither did it work when I was being dragged along the ground by a hot air balloon that didn't want to stay there.' ■ Likes pub preservation and specific gravity testing. Dislikes closing time, getting up and bosses who find out what I'm up to.
■ Lives in Yorkshire.

ROGER FINNIGAN
'I persuaded John Cleese to mime to a record on radio. . .'

BORN: 9th April 1950 in Manchester. Father managing director of a hat manufacturing

company. EDUCATED: William Hulme's Grammar School, Manchester. York University (B.A.Hons in English and Related Literatures). FIRST JOB: After a year spent abroad in North and Central America, following University, he became a general reporter for BBC Radio Nottingham. FIRST BROADCAST: Reviewing a newspaper that he came to loathe in Nottingham! In 1974 he moved to Manchester and became features editor/presenter for Piccadilly Radio. In 1975 presented one of the first genuinely frank sexual advice phone-in programmes on British radio. Produced and reported 'An 8.3 in Business Hours', which was the runner-up in the Best Documentary section of the 1980 British Local Radio Awards. Returned to America in 1979 and spent two years on the West Coast as a freelance reporter for BBC, IRN and the BBC World Service. Is a reporter for BBC Radio 4's *File on 4* programme, making weekly current affairs documentaries.

■ Most exciting moment of career: Several! 'Flying by the seat of our pants in the opening weeks of commercial broadcasting . . . persuading motor cycling champion Mick Grant to ride pillion behind *me* in a 100mph circuit of Oulton Park . . . Flying Chinook helicopters whilst covering an earthquake simulation exercise in California and finally getting a break with a current affairs outfit that doesn't regard any of these things as extraordinary.' ■ A moment to remember: 'I wonder if John Cleese recalls the occasion I got him to mime (for a radio audience) to a Mitzi Gaynor record.' ■ Likes vintage motor cycles, photography, and fishing. Dislikes most American television, Sony Walkmans (men) and programmes made with either the ratings or the Review Board in mind. ■ Is a bachelor and lives in Lancashire.

MIKE FLYNN
'Goes to work by airplane. . .'
Started in radio through a factory station in Wrexham in 1973. Has worked for Radio City

and Radio Merseyside. Has been with BBC Radio Wales since it first started in 1978. Presents his own daily show also does a weekly outside broadcast from different locations in Wales called *On the Road*.

■ Most exciting moment of career: 'Landing my aeroplane in a field near Prestatyn for a programme one morning.' ■ Likes flying his own Piper Cherokee airplane. This includes flying to programmes in North Wales and trips to Europe in the summer. Also likes cars and drives XJS and Triumph Roadster 'Bergerac'.

FRANK FORBES
'The Best of Scottish. . .'
BORN: 15th May 1932 in Port Glasgow, Scotland. Father a Scottish Gas Board official. EDUCATED: Greenock High School. Glasgow University. FIRST JOB: Teacher of Modern Languages. Has also been an actor and a singer. Became the Head of Department of Modern Languages at Ipswich Civic College from 1960–65. Was Head of Department of Drama at Moray House College of Education, Edinburgh 1965–79. FIRST BROADCAST: 1966 as a newsreader/announcer for BBC Radio Scotland having applied for and passed an audition. Is a newsreader/presenter for BBC Radio Scotland based in Edinburgh and presents *Best of Scottish*, Radio Scotland's equivalent of Radio 4's *Pick of the Week*.

■ Likes travel, directing for the theatre, singing, music and reading biographies. Dislikes cold climates. ■ Lives in Edinburgh.

BRIAN FORD
'Determined to get into broadcasting. . .'
BORN: March 6th, 1952 in Edinburgh. Father a
teacher. EDUCATED: Leith Academy,
Edinburgh. FIRST JOB: Editorial assistant on the
'Scottish Daily Mail'. Also worked as a sales
promotion assistant and a recording engineer.
FIRST BROADCAST: On Radio Clyde in 1974.
Presented Radio Clyde's *Homeward Bound,
Stick it in Your Ear* and *Streetsounds*. Then
moved to Radio Forth to present the *Lunchtime
Show* and *Ford's Emporium*. Now presents the
Brian Ford Show Monday to Friday on Radio
City in Liverpool, also their Top 40 show on
Saturdays.

■ Most exciting moment of career: Hasn't
happened yet.　■ Likes swimming, squash,
running and photography. Dislikes filling in
forms.　■ Married to Margaret and has two
sons.

BRIAN J. FORD
'Founder of Radio 4's Science Now. . .'
BORN: 13th May 1939 in Corsham, Wiltshire.
Father (a descendant of Sir James Watt) an
engineer, designer and company director.
EDUCATED: King's School, Peterborough.
University College, Cardiff. FIRST JOB: A year
on the junior staff of the Medical Research
Council. He was also writing a weekly
newspaper column on science at the time. Has
lectured in Asia and the East for the Foreign and
Commonwealth Office. Is editor of many

publications including 'Science Diary' and
'Broadcasting Bulletin' and has written many
books. Plays good rhythm and blues piano!
FIRST BROADCAST: A Sunday morning talk for
the Welsh Region of the BBC at the age of 21,
the title, *A Fossil Tree That Survived*, the fee,
three guineas. Was given his first television
series three years later but radio has remained
his first love and what's more he doesn't own a
television set! Was a regular member of the
team on *Dial a Scientist*. Was the founder of
Science Now on Radio 4 and has contributed to
a wide range of programmes across the
networks such as *Woman's Hour*, Radio 1's
*Newsbeat, Start the Week, Stop the Week, It's
Your Line, A Word in Edgeways* and his own
series *Where Are You Taking Us?*

■ Most exciting moment of career: 'Pioneering
a two-hour programme on cancer for Radio 4.
Controller Tony Whitby described it as an
"epoch making programme" and it gained the
highest ever Audience Research Index in the
BBC's history. There was a tragic post-script.
Tony Whitby died soon after, from cancer.'
■ A moment to remember: 'I was due to guest
on a chat show with Katie Boyle and had to
rush back from a weekend house-party in
Somerset. As I parked outside Broadcasting
House and breathed a sigh of relief, I heard
another sigh from the back seat – it was my
host's pedigree dog, fast asleep! Katie was
marvellous and took care of the animal. We
joked about it on the air and the owner heard
and drove over to collect his dog. In the end we
used it as an excuse to continue the party at our
place.'　■ Likes travelling with his family and
going to rock'n'roll gigs. Dislikes hypocrisy and
canned sauerkraut.　■ Married to Jan, has six
children and lives in Glamorgan, handy to the
sea, the mountains and the West End.

GERRY FORD
*'The cop who became a Country
singer/DJ. . .'*
BORN: 25th May 1943, in Athlone, County
Westmeath, Ireland. Father a motor mechanic.

EDUCATED: St. Mary's College, Athlone. He sang in his local church choir and at the age of 17 bought his first guitar for £14 and taught himself to play. FIRST JOB: Apprentice baker and confectioner. Continued his training in Edinburgh and then in London where he qualified. While working as a baker in London he took a part-time job as compère/DJ at the Majestic Ballroom, Finsbury Park where he introduced the Beatles on their first London appearance. In 1965 he returned to Edinburgh and joined the Edinburgh City Police. He was a policeman for 11 years. FIRST BROADCAST: The summer of 1974 as a guest on Country Sounds on Radio Clyde. The following year, when Radio Forth opened up in Edinburgh he sold them the idea of letting him present a country show, *Forth Country Special*. In 1976 he was nominated Top Country DJ by the Country Music Association and that same year he resigned from the Police and turned professional as a singer. In 1977 and 78 he won the Top Country DJ Award from the CMA. He then joined BBC Radio Scotland and has been presenting their *Country Corner* ever since. As a singer he has been heard on Radio 2's *Country Club, You and the Night and the Music* and *The Truckers' Hour*.

■ Most exciting moment of career: 'Appearing at the Grand Ole Opry in Nashville, performing one song and getting an encore. Since then I've made seven appearances there; plus recording two albums in Nashville and duetting with country star Jean Shepard on one of them.' ■ Likes researching country music, the movies and swimming. Dislikes insects and insincerity. ■ Married to Joan, has one son and lives in Edinburgh.

KEITH FORDYCE
'Running an aircraft museum between broadcasts. . .'
BORN: 15th October 1928 in Lincoln. Father a Civil Servant. EDUCATED: The Lincoln School. Emmanuel College, Cambridge. FIRST JOB: RAF. FIRST BROADCAST: 1948 in the RAF when

he was seconded to the British Forces Network in Hamburg as an announcer. Since then has done numerous programmes for BFBS, Radio Luxembourg and BBC Radio. He's the chairman of *Town and Country Quiz* and introduces *Sounds of the Sixties* and *Beat the Record*, all on Radio 2. Apart from his radio and television commitments, he manages to run the Torbay Aircraft Museum, near Paignton in Devon, an extremely successful second string to his bow!

■ Most exciting moment of career: 'Every time I start a new series'. ■ Likes flying, travel and gardening. ■ Married to Anne, has four children and lives in Devon.

RODNEY FOSTER
'The bull didn't appreciate the finer political points. . .'
BORN: 18th June 1938 in Sutton Coldfield, Warwickshire. Father in the furniture trade. EDUCATED: Bishop Vesey Grammar School, Sutton Coldfield. John Bright Grammar School, Llandudno. FIRST JOB: Trainee reporter on 'North Wales Weekly News', Conwy. Was local government correspondent for the 'Express and Star', Wolverhampton. Then joined the 'Daily Sketch' as their parliamentary correspondent. FIRST BROADCAST: 1970. 'I took a six-month contract as TV News scriptwriter before "helping out" at Westminster as political correspondent.' Is one of the BBC's political correspondents at Westminster and contributes to all the news and current affairs programmes.

■ Most exciting moment of career: 'Being lowered 60 feet from a Sea King helicopter onto the deck of a fishery-protection frigate in the Western Approaches, to film with a Select Committee.' ■ A moment to remember: 'The day I tried to compete with a rutting bull (if that's the phrase) while trying to do a piece to camera in the middle of the North Wales countryside. I eventually had to abandon my position and move to a somewhat quieter spot.

Obviously the bull didn't appreciate the finer political points of my piece.' ■ Likes music, gardening and golf. Dislikes untidiness. ■ Married to Joyce and lives in Essex.

ROBERT FOX
'Reporting from the Falklands. . .'

BORN: 21st September 1945 in Ratley, Warwickshire. Father a farmer. EDUCATED: Blundell's School, Tiverton. Magdalen College, Oxford. (B.A. 2nd Class Hons Modern History). FIRST JOB: Producer/reporter in the London office of the Australian Broadcasting Commission. Has also been a teacher and a cider factory hand in Taunton. FIRST BROADCAST: To Australia in 1967. He applied to the BBC for a job in radio in August 1968 and was appointed a producer for Radio Newsreel. Programmes include *Analysis* on Radio 4 and several talks and documentaries for Radio 3 between 1970 and 1973. Was the guest correspondent for Corriere Dela Sera Milan 1976–77. As a BBC Radio news reporter he has reported on four earthquakes in five years; the assassination of Aldo Moro; attempted assassination of the Pope; the 1976 Cod War; Red Brigades terrorism; the Mountbatten funeral; the Royal Wedding; twelve elections in seven countries and the Falklands Campaign. Has written two books, *I Counted them All Out and Counted Them All Back* with Brian Hanrahan and *Eye Witness Falklands*, which is his own personal diary. He was awarded the MBE for his coverage of the Falklands Campaign in 1982.

■ Most exciting moment of career: 'My involvement in interpreting for the surrender of 1,200 Argentine soldiers at Goose Green on May 29th, 1982.' ■ A moment to remember: 'Being spotted on a bus going into Venice. After asking the price of the fare, a couple said they recognized my terrible Italian accent from a TV broadcast the evening before!' ■ Likes history, the theatre, small boat sailing, opera, and viewing Broadcasting House over left shoulder. Dislikes central heating and air conditioning, Broadcasting House. ■ Married to Dutch painter Marianne Ockinga and has two children.

ASHLEY FRANKLIN
'A pail of water over his head. . .'

BORN: 15th December 1954 in Cwmbran, Gwent. EDUCATED: Henry Mellish Grammar School, Nottingham. City of Birmingham Polytechnic. FIRST JOB: Sales ledger clerk. Has also been a paperboy, a blackberry picker, Smith's Crisps factory packer (I spent two weeks shovelling 'Quavers' into a vat). FIRST BROADCAST: October 1971 *Extravaganza* on BBC Radio Nottingham having won their DJ contest. From Nottingham he moved to BBC Radio Derby to present their early morning news magazine, *Up and About* followed by weekday mid-morning programme *Line Up*.

■ Most exciting moment of career: 'Being asked by Sheila Tracy to fill in a questionnaire about my career. [The best is definitely yet to come!] ■ A moment to remember: 'I was on an outside broadcast which took us down an historic street in Derby. While standing outside a block of flats our resident architectural historian was telling us how the old building opposite used to be the site of executions. As if on cue, a resident of the flats carried out her own "punishment", as we had the audacity to loiter around her block, and executed the throwing of a pail of water, mainly over me! Violà, one drowned rat. Is this how you "leak" a story?" [At least it was a pail of *water*, it could have been something worse] ■ Likes music, the cinema, photography, all sports, telling jokes. Dislikes beetroot, arrogance and party bores (to get rid of them I talk about myself). ■ Married to Francine and lives in Derbyshire.

STUART FREEMAN
'A wide variety of jobs. . .'

BORN: 4th October 1952 in Blackpool, Lancashire. Father worked for the GPO.

EDUCATED: Highfield Secondary Modern, Blackpool. Blackpool College of Technology and Art. FIRST JOB: Insurance clerk, while working as a mobile DJ in the evenings. Has had a wide variety of jobs; van driver, Encyclopedia salesman, fairground worker, ice cream salesman, waiter, boutique owner and concert promoter! FIRST BROADCAST: October 1976, *Soul Time* on Swansea Sound. 'I was on the panel of a Pop Quiz programme on BBC Radio Blackburn and the bug got to me. I then started working in hospital radio and from there on to the "Big Time" *Soul Time* on Swansea Sound.' Has done just about everything there is to do at Swansea Sound and presents the weekday morning show. Also announces and reads news for HTV.

■ Most exciting moment of career: 'Every Friday when I receive my pay cheque! Also working in the USA on station WMMR in Philadelphia and station WNET in Boston.' ■ Likes squash, football, cinema, theatre, wine, women and song, and travelling. Dislikes queuing, bad tempered people and moody people. ■ Married to Shann and lives in West Glamorgan.

BILL FRINDALL
'Dear Sir, You must be one short...'
BORN: 3rd March 1939 in Epsom, Surrey. Father a research chemist specializing in yeast fermentation. EDUCATED: Reigate Grammar School. Kingston-upon-Thames School of Art

(I retired as it interfered with cricket') FIRST JOB: In publishing – production department of Lutterworth Press, but was called up for National Service after eight months. Trained in statistics and accountancy by the RAF and was commissioned in Secretarial Branch as an accountant officer. Was seconded to NATO and AFCENT (Fontainebleau) and retired after six and a half cricket seasons. FIRST BROADCAST: April 1966, scoring the match at Worcester between Worcestershire and the West Indians for a radio Outside Broadcast. 'That was my first meeting with John Arlott. When I heard about the death of my predecessor on BBC Radio News, I found out who was the Head of OB's Radio and wrote to him (Dear Sir, You must be one short!) Moral! watch the obituaries!' As official scorer and statistician to BBC Radio's *Test Match Special*, he has scored every home Test since 1966 which is something of a record in itself. His 100th test score comes up with the first test between England and the West Indies in the summer of 1984. Is the cricket statistician to the 'Daily Telegraph' and the 'Guardian' and has compiled and edited 11 books on cricket.

■ Most exciting moment of career: 'It's all been exciting I'm being paid to carry out a hobby that's got out of control, but probably none surpasses the Melbourne Test of Christmas 1982 which England won by 3 runs.'
■ A moment to remember: 'Thanks to Brian Johnston ("and Massive Arsood, (Asif Masood) comes in to bowl"), I am known as the "Bearded Wonder". It prompted my being sponsored for Cancer Research, to dress as an Arab for the entire third day's play between England and Australia at The Oval in August 1977 – the only time that *Test Match Special* has been on *Pick of the Week!*' ■ Likes cricket, travel, women, wine and philately. Dislikes dogs, snobs, TV commercials, pasta, junk food, pop music and cricket eccentrics (retired military, clergy and small boys) who expect their incredibly long and demanding letters to be answered. ■ Is divorced, has one manic cat, Bonkers, and lives in East Finchley.

PAUL GAMBACINI
'A Yank at Oxford...'
BORN: 2nd April 1949 in New York City. Father a partner in a photo-engraving corporation. EDUCATED: Dartmouth College, USA. University College, Oxford. FIRST JOB: Afternoon paper-round after school. Was a delivery boy for a chemist in the summer of 1966 and was bitten by a dog on his first delivery. A lot later became executive producer

at station WBZ Boston, Massachusetts. FIRST BROADCAST: A newscast on WDCR Hanover, New Hampshire, USA. WDCR was the nation's largest radio station run by students, and owned by the Dartmouth College Trustees. While he was a student at Oxford and contributing editor of 'Rolling Stone' magazine, he was invited by BBC producer John Walters to give a weekly talk on Radio 1. Has since contributed to a wide variety of radio programmes; *All American Heroes, Kaleidoscope*, the *Elton John Story*, the *Bee Gees Story, Roundtable, What Next*. Television credits include *Pebble Mill at One* and the *Old Grey Whistle Test*. He presents the *Paul Gambacini US Hits Show* on Radio 1 and is the co-author of the 'Guinness Book of British Hit Singles.'

■ Most exciting moment of career: 'When I opened 'The Sunday Times' and saw the 'Guinness Book of British Hit Singles' had gone to Number One in the Best Sellers.' ■ Likes softball, squash, collecting Carl Barks comics. Dislikes winter drizzle. ■ Lives in London.

NORMA GAMBLE
'A second career in broadcasting. . .'
BORN: 8th June 1939 in Belfast, Northern Ireland. Father a Civil Servant. EDUCATED: Belfast Royal Academy. FIRST JOB: A nurse. Has also worked as a personnel officer. FIRST BROADCAST: October 1980. Having gained experience in hospital radio, joined Radio Tay

in Dundee and has presented a wide variety of their programmes. Is the presenter of *Afternoon Affair*, Monday to Friday on Radio Tay.

■ Most exciting moment of career: Broadcasting from a hot air balloon and while power hang gliding. ■ A moment to remember: 'Chatting to a quiz contestant who turned out to be 17 and married with a baby and then putting the question "Complete the proverb 'Marry in haste'. . .!"' ■ Likes amateur theatre, gardening, sewing and swimming. ■ Married to Brian, has two children and lives in Tayside.

BRIAN GEAR
'Adapted 'Lorna Doone' and 'The Moonstone' for radio. . .'
BORN: 22nd September 1936 in Redhill, Surrey. EDUCATED: Reigate Grammar School. FIRST JOB: Reporter on the 'Surrey Mirror'. FIRST BROADCAST: As a reporter on *Today in the South and West*. Programmes include *Home in the Afternoon*, Radio 3's *Music in Question, Woman's Hour* and several features for Radio 4 – *Clara Butt, The Storyteller, A Portrait of Saki, Going to Extremes*. Has adapted 'Lorna Doone' and 'The Moonstone' as radio plays. A freelance radio and television reporter specializing in the arts.

■ Most exciting moment of career: 'Still waiting for it.' ■ Dislikes pop music.

DAVID GEARY
'Many years as a West End actor. . .'
BORN: 7th March 1928 in Welwyn, Hertfordshire. Father a schoolmaster. EDUCATED: Cheltenham College. Royal Academy of Dramatic Art. FIRST JOB: Understudying in *Who is Sylvia* at the Criterion Theatre. Other theatre credits include *Hobson's Choice* at the Grand Theatre, Blackpool; *Aren't We All?* at the Theatre Royal, Haymarket; *Summer Song* at the Princes Theatre, Shaftesbury Avenue. FIRST BROADCAST: Scipio

48

in *The Road to Rome* on the BBC Light Programme. After many years as an actor, he wrote to the BBC, was interviewed, auditioned and invited to join the staff as an announcer. He has also worked for Anglia Television *Anglia News, Anthology, Probe, Police Call* and for LBC Radio on *Artsweek*. He is a Radio 2 newsreader/announcer.

■ Most exciting moment of career: 'Playing the lead during Kenneth More's holiday, in Terence Rattigan's *The Deep Blue Sea* at the Duchess Theatre. ■ A moment to remember: 'A moment of linguistic revelation, *c.* 1959. I entered the BBC's Aeolian Hall studio to present a lunch-hour music show billed as ''Hermanos Deniz and the Band''. ''Which is Hermanos?'' I asked. The reply: ''They're both over there'' . . . it effectively taught me that ''Hermanos'' is Spanish for ''brothers''!' ■ Likes photography and boatbuilding. Dislikes yoghurt and chilled Guinness (surely it spoils the flavour?) ■ Married to Sheila, has two children and lives in Buckinghamshire.

MIKE GEORGE
'Broadcasting with a bucket. . .'

BORN: 4th May 1945 in Harrow, Middlesex. Father a Royal Marine. EDUCATED: Bushey Grammar School, Watford (Now Queen's School). FIRST JOB: Meteorological instrument-maker. Spent ten years in the Royal Navy and then became a representative for a pharmaceutical company. FIRST BROADCAST: In the Royal Navy on Beira patrol. Is presenter of *Mainline Drivetime* for Radio Wyvern. Also presents their Saturday *Family Show.*

■ Most exciting moment of career: Being in at the start of Radio Wyvern and seeing it develop into a successful radio station. ■ A moment to remember: 'Broadcasting in the Navy when I sat at the microphone with a pile of records on one side and a bucket on the other — I wasn't a very good sailor.' ■ Likes television, walking and his kids. Dislikes lies, except white ones to avoid hurting people. ■ Married to Janet, has two children and lives in Worcester.

ANDREW GIDLEY
'Supports Crystal Palace . . . someone has to!'

BORN: 3rd January 1954 in London. EDUCATED: Ashburton High School, Croydon. FIRST JOB: Invoice clerk in an office at Aldgate, London. Has also worked in public relations. FIRST BROADCAST: Reporting on Crystal Palace v Hull City at Selhurst Park. He freelanced for some time before joining the staff of LBC in London in October 1979. Was one of the commentators at the FA Cup Final Spurs v Manchester City replay in 1981. Is LBC's tennis correspondent.

■ Most exciting moment of career: 'Commentating on Ricky Villa's winning goal in the 1981 FA Cup Final replay against Manchester City and being ''on air'' at the very moment. Also attending my first Scotland-England international at Hampden Park, Glasgow.' ■ Likes supporting Crystal Palace (someone has to). Dislikes Chinese food, cross channel ferries, *Crossroads* and losing on the horses. ■ Married to Sue and lives in Sussex.

ANDY GILLIES
'Cupid of the airwaves. . .'

BORN: 21st December 1959 in Perth, Scotland. Father a teacher. EDUCATED: Trinity College, Glenalmond. Corpus Christie College,

Cambridge (Classics degree). FIRST JOB: Joined Hereward Radio straight from University. FIRST BROADCAST: August 1981 on Hereward Radio, having gained experience with Cambridge University Radio over the previous two years. Has presented the weekend *Breakfast Shows*, the *Exploding Wireless Show* and the Saturday *Late Show*. Is presenter of the daily lunchtime news magazine on Hereward Radio.

■ A moment to remember: 'The night I was asked to propose to a girl on someone else's behalf on the air! It's the first time I'd ever done anything like that but it was great. I wouldn't mind it happening every Saturday night. Oh, she said "yes" by the way!' ■ Likes most traditional sports, Wimbledon fortnight and expensive (and good) restaurants. Dislikes inane TV quiz shows, football hooligans and expensive (but bad) restaurants. ■ Married to the job and lives in Cambridgeshire.

JAMES ALEXANDER GORDON
'A never-to-be-forgotten news flash. . .'
BORN: 10th February 1936 in South Queensferry, Scotland. Father a publican. Adopted at 6 days old, at 6 months old, he contracted polio and was completely paralysed. EDUCATED: In hospital, where he spent his childhood up to the age of fifteen, by which time he was walking again due to the determination and encouragement of his parents. FIRST JOB: Clerk with ICI. He became a song plugger for Noel Gay Music and then

joined the production department of Deutsch Grammophon in London. A job as a researcher on television music programmes followed. FIRST BROADCAST: *All Things Considered* on BBC Television. 'I was working as a researcher, but someone who had written a piece for the programme failed to turn up, so I did the commentary and reporting. They liked what I did and I was asked to do other things.' He joined Radio 2 as a newsreader/announcer in 1971. Has presented many Radio 2 programmes including *Brass and Strings* and is heard reading the football results on Saturdays in *Sport on 2*.

■ Most exciting moment of career: 'Introducing my first concert at the Royal Festival Hall, *Brass and Strings*.' ■ A moment to remember: 'The day I read a news flash on Radio 2 and said, "The Chancellor of the Exchequer has just announced his new Bunny Midget." A communication arrived from the House of Commons saying that the Chancellor (Anthony Barber) liked it very much and no action was to be taken against me!' ■ Likes cooking, music and current affairs. ■ Dislikes nothing! ■ Has one son, David and lives in Berkshire.

LOU GRANT
'A stand up comedian before becoming a DJ. . .'
BORN: 3rd November 1936 in Ayr, Scotland. Father an aircraft fitter. EDUCATED: Newton-Head Sch⁓ ., Ayr. FIRST JOB: Apprentice piano⏑ ⎯ner. Has also been a Butlin Red-Coat and progressed into Show Biz proper as a stand-up comedian and entertainer. FIRST BROADCAST: Showtime on BBC Scotland in the early 70s. Appeared on many television programmes in Scotland such as STV's *Big Night Out, Battle of the Comics*. Network television shows include *Startime* and *Search for a Star*. Was approached by West Sound to write and submit some ideas for programmes. They were accepted and he was offered the *Good Morning* programme Monday to Friday and the Sunday *Family Request* programme.

■ Most exciting moment of career: 'Compèring the Festival of Scotland from the Royal Albert Hall in London, and my first tour of America and Canada with the White Heather Club stage show!' ■ A moment to remember: 'I was sitting in a restaurant discussing an important business transaction when the lady opposite who had been staring at me for some time, eventually came over and said without as much as an "excuse me", "Are you Lou Grant?" Somewhat irritated, I retorted "no" and thought that would be the end of the matter. However the staring match continued. Over she came again . . . "Are you Lou Grant?". "Look Madam", I said, "I know who I am, and I am not Lou Grant". Like all good fans, she was persistent and when she came back for the third time I had had enough. "Madam, if it will make you happy and allow me to finish my lunch, I am Lou Grant." To which she replied " I thought you were but you don't look like him. I thought you were much taller". True . . . True . . . True!' ■ Likes horse racing and tropical fish. Dislikes insincerity, 'hangers-on', people who block shop doorways and sidewalks. ■ Lives in Ayrshire.

RICHARD GRAVES
'A choirmaster for over twenty years. . .'
BORN: 21st June 1926 in Harrogate, Yorkshire. Father an engineering consultant and musician. EDUCATED: Lanesborough Prep. School, Guildford. Lewisham School, Weston-super-Mare. Taught to play the piano by his father, but later studied under Samuel Popplestone and F.C.Rowles. FIRST JOB: As part-time school music teacher and private music teacher. Almost first job as a writer was compiling an instruction brochure for the 'Tin Whistle'. He then gave up teaching to become a freelance musician, writing, composing, conducting and lecturing. For several years was the pianist in The Palm Court Trio and a freelance flautist. He was also organist and choirmaster of St. Saviour's Church, Weston-super-Mare for over 20 years. FIRST

BROADCAST: Talk for *Children's Hour* in 1948, having submitted a script on spec, which was accepted. A variety of other broadcasts quickly followed. 'I was greatly helped by the then West Region's *Children's Hour* Organizer, Mollie Austin, who gave tremendous encouragement and technical advice.' Has presented *Music Magazine* and *Mainly For Pleasure* for Radio 3; *Postmark UK* for the World Service. Has appeared as a singer/presenter of Victorian/Edwardian songs on *Woman's Hour* and the *Charlie Chester Show*. Has also produced many of Jack Brymer's *At Home* programmes. Presents the World Service series, the *Golden Age of Operetta*.

■ Most exciting moment of career: 'Making my first appearance on a "live" television show, *Pebble Mill at One*.' ■ A moment to remember: 'During the presentation of a music programme, finding that the studio "talkback" had been accidentally plugged into the network, thus enabling listeners to hear the "private" conversation between presenter and producer!' ■ Likes travel. Dislikes dieting, intellectual hotels and boarding houses masquerading as hotels. ■ Married to Mary Ketley-Roberts, has three children and lives in Avon.

BENNY GREEN
'Flat on his back on the studio floor. . .'
BORN: 9th December 1927 in Leeds. Father a professional musician. EDUCATED: St. Marylebone Grammar School, London. Was taught to play the tenor sax by his father. FIRST JOB: Playing gigs. He spent 20 years as a professional musician playing with such bands as Roy Fox, Kenny Baker, Stan Kenton and Ronnie Scott. As a musician he also pursued a writing career and wrote a weekly column for the 'New Musical Express' from 1955 to '57. He was jazz critic of the 'Observer', 1958 to '77. He now writes a Saturday column for the 'Mirror'; a weekly TV column for 'Punch'; a

weekly column in 'Where to Go in London'; and a monthly column in 'Ideal Home'. He has written biographies of P.G. Wodehouse and Fred Astaire and a book on Bernard Shaw. He has also edited four books on cricket. FIRST BROADCAST: (Not as a musician) A talk on jazz in 1955. In 1959 he did a monthly review of jazz records on the Third Programme. Has written many series for Radio 2 which have been broadcast by others; *History of Pop Music* (Kenneth More); the *Life of Fred Astaire* (David Niven); *Life of Ella Fitzgerald* (Andre Previn); *History of the Hollywood Musical* (Douglas Fairbanks) and the *Hollywood Moguls* (Orson Welles). 'Out of the eight scripts I wrote for him, he only changed a few words in one of them. I felt quite bucked'. But although he writes for the stars, he's a very popular broadcaster in his own right with his weekly Sunday afternoon show on Radio 2 and his *Jazz Score* series, of which he is chairman. He also makes regular appearances on Radio 4's *Kaleidoscope* and *Stop the Week*, along with a regular Friday morning slot on the *Mike Aspel Show* for Capital Radio. Always thought of as a Cockney although he was born in Leeds ('I only spent 3 weeks there') he has spent most of his life in the Euston road area of London. 'I can't drive, I can't swim, I can't dance, I can't skate and not only can I not speak any foreign languages, I have a lot of trouble with English!'

■ Most exciting moment of career: 'Being sent by the BBC in 1976 to Beverly Hills to interview 28 people for the *Hooray for Hollywood* series and for the BBC Archives, including Ira Gershwin, Harry Warren and Gene Kelly.' ■ A moment to remember: 'In 1965 I was doing a radio series called the *Jazz Scene*, when I slipped a disc. In the studio I would lie flat on my back on the floor, with my producer lying beside me and in that position we would go through the script. On one such occasion a young man from the Iranian Broadcasting Company, who was studying production, came in with his note book to see how things were done at the BBC. Nobody explained to him why we were lying on the floor, and he scribbled away taking notes. I wouldn't be surprised if that's the way they do it in Iran now, flat on their backs on the studio floor.' ■ Likes popular music à la Gershwin, Porter, Berlin; and cricket. Dislikes the worst elements of modern pop music. ■ Married to Toni, has three sons and one daughter and lives in Hertfordshire.

ANNE GREGG
'Two and a half hours talking to a minah bird. . .'

BORN: 11th February 1940 in Belfast. Father a Civil Servant. EDUCATED: Strathearn School for Girls. FIRST JOB: On leaving school, a fill-in job with the Ministry of Finance. At the age of nineteen became a reporter on Ulster Television's nightly current affairs programme. Worked as an announcer on BBC television and as a reporter on Anglia's *About Anglia*. Has been the deputy editor of 'Good Housekeeping' and the editor of 'Woman's Journal'. FIRST BROADCAST: (On radio) *Woman's Hour* in 1965. Has contributed to *Today* and the *World at One*. 1977/78 presenter of *Weekend Woman's Hour*. 1981, presenter of *Rags to Riches*. 1982 guest announcer on Radio 4 and presenter with Anthony Holden of Radio 4's *In the Air*. Television credits include *Holiday* on BBC 1.

■ Most exciting moment of career: 'Landing my first presenting/reporting job at the age of 19 after being short listed from 1,000 applicants. But there was also the excitement of interviewing Hope and Crosby; and ballooning over Dunstable for *Woman's Hour*!' ■ A moment to remember: 'I once spent two and a half hours talking to a minah bird at the Talking Birds Exhibition at Olympia. It took another two and a half hours to edit down to two and a half minutes of quite hilarious "proper" conversation for *Woman's Hour*. The fee was hardly commensurate with the time involved, but I think it made *Pick of the Week!*' ■ Likes travel, painting, cooking, gardening and DIY. Dislikes pseuds, jargon, aggressive drivers, closed minds and oysters. ■ Lives in Middlesex.

HUBERT GREGG
'Maybe it's because I'm a Londoner. . .'

BORN: London. EDUCATED: St. Dunstan's College and Webber Douglas School of Singing and Dramatic Art. FIRST JOB: Singing 'the

gardener' in *The Marriage of Figaro* with the
Chanticleer Opera Company. Played many
Shakespearean roles at the Old Vic and the
Open Air Theatre Regent's Park. West End
plays include *French Without Tears* (London
and New York), *While the Sun Shines,
Chrysanthemum* (first musical). Chichester
Festival Theatre 1968/71. Has presented his
one man show on both sides of the Atlantic.
Films include Walt Disney's *Robin Hood,
Doctor at Sea, Simon and Laura.* Has written
over a hundred songs, many of them big hits.
*I'm Going to Get Lit Up, Maybe it's Because
I'm a Londoner.* Has written two novels *April
Gentleman* and *A Day's Loving.* Non-fiction
works include *Agatha Christie and all that
Mousetrap* and *Thanks for the Memory.* FIRST
BROADCAST: With the Birmingham Repertory
Theatre in *Cabbages and Kings* from the BBC
Midland studios in 1933. In the 60s he adapted
Jerome K. Jerome's *Three Men in a Boat* as a
musical for radio, appearing in it along with
Kenneth Horne and Leslie Phillips. Nowadays
well known and loved for his 'nostalgic
programmes on Wireless 2, as he calls it, *A
Square Deal* which ran for seven years and
Thanks for the Memory which has been
running since 1970. Other series include
Hubert Gregg at the London Theatre, and more
recently *I Call It Genius* and *I Call it Style,* all on
Radio 2.

■ Most exciting moment of career: 'Holding a
conversation with Winston Churchill on the
telephone when he called the Empire Service
(as the World Service was called in the 30s) at
1am, and I, as a part-time announcer, was the
only person in authority in the building.'
■ A moment to remember: '2nd April 1949
when the lights went on in Piccadilly Circus
and they sang *I'm Going to Get Lit Up* on the
Criterion balcony. I was on *In Town Tonight*
that night.' ■ Likes cinematography,
videography and anything connected with
yesterday. ■ Married to Carmel, has three
children and lives in Kent.

TIM GUDGIN
'You name it, he's done it. . .'

BORN: In Croydon, Surrey. 'I'm older than Terry
Wogan and younger than Jimmy Young!'
EDUCATED: Hardy's School, Dorchester. Bishop
Wordsworth's, Salisbury, Whitgift, Croydon.
FIRST JOB: Newsreader/scriptwriter Forces
Broadcasting Service, BFN Hamburg. FIRST
BROADCAST: Reading a five minute News for
CCG (Control Commission for Germany.)
Doing National Service, he was seconded from
5th R.T.R. at Belsen as Acting Captain to British
Forces Network, Hamburg as
DJ/producer/scriptwriter/actor etc. On
returning to civvy street, he established himself
as a leading broadcaster with such programmes
as *Family Favourites, Today, Housewives'
Choice, Round the Bend, Music Box, 12
o'clock Spin, Listen With Mother, Friday Night
is Music Night, Saturday Night on the Light,
Treble Chance, Top of the Form, Maestro,
Swingalong* and many others. He was
anchorman on the forerunner of TV's
Grandstand and Radio's *Sport on 2,* i.e. Light
Programme's *Out and About.* Television credits
include *Blue Peter, Town and Around* and
Grandstand. He was the Chairman of the
Square Deal Surf Forum advertisement on
television, the proceeds of which bought him
his first brand-new house! He is a Radio 2
newsreader/announcer and is one of the
presenters of *You and the Night and the Music.*
He is also heard on Radio 4's *Top of the Form*
and BBC 1's *Grandstand.*

■ Most exciting moment of career: 'The red
light going on in the Hamburg Concert Hall at
the start of the very first programme in a "live"
BFN Concert series (*Rhineland Serenade*) that
was broadcast simultaneously by the Light
Programme.' ■ A moment to remember:
'When I was presenting *Music Box* in the 60s, I
went on an overseas trip as question master
with the long running quiz show, *Treble
Chance,* visiting service bases in Germany,
Malta, Cyprus, Gibraltar and N. Africa. At each
destination the *Music Box* producer, John

Fawcett Wilson, had made arrangements with the local broadcasting service for studios and lines to be available to present the programme "live" as usual. All went well until Cyprus who were having certain troubles between the Greeks and Turks. I found it off-putting to say the least to find myself in a studio at the end of Nicosia Airport runway, and being greeted on arrival by Cypriot troops with fixed bayonets. They turned out to be friendly and guarded me and the sand-bagged building, while inside I tried to sound my cheery self, full of jolly banter presenting our usual banal music mixture to the accompaniment of jet fighters and bombers taking off and landing just above the roof. A memorable occasion!' ■ Likes playing jazz clarinet, collecting records, squash, tennis, golf and sailing. Dislikes opera, joggers, letter writing and interviewing politicians.
■ Married to Jenny, has six children and lives in Kent.

RICHARD GWYNN
'Eight years with BFBS. . .'
BORN: 7th September 1949 in Bournemouth. Father a bank manager. EDUCATED: Clifton College, Bristol. FIRST JOB: In Public Relations for BP Chemicals. FIRST BROADCAST: 1972 on BFBS Cyprus. 'I was hitch hiking around Europe and I landed a three-month temporary job as an announcer for BFBS in Cyprus I also worked for the Cyprus Broadcasting Corporation while I was there.' He remained with BFBS for eight years working in Cyprus, Malta, Gibraltar and Germany. He also became Station Manager for BFBS Television. He then joined Two Counties Radio in Bournemouth where he is Programme Controller and presents the 9 to 12 noon show daily.

■ Likes sport, especially golf and cricket. Dislikes filling in forms. [Sorry!] ■ Married to Linda, has two sons, Phillip and Jonathan, and lives in Dorset.

ROBIN HALL
'An avid football freak. . .'
BORN: 27th June 1937 in Edinburgh. Father an upholsterer. EDUCATED: Allan Glen's School, Gasgow. FIRST JOB: Chef. Has also worked as a swimming instructor, an actor and a fisherman. FIRST BROADCAST: 1946 singing and reading a short story on *Children's Hour*. Has made hundreds of television and radio performances as a folk singer. Became a household name along with Jimmie Macgregor when they appeared nightly on BBC Television's *Tonight* programme for four years. The two of them became one of the most famous folk singing duos in the country. In recent years has become a presenter/producer/researcher as a result of being asked by Radio Clyde to make a documentary on Glasgow, the *Sing Song Streets*. He's the presenter of Radio Scotlands *Travelling Folk* and *Robin's Review*. Also presents a children's music programme *Make Minor Music*.

■ Most exciting moment of career: 'Re-joining all my old colleagues and friends for the special 25th anniversary of the *Tonight* programme; and being presented with two awards by Professor Asa Briggs in the Imperial Tobacco Radio Awards of 1977 . . . Best Radio Documentary and Best Radio Presenter for the *Sing Song Streets.'* ■ A moment to remember: 'Being an avid football freak, I was delighted to have been given the chance to produce a Radio Scotland documentary, the *50/50 Ball*, to commemorate the 50th anniversary of the death of the famous Celtic and Scotland goalkeeper, John Thompson.' ■ Likes cooking, jazz and is a fervent supporter of Partick Thistle F.C. Dislikes wallpaper music, fascism and Glasgow sectarianism. ■ Married to Andy, has two children and lives in Glasgow.

STUART HALL
'Clocks make him tick. . .'
BORN: December 25th, 1934, in Hyde,

politician? She smiled winsomely and said "I always thought you voted Tory, Stuart."'
■ Likes collecting clocks (he has over 200 of them), watches, motorbikes. Dislikes snobs and pseuds. ■ Married to Hazel, has a daughter and a son and lives in Cheshire.

Cheshire. Father a master baker. EDUCATED: Glossop Grammar School. University of Manchester Faculty of Technology. FIRST JOB: In the family catering and garage businesses. 'I sold hot loaves and hotter motor cars to some even hotter folk'. FIRST BROADCAST: 1958, commentating on a football match between Manchester United and Leicester City in which he saw only two of the seven goals scored because of thick fog. It all came about because of his interest in football and motor racing, 'I played at both in typical amateur, laissez-faire style' and after hearing him do a couple of commentaries at the racing circuits, the BBC came up with an offer to work for them. His first boss told him to use his personality when broadcasting, advice he has followed to such good effect that nowadays people either love or loathe him! Moved into television in the mid 60s as anchorman of the nightly magazine *Look North*, but found national fame, if not a fortune, as compère of *It's A Knock Out*. Is still a regular commentator on football matches, much to the irritation of certain footballers who shall be nameless! Has been entertaining Radio 2 audiences in his own inimitable style, with the *Stuart Hall Late Show* from Manchester.

■ Most exciting moment of career: Compèring a Variety Show for Her Majesty the Queen, and riding a motor cycle down Snaefell on the Isle of Man. ■ A moment to remember: 'In the early days of my career, I'd been to Ramsbottom to interview a mountain climber in the pouring rain. When I got back to the television studio in Manchester for the evening programme, I was soaked through and as I had no intention of ruining my one and only good suit by sitting around in it, I went into the studio in a cardigan, shirt and tie and underpants. They were pretty daft underpants, given to me by a fan and they had "I love you" across the crotch and silly red hearts. There I sat flaunting myself, telling the cameramen to keep in close, when suddenly the door opened and in walked a leading Labour lady politician. I'd never been so embarrassed in all my life. And the lady

DAVID HAMILTON
'I love the one-to-one contact of radio. . .'
BORN: 10th September 1941 in Manchester. Father a journalist. EDUCATED: Glastonbury Grammar School. FIRST JOB: As a script writer for ATV. FIRST BROADCAST: The *Beat Show* from Manchester in 1963. Has always been in show business. From script writing he moved to television announcing to acting, to compèring and to becoming a DJ. Has hosted many TV shows including *Top of the Pops, World Disco Dance Championships, Miss TV Times, TV Times Gala Awards, Up for the Cup, Chipperfield's Circus, Seaside Special*. Has had his own daily show on BBC Radio 2 since 1973.

■ Most exciting moment of career: (Three!) Working on television in America; Compèring a show at the London Palladium; Playing in a football match with the team that won the World Cup in 1966. 'Although my career started in television and I have done stage work, pantomime etc:, radio has always been my favourite medium. I love the one-to-one contact, the feeling of communication with the listener. And the good thing about radio is that you don't have to dress up for it!' ■ Likes playing football for the Showbiz Eleven, tennis, music and watching Fulham. Dislikes Chelsea and any other football team except Fulham. ■ Divorced, has two children and lves in south-west London.

JIM HANCOCK
'In at the start of Piccadilly Radio. . .'
BORN: 10th October 1948 in Plymouth, Devon. Father a quantity surveyor. EDUCATED:

Shebbear College, North Devon and Manchester University. FIRST JOB: Assistant to Managing Director, Piccadilly Radio, having been introduced to him while President of the Student's Union at Manchester University. FIRST BROADCAST: 2nd April 1974 in *Time to Talk*. Then went on to become a reporter for BBC TV North West and then to London as lobby correspondent for Independent Radio News at Westminster. Programmes include *Decision Makers* for IRN, *Piccadilly Line, World from the NW, Hancock* (3-hour magazine) on Piccadilly Radio. Also holds the position of Current Affairs Editor for Piccadilly Radio.

■ Most exciting moment of career: Interviewing the Prime Minister at Number 10. ■ A moment to remember: 'Being in at the start of Piccadilly Radio when there were no studios, and record pluggers had to negotiate wood and wires to get to my desk to urge me to play their records on non-existent programmes!' ■ Likes History and Plymouth Argyle. ■ Married to Frances, has one child and lives in Manchester.

DOMINICK HARROD
'A prediction that came true. . .'

BORN: 21st August 1940 in Oxford. Father the distinguished economist and Don at Christ Church Oxford, Roy Harrod. EDUCATED: Westminster School. Christ Church, Oxford. FIRST JOB: Assistant gossip columnist of the 'Sunday Telegraph'. 1966–69 Washington correspondent of the 'Daily Telegraph'. FIRST BROADCAST: 1968 in Washington DC on a chat show. Joined the BBC in 1971 as economics correspondent. Left the Corporation in 1978 to spend a year in the head office of Dunlop's. Returned to the BBC in 1979 as Economics Editor. Is heard regularly on all the news and current affairs programmes and usually partners Jimmy Young on Radio 2 on budget specials.

■ Most interesting period of career: 'The three years I spent in Washington.' ■ A moment to remember: (or maybe savour) 'It was the summer of 1975 during the experimental broadcasting of Parliament when I received some exclusive information that enabled me to put two and two together and predict that Denis Healey, the then Chancellor of the Exchequer would make a statement in the Commons on a pay policy. On the Jimmy Young programme in the morning I predicted what that pay policy would be limiting pay rises to £6 per week. When, at lunch time, it was announced that the Chancellor was to make a statement that afternoon, I persuaded Radio 4 to ditch their *Afternoon Theatre* and go over to the Commons "live" for the Chancellor's speech. They did and Denis Healey duly announced what I had predicted some four hours earlier. Very gratifying.' ■ Likes dinghy sailing. Dislikes people who are rude to waiters in restaurants. ■ Married to Christina, has one son and lives in London.

DICK HATCH
'Parish priest for sixteen years. . .'

BORN: 24th September 1936 in St. Vincent, British West Indies. Father a priest. EDUCATED: Yarlet Hall, near Stafford. St. John's, Leatherhead. Queen's College, Cambridge. FIRST JOB: Curate at St. Mary's Leigh, Lancashire. Spent sixteen years as a parish priest. FIRST BROADCAST: Religious contribution in 1972. As his contributions to religious programmes increased, his broadcasting career gradually took over from his career in the

Church. Has presented many programmes for BBC Manchester including *Changing Scenes, Up and About, Late Night Manchester, Ever Singing, Nine till Noon, Midday Talk-In,* and now presents *206 Tonight.*

■ Most exciting moment of career: Interviewing the President of Pakistan. ■ Likes music. Dislikes crabs. ■ Married to Gillian, has three daughters and lives in Greater Manchester.

DESMOND HAWKINS
'Half a century in broadcasting. . .'
BORN: East Sheen, Surrey. Father an ironmonger. EDUCATED: Cranleigh and Grub Street. FIRST JOB: Trainee for the Willen Key Co in London. FIRST BROADCAST: A book talk on the BBC Empire Service. As a freelance scriptwriter and critic he was invited by Lawrence Gilliam to join the BBC's wartime features department as a scriptwriter working with Francis Dillon. He remained on the BBC staff for 25 years and in 1983 clocked up another 25 years as a freelance author and broadcaster. During his time on the staff he progressed from Features Producer to Head of Programmes to Controller of West Region, but never stopped broadcasting. Programmes have included *Country magazine,* the *Naturalist, Birds in Britain, Pass the Salt* (with Johnny Morris), *Look* (TV), *Time for Verse, In the Words of the Poet* and *War Report.* He has written many books, his latest being 'Hardy's Wessex'.

■ Most exciting moment of career: 'Sharing with Christopher Parsons (Head of Natural History Unit) the Royal Television Society's Award to the National History Unit in it's Jubilee year (1982).' ■ A moment to remember: 'When I was in Tripoli to advise the Libyan government on the introduction there of a television service, I interviewed a local Arab journalist who told me about the one great pilgrimage he had made. To my surprise it was not to Mecca but to Madrid, to see Real Madrid play Manchester United in the European

Cup!' ■ Likes bird watching, touring and gardening. Dislikes the poor presentation of radio programmes in 'Radio Times.' ■ Lives in Dorset.

BRIAN HAYES
'Lethal on the end of a telephone. . .'
BORN: 17th December 1937 in Perth, Australia. Father was a miner (gold)! EDUCATED: Left school at 15. FIRST JOB: Junior clerk in a mining company. FIRST BROADCAST: Reading the local news on 6KG Kalgoorlie, Western Australia at 8am on a November day in 1955. Having become very frustrated with an office job in a gold mine, and having heard that the local radio station were desperate for a new announcer, he rang the station manger, did an audition, and was offered the job. Since coming to the UK he has worked for Capital Radio producing *Capital Open Line* and their General Election coverage. In January 1976 he moved from Euston Road to Gough Square to present his own weekday programme from 10am to midday on LBC and has established quite a reputation for himself as an interviewer and a handler of 'phone-ins'. He's also consultant on presentation for LBC.

■ Most exciting moment of career: 'Interviewing some of my literary heroes including Joseph Heller and John Updike; receiving an award for 'best phone-in' for a series of programmes from Belfast, and being on the radio every weekday.' ■ Likes reading fiction, going to the cinema and watching television. Dislikes people who don't enjoy the sport of argument. ■ Lives in London.

HENDI. (MICHAEL HENDERSON)
'Likes working late. . .'
BORN: 1942 in Nottingham. Father a Civil Servant. EDUCATED: Local grammar school. FIRST JOB: Bank official. FIRST BROADCAST: In Belfast on the *Radio 1 Club* with Tony Brandon

in 1967, having asked producer Aidan Day if he could be the guest DJ. Freelanced for the BBC in Ulster and also appeared on Ulster Television in *Zoom In*. Joined the Independent Local Radio Station, Downtown Radio, in March 1976. Has presented their *Breakfast Show*, *Mid-Morning Show* and the *Late Nite Programme* (lovely time to work), is now the *Mid-Afternoon* presenter on Downtown Radio.

■ Most exciting moment of career: Still waiting! ■ A moment to remember: 'On a phone-in, I asked an Ulster lady, "Have you any children?" She replied, "Yes I have two". "What are they?" I enquired and she quickly said, "Oh they're Protestants like myself".' ■ Likes swimming, gardening, admiring beautiful women. Dislikes tripe. ■ Married to Dee Dee, has two girls and a boy and lives in Northern Ireland.

NICK HENNEGAN
'Police cadet to DJ. . .'
BORN: 14th August in Birmingham. Father a sewing machine mechanic. EDUCATED: Wheelers Lane School, Birmingham. FIRST JOB: Police cadet with the City of Birmingham Police. Has also been a social worker in London, and it was this social work that got him into broadcasting. FIRST BROADCAST: 12th December 1981 on BRMB. Has presented their *Morning Call* and *Whaddyawant* (young persons' show). Is the presenter of BRMB's *Romantics* music to make love by!

■ Most exciting moment of career: 'Saving a drowning boy while conducting an interview near Redditch, Worcestershire! The boy was OK; the interview wasn't.' ■ Likes playing the guitar, sailing and kids. Dislikes bigots, pretention and most school teachers. ■ Is a bachelor and lives in the West Midlands.

LENNY HENRY
'Too much bad pop on the airwaves. . .'
BORN: 29th August 1958 in Sedgely. Father employed by British Leyland. EDUCATED: Blue Coat Secondary Modern School. FIRST JOB: Apprentice engineer at British Leyland in Dudley. Has also worked in Dudley Zoo on the catering side (washing glasses and stacking bottles in crates). FIRST BROADCAST: *New Faces*, January 1975. His first radio broadcast was on Radio 1's *Newsbeat*. After appearing on the Radio 1 Roadshow in Great Yarmouth, he was asked if he would like to do some radio and was eventually given his own show. Apart from appearing on *Wit's End* on Radio 2, all his shows have been for Radio 1. *Roundtable, Lenny Henry Easter Egg, My Top 12* and *The Sunday Hoot*.

■ Most exciting moment of career: Appearing in the Royal Variety Performance and working with Muhammad Ali. ■ A moment to remember: 'While doing a *Roundtable* with Darryl Hall (of Hall and Oates fame), myself and Mike Read were messing about and doing various characters and basically saying that a lot of the records were awful, in a funny sort of way! On leaving the building Darryl Hall was heard to remark, "If these guys decide the hits, no wonder it's such a hard market to crack!"' ■ Likes listening to soul music and reading. Dislikes saturation of the airwaves with bad pop music. ■ Lives in the West Midlands.

STUART HENRY
'A pirate DJ and the world's worst sailor. . .'
BORN: 24th February 1942 in Edinburgh.

EDUCATED: Glasgow Drama College. FIRST JOB: Actor on a six month contract with the BBC in Scotland. He then joined a repertory company in Dundee and while there decided he wanted to become one of the new breed of 'pirate disc jockeys'. One thing he hadn't catered for was the fact that the pirate stations were all at sea. He was the world's worst sailor and it wasn't long before he was back on dry land. FIRST BROADCAST: (As a DJ) on Radio Scotland [the pirate station] Soon transferred to their land-based studio in Glasgow. At this time David Jacobs heard him and told his agent Bunny Lewis about the young Scottish DJ. An audition in London followed and when Radio 1 opened he was given a weekly show, *Mid-day Spin*. Between 1967 and '74 he presented many shows on Radio 1. In 1974 he moved to Radio Luxembourg. Two years later he became a victim of Multiple Sclerosis but hasn't allowed it to disrupt his career saying 'It is fortunate that fate determined that I should be a radio disc jockey, since in that capacity, one works seated behind a console, and I know that as long as I am sitting down, I can function normally.' Is greatly helped by his wife Ollie who co-presents many of his programmes with him and has become a popular broadcaster on Radio Luxembourg.

■ A moment to remember: '28th April 1981 when the Stuart Henry Multiple Sclerosis Research Appeal was launched in London. The success of that evening was due almost entirely to the efforts of one man, my friend and Luxembourg programme director, Tony Prince. Tony and the RTL team made that a night to remember.' ■ Married to Ollie Henry and lives in Luxembourg.

JOHN HENTY
'To Istanbul with James Bond. . .'
BORN: 25th March 1936 in Croydon, Surrey. Father was an accountant. EDUCATED: Whitgift School, Croydon. FIRST JOB: Clerk for the Shell Petroleum Company in the Hounsditch

Warehouse! Went on to work as a newspaper reporter then spent five years with BEA as an airline public relations officer helping the Beatles through the hordes of fans at Heathrow and flying to Istanbul with Sean Connery. Is a member of the Guild of British Travel Writers. FIRST BROADCAST: Reading the news on Station K15T in Santa Barbara, California, in March 1960. First outside broadcast was from the top of Brighton's tallest block of flats on the opening day of BBC Radio Brighton on 14th February 1968, having successfully applied for a producer's job with them after gaining initial experience with Croydon Hospital broadcasting. Has made regular contributions to *You and the Night and the Music* on Radio 2. Presented first travel programme, *Travel Bag*, on local radio. Does *Saturday Session* on Radio Brighton and is now a freelance broadcaster.

■ Most exciting moment of career: The early days of local radio and working in Brighton, Michigan for two weeks. ■ A moment to remember: 'My Early Bird Club on Radio Brighton was a feature of the *Breakfast Show* in the mid 70s and was introduced by a worm named Wurley, probably the world's first broadcasting worm. My style of broadcasting has been described as "Idiosyncratic of Brighton" . . . or maybe that was the person who signed the letter?' ■ Likes anything associated with Mabel Lucie Atwell and running a Nostalgia Museum on Hastings pier, 'Remember When'. Hates garlic, *Nationwide* and people who jump on bandwagons. ■ Married to Sylvia, has one son Andrew and lives in Sussex.

ROBIN HICKS
'Down on the farm. . .'
BORN: 6th December 1942 in Purley, Surrey. Father in insurance. EDUCATED: Bancrofts School, Essex. Seale-Hayne College of Agriculture, Newton Abbot, Devon. University of Reading. FIRST JOB: Farm labourer/undershepherd. Has been an Agricultural Adviser and Head of Marketing

and Development Royal Agricultural Society of England. FIRST BROADCAST: July 1968 as a special reporter. Since then has been associated with most of the BBC's programmes on farming including Radio 4's *Farming Today, In Your Garden* and *Farming Week.* And on Radio Scotland, the *Scottish Garden* and *Crofting.* Television credits include *Farming* and *Dig This* for BBC 1. Has moved from presenting into producing programmes and is the Head of Network Radio Bristol, but is still heard regularly on the air.

■ Most exciting moment of career: 'Every time I'm "live" in front of a microphone.'   ■ Likes boating, the theatre, photography and playing tennis badly. Dislikes instant coffee in general . . . with powdered milk.   ■ Married to Sue, has two children and lives in Avon.

PETER HILL
'Denounced by a Minister in the Lords. . .'
BORN: 22nd April 1937 in Scunthorpe, Lincolnshire. Father a bank manager. EDUCATED: Christ's Hospital and Trinity Hall, Cambridge. FIRST JOB: BBC general trainee. Was the editor of the Cambridge student paper 'Varsity'. Acted as a Russian interpreter while in the Royal Navy and later in the RNR. FIRST BROADCAST: On the BBC European Service in 1961. Is one of the BBC's political correspondents at Westminster and contributes to all news and current affairs programmes for both radio and television.

■ Most exciting moment of career: 'Seeing CS gas bombs thrown into the Commons chamber.'   ■ A moment to remember: 'I broadcast an exclusive story during the Falklands conflict and was roundly denounced by a Minister in the Lords for it. Within six months, the Prime Minister had sacked him.'   ■ Likes cricket, picture framing, gemmology, skiing, and growing vegetables. Dislikes wrong stresses on Russian names and the use of children in TV adverts.   ■ Married to Rosemary, has two children and lives in Middlesex.

PETER HOBDAY
'With Mrs Thatcher in the Powder Room. . .'
BORN: 16th February 1937 in Dudley, Worcestershire. Father a Civil Servant. EDUCATED: St. Chad's College, Wolverhampton. Leicester University. FIRST JOB: National Service in the Army in Paris. FIRST BROADCAST: On an early version of the *Today* programme around 1957 . 'My brother John was in broadcasting and I tried for years and years not to do it, but I kept on meeting people who did and finally producer Brian Sharp at Bush House said 'Come along and talk on this programme', so I did . . . the programme was *Forum.* Then somebody else rang me up and so on.' Programmes for the World Service include *Business Industry, Outlook* and many contributions to the French service. He has presented the *Financial World Tonight* and the *World at One* for Radio 4. Since February 1983 has been one of the presenters of Radio 4's *Today* programme.

■ A moment to remember: 'Way back, when I was working on the *Financial World Tonight* I interviewed Mrs Thatcher who was then a little-known politician in opposition. She was attending the Annual Conference of the Institute of Directors at the Royal Albert Hall, a noisy and echoey building at the best of times. The only place we could find to tape this little interview was in the Executive Powder Room, as it was delicately called. So there we sat, talking about tax incentives for the businessman in the lavatory, and it was a relief to us both when we had finished!' ■ Likes travelling and eating, not necesarily in that order. Dislikes boring people and anyone who talks 'shop'. ■ Has one son and one daughter and lives in Hertfordshire.

ANTHONY HOLDEN
'Two incongruous obsessions, Princes and Presidents'.

BORN: 22nd May 1947 in Southport, Lancashire. Father a retailer EDUCATED: Merton College Oxford. (M.A. Hons Eng. Lit.) FIRST JOB: Trainee reporter on the 'Evening Echo', Hemel Hempstead (1970–'73) From there joined 'The Sunday Times' as a general reporter. 1977–'79 Atticus, 'The Sunday Times' (Columnist of the Year 1977). 1979–'81 Washington correspondent of 'The Observer'. 1981–'82 Features Editor of 'The Times'. FIRST BROADCAST: As an Oxford student on the *World Tonight*, Radio 4 during 'les evennements' of 1968. After frequent freelance appearances was invited to host Radio 4's new 'diary column of the air' *In the Air*, by producer Julian Hale, in 1982 and has been presenting it ever since. Has appeared on most news programmes, *Start the Week, News Quiz, Jimmy Young Show* usually in connection with US politics and/or the Prince of Wales. Published a biography of the Prince of Wales in 1979.

■ Most exciting moment of career: Resigning from 'The Times'. ■ A moment to remember: 'A transatlantic interview with Jimmy Young in which my two incongruous obsessions, princes and presidents were the subject of one double-barreled interview when rumours of the Prince of Wales' engagement coincided with the US presidential elections in November 1980.' ■ Likes music, poker, computers, 'movies. Dislikes VAT, cheese, unpunctuality, cults. ■ Married to Amanda Warren, has three children.

JOHN HOLMSTROM
'Got into broadcasting unintentionally. . .'

BORN: 9th September 1927 in Worksop, Notts. Father a steel manufacturer. EDUCATED: Haileybury. King's College, Cambridge. FIRST JOB: BBC Radio announcer 1951, on the Third Programme from 1954. Was Literary Adviser to the Royal Shakespeare Company 1959–'61. Theatre and Television Critic of 'New Statesman' 1961–'65. Director of Colts children's shops 1965–'74. Governor of British Film Institute 1980–'82. Radio programmes include *The Critics* on the BBC Home Service. Is a Radio 3 newsreader/announcer.

■ Most exciting moment of career: 'Best forgotten!' ■ Likes gardening, travelling, languages and computerised cricket. Dislikes disco music and fruit jelly. ■ Lives in London.

BOB HOLNESS
'Independent Radio Personality of the Year. . .'

BORN: 12th November Vryheid, Natal, South Africa. Father a motor engineer. The family returned to the UK just after Bob was born. EDUCATED: Ashford Grammar School, Kent. Maidstone College of Art. FIRST JOB: Printing in Art and Design. Returned to South Africa as a printer but on discovering a new theatre opening in Durban 'The Intimate Theatre' being run entirely by English actors and actresses, he walked in and talked himself into a job. He also picked up a wife . . . actress Mary Clifford who was out there on a year's contract. A regular first-nighter at the theatre was Cedric Messina, then senior producer with the South African Broadcasting Corporation, and when Bob decided the theatre was in no way going to pay him enough to support a wife, Cedric Messina offered him some radio work. FIRST BROADCAST: As an actor in a radio serial in 1955. But he soon branched out into presentation and DJ work. He returned to the UK in 1961 and never having even seen a television camera, started to work in television. *Junior Criss Cross Quiz, World in Action, Today, Transworld Top Team.* Latest TV show is *Blockbusters* for Central TV. In radio he has presented *Housewive's Choice, Roundabout, Playtime, Newly Pressed, Swingalong, Late Night Extra,* and *Anything Goes* (for the World Service). But by far his biggest success has been as the co-presenter of LBC's top-rating *Breakfast show AM,* for which he won the Variety Club's Independent Radio Personality of the Year Award.

■ Most exciting moment of career: Landing a three year contract with Granada Television after landing at Southampton, upon return from South Africa in 1961. ■ A moment to remember: 'The organizing by my co-presenter Doug Cameron, of a visit to the AM studio by two ladies (?) from what one can only describe as "Rent a Slut" to wish me a happy birthday on air. They couldn't sing, though they tried to and they looked ghastly, a fact somewhat lost on our listening audience. I was almost at a loss for words. Currently planning revenge.'
■ Likes music and gardening. Dislikes broadcasters who rely on jargon. ■ Married to Mary Clifford, has three children and one grandchild and lives in Middlesex.

ANTHONY HOPKINS
'The most radio minded of all who write music for wireless features. . .'
BORN: 21st March 1921, in Bush Hill Park. Father a writer and excellent amateur pianist.

EDUCATED: Berkhamstead School. Royal College of Music where he won the Chappell Gold Medal and the Cobbett Prize. Plays piano and organ. FIRST JOB: Schoolmaster at Bromsgrove School, before going to the Royal College of Music. FIRST BROADCAST: of incidental music for a radio play was in November 1944. It was the start of his successful career as a composer. The radio critic of the Observer once wrote 'He is to my mind, the most radio minded of all who write music for wireless features.' In 1952 he signed a contract to do six programmes of *Talking About Music* and it has been running for the greater part of each year ever since. Was awarded the CBE in 1976.

■ Most exciting moment of career: 'Recording my music with the BBC Revue Orchestra for the very first time. Not in my wildest dreams had I ever visualised myself in such a situation. To hear my music played by a professional orchestra was thrill enough; for the experience to happen in a huge drama studio with a distinguished cast of actors and actresses was an immeasurable bonus.' ■ A moment to remember: 'One of the nicest amateur groups I have ever worked with was a choir formed from members of the Women's Institutes. We were giving a concert at the Purcell Room on the South Bank. The rehearsal went well, but backstage it was chaos with 45 women trying to change into evening dress in space designed for a string quartet at most. I put my suitcase in a corner and, trying to avert my gaze from the unprecedented display of undergarments, began as modestly as I could to exchange my grubby cords for a respectable dinner jacket. I started to unpack. Jacket, shirt, tie, socks, shoes . . . but no trousers! In a flash of inspiration I remembered that one of my keenest singers had been wearing black slacks all day. "Ros", I called to her; "I'll have to wear your trousers. Can I try them on?" Looking at myself in the mirror I saw there was a very visible bright chrome zip drawing attention to those parts men's trousers are supposed to conceal. I took my bows very demurely that night, hands folded in front of me to hide my shame.' ■ Likes motoring and golf. Dislikes people who smoke next to him in the cinema and policemen who stop him for exceeding the speed limit. ■ Married to Alison Purves and lives in Hertfordshire.

MATT HOPPER
'Meeting with Mick Jagger . . . enlightening!'
BORN: 26th May 1956 in Harpenden, Herts.

Father a Chartered Surveyor. EDUCATED: Moreton End School and Aldwickbury School, Harpenden. The Leys School, Cambridge. Portsmouth Polytechnic. FIRST JOB: Milkman. Also worked as a waiter, chef, hotel receptionist and hotel manager. FIRST BROADCAST: 1978 on Radio Victory, although he had done some pirate radio in the early 70's. Presents *Morning Call* on Radio Victory Monday to Friday and is also an interviewer and presenter for features and specials on the station.

■ Most exciting moment of career: 'Meeting Mick Jagger for the first time in 1980 . . . an enlightening experience!' ■ Likes driving, travelling, sunbathing, swimming and music. ■ Lives in Hampshire.

JOHN HOSKEN
'We were brought up as a radio family. . .'
BORN: 31st October 1937 in Cornwall. Father a Bank Clerk. EDUCATED: Truro School. (There is nothing else a Westcountryman need add.) FIRST JOB: Potato picking up Threemilestone at 14. On leaving school, reporter on the 'West Briton' in Truro. National Service in the RAF followed. Was film critic for the 'Western Morning News' and Northern Industrial Correspondent of the Daily Herald. FIRST BROADCAST: April 1966 introducing Voice of the North, 'live' with interview (Terrified!). Has introduced Radio 4 *Newsdesk, World at One, Election Platform, Referendum Special,*

International Assignment and many other specials. On Radio 2 has contributed to the *John Dunn Show* and the *Jimmy Young Show* which he has also introduced in the absence of JY. Has commentated on State occasions such as the *Queen Mother's Birthday* and the *Royal Wedding.* Is the BBC's Environment/Transport Correspondent.

■ Most exciting moment of career: 'Being helicoptered into Baginton Airport, Coventry on Pentecost Sunday 1982 to join a crowd of 400,000 and give a "live" commentary on the Pope's visit. Also commentating on the fly past over the City of London during the Falklands Parade.'
■ A moment to remember: 'When I was presenting *Voice of the North* in Manchester, a man aproached me in a pub and said "You're John Hosken aren't you? My friend recognised your voice and would like to meet you." I did so, and the friend was blind just as my mother had been since I was 2 years old. Like my mother he had an excellent ear for voices and had picked out mine in the pub. Because my Mother was blind, we were brought up as a "radio" family and it was a great delight to her when she began to hear me on the radio. She once told me that her two favourite broadcasters were John Hosken and (God help me) Monty Modlyn. I refused to speak to her ever again! I am constantly aware that on radio, all our listeners are "blind" and that it is necessary to paint vivid pictures with our voices while muting the verbiage.' ■ Likes writing, reading, running, the Spanish language and flying light airplanes. Dislikes busybodies, rules, neighbours, deceit, the Irish and lorries. ■ Married to producer Gillian Gray, has three children by a previous marriage and lives in Essex.

DAVID HOULT
'A musical career. . .'
BORN: In Birmingham. EDUCATED: Redditch High School, Manchester University and Royal

Manchester School of Music. FIRST JOB: As a
musician, teaching, playing the French Horn
and conducting. He later took up singing.
FIRST BROADCAST: As a singer in 1975 and as a
presenter of Radio 3's *Mainly for Pleasure* in
1982.

■ Likes walking, brewing and consuming the
result.　■ Married to Mary, has one child and
lives in Manchester.

MARGARET HOWARD
'Pick of the Week'.

BORN: Esher, Surrey. Father a jeweller.
EDUCATED: Various convents and a year at
Indiana University, USA. FIRST JOB: BBC
clerk/messenger, having written to the BBC
asking for a job as an announcer! But made the
grade in the end. Also worked as a PA and
Director for BBC Television, and became a
teaching assistant in the Radio and Television
Dept. of Indiana University. FIRST BROADCAST:
As a bicycle bell on *Listen with Mother.*
Programmes have included *Forces Favourites,
Listener's Choice, Calling the Falklands, Date
with a Disc, Outlook, The World this
Weekend, Today, News Quiz, Law Game*, and
Pick of the Week which she produces and has
been presenting since 1974. Has appeared on
Horizon and *Call My Bluff* on television.

■ Most exciting moment of career: 'Chairing
the first ever world-wide phone-in "live" on the
BBC World Service in December 1982. Before
that announcing the Last Night of the Proms
with Sir Malcolm Sargent conducting'.
■ A moment to remember: 'Having been
offered the job of Editor of Radio 4's *Pick of the
Week*, suggesting that I might also present it, to
be met with the reply "Do you think a woman
could sustain an hour's broadcasting?"
Reluctantly it was agreed I might have a go at
introducing it, but only for a trial period lest the
audience should be up in arms. Eight years later
I'm still doing it!'　■ Likes riding, dog walking,
wine drinking. Dislikes ash left in studio ash
trays.　■ Lives in London.

ROY HUDD
'Here are the News Huddlines. . .'

BORN: 16th May 1936 in Croydon, Surrey.
Father a carpenter and joiner. EDUCATED:
Tavistock Secondary Modern, Croydon and
Croydon Secondary Technical School. FIRST
JOB: Messenger for an advertising agency.
Progressed to becoming a sugar shoveller,
window dresser and a commercial artist. FIRST
BROADCAST: *Worker's Playtime* in 1959 after
being seen by producer James Casey while
appearing in a summer season in Babbacombe,
Devon. One of our best known comedians
whose impersonation of the late Max Miller is
brilliant by any standard. He hasn't done too
badly either with his portrayal of Bud Flanagan
in 'Underneath the Arches' which opened at
Chichester and transferred to Prince of Wales
Theatre in London's West End. Has appeared
on radio in all sorts of variety shows, *The Roy
Hudd Show, Udd's 'Our an 'Arf, Roy Hudd's
Vintage Music Hall, Stick a Geranium in Your
Hat*. But by far his biggest success on radio has
been *The News Huddlines* on Radio 2 which
scores heavily because of it's topicality and
because Roy is such a super person that he can
get away with saying anything about anybody!

■ Most exciting moment of career: Every time
the Governor says 'We'd like some more
"Huddlines"!'　■ A moment to remember:
'Struggling to make some impossible lyrics fit a
well known tune for fifteen minutes on a
"Huddlines" rehearsal and then being told by
producer Alan Nixon to leave it as it was April
1st. The swines had written it especially for the
occasion!'　■ Likes walking and sleeping (not
at the same time!) Dislikes aggressive
people.　■ Married to Ann, has one child and
lives in London.

GRAHAM HUGHES
'A hard landing. . .'

BORN: 5th October 1953 in Shrewsbury,
Shropshire. Father a bank manager. EDUCATED:
Ross Grammar School. Hereford Technical

College. Gloucester City College of Technology. FIRST JOB: Industrial buyer. Also worked as a Counsellor in Pennsylvania, USA, teaching American kids (8–11 year olds) various sports. FIRST BROADCAST: On Cotswold Hospital Radio in 1976. From then on presented everything from news and sport to easy listening to rock. Joined Severn Sound as a freelance in the Spring of 1981 presenting *Rock and a Cast of Thousands* and *Saturday Night on Severn* plus various sports fixtures. Then joined Radio Wyvern presenting the *Afternoon Shows* Monday to Friday and the Rock Shows on Monday, Tuesday and Wednesday.

■ A moment to remember: 'The terror that followed 90 seconds of bliss floating through the Herefordshire sky making a parachute jump for a report. The landing (splat) was harder than expected!' ■ Likes walking, swimming, and lazing around in the sun. Dislikes motorists who are crazier than me. ■ Married to Christine and lives in Herefordshire.

IAN HUGHES
'Planning to work on children's television. . .'

BORN: 18th July 1954 in South London. Father the owner of a Hire Purchase Company. EDUCATED: Secondary School followed by seven years at College studying to be a motor vehicle technician. FIRST JOB: motor vehicle technician. Has also been a windsurfing instructor. FIRST BROADCAST: On Radio Tees,

Easter 1978. 'I kept on sending in Demo tapes and interviews until I got a programme and proved I could do it!' Has presented the *Breakfast, Lunchtime* and *Late Night shows* for Radio Tees. Presents the *Drive Time* programme on weekdays and the Sunday kid's show *Hubble Bubble*. Is also Head of Children's Programming at Radio Tees.

■ Most exciting moment of career: Flying with the Rothman's Aerobatic Team, piloting a lifeboat, taking part in a sponsored parachute jump and taking a trip in a hot air balloon. ■ A moment to remember: 'Coming Second to Radio 1 in Best Children's Education Programme. I'm planning to work on Children's television programmes . . . any offers?' ■ Likes motor racing, windsurfing and skiing. Dislikes boring people or bucket mouths. ■ Lives in Durham.

GLORIA HUNNIFORD
'A meteoric rise to radio fame. . .'

BORN: 10th April in Portadown, Co. Armagh, Northern Ireland. Father the advertising manager of a newspaper group. EDUCATED: Portadown College. FIRST JOB: Assistant to an accountant in Old Fort Henry, Ontario, Canada. While in Canada became a professional singer working in cabaret and on radio and television. FIRST BROADCAST: In Kingston, Ontario, Canada as a singer. On returning to the UK she joined the BBC in Belfast as a production assistant, but still continued to sing. The release of a record led to her doing some interviewing for Radio Ulster. Radio programmes in Northern Ireland include *Good Morning Ulster* and her own daily show *A Taste of Hunni*. She deputized for Jimmy Young on Radio 2 in the spring of 1981 and later that year was given her own daily show on the network. She also presents *Album Time* for the World Service. From being virtually unknown outside Northern Ireland, she had a meteoric rise to fame, appearing in the 1982 Royal Variety Performance, being confronted by Eamonn Andrews uttering those immortal words, 'This Is Your Life' and in 1983 winning the Variety Club's Radio Personality of the Year Award.

■ Most exciting moment of career: 'Interviewing the Duke of Edinburgh at Buckingham Palace; appearing in the 1982 Royal Variety Performance and winning the Variety Club's Radio Personality of the Year Award in 1983.' ■ A moment to remember: 'I was interviewing Esther Rantzen about a documentary she was making on the subject of "Having Babies". She had her new baby with her in the studio but didn't want the listeners to know that she was actually having to breast feed the baby "on air". However after endless sucking noises, she had to explain what was happening . . . that nature had called urgently, feeding time was feeding time! So Master Wilcox made his broadcasting debut on Radio 2 at a *very* early age!' ■ Likes collecting antiques and playing tennis. Dislikes injustice, snails, rain and Mondays. ■ Married to television producer Don Keating and has two sons and one daughter.

LIBBY HUNTER
'Pestered the BBC until they gave in. . .'
BORN: 31st May 1942 in Belfast. Father a factory manager. EDUCATED: Down High School, Downpatrick, Co. Down. FIRST JOB: bank clerk. Also worked as a personnel officer. FIRST BROADCAST: May 1979 . . . 'after continually pestering the BBC until they finally gave in!' Has presented *Day by Day* and *What's West* and is now the presenter of the *Afternoon Show* and also a daily contributor to Paul Clarke's *3 to 5* on Radio Ulster.

■ Most exciting moment of career: 'Going into a cage full of tigers, to interview their trainer!' ■ A moment to remember: 'I've had great "crock" with phone-ins, eg: asking a young boy which was his index finger, to which he replied "The one I pick my nose

with". I also had half the country making pancakes a week before Shrove Tuesday . . . I got my date wrong!' ■ Likes squash, sailing (in good weather) and water skiing. Dislikes pineapple and bad manners. ■ Married to Alistair, has two children and lives in Londonderry.

MARK HURRELL
'A sausage fan. . .'
BORN: 31st July 1954 in Poole, Dorset. EDUCATED: King's College Taunton. Grenoble University, France. FIRST JOB: Retail assistant in the petro-chemical industry (Petrofina UK) in London. Became a self employed UK rep for *The People Ship* in 1977 and during that period ran the CBS/Wrangler Road Show and was tour manager for a six month promotion with EMI Cassettes. In 1978 he joined the BBC as a travelling station assistant, working on twelve different radio stations. Also did a week on Radio One in 1980 before joining Centre Radio in 1981. FIRST BROADCAST: August 1976 on *The Peace Ship*. He had gained experience working in discos and on hospital radio (Radio Wey in Weybridge, Surrey) between 1974 and 1976. Has presented all kinds of local radio programmes from phone-ins to sport, serious talks, news reading to documentaries. Presents the mid-morning show *Mark Hurrell at Home* on Centre Radio Monday to Friday and a *Jazz Funk* programme on Monday nights.

■ Most exciting moment of career: Being on Radio 1; being on air on Day One of Centre Radio; and trying to do a programme during a Force 9 gale in the Eastern Mediterranean.

■ A moment to remember: 'The occasion on Radio Derby, when I mentioned on air that I was a sausage fan. Much to my surprise and joy there were 2lbs of freshly made sausages waiting for me at reception after the show. A good lunch was had by all!' ■ Likes his wine cellar, good food [including sausages?], sport, and (reluctantly) DIY. Dislikes bad manners and amateurs. ■Married to 'my wife', has one child and lives in Northamptonshire.

BERNARD JACKSON
'Ordered off the set by Billy Wilder!'
BORN: 28th October 1940 in Bradford, Yorkshire. Father a haulier. EDUCATED: St. Bede's Grammar School, Bradford. FIRST JOB: Salesman. But then decided to become an actor [good salesmen always are]. Between 1968 and '72 appeared in repertory, radio and television and did some film extra work. Then while resting picked a producers name out of the 'Radio Times', rang him up and asked if they took free-lance contributions. FIRST BROADCAST: An illustrated talk on Gregorian Plainsong for Religious programmes in June 1974. Since then has made quite a niche for himself in the religious sector of the broadcasting business and has introduced *Songs of Praise* on television.

■Most exciting moment of career: 'Appointment as a researcher for *Radio Speakeasy* with Jimmy Savile at a salary of £30 per week in 1974. Also securing an ID card to get into Broadcasting House.' ■A moment to remember: In my film extra days, I was at Pinewood Studios, cast as a banker in the period film *The Diary of Sherlock Holmes* directed by Billy Wilder. One hot summer's day we were shooting on a studio lot which was a mock-up of Baker Street. There were horses, carts, milkmen and postmen and hundreds of us extras. Finally after many rehearsals the scene was set to shoot. "Action" screamed Wilder and the whole scene became instantly animated. I, with fellow banker, strolled down the street straight past the camera as directed. All seemed to go well until the fuming Wilder shrieked "Cut, Cut" Pointing directly at me he bellowed "Get that guy out of here". It took me a few moments to realize the whole scene had been ruined because I was wearing a pair of sun-glasses! It was then I decided to turn to broadcasting. ■Likes

criticising other people's programmes. Dislikes other people's programmes. ■Married to Alison, has three boys and lives in Middlesex.

NICK JACKSON
'A DJ convention led to a career in broadcasting. . .'
BORN: 27th May 1952 in Tanzania. Father an Antiques Exporter. EDUCATED: Rivington and Blackford Grammar School, Horwich, Bolton, Lancashire. FIRST JOB: Trainee accountant. Has also worked as a forecourt attendant, entertainments manager and consultant and has been in the RAF. FIRST BROADCAST: August 1975 on Radio Victory in Portsmouth, having met David Symonds at a DJ Convention and been invited by him to join Radio Victory. In 1979 he joined BBC Radio 2 as a newsreader/announcer. He has presented *You and the Night and the Music* and the BBC entry for the 1982 Monaco Radio Prize, which came second. He regularly presents *Star Sound* on Radio 2.

■Most exciting moment of career: 'Being offered my first job on Radio Victory.' ■Likes cooking, photography, gardening and home brewing. Dislikes cornflakes. ■Married to Barbie, has two children and lives in Sussex.

CLIVE JACOBS
'The night the DG bought me a drink. . .'
BORN: 9th April 1939 in London. Father a senior executive with Marks and Spencer. FIRST JOB: National Service in the Royal Navy which led to a 5 year Supplementary Commission in the Fleet Air Arm. A brief brush with Marks and Spencer followed but he decided merchandizing corsetry and bras wasn't really his scene! Off to Henleys which allowed him to pursue his love of motor racing and rallying. FIRST BROADCAST: Was for BBC Television in the South in the summer of 1966. 'Six months earlier I had written to the BBC asking for an audition and had forgotten all about it until it

turned up! There were twelve of us and when it was over, I felt as if I'd been put through a washing machine! I had no idea what I was being auditioned for and a week later I was asked to go through it all again. But then came the letter saying "Come and join us to present and report for *South Today*".' First radio work was as a features reporter for Radio 4's *World Tonight*. There have been regular reports for *Woman's Hour, You and Yours* and *Today*, all on Radio 4. Now a regular presenter of Radio 4's *Going Places* and *Sunday*.

■ Most exciting moment of career: 'While working on a documentary on the Red Arrows, I flew with them several times and on my last trip with the team, they decided to give me a "surprise" I was commentating on our gentle approach in formation to the runway and just as we were about to land, the formation suddenly turned at right angles and headed for the sky, eventually rolling upside down so I was hanging by my straps, and then screaming towards earth before pulling out with incredible G force. It's the only time I've ever uttered an oath on the air!' ■ A moment to remember: 'The night the new DG came to Southampton to see how we did things and everything went wrong. The film broke, another didn't appear. To fill time I had to over-run an interview with an interviewee who had nothing to say and on the final item, a film cut to music, the telecine operator pressed the stop button by mistake and the whole thing ground to a slurring halt. I threw up my hands, said goodnight to the viewers and the DG bought me a drink!' ■ Likes sailing, playing squash, making furniture. Dislikes fancy dress parties and keeping accounts. ■ Married to broadcaster Frances Dymock, has two children (one of her's and one of his) and lives in Hampshire.

DAVID JACOBS
'All the melodies are for you. . .'
BORN: 19th May 1926 in Streatham Hill,

London. Father was a fruit broker. EDUCATED: Belmont College and Strand School. FIRST JOB: As a groom in a riding stables. A series of jobs followed . . . salesman in men's outfitters in Haslemere; office boy/general help in a leather warehouse; the tobacco trade, crawling from the tobacco floor to analytical chemist with no qualifications, but it was wartime and someone had to do it! Joined the Royal Navy. FIRST BROADCAST: *Navy Mixture* 1944. It all came about because the girl next door heard his impressions [a variation on the 'Come up and see my etchings' theme?] which he had started doing while in the Navy, and as she worked for the producer of *Navy Mixture*, got him an audition. Made a big name for himself on television as well as radio with such long running series as *Juke Box Jury*. Very much thought of in the early days as a DJ, David's career took a change in direction when he took over from Freddy Grisewood as the question master for *Any Questions*, on Radio 4, a difficult job which he handles superbly. He also of course presents *Any Answers* on the same network. Across on Radio 2, he has built up a huge following for his *Melodies for You* on Sunday mornings, and equally as successful has been his Saturday morning show with its standards and music from the musicals, which he calls 'my other side'. He introduces countless concerts on Radio 2 and has undoubtedly become one of Radio's top personalities. In January 1983 he was made a Deputy Lieutenant of and for Greater London and being interested in initials David pointed out that as his middle initial is L, DJ the DJ will now become DLJDL.

■ Most exciting moment of career: Introducing Judy Garland at a Variety Club lunch.
■ A moment to remember: 'The day I got the sack from the BBC for laughing while reading a news bulletin'. ■ Likes collecting porcelain. Dislikes bad drivers. ■ Married to Lindsay Hutcheson, has three daughters, one step-son, two grandsons and lives in London.

SUE JAMESON
'Knocked 50 points off the FT Index. . .'

BORN: 3rd July 1955 in Sydney, Australia. Father an orthodontist. EDUCATED: Surbiton High School. Liverpool University. FIRST JOB: Radio City in Liverpool after dabbling as a student on BBC Radio Merseyside. FIRST BROADCAST: On a student programme called *Precinct* on BBC Radio Merseyside. 'I had a lot of luck, far too much self confidence and programme controllers who believed in gambling!' Joined LBC/IRN in London in 1980. Is their Arts Correspondent. Presents *Artsweek* and contributes to all the news programmes.

■ Most exciting moment of career: 'The first time I went "live" on radio. It was only a traffic report but I think I lost 2 lbs in weight in 30 seconds and in broadcasting excitement and terror are inseparable!' ■ A moment to remember: 'Most broadcasters only remember other people's mistakes or their own very early ones. True to form the things that now make me laugh are slips of the tongue committed during my first couple of bulletins. I lost 50 points off the 'Financial Times' Index one day through nervousness, no doubt causing several Liverpool business people to contemplate the open 12th floor window; and followed it by "The Welsh Gas Board is investigating a leak". They still kept me on!' ■ Likes yoga and sleeping. Dislikes marzipan, overnight shifts and heavy tape recorders.

DAVE JAMIESON
'Waited to be on the wireless. . .'

BORN: 'A closely guarded secret'. Father a quantity surveyor. EDUCATED: Daniel Stewart's College, Edinburgh. Heriot-Watt University, (failed!) FIRST JOB: Selling space in an advertising magazine (it lasted 6 weeks) Also worked in Heriot-Watt University (where he'd just failed) making television programmes. FIRST BROADCAST: 1969 *Radio One Club* as the guest DJ from the Edinburgh venue. Went on to do several more such programmes, having

spent six years working in Hospital Radio in Edinburgh. 'My father taught me all about record players and things'. Has worked on several different local radio stations. BBC Radio Leicester (*Good Morning Leicester*); BRMB (*Late Night Shows*); BBC Radio Clyde (*Clydewide Tonight*). Is Head of Music at Mercia Sound and presents their *Through 'till One*, Monday to Friday, also *Mercia Memories* on Sundays.

■ Most exciting moment of career: 'First employment by the BBC in 1969. After waiting to be on the wireless for so long, it was quite a moment!' ■ A moment to remember: 'The time I interviewed Edward Heath at BRMB Radio and stated that the station was doing OK "now". "Now?" he asked. "Yes, we couldn't have started at a worse time" I replied. "It was right in the middle of that dreadful 3 day week" . . . exit Mr Heath.' ■ Likes collecting records (surprise, surprise!), home computers, inland waterways. Dislikes anyone unprofessional.

CHRISTINE TRUMAN JANES
'A voice admirably suited to radio. . .'

BORN: 16th January 1941 in Loughton, Essex. Father a Chartered Accountant. EDUCATED: Braeside School. FIRST JOB: Playing tennis! FIRST BROADCAST: As a commentator in 1975 at Eastbourne and at Wimbledon for BBC Radio 2. Before that of course, appeared on both radio and television many times as a tennis star. Many players move into the commentary box after they retire from competitive sport, few have done it more successfully than Christine who's voice is admirably suited to radio.

■ 'I consider being a part of the Wimbledon Commentary team my most enjoyable radio achievement.' ■ Likes golf and writing. Dislikes sewing. ■ Married to Gerald Janes, has four children and lives in Essex.

to admit that the combined assault had the desired effect. I dissolved into giggles, which in turn had the effect of my being left very suddenly alone in the studio . . . thank goodness.' ■ Likes photography. Dislikes insincerity, people who panic, cold hard-boiled eggs and spinach. ■ Married to Penny, has one daughter, Clare, and lives in Surrey.

PETER JEFFERSON
'We only had radio at home, no television. . .'

BORN: 12th May 1945 in London. Father a Writer/broadcaster/orchestral manager. EDUCATED: St. Martin's Prep School, Walton-on-Thames. Halliford Grammar School, Shepperton, Middlesex. FIRST JOB: Estate agent's clerk in London's West End. He then joined the BBC as a Tape Library clerk in the Overseas Service, graduating to studio manager. FIRST BROADCAST: BBC World Service. (One of the many Studio Managers who have become announcers). Programmes include *Nightride* on Radio 2 and *From Our Own Correspondent* on the World Service and on Radio 4. Has been a Radio 4 newsreader/announcer since 1974.

■ Most exciting moment of career: 'Being on duty, the night man landed on the moon and the evening when Princess Anne and Captain Mark Phillips were shot at in the Mall. There was also the occasion when there was such a commotion during an *Any Questions* programme that David Jacobs had to hand back to me in the studio at Broadcasting House until peace had been restored.' ■ A moment to remember: 'One day, very early on in my broadcasting career, two of my World Service colleagues, who shall remain annonymous, had partaken of a liquid lunch and thought it would be good fun to put me to the test. The script I was reading, was pulled from my hand so that it began noisily to rip. While this was happening, my other colleague poured water from a tea-pot over my head. I'm afraid I have

DAVID JENSEN
'Sold his trumpet for an airline ticket to Luxembourg. . .'

BORN: 4th July 1950 in Victoria, B.C. Canada. Father a musician. EDUCATED: In various schools in Canada. (We moved around a lot) FIRST JOB: Radio announcer on a classical music station at the age of 16. Also played trumpet in a symphony orchestra. 'I always wanted to play the saxophone, but we couldn't afford one, so I learnt the trumpet instead.' FIRST BROADCAST: In the UK was for Radio Luxembourg in October 1968. 'When I was working on the Canadian Radio Station we had a DJ from Radio Caroline visit us. I didn't know anything about Pirate radio stations, and as I wanted to go to Europe anyhow, I sat down and wrote to Radio Luxembourg, and then sold my trumpet to get enough money to buy the plane ticket.' From being the youngest DJ on Canadian radio, he was given his own show on Radio Luxembourg at the age of 18 and with it the nickname of 'Kid'. He stayed for eight years, then in September 1976 joined BBC Radio 1, presenting such shows as *B 15, Staying Alive, Roundtable, Mailbag* etc as well as his own show. Television credits include *Top of the Pops, Pop Quest, Rock on 45, Coast to Coast*. He took an 18 month break from Radio 1 to go to the USA to work on cable television presenting news and current affairs. 'They offered me so much money I couldn't refuse'. He returned to the UK to present his weekday evening show and Sunday show on Radio 1.

■ Most exciting moment of career: 'Coming to Europe and joining Radio Luxembourg.'
■ A moment to remember: 'The day I was reading the News at Luxembourg and somebody took my trousers off and removed them from the studio. At the end of the bulletin I stood up in my underpants and outside the glass was a party of Girl Guides. No worse than the time I was doing the Top 40 from Southampton University when a producer who shall be nameless set fire to the chart I was reading . . . luckily the fire was going the same way as I was!' ■ Likes reading and collecting rare books. Dislikes sea shanties. ■ Married to Gudrun (Icelandic), has a daughter and a son and lives in Surrey.

BROADCAST: 1979 on Radio 1 reading motoring flashes and acting as a stand-by DJ providing studio cover for Outside Broadcasts. Presents Radio 1's *Early Show* Monday to Friday and *Wake Up to the Weekend* on Saturday. 'I have to get up in the middle of the night six days a week, I don't mind, but the dog gives me a few strange looks!'

■ Likes video photography, playing keyboards, collecting records, writing lyrics and swimming. ■ Married to Joy, who's a nurse, and lives in Kent.

STEPHEN JESSEL
'Foreign Correspondent. . .'
BORN: 9th August 1943 in Burnham, Bucks. Father a journalist. **EDUCATED:** Dragon School, Oxford. Shrewsbury School. Balliol College, Oxford. **FIRST JOB:** Editorial trainee with 'The Times'. **FIRST BROADCAST:** While still at school. Is the BBC's Peking correspondent and contributes to all news and current affairs programmes on both radio and television.

■ Most exciting moment of career: The French Presidential Election in 1981. ■ Likes travel, food and wine. Dislikes dogs. ■ Married to Sarah Marshall, has one child and lives in Peking, China.

ADRIAN JOHN
'The dog gives me a few strange looks. . .'
BORN: 1954 in London. **FIRST JOB:** Working as a DJ at parties and discos. In 1972 was a DJ aboard the QE 2. He sent an audition tape to Radio 1, when he was fifteen and spurred on by an encouraging reply set about gaining experience as a club DJ. He even took his huge record collection to a famous West End fashion store and entertained the customers. **FIRST**

BRIAN JOHNSTON
'It's been a lot of fun. . .'
BORN: 24th June 1912 in Little Berkhamsted, Hertfordshire. Father a coffee importer. **EDUCATED:** Eton. New College, Oxford. (B.A.) **FIRST JOB:** Worked in the family coffee business 1934–'39. He joined the 2nd Battalion Grenadier Guards and took part in the Normandy campaign, the advance into Brussels and crossing of the Rhine into Germany. He was awarded the MC in 1945. After being demobbed, a chance meeting with Stewart Macpherson and Wynford Vaughan-Thomas got him an introduction to the Head of Outside Broadcasts at the BBC, Seymour de Lotbinière. **FIRST BROADCAST:** 'Early in 1946, just after joining OB's, I had to describe the blowing up of an unexploded bomb in St. James's Park. I was told afterwards that I got very excited and finished the broadcast by

promising the listeners to bring them a bigger and better bomb next week!' During his 27 years on the BBC staff, he became one of radio's most popular broadcasters with such programmes as *Let's Go Somewhere* (a regular feature on *In Town Tonight*), *Spot the Headliner, Twenty Questions, Sporting Chance* and *Housewife's Choice*. In 1972 he took over *Down Your Way* and has been with the programme ever since. He has commentated on many royal occasions including the funeral of George VI and the coronation of Elizabeth II. He was the BBC's cricket correspondent from 1963 until he retired from the staff in 1972 to lead an even busier life as a freelance broadcaster, which includes being one of the commentary team for *Test Match Specials* on Radio 3. He has written several books including, 'It's Been a Lot of Fun' and 'It's a Funny Game'. Was named Radio Male Personality of the Year in 1983.

■ A moment to remember: 'My first commentary on a serious occasion was the funeral of George VI. I discovered that at the head of the procession would be 5 mounted policemen on white horses, so wanting to get off on the right note, I did something I had never done before, I wrote out my opening sentence. "And here comes the procession now led by 5 Metropolitan policemen mounted on white horses". On the day, I got my cue and at that moment could just see the caps of the 5 policemen coming into sight up the slope. "Yes, here comes the procession led by 5 Metropolitan policemen mounted on . . ." and to my horror I realized they were not white horses but black. I had rehearsed white horses so often that I panicked and couldn't think of any other colour. So what I said was . . . "mounted on (pause) . . . horseback". This brought an immediate response from my producer in my headphones . . . "What on earth do you think they are mounted on, camels!".' ■ Likes cricket, golf, the theatre and reading newspapers. ■ Married to Pauline Tozer, has 3 sons and 2 daughters and lives in London.

CHRISTOPHER JONES
'I find the Palace of Westminster deeply absorbing as a place'.
BORN: 17th December 1928 in Folkestone, Kent. Father the editor of a local paper. EDUCATED: Harvey Grammar School. St. Michael's College, Hitchin, Hertfordshire. FIRST JOB: As a reporter on his father's newspaper. He then worked in Bradford and Fleet Street before joining the BBC as a general

reporter in 1959. FIRST BROADCAST: 1959. He did occasional reports from Parliament over the years but joined the Parliamentary Unit full time in 1964. In 1975 he did the first commentary on the first ever broadcast of Prime Minister's Question Time, during the Broadcasting from Parliament Experiment. As the BBC's Parliamentary Correspondent, he contributes to all the news and current affairs programmes on both radio and television.

■ Most exciting moment of career: 'Writing and presenting a series of eight 50-minute programmes for BBC Television on The History of Parliament and the Palace of Westminster. Also writing a book to accompany the series, 'The Great Palace – The Story of Parliament.' ■ A moment to remember: 'On the very first day of the broadcasting from Parliament Experiment in 1975, I had five inserts lined up for the 5-45pm television news. I introduced the first one and the telephone rang to say that had gone down, so I went on to the second insert, but that had gone down too. The gremlins were really at work because all five failed to materialize and I was left with a certain amount of egg on my face!' ■ Likes music, the history of Parliament. Dislikes sloppy English and bad pronunciation. ■ Lives in London.

DEREK JONES
'The countryside my hobby as well as my work. . .'
BORN: 10th January 1927 in Buxted, Sussex. Father a gamekeeper. EDUCATED: Lucton School, Hereford. Huish's Grammar School, Taunton, Somerset. FIRST JOB: In the BBC Engineering Division at the Taunton transmitter. FIRST BROADCAST: British Forces Network in Hamburg 1946. 'For my National Service, I was conscripted as a recruit to BFN Engineering, but they were more short of broadcasters than technicians, so I began broadcasting almost straight away. The first broadcast was as an American voice in a

programme produced by Raymond Baxter. The accent came fairly easily to me with my West Country burr and the influence of working with Americans and Canadians at Broadcasting House in London in the latter days of the war.' While in Hamburg he sometimes presented that end of *Two Way Family Favourites* in the pre-Cliff Michelmore days. With Alan Gibson he presented *Good Morning* on BBC West Region for eleven years, the first (he thinks) unscripted DJ programme on BBC Radio. He now presents Radio 4's *Wildlife* and *The Living World* for the BBC Natural History Unit. Also co-presents the BBC West television series *Day Out*. 'Today I regard myself as a very lucky man since the countryside and the life in it are my hobbies as well as my main work. Every radio trail for the *Living World* is exciting, something is always happening be it a raven flying overhead proclaiming it's territory or a Great Crested Newt in a London pond; a rare visitor to my garden birdtable or a hedgehog coming in the french windows for its evening meal.'

■ Most exciting moment of career: 'Working as a "Ham" operator on the BBC Beachhead Transmitter linking London with the Mobile Transmitters and War Correspondents during the Normandy invasion and subsequent advance into Hitler's Europe.' ■ A moment to remember: 'The ill-fated Beaulieu Jazz Festival of 1956. We were "live" on BBC television that Saturday night when all the fans wanted "Acker" and were saying so with words, and subsequently bottles and other missiles. Our lighting scaffold collapsed under the weight of fans looking for vantage points, but we stayed on the air. My commentary point was alongside the merry-go-round stage and I shall always remember the voice of Peter Bale, the producer, coming through my earpiece saying "Derek, you're on your own". I'd never felt more so.' ■ Likes golf and the countryside. Dislikes people who can't keep appointments on time (the natural reaction of all pro broadcasters). ■ Is a widower, has one daughter and lives in Avon, 'but we still regard it as Somerset!'

GETHYN JONES
'Started on the bottom rung. . .'

BORN: 7th May 1952 in Reading, Berkshire. Father a headmaster. EDUCATED: Portsmouth Grammar School. Brune Park School, Gosport. FIRST JOB: Delivering paraffin! FIRST BROADCAST: February 1972 on BBC Radio Solent. 'I was searching for something to do with rock music and the post of Record Librarian seemed better than an office job! I applied successfully and found myself on the bottom rung of a ladder which led to sitting behind a microphone.' Has presented many programmes on Radio Solent and has also contributed to Radio 2's *Blooper* programme! Presents the *Afternoon Show* on Radio Solent also *Solent Rock*. As a producer/presenter, he is responsible for local recordings and produces jazz, folk and classical programmes.

■ Most exciting moment of career: Covering the making of the film 'Tommy' in the Portsmouth area and watching Keith Moon and Oliver Reed 'enjoying' themselves. ■ A moment to remember: 'When a well-known blonde TV actress stopped me during a recorded interview to tell me how good we sounded together! (Gulp!)' ■ Likes songwriting, renovating and maintaining his cottage. ■ Married to Nicole, has one child, Pascal and lives in Hampshire.

NICHOLAS JONES
'Countless BBC application forms. . .'
BORN: 1st October 1942 in Abergavenny,

Gwent. FIRST JOB: Left school at 16 to work as an editorial assistant on a weekly trade magazine, 'Advertisers Weekly'. For seven years worked as a reporter on evening newspapers in Portsmouth and Oxford. In 1968 he became a parliamentary reporter for 'The Times'. After completing countless BBC application forms, he joined BBC Radio Leicester as a news producer in 1972. Within eighteen months had moved to London as a reporter for BBC Radio News. Was acting political correspondent at Westminster during the Broadcasting from Parliament experiment in 1975. In 1979 he switched to Labour and Trade Union affairs and the following year became Labour Correspondent.

PETER JONES
'Sharing a lift with Dorothy Dandridge. . .'
BORN: Wem, Shropshire. EDUCATED: Wem Grammar School. FIRST JOB: In repertory at the Grand Theatre, Wolverhampton. It didn't last long, he was sacked after the first house Monday night! FIRST BROADCAST: In 1938 in Arnold Bennett's *The Card* from Birmingham. Was offered a small part after having been seen in an amateur production of *The Wind and the Rain*. Has established himself on radio quite literally *In All Directions* . . . (the title of one of his programmes) as question master, panellist, raconteur, comedian, narrator [I've probably missed something out] Programmes include *Talk About Jones, We're in Business, Twenty Questions, Hitch-hikers' Guide to the Galaxy* and *Just a Minute* all on Radio 4.

■ Most exciting moment of career: Sharing a lift with Dorothy Dandridge. ■ Likes making plans. Dislikes milk cartons, shopping trolleys, and recorded music in shops and pubs. ■ Married to Jeri Sauvinet, has three children and lives in London.

ROB JONES
'It's great talking on the radio. . .'
BORN: 30th April 1955 in Liverpool.

EDUCATED: Liverpool College. FIRST JOB: Trainee accountant. FIRST BROADCAST: Radio City in Liverpool. He sent an audition tape, having decided he didn't care for accountancy, and was taken on by Programme Controller Gillian Reynolds who gave him the job on condition he studied accounting at night school. 'I never got around to it and we still joke about it when we meet.' At Radio City he presented everything from record programmes to phone-ins. Sitting in the studio one day he got a phone call from Radio Luxembourg. 'I just picked up the phone and said, "OK what do you want", I could have choked when I realized who it was.' He went to London for an interview, passed with flying colours and was given the *Early Show* on Radio Luxembourg. 'Working on Luxembourg is very different from local radio where the listener can easily relate to what you are saying because you talk about things he knows about like "What about the pile up in Queen's Drive today!". But you can't do that on Radio Luxembourg, so I go into the studio with a clip board of at least five topics which I know I can talk about. And I always read as many papers as I can lay my hands on. It's important to sound informed on the air . . . It's great talking on the radio. You can strike up such a good relationship with people, just like you were sitting in a pub with them.' ■ Likes all kinds of sport. ■ Married to Jackie and lives in Luxembourg.

STEVE JONES
'Bass player with Lonnie Donnegan. . .'
BORN: 7th June 1945 in Crewe, Cheshire. Father a teacher. EDUCATED: Crewe Grammar School. College of St. Mark & St. John, Chelsea. FIRST JOB: Bass player with Lonnie Donnegan in 1967. But has also worked as an ice cream salesman, a school teacher, a market researcher and a lorry driver. FIRST BROADCAST: 31st July 1972 on *Rosko's Round Table* on BBC Radio 1. 'I had been plugging a record to Radio 1 when I met producer Ron Belchier who hated the disc but fortunately spotted my immense

natural talent!'. Went on to present *Radio 1 Club, Pop Club* for BBC World Service, *Early Show* on Radio 2, has had his own daily show on Radio 2, and sits in occasionally for Jimmy Young, and other Radio 2 DJs. Presented *Nightline* for LBC in 1978/'79, having spent the previous four years with BBC Radio Clyde. Has become a well known face on television, hosting many quiz shows.

■ Most exciting moment of career: 'My first "self-op" show for Radio 1 in 1972 . . . most exciting and the most frightening! And being voted Scottish Radio Personality of the Year in 1977 . . . felt particularly proud because I'm English!' ■ A moment to remember: 'Commentating on the 1981 Eurovision Song Contest from The Hague. A carefully fixed introduction had to be thrown out when we were informed the lines had gone down. We had to start all over again, condensing five minutes of information into two. It does wonders for the concentration!'. ■ Likes golf, the theatre, current affairs and swimming. Dislikes litter, chewing gum and frustration. ■ Married to Lolita and has three children.

WENDY JONES
'Like pressing the button for World War Three. . .'

BORN: 26th September 1949 in Loughborough, Leicestershire. EDUCATED: Loughborough Girl's

High School. Hull University. FIRST JOB: Barmaid. Then became a reporter with the 'Slough Observer'. FIRST BROADCAST: July 1974 on BBC Radio Carlisle. Was considering taking a job on a Canadian newspaper in Calgary, when she was diverted by an article on BBC Local Radio. Saw a vacancy advertised at Radio Carlisle, applied and got the job. Presented news and current affairs programmes for Radio Carlisle 1974–'75 and then moved to Radio Oxford for the next three years. Joined the *Today* programme on Radio 4 in 1978 as co-presenter along with John Timpson and Brian Redhead. Also contributes to a number of other Radio 4 and World Service magazine programmes.

■ Most exciting moment of career: 'Reporting abroad for the first time, in El Salvador. A novice among experienced reporters, I felt a bit like the hero in Evelyn Waugh's "Scoop".'
■ A moment to remember: 'Much as I loved local radio, I never felt happy in charge of buttons, faders and the like. Once a week at Radio Carlisle I had to "opt out" of Radio 2, read the local news and "opt" back to Radio 4. Every time I went into a cold sweat . . . taking control was like pressing the button for World War Three!' ■ Likes family, friends and her tiny garden. ■ Married to a chemical engineer, has two children and lives in London.

ADRIAN JUSTE
'I'm a radio nutcase. . .'

BORN: 21st April 1947 in Kirby Muxloe, Leicestershire. Father owner of a Private Hire Company. EDUCATED: Guthlaxton Grammar School, Wigston. FIRST JOB: Car mechanic at 1/7d an hour. 'It lasted eight weeks and then I was offered a job as a shoe salesman.' FIRST BROADCAST: 1969 on BBC Radio Leicester. He joined BRMB Radio in 1974 and for nine months presented their *Early Show* 5am to 9am. 'I'm not at my best at that end of the day and it nearly killed me so they put me on to the weekend show, and that's when I started introducing comedy excerpts into my show.' In 1977 he sent a tape to Radio 1 and two weeks later got a reply asking him to make some trails for Radio 1. He got his first break as a DJ on Radio 1 in April 1978 when he hosted a two hour Saturday morning show. His quick fire cutting from music to comedy clips is not unlike the style of the late Jack Jackson and he has built a complete radio studio in his front room where he makes all the inserts for his programme.

■ Most exciting moment of career: 'An hour long interview with Elton John on BRMB Radio in 1975. He arrived with his Rolls Royce and a whole entourage but he was terrific. A bit of a frustrated DJ and he read out the letters and the weather reports throughout the show.'
■ A moment to remember: 'Working from 5am to 9am five days a week kills your social life stone dead but one night I had been out somewhere and decided to get a couple of hours' kip on the studio floor instead of going home so I would be ready to go on the air at 5am. At BRMB Radio there was just the news guy and me in at 5am to open up the station. He overslept and the first thing I knew was the telephone ringing with BBC Radio Birmingham on the line asking why we weren't on the air as it was 5.30! I fell into the chair and opened up the microphone, not really knowing where I was, but just hoping not too many people would have noticed at that unearthly hour. What a hope, in the pub at lunch time a steady stream of people came up and said "What happened to you this morning then?".' ■ Likes watching speedway and horse racing. Dislikes getting up in the morning and driving. ■ Is a bachelor in need of cosseting and care but no one will take the job on! Lives in Northamptonshire.

MARK KASPROWICZ
'Catfish, Kaspreene and Kas-oh-I-can-never-get-it-right. . .'
BORN: 17th August 1947 in Cambridge. Father

a re-insurance clerk. EDUCATED: St. Aloysius College, Hornsey Lane, London. FIRST JOB: Freelance photographer. Has also worked as a dustman and a film sound recordist. FIRST BROADCAST: August 1973, reading the News on BBC Radio Oxford. 'I had no qualifications and no ambitions, so becoming a broadcaster seemed the natural thing to do! Seriously though, it was a natural extension to skills learnt in television and it seemed fun.' Has presented a wide range of programmes for Radio Oxford and is the presenter of the breakfast programme *Oxford A.M.* His Polish surname is pronounced correctly by relatively few!

■ Most exciting moment of career: 'Every morning is exciting, it sounds corny I know, but I wouldn't do it if it wasn't. But one programme I'll never forget was a "live" concert given by the English Youth Orchestra and ten minutes before the broadcast I learnt I was to be the balance engineer. I shed a stone and gained five years in age during those two hours.'
■ A moment to remember: 'I suppose the early days of local radio are those where most of the anecdotes stem from. There always seemed to be someone willing to corpse you. Everything was tried from setting fire to your script, pulling the hairs out of your legs (men only) while you were trying to read a serious item of news to the worse situation of all – the self corpse. On one occasion I read "the meeting of the Common Market ministers was delayed for two months because of the French presidential erection" instead of the presidential election. Knowing that I'd said what I'd said was compounded by the fact that everyone on the other side of the glass had heard it and mirth was rife. I managed to read another two minutes of news summary before collapsing in laughter during the weather forecast.' ■ Likes windsurfing, photography and writing. Dislikes chartreuse, tripe and onions, CB, and cars that won't start in the morning. ■ Married to Pauline, has two children (enough) and lives in Oxfordshire.

P.J. KAVANAGH
'Son of Ted Kavanagh of ITMA fame. . .'

BORN: 6th January 1931 in Worthing, Sussex. Father Ted Kavanagh who wrote the scripts for ITMA. EDUCATED: Merton College, Oxford. FIRST JOB: Teacher. FIRST BROADCAST: 1941 at the age of ten. Is heard on many book and poetry programmes. Also *Any Questions* and *Quote/Unquote.*

■ Has two children and lives in Gloucestershire.

BRIAN KAY
'Carnegie Hall and custard pies. . .'

BORN: 12th May 1944 in Grappenhall, Cheshire. Father a solicitor. EDUCATED: Rydal School and King's College Cambridge. FIRST JOB: Member of Westminster Abbey Choir 1968–'71. Sang bass with the King's Singers 1968–'81. FIRST BROADCAST: As a King's singer in 1969. As a presenter in 1981. Now divides his time equally between music and the spoken word, presenting a series of Cheltenham and Edinburgh Festival concerts for the Transcription Service of the BBC; presenting *Mainly for Pleasure* Radio 3; writing and presenting a Radio 4 special about the Festival of 9 Lessons and Carols at King's Cambridge, *At Home*, a series of chat programmes with distinguished musicians and many contributions to the BBC Schools programme *Singing Together*. He works as a solo singer and as a Review artist with Donald Swann and is Chorus Director of the London Choral Society.

■ Most exciting moment of career: Appearing as a King's Singer in Carnegie Hall.
■ A moment to remember: 'Many of them on television with the King's Singers . . . in a bath as the recipient of a Spike Milligan custard pie; as one of the six wives of Harry Secombe's Henry VIII. Life as a presenter is comparatively calm and dignified. This at least is the theory!' ■ Likes reading, the theatre, pottering about and the local pub. Dislikes anything

cheap, babies on aeroplanes, being late and going to the dentist. ■ Married to the soprano Gillian Fisher, has two children and lives in the Cotswolds.

STEVE KAYE
'From London to Merseyside. . .'

BORN: 31st October 1955 in Hampstead, London. EDUCATED: In London. FIRST JOB: In sales administration for Border Television. FIRST BROADCAST: June 1976 on BBC Radio London, having gained experience in Hospital Radio. Has presented all the main shows on BBC Radio London as well as presenting General/Local Election programmes and phone-ins. Moved to BBC Radio Merseyside where he is presenter/producer of the *Steve Kaye Show* Monday to Friday afternoons.

■ Most exciting moment of career: 'Being nominated twice by British Local Radio Awards for best phone-in programme. Meeting Prince Charles in April 1982.' ■ Likes cars, travel, radio, television, music, current affairs and limbo dancing. Dislikes getting in the wrong queue at the Post Office. ■ Married to Helen and lives in Merseyside.

ALAN KEITH
'Your hundred best tunes. . .'

BORN: 19th October 1908 in London. Father a shopkeeper. EDUCATED: Dame Alice Owen's School. Royal Academy of Dramatic Art. FIRST

JOB: Understudying in *The Moving Finger* at the Garrick Theatre in 1928. Other West End plays include *Late Night Final* at the Phoenix 1931; *Dinner at Eight* the Palace 1933; *Magnolia Street* the Adelphi 1934. Also appeared in *The Matriarch* in America in 1930. **FIRST BROADCAST:** Compèring a variety show at St. George's Hall in 1935. He presented his first record programme in 1936. Was an interviewer for *In Town Tonight* and has introduced the many musical programmes produced by Charles Chilton over the years. Presents two extremely popular weekly programmes on Radio 2, *Among Your Souvenirs* and *Your Hundred Best Tunes* which he devised, compiles and presents. The programme has been running since 1959, which makes Alan one of the longest serving regular broadcasters and long may he continue. Over three million albums of *Your Hundred Best Tunes* have been sold for which he has been awarded a gold and five silver discs. He has also published his autobiography, 'Your Hundred Best Tunes'.

■ Most exciting moment of career: 'When Nancy Mitford, in an autobiographical feature on Radio 4, said that listening to *Your Hundred Best Tunes* was her idea of heaven.'
■ A moment to remember: Presenting a programme of gramophone records on Radio 4 on the day of Sir Winston Churchill's funeral, when the proceedings were off the air during the coffin's journey by train to its resting place in Bladon Churchyard. ■ Likes reading and political discussion. ■ Married to Pearl Rebuck, has two children and lives in London.

SARAH KENNEDY
'Matron at a boy's prep school...'
BORN: 8th July 1950. **EDUCATED :** Notre Dame Convent, Lingfield. **FIRST JOB:** Peeling potatoes and selling raffle tickets. Has also been a teacher, teaching English to the sons of Leekuan Jews, and a Matron at a boys prep school. **FIRST BROADCAST:** A roundtable

discussion on cystitis for British Forces Broadcasting service. After applying to the BBC for a job as a studio manager and being turned down, she bullied BFBS into employing her! From BFBS, she moved to BBC Radio 2 for a short spell as a staff announcer/newsreader during which time she hosted *Family Favourites* as holiday relief. Since going freelance, has made her mark in television with such programmes as LWT's *Game for a Laugh* and BBC 1's *Holiday* and *Looking Good and Feeling Fit*. She is also producing and reporting for a Channel 4 Current Affairs Documentary. Radio 2 programmes include *String Sound* and sitting in for John Dunn.

■ Most exciting moment of career: 'Far too young to say yet!' ■ Likes running, tennis, swimming and staying in bed. Dislikes people with no sense of humour. ■ Lives in London.

JUNE KNOX-MAWER
'Reporting on the King of Tonga's coronation...'
BORN: 10th May 1930 in Wrexham, N. Wales. Father an accountant. **EDUCATED:** Grove Park Girls Grammar School, Wrexham. **FIRST JOB:** Junior reporter on the 'Chester Chronicle'. Also did freelance work for the 'Manchester Guardian' and women's magazines. Has written several travel diaries ... 'Sultans Come to Tea', 'A Gift of Islands', 'A World of Islands', 'A South Sea Spell', and one novel ... 'Marama'. **FIRST BROADCAST:** 1958 on BBC Television talking on Travels in Arabia. That same year her husband was appointed a Judge in Fiji and while there, June took part in an English for You series for the Fiji Broadcasting Commission. She was taken on as a continuity announcer/presenter and from then on did just about everything, features, DJing, commercials etc. She stayed with FBC until 1970 when the family returned to the UK. Between 1971 and 1975 she presented the afternoon show on BBC Radio Merseyside. Since then has presented

Woman's Hour from both Manchester and London, has occasionally presented *Pick of the Week* on Radio 4 and has written and presented many documentaries on literary and travel themes. She has also done several programmes on psychical research. A recent documentary is about dream control and called *The Dream Makers* and another investigates re-incarnation. She presents *Weekend* on Radio 4.

■ A moment to remember: 'The coronation of the King of Tonga in 1967 and I was recording a three hour commentary for posterity on a cat-walk outside the Royal Chapel. It was a great thrill to be there but on descending to earth after the ceremony I was informed by a beaming Tongan engineer that "machine pack up". A desperate drive followed through the cheering throngs to Broadcasting Centre and an even more desperate attempt to recall the whole thing from memory in a deserted studio. It turned out to be a much shorter programme than anticipated!' ■ Likes having friends to dinner, weekends in Wales and bargain hunting at country sales. Dislikes electronic mod-cons, travelling on the tube and pompous people. ■ Married to Ronald Knox-Mawer, has a daughter Vanessa who's an actress and a son Howard who's a freelance writer. Lives in London and Clwyd, North Wales.

on the Arts. Joining the BBC, he presented Radio Ulster's *Early Call* music programme and has introduced many concerts on Radio 3 from Northern Ireland. He is a BBC Northern Ireland announcer for both radio and television.

■ Most exciting moment of career: 'I find every day in broadcasting exciting and full of new challenges.' ■ A moment to remember: 'I had been on holiday in Teneriffe and as I was waiting in the airport departure lounge a lady recognized me from my television appearances and she started to nudge her husband frantically. Once on board the plane I found the same woman was sitting directly behind me. She proceeded to tell me how much she enjoyed my work and continued in the same vein for several minutes. You can imagine how embarrassing it was, when after asking for my autograph she declared in a very loud voice that I wasn't who she thought I was!' ■ Likes swimming, travel and driving. Dislikes wet weather and early morning shifts. ■ Lives in Northern Ireland.

STAN LAUNDON
'CB handle 'Alabama Wildman. . .'

BORN: 15th June in Hartlepool, Co. Durham. Father a fitter/turner/engineer. EDUCATED: Dyke House Secondary School, Hartlepool. FIRST JOB: An apprentice engineer. 'I then became secretary of Joe Brown's fan club, a part-time job when I started, but when he had a smash with *A Picture of You* in May 1962, I had to go full time. I then went on the road with Joe, working as his right hand man and ghost writer.' FIRST BROADCAST: Radio 2's *Country Style* recorded at BBC Radio Durham. 'Being interested in Country Music, I applied for a position with BBC Radio Teeside in 1970'. Teeside became Radio Cleveland and Stan has presented a variety of shows for them, pop, folk, country, news and current affairs and request shows. Is the presenter of *AM 194*, early morning news and current affairs

ROY LARMOUR
'Recognition at last. . .'

BORN: 19th June 1955 in Belfast. Father an engineer. EDUCATED: Newtownbreda High School, Belfast. FIRST JOB: Solicitor's clerk. Has also worked on the 'Belfast Telegraph' and the 'Newsletter' and was manager of Morton Newspapers London office. Has been an actor in repertory and the touring theatre. FIRST BROADCAST: A Radio 4 Drama production, *A Broach You'd Throw Away*. Gained his first experience in broadcasting on the Belfast ILR station Downtown Radio where he presented a book at bedtime form of programme and items programme. Is also producer/presenter of their weekly, *Country Time*.

■ Most exciting moment of career: 'Meeting twice and interviewing Jerry Reed, the *Snowman* from the movie *Smokey and the Bandit*. ■ Likes motor racing, country music, driving and travel. Dislikes know-alls.
■ Married to Karen and lives in Middlesbrough, Cleveland.

the West Country, I dropped a clanger whilst doing a commentary high up on the roof of the Grand Atlantic Hotel at Weston-Super-Mare. As I looked down on what seemed like a million spectators 150 ft below me, I promoted HRH by saying 'The King seems to be enjoying himself talking to the crowd'. An amused producer whispered in my ear "You after an OBE then?"!' ■ Likes drawing and sketching. Dislikes pompous people and selfish drivers. ■ Lives in Avon.

PETER LAWRENCE
'You after an OBE then?. . .'
BORN: 12th November 1925. Father an engineer-fitter. EDUCATED: St. Brendans College, Bristol. FIRST JOB: Clerk at a 'one-man' garage. Has also worked for the British Egg Marketing Board where he was Regional Manager, but the Egg Board was disbanded and all the staff made redundant! FIRST BROADCAST: In Children's Hour Serials 1937–'39. When he was made redundant by the termination of the Egg Board, he wrote a short straight piece in Bristol dialect which eventually became a weekly series of 3 minute pieces on Radio Bristol. It has since developed into an hour's request programme each Saturday called *Pete and Eval . . .* Eval being a lady co-presenter (The name is Eva, but Bristolians always add an 'L' to words ending in 'A'!) Has also been a freelance reporter and newsreader for 10 years and contributed to various OB's. Presents Radio Bristol's tea time news magazine each weekday.

■ Most exciting moment of career: 'I was sent to a boxing exhibition to interview local sports personalities and was suddenly offered an interview with Lord Louis Mountbatten, whom no-one had realized would be attending. As I had served under Lord Louis in the 14th Army in Burma, it was quite an exciting moment to be able to talk to the great man. I still have, and treasure, a recording of that interview.'
■ A moment to remember: 'During a visit of H.M. The Queen and the Duke of Edinburgh to

DOUGLAS LEACH
'An affinity with the works of Thomas Hardy. . .'
BORN: Exeter Devon. Father a garage proprietor. EDUCATED: Hele School, Exeter. Central School of Speech and Drama. FIRST JOB: Called up for military service in January 1942, after one term at the Central School of Speech and Drama, he served with the Black Watch Regiment in Italy and was wounded at Rimini in September 1944. In 1945, he returned to the Central School for a three year drama course. FIRST BROADCAST: September 1946, *Time for Verse* on the BBC Home Service. 'Having been awarded first place in the English Festival of Spoken Poetry in August 1946, I was invited to make my first broadcast by BBC producer Patrick Dickinson who was one of the judges at the Festival.' In 1953 he joined BBC West Region in Bristol as an announcer/newsreader, a post he held until 1968. The following two years were spent mainly with Radio 3. Programmes include *Story Time, Morning Story* on Radio 4 and he has played character parts in radio plays and dramatizations of Hardy's novels. He is heard on Radio 4's *Time for Verse* and *Any Answers*. Television narrations include *West Country Tales, The Poacher* (BBC 2) and two series of *Cameo* (BBC 2). With Desmond Hawkins and Pauline Wynn he presents *An Evening With Thomas Hardy* for arts centres, schools and colleges on both sides of the Atlantic.

■ Most exciting moment of career: 'My first broadcast.' ■ Likes gardening and music. ■ Lives in Somerset.

GRAHAM LEACH
'A glass of water over Idi Amin. . .'
BORN: 1st October 1948 in London. Father a Civil Servant. EDUCATED: Battersea Grammar School, London. University of London. FIRST JOB: BBC News trainee. Has also been a stage hand at the Wimbledon Theatre; a school teacher, a reporter on the Guardian and Editorial Assistant to Radio Times. FIRST BROADCAST: University News programme on BBC Radio Merseyside in 1969. Is one of the BBC's Foreign Correspondents, having covered Bonn, The Middle East and Southern Africa.

■ Most exciting moment of career: (Dramatic!) The seige of Beirut in the summer of 1982.
■ A moment to remember: 'Ten days after the Israeli raid on Entebbe, I flew to Uganda to interview Idi Amin. I placed my tape recorder on a table in front of him. One of the table legs gave way and President Amin ended up with the contents of a glass of water over his trousers. He laughed the matter off although his bodyguards were fingering their weapons and giving me all sorts of threatening looks.'
■ Likes going to the theatre, cricket and photography. Dislikes airports. ■ Married to Ruth, has one child and when in the UK lives in Berkshire.

GRAHAM LEDGER
'Will try anything once. . .'
BORN: 7th February 1955 in Littlehampton, West Sussex. Father a self employed greengrocer. EDUCATED: Andrew Cairns Secondary Modern School (The Littlehampton School) Plus private tuition in speech and drama, and qualified as a Licentiate of the Trinity College London. FIRST JOB: 'As I was born in a trug basket, I worked for my father while continuing my studies'. Went on to work

in summer seasons and pantomimes including a season with the Black and White Minstrel Show. Worked as a mobile disc jockey compèring one night stands with stars such as Michael Bentine. FIRST BROADCAST: 4th April 1977 from The Voice of Peace radio station anchored off Tel Aviv to a potential audience of 18,000,000. 'I had tried very hard to get into broadcasting but was always met with the old "no previous experience" syndrome. So after a thousand letters I phoned the London office of the Voice of Peace. Crispian St. John was Programme Controller, he liked my tape, needed someone quickly and flew me out to the ship within a week of my application.' With the necessary experience behind him, Graham went on to work for several Independent Local Radio stations contributing feature programmes on subjects such as parachuting (and yes, he did jump!), life boats, hot air ballooning and submarines (including a three day trip in one). 'I'm prepared to try anything adventurous once'. Joined Radio 210 (Thames Valley) where he produces and presents the *Weekend Breakfast Shows*, a country music programme, a medical 'phone-in programme and *Black Expressions*, a programme aimed at their West Indian audience.

■ Most exciting moment of career: 'Getting my first long term contract in Local Radio'.
■ A moment to remember: 'Early in my career I was doing continuity announcements from a studio in the process of being repaired. In other words the engineers had to hold various bits of studio together while I was on the air. Self control was tested to the limit at the sight of two engineers with various limbs in various positions looking at me as if to say "Come on mate we've got our job to do". It was a humorous link to say the least.' ■ Likes the theatre, driving and adventurous stunts. Dislikes bullies and stalky cabbage.

CHRIS ELDON LEE
'I had to edit the tape with my teeth. . .'
BORN: 19th November 1952 in Manchester.

EDUCATED: Nailsea Grammar School. Gloucestershire College of Art and Design, Cheltenham. FIRST JOB: A residential house father in a county council children's home in 1975. Has also worked as a kindergarten teacher, a gardener and decorator, sales assistant in a record shop, feature writer and a disco DJ. FIRST BROADCAST: As a film critic for Severn Sound Radio in Gloucester on October 27th 1980. Was a founder member of Cotswold Hospital Radio in 1974 and bluffed his way into Severn Radio! Produced and presented the Outward Bound series of Outside Broadcasts for Severn Sound on which he starred with a baby otter. Devised and presented *388 Tonight* (current affairs magazine on Severn Sound), also a documentary *The Janos People*. Moved to BBC Radio Merseyside where he presents *Morning Merseyside*, their daily current affairs breakfast show. Also reports for the lunchtime magazine *Town and Around*.

■ Most exciting moment of career. 'When my first documentary *The Janos People* was the British entry in the Radio Documentary section of the Prix Italia 1982 in Venice.' ■ A moment to remember: (several!) 'The worst one was when I made an on-air spoonerism of "Fits and Starts". Doing the *Early Morning Show* from a hot air balloon and having to hang half-way out of the basket in order to get the signal back to the studio. Reporting a story which involved making a recording and playing the tape "live" into the News bulletin. The engineer dropped the razor blade down a grid and I had to edit out an expletive with my teeth. We made it on air with seconds to spare!' ■ Likes the theatre, railway engines, long walks, good beer and Italy. Dislikes Greenwich Mean Time signals. ■ Married to the job (who will marry someone who gets up at 3.30am!)

STEPHEN LEFEVRE
'The whole job is exciting. . .'
BORN: 9th June 1957 in Larne, Co. Antrim, N. Ireland. Father a GEC training officer. EDUCATED: Larne Grammar School. New

University of Ulster, Coleraine, Co. Londonderry. FIRST JOB: Hotel Management trainee. Also worked as a salesman and as a manager for Visionhire. FIRST BROADCAST: Voice over for a commercial on the local radio station, in 1979. Joined the BBC as an announcer in 1981. 'I had originally wanted to become an actor and while doing various jobs to earn a living, I applied to stage schools as well as the media.' Has presented the *Early Show* for BBC Radio Ulster and *Play Review* for the arts programme *Auditorium*. As a BBC Radio Ulster newsreader/announcer he reads news on both radio and television and is responsible for both radio and television continuity.

■ Most exciting moment of career: 'As I haven't been in the business for very long, the whole job is exciting and I'm constantly coming across fresh challenges and new aspects to the work.' ■ Likes drama, tennis, squash and football. ■ Is a bachelor and lives in Northern Ireland.

PAUL LEIGHTON
'An early morning dash to fetch the news. . .'
BORN: 28th June 1951 in Birmingham. EDUCATED: St. Philip's Grammar School, Edgbaston. University of Nottingham. FIRST JOB: Trainee reporter on the Birmingham Post. FIRST BROADCAST: As newsreader for the University programme *Campus* on BBC Radio

Nottingham in 1971. 'Having served as a reporter on the University newspaper, and hoping to return to the 'Birmingham Post', I was persuaded to join the University radio team and on graduation, joined BBC Radio Derby as a reporter.' In local radio he worked chiefly in local government coverage and was Political Affairs Producer for Radio Derby 1977–'79. He also produced and presented Radio Derby's breakfast show *Up and About*. Presented Radio 4's *Morning Has Broken* for 18 months when he was an announcer on the network. Is now a newsreader/announcer on Radio 2 and presented the *Nordring '82* series. He occasionally presents *You and the Night and the Music*.

October 1982. ■ Likes the theatre, opera, squash and swimming. Dislikes people who aren't punctual. ■ Married to the job, like all broadcasters, and lives in Worcestershire.

■ Most exciting moment of career: A highlight, was presenting Radio Derby's breakfast show 'live' from Osnabruck in West Germany for one week during 'Friendship' celebrations . . . followed by one week recovering from German hospitality.' ■ A moment to remember: 'The morning the Radio Derby newsreader overslept while I was fronting the breakfast programme. The man in question (who's blushes should be spared) had taken the vital lead story home with him. During our 7 o'clock relay of the then ten minutes national news from London, I left the studio, drove the mile to his flat, knocked him up, siezed details of the lead story, drove back, leapt upstairs to the studio and practised two minutes deep breathing prior to reading the local news myself. Aah . . . the charms of local radio!' ■ Likes politics, wine, historic buildings and good company. Dislikes language pedants . . . 'Of which I am one!' ■ Married to Margaret, has one son and one daughter and lives in Derbyshire.

ROY LEONARD
'In at the start of Radio Wyvern. . .'
BORN: 25th April 1948 in Bedford. Father a confectioner. EDUCATED: Bedford Modern School. FIRST JOB: Trainee apprentice draughtsman. FIRST BROADCAST: 1966 from RAF Watton. Having started broadcasting while in the RAF, he went on to Hospital Radio and from there to Community Radio. Made his first local radio broadcast in 1972 on BBC Radio Medway. Freelanced with Chiltern Radio presenting their *Top 40* show and the Sunday and weekday lunchtime shows. Joined Radio Wyvern and has presented their mid morning and Saturday breakfast shows. Presents the *Morning Show* and *Wyvern Weekend*.

■ Most exciting moment of career: 'Must be the opening morning of Radio Wyvern on 4th

PETER LEVY
'Enjoys meeting his childhood heroes. . .'
BORN: 5th September 1955 in Farnborough, Kent. Father a jeweller. EDUCATED: Hammersmith College of Further Education. Mountview Theatre School. FIRST JOB: Playing clown with a touring company including clown tricks. Has acted in many television plays and series, including *Dixon of Dock Green, Man About the House* and *Comedy Playhouse*. FIRST BROADCAST: 20th September 1975 on Pennine Radio in Bradford. Out of curiosity he applied for a job with Pennine Radio, got it and never looked back. Has been hosting a daily radio programme non stop since 1975. *The Peter Levy Show* on Pennine Radio for four and a half years, *City Extra* on Radio City for two years. Is producer and presenter of the *Peter Levy Show* on Radio Aire in Leeds.

■ Most exciting moment of career: Winning the runner-up award for the Best Produced and Presented Radio Programme in the Local Radio Awards 1979. 'The thing I have enjoyed most working in radio, is meeting many "names" who as a child I could never have guessed I would have met. I was most nervous interviewing Michael Parkinson who turned out to be great.' ■ Likes gliding, badminton and walking on the moors. Dislikes untidy people. ■ Engaged to Hilary. Lives in Yorkshire ('And I *LOVE* it')

NOEL LEWIS
'Got bored with newspapers. . .'
BORN: 25th December 1932 in Newport, Monmouthshire. Father an engineer.
EDUCATED: St. Julian's School, Newport, Monmouthshire. FIRST JOB: Junior reporter on 'South Wales Echo', 'Western Mail'. Has been Political Correspondent for Westminster Press Newspapers. FIRST BROADCAST: 1964 for the Australian Broadcasting Corporation. Is one of the BBC's Political Correspondents at Westminster and contributes to all news and current affairs programmes on both radio and television.

■ Most exciting moment of career: 'The day I joined the BBC having got bored with newspapers.' ■ Likes kite flying.

TONY LEWIS
'The winter job of a county cricketer. . .'
BORN: 6th July 1938 in Swansea. Father a civil servant. EDUCATED: Neath Grammar School. Christ's College, Cambridge. FIRST JOB: Playing cricket for Glamorgan. Became Cricket Correspondent of the 'Sunday Telegraph'. Is

also the director of a travel agency. FIRST BROADCAST: As a reporter on a Rugby Sports Medley programme for BBC Wales in 1964, doing what he describes as 'the winter job of a County cricketer.' As well as being associated with sport's programmes has done some general presenting on both radio and television . . . *Good Morning Wales*, and *Saturday Night at the Mill* for BBC Television. Has presented *Sports Arena* for HTV since 1973. Presents *Sport on Four* for Radio 4 and is one of the radio commentary team for *Test Match Special* on Radio 3.

■ Most exciting moment of career: 'Presenting *Sport on Four* from Moscow, Melbourne, Sydney, Perth, Aintree, Turnbery, Troon, Wimbledon, Silverstone, Paris . . . wherever.' ■ A moment to remember: 'At the Commonwealth Games in Edmonton I did my first ever commentary . . . on an African in a loin cloth climbing up a 50 foot pole . . . unprintable. I should have been banned from the airwaves. "Shining black thighs wrapped around . . . etc, etc."' ■ Likes golf and music [Plays the violin although he hasn't said so!] Dislikes smoking. ■ Married to Joan, has two daughters and lives in Middlesex.

TIM LLEWELLYN
'Arrested in many places gathering news for the BBC. . .'
BORN: 6th June 1940 in Broadway, Worcestershire. Father an RAF pilot.
EDUCATED: XIV School, Bristol. Monkton Combe School, Nr. Bath, Somerset. FIRST JOB: Reporter for Bristol morning newspaper, 'Western Daily Press'. Has been a reporter and sub on the 'Globe' and the 'Mail' in Toronto and the 'Daily Sketch', 'The Times' and the 'Sunday Times' in London. FIRST BROADCAST: Covering the Beatles concert in Toronto in 1964, on CBC Radio. He reported from the Middle East and Africa for CBC and also as a freelance reporter worked for NBC News, New York. Returning to the UK he joined the BBC as

a chief sub in their External Services newsroom in 1971. As a reporter/correspondent for BBC Radio News he contributes to all the news and current affairs programmes.

■ Most exciting moment of career: 'Being one of the first people to discover the Palestinian bodies in the massacre at Shattila/Sabra camp in September 1982, although the taking of the US hostages in Iran and the Israeli invasion of the Lebanon in 1978 are close runners.'
■ A moment to remember: (Several!) 'I was once set fire to by ace BBC TV reporter Keith Graves in the King David Hotel in Jerusalem, while doing a two way interview with *PM* and I was shot at by a sniper in Beirut in 1976, but still didn't get a substantive upgrading. I've been arrested while gathering news for the BBC in many places, but I liked it in Cameroon the most (French educated) and Uganda the least (British educated). I think the most green making moment was in 1979 when Iran's revolutionary guards were combing the Intercontinental Hotel looking for anyone from the US network NBC, with a view to arresting them and seizing video tape of the US Embassy occupation. I hid NBC's videos and tapes and an Iranian secretary in my lavatory. The revolutionary guards got the room numbers wrong and burst into my place, guns first. It was the only time in my life being with the BBC has helped. They saw my ID card, put away their pistols and stormed off. Thank God they didn't even look in the lavatory. If they had, something fairly Islamic might have happened to me, not to mention the girl.' ■ Likes photography, reading, serious drinking and beautiful young women, preferably Thai, North American or African. Dislikes almost everyone except the young women mentioned above, English licensing laws, package holidays, dogs, cyclists, Women's Lib, Royalty, CND and all modern music. ■ Married to no one at present and has one child.

DAVID LLOYD
'A Mayday call on the air. . .'

BORN: 3rd January 1948 in Leigh-on-Sea, Essex. Father owned a sports shop. EDUCATED: Southend High School. FIRST JOB: Working in a sports shop, coaching tennis before becoming a professional tennis player. FIRST BROADCAST: The Benson and Hedges Tournament in 1977, summarizing play between games. Now summarizes for all outside broadcasts from tennis tournaments, including Wimbledon for BBC Radio.

■ Most exciting moment of career: 'Winning the Doubles match with my brother John against Italy in the 1976 Davis Cup tie at Wimbledon, and beating Australia in the 1978 semi-final of the Davis Cup at Crystal Palace.' ■ A moment to remember: 'During a very rainy Wimbledon, whilst commentating with John Motson on a match, a bolt of lightning struck the commentary box and I felt it through my headphones, so I issued a Mayday call on the air!' ■ Likes golf and any sport. (supports Tottenham Hotspur). Dislikes flying and people who turn right at traffic lights without signalling. ■ Married to Veronica McLennan, has three children, Scott, Camilla and Laura, and lives in Surrey.

JIM LLOYD
'From popcorn to folk. . .'

BORN: 17th June 1932 in Selsdon, Surrey. Father a company director. EDUCATED: Whitgift Middle School, Croydon. Central School of Speech and Drama. FIRST JOB: With a repertory company at Southwold, but more exciting things were on the way like selling popcorn at Bertram Mills' Circus, acting with Mary Ure, John Clements and Jimmy Logan. Dressing Trevor Howard and Paul Schofield and almost being undressed by Diana Dors. FIRST BROADCAST: *Twelve O'clock Spin*. Had left the acting profession in 1959, joining Tyne Tees Television as an announcer. Two years later he left to go to ATV and his place was taken by newcomer David Hamilton. On leaving ATV, Jim's place was taken by another new boy, Ray

Moore. After a spell introducing *Midlands Today* for the BBC, he became a regular contributor to *Today, Roundabout* and *Woman's Hour.* In 1964 a meeting with The Spinners got him interested in Folk Music and he soon established himself as something of an authority on the subject. In 1969 he persuaded BBC producer Frances Line to allow him to introduce a series of folk programmes on Radio 2. [He also persuaded her to become Mrs Jim Lloyd, but that's another story] *My Kind of Folk* was followed by the popular *Folk on Friday* series which in turn gave way to *Folk on 2.* Also presents *These Musical Islands* for the World Service.

■ Most exciting moment of career: Discovering the Yetties, becoming their manager and turning them into one of the most popular folk groups in the country with ten albums to their credit.   ■ A moment to remember: 'Booking the Theodorakis Ensemble into London's Scala Theatre, feeling sure there was a big market for Greek music in London, and sitting in an empty theatre for five weeks (matinees Wednesdays and Saturdays) applauding the most expensive show we had ever seen. I still feel my stomach tighten every time I hear a bouzouki!'   ■ Likes walking and talking, not necessarily at the same time. Dislikes people who say they don't like folk music when they don't bother to find out what it is.   ■ Married to Frances Line, has two children from a former marriage and lives in Surrey.

HOWARD LOCKHART
'Looking back on a long and varied career. . .'

BORN: 29th March 1912 in Ayr, Scotland. Father a lawyer. EDUCATED: Ayr Academy. High School of Glasgow. Glasgow University. M.A. FIRST JOB: Law apprentice. FIRST BROADCAST: In 1923 as a child of eleven, reading his own story on *Children's Hour,* broadcast from Bath Street studios in Glasgow. He became a BBC announcer while still in his teens, joining the permanent staff of the BBC in Edinburgh in 1935. He moved to Aberdeen as a producer/announcer until the outbreak of war when he joined the Royal Artillery. After the war returned to BBC Glasgow first as a general producer and then as the Head of Variety. Worked with all the big stars of the day and also produced the famous *McFlannels* family series in Scotland. Since 1957 he has been arranging and presenting programmes of greetings and music for hospitals etc. on BBC Radio Scotland, and in 1981 was awarded a silver disc by Radio Scotland to celebrate 25 years of his weekly programme. Was awarded the MBE in 1976.

■ Most exciting moment of career: Receiving the MBE from Her Majesty the Queen in 1976. Also spending six wonderful months with the Australian Broadcasting Commission in Australia.   ■ 'Having been twice around the world, I now look back on a long and varied career.'   ■ Likes silent films.

MARJORIE LOFTHOUSE
'Left the security of ten years in the classroom. . .'

BORN: 3rd March 1943 in Poona, India. Father in the Army. EDUCATED: City of Bath Girl's School. County of Stafford Training College. FIRST JOB: Teaching games, needlework, drama and English at the Ralph Allen School in Bath. Had as a student, packed plasticine for Harbutts Ltd in Bath and washed lettuce in the famous 'Hole in the Wall' restaurant in Bath. Became Senior Mistress at a comprehensive school in Newcastle. FIRST BROADCAST: Voice over on a history programme on BBC Radio Durham. Was asked back to take part in a weekly educational programme. Continued broadcasting on a part time basis while still teaching. In June 1978, finally took the plunge and left teaching. Presented an afternoon magazine television programme for HTV *Here Today. Yours for the Asking* (the North East's answer to *Family Favourites*) on Metro Radio and presented a Saturday evening album track music programme. Regularly presents *Woman's Hour* from Manchester on Radio 4 and presents light orchestral programmes for Radio 2. Reporter/presenter for Radio 4 documentary *Enterprise*. Is also, one of the presenters on *Pebble Mill at One* on BBC 1.

■ Most exciting moment of career: 'When I left the security of ten years in the classroom as a teacher and faced the insecurity of a free-lance broadcaster's life. Now it's exciting every time the red light goes on! ■ A moment to remember: Getting a fan letter from an ex-pupil who used to hate me as a teacher, which began 'Please Miss . . ,' ■ Likes gardening, entertaining at home, walking. Dislikes smokey pubs and people who don't talk loudly enough in restaurants for me to hear!' ■ Married to Ken Stephenson and lives in West Yorkshire.

JANICE LONG
'Famous sister of a famous brother. . .'
BORN: 5th April 1955 in Liverpool. Father a sales representative. Her brother is Keith Chegwin. FIRST JOB: Air hostess with Laker Airways for two and a half years. Has also worked as an insurance clerk, a cashier, waitress, grape picker, shop assistant and telephone sales person for the local evening paper. FIRST BROADCAST: BBC Radio Merseyside in 1979 presenting their *Streetlife* show and then the afternoon show. She joined Radio 1 on 4th December 1982 where she hosts her own Saturday evening show and presents *Platform 9* on Monday evenings. Television credits include *Top of the Pops*, *Oxford Road Show*, *YES* (Youth Enterprise Show) and *Stopwatch*.

■ Most exciting moment of career: 'I was on the air with the afternoon show on Radio Merseyside, when the telephone went and it was Derek Chinnery, Controller Radio 1 who said "Put on a long record, I've got something to ask you." That invitation to join Radio 1 came right out of the blue.' ■ A moment to remember: 'It wasn't long after I joined Radio 1

that I fell off my chair, knocked the needle off the record and ended up on the floor. So there I was on my knees trying to explain the extraordinary sound effects!' ■ Likes going to see bands, watching American television programmes, collecting earrings and frogs. Dislikes British Rail. ■ Lives in Merseyside.

ADRIAN LOVE
'Three Russian names in his first news bulletin. . .'
BORN: 3rd August 1944 in York. Father Geoff Love (qv). EDUCATED: Under protest at Tottenham Grammar School. FIRST JOB: Selling suits at Burton's the Tailors. Has been a bass player and singer with several groups and has appeared at Ronnie Scott's as one of the Jon Hendrix Singers. FIRST BROADCAST: 1966 on Radio City, the pirate station in the Thames Estuary. 'I walked into their London office and asked for a job. They asked for a tape, which I knocked out and then went on holiday. When I got back there was a message asking me to call them. The very next day I was reading the 1 o'clock news and I've never been so scared in all my life, there were three Russian names in the first story!' In 1967 he presented a late night show for the BBC Light Programme and several programmes for the World Service. Two and a half years with the United Biscuit Network followed, where he ended up as Programme Controller. LBC had only been on the air for six weeks, when he joined them with his first phone-in programme. He then joined Capital Radio presenting a nightly phone-in and also presenting their Arts programme, *Alternatives*. An 18 month spell with Radio One ended in February 1982 when he went freelance, doing programmes for Capital Radio, LBC, BFBS and County Sound.

■ Most exciting moment of career: 'Winning the Pye Award for the Best Children's Programme, Radio 1's *Talkabout* in 1981. My most memorable programme was an hour long Special I did with Peter Ustinov.' ■ A moment to remember: 'During a phone-in I was doing

for Capital Radio, I had Cyril Fletcher as my
guest who is quite an expert on gardening and
people were phoning in with their gardening
queries . . . not a subject close to my heart! A
lady called Barbara came on the line and went
on at great length about how she had this
garden in the country which had got
completely out of hand and how her husband
was quite useless when it came to gardening
and was far too lazy anyway to do anything
about it. Cyril gave her lots of advice and
winding up the conversation I asked her if there
was anything else she wanted to ask, to which
she replied "Will liver and bacon be alright for
supper?" . . . it was my wife and I hadn't even
recognized her voice! Cyril nearly fell off his
chair!' ■ Likes his daughter and motor boat
racing. Dislikes sport generally apart from
American football. ■ Has one daughter,
Helen Peta, and lives in Middlesex.

CHRIS LOWE
'Interviewed every PM since Eden. . .'
BORN: 25th January 1949 in Prestwick,
Ayrshire. Father an RAF officer. EDUCATED:
Haileybury College, Hertford. Brasenose
College, Oxford. FIRST JOB: Teaching. FIRST
BROADCAST: 'A few words on a record
programme in Scotland, presented by my
uncle, Howard Lockhart (qv) in 1959.' In 1972
he applied from Oxford for a Graduate News
Traineeship with the BBC. Worked as a
political correspondent for local radio and the
regions, at Westminster between 1975 and
1980. Has presented the *Today* programme on
Radio 4. Is a reporter for Radio News based in
London. 'I have interviewed every Prime
Minister since Eden, though they weren't all in
office at the time. And I've interviewed Tony
Blackburn as well!'

■ Likes sport, travel and sleep. Dislikes hot
curries and interviewees who won't give
straight answers. ■ Married to Judith Fielding,
has two children and lives in West London.

DAVE LUCK
'It's a funny old world. . .'
BORN: 30th July 1953 in London. Father
council worker (Schools) EDUCATED: Albany
Boys School, Bell Lane, Enfield, Middlesex.
FIRST JOB: Apprentice toolmaker. Has also
worked as a holiday camp cleaner ('very
interesting, you should have seen the ladies'), a
baker, a salesman and a sales rep. FIRST
BROADCAST: *The Peoples Chart* on Radio West
in October 1981. 'I spent five years working in
Hospital Radio in which time I had auditions
with the BBC and Radio Hallam in Sheffield. I
then went to the National Broadcasting School
in London and from there got a job at Radio
West.' While with Radio West Dave presented
their Arts programme *Western Arts* and also
covered many of the daily shows. He then
moved to Radio Orwell and presents *Mid
Morning and More* Monday to Friday and also
the *Sunday Request Show* on its twin station
Saxon Radio.

■ Most exciting moment of career: 'I've never
had the adrenalin pumping through me quite
like the first time I went on the air at Radio
West. Interviewing George Best on Radio West,
being a keen football fan I had admired him for
years. Funny old world!' ■ A moment to
remember: 'My first day at Radio Orwell I had
the Nolans as guests on my show. We had a
chat on air, I then proceeded to play a track
from their latest album. I remembered to turn
their mikes off, but like a lemon, left mine
open, so there I was nattering away to them all
over the disc. I thought "great, my first morning
and I've handed in my notice already".
Another dreadful experience was waking up
late for the *Breakfast Show* on Radio West. I
turned up 45 minutes after I was due on the air.
You only ever do that once in your career.'
[And you're not the first person to have done
it!] ■ Likes football, tennis, record collecting
and work. Dislikes aggressive people and
getting out of bed, yuk! ■ Lives in Suffolk.

PATRICK LUNT
'Built first dry ski slope south of Edinburgh. . .'

BORN: 15th February 1949 in Liverpool. Father a schoolmaster. EDUCATED: Radley College. St. Andrews University, Scotland. FIRST JOB: Bank clerk. Has also worked as a farmhand, a hospital porter and was the builder of the first dry ski slope south of Edinburgh at Dudley Zoo. FIRST BROADCAST: 1973 with BFBS in Germany, having been working in the BBC's Gramophone and Music Libraries. Rejoined the BBC as a Radio 2 newsreader/announcer in 1978. Is one of the presenters of *You and the Night and the Music.*

■ A moment to remember: 'This is the sort of thing that happens to everyone else but never to you, only this time it did! My job as a staff announcer involves sitting in the studio in case somebody drops dead, or worse. One evening at 9pm doing a continuity shift and minding my own business, in comes a producer who says "You're on, you're doing *Round Midnight.* Brian Matthew's not well, and in three minutes you've got to interview Yehudi Menuhin who's waiting in the studio." So, I did the interview and the programme.' ■ Likes photography, squash, driving, swimming, anagrams, singing and playing the piano. Dislikes untuneful music and cars that break down. ■ Married to Jan Leeming, has one son and lives in Buckinghamshire.

HUMPHREY LYTTELTON
'The only way to avoid embarrassment is to own up. . .'

BORN: 23rd May 1921 in Eton College. Father a teacher at Eton. EDUCATED: Eton College. A self-taught musician. 'I taught myself to play the trumpet while at Eton and frequently had it confiscated.' FIRST JOB: Joined the Army straight from school, for the duration of World War 2. After the war went to Art School and then got a job in Fleet Street as a cartoonist,

spending five years on the 'Daily Mail'. Was also working as a musician playing with George Webb's Dixielanders in 1947 and forming his own band in 1948. That same year went to the Nice Jazz Festival which led to him being interviewed by Joan Gilbert on television from Alexandra Palace. This in turn led to him being invited to take part in a radio series called *Red Letter Day.* FIRST BROADCAST: (as a broadcaster, not a musician) *Red Letter Day* on the BBC Third Programme. . . 'talking about how I bought my first trumpet . . . very much a scripted affair.' Various jazz quizzes followed and from 1963 he shared the presentation of the *Jazz Scene* with Peter Clayton. Part of that programme was BBC Jazz Club and he compèred that for ten years. Was given his own jazz programme in 1968 and has been presenting the *Best of Jazz* on Radio 2 ever since.

■ Most exciting moment of career: 'Undoubtedly the Nice Jazz Festival in 1948, seeing and meeting Louis Armstrong for the first time. Not only Louis, but he had his All Stars, Earl Hines, Jack Teagarden and Barney Bigard. I sent a telegram home from Nice saying "Have shaken hands with Louis Armstrong".'
■ A moment to remember: 'Since the 1950's I've always considered Spike Milligan to be the patron saint of performers. He did a play and when he forgot his lines, he not only turned to the prompter but brought her on to the stage complete with book. He proved that the only way to avoid embarrassment if you make a mistake, is to own up. One of my earliest broadcasts was introducing *Jazz Record Requests.* I laid all the cards face up on the table in front of me so I could read them easily without transferring them to a script. The red light went on and I promptly upset the water jug over everything, so I simply said "I've upset the water jug all over your requests and I can't read any of them, so let's listen to some music." Nobody to my knowledge complained!'
■ Likes birdwatching as an alternative to playing golf or sitting watching wrestling on the

television, and Caligraphy. Dislikes musical wallpaper and being 'sung at' in hotel lifts, supermarkets etc. ■ Married to Jill, has two sons, two daughters and two grandchildren. Lives in Hertfordshire.

TIM MABY
'Reported the Penlee lifeboat disaster...'
BORN: 26th August 1947 in Buenos Aires. Father a diplomat. EDUCATED: Shrewsbury Public School. New College, Oxford. FIRST JOB: Presenter/reporter for *Good Morning Wales*, 'having talked my way into the building and persuaded them to let me do some interviewing'. FIRST BROADCAST: 'Many years before the above. As a diplomat's child at the age of 9, I was interviewed in Welsh about my experiences in South East Asia.' As well as working for BBC Wales, he has been a television reporter in Newcastle and has presented International Assignment on Radio 4. He is the BBC's Welsh Affairs Correspondent for Radio News.

■ Most exciting moment of career: (The saddest too) . . . reporting on the Penlee-Lifeboat disaster in 1981. ■ Likes music (plays recorder and guitar), sport (ski-mountaineering, rugby, tennis, squash). Dislikes eating fish.
■ Lives in South Glamorgan.

DENNIS McCARTHY
'Dislikes women broadcasters...'
BORN: 7th May 1933 in London. Father a painter and decorator. EDUCATED: Elementary schools in London and Nottingham. FIRST JOB: Office boy. Has also been a washing machine salesman and a tripe procurer (for dogs). FIRST BROADCAST: February 1968. Reporting on Crufts Dog Show for which he got paid £1. Since then has reported for *Woman's Hour, Today, After Seven, Late Night Extra* and *Radio Newsreel*. Local radio programmes include *Date with Dennis, Soundtrack, Take the Lead, Local Boy Makes Good*, all for BBC Radio

Nottingham. For Radio 4, two series of *Animals at Home, Just the Job*, and *It's an Odd World*. Presents and produces *Afternoon Special* which is networked over the East Midlands on BBC Radio Nottingham, Derby, Leicester and Lincolnshire. has written several books including 'The Afghan Hound' and 'The Cocker Spaniel'. Has won a Radio Award for the 'Best Outside Broadcast' and 'Best Jubilee Event'. Has also been nominated for Radio Personality of the Year.

■ Most exciting moment of career: Interviewing Red Rum; first 'live' broadcast from Lourdes; first 'live' broadcast from down a sewer; first 'live' broadcast from Crufts Dog Show 1982.
■ Likes looking at old Hollywood movies. Dislikes women broadcasters (with just a few exceptions) [Cheek!]. ■ Married to Marjorie, has four children and lives in Nottinghamshire.

JOHN McCAULEY
'I must learn to write things down...'
BORN: 25th October 1954 in Croydon, Surrey. FIRST JOB: A filing clerk. 'I was a civil servant for years and years. You know people say it can be boring, and it can.' FIRST BROADCAST: October 1981, the Saturday *Breakfast Show* on Radio West. 'Thanks to Programme Controller Robin Wyllie who eventually gave me the chance to prove myself'. Having presented the Saturday and Sunday *Breakfast Shows*, he has now moved to the mid morning slot and also presents *The Dolphin Club* and *Album Choice* for Radio West.

■ Most exciting moment of career: 'My career is constantly exciting.' ■ A moment to remember: 'Having presented a magazine programme, coming to the end and starting to thank all concerned, got to my producer who was sitting opposite me, a close colleague . . . and could I think of his name? . . . No I couldn't. An awful experience. I must learn to write things down . . . I must learn to write . . . I must learn . . .' ■ Likes music, cars and nice things to eat. Dislikes people who are loud, bills and mince. ■ Lives in Ayrshire.

ANGUS McDERMID
'Four generations of journalists. . .'
BORN: 14th December 1920 in Bangor, Gwynedd. Father and grandfather both journalists (four generations of journalists). EDUCATED: Friars School, Bangor. FIRST JOB: Junior reporter on 'North Wales Chronicle' in Bangor. Was in the RAF 1939–'46. FIRST BROADCAST: October 1948 as a freelance sports reporter for the Welsh Region of the BBC. In 1957 became the BBC's Home Reporter, in 1963 their Central Africa Correspondent; 1964 West Africa Correspondent; 1970 Southern Africa Correspondent; 1972 Washington Radio Correspondent; 1977 Chief European Correspondent in Brussels; 1979 Diplomatic and Court Correspondent (Radio). Retired December 1980 and as a freelance presents *International Assignment, Six Continents* and contributes to many radio news productions on both Radios 3 and 4. He was made a Freeman of the City of Bangor in 1974 and Honorary Druid of Welsh Gorsedd of Bards in 1977. In 1980 he received the OBE and the Order of Ouessam Alouite (Morocco).

■ Married to Myfanwy Jones, has one child and lives in Gwynedd and London.

IAN McDOUGALL
'A BBC Foreign Correspondent for 27 years. . .'
BORN: 6th January 1921 in Wakefield,

Yorkshire. Father a doctor. EDUCATED: Uppingham School and Magdalen College, Oxford. (M.A.Oxon Mod. Languages). FIRST JOB: Sub-editor Agence France-Presse in Paris 1947–'48. FIRST BROADCAST: In Paris in 1949, having successfully applied for the post of sub-editor for the BBC External Services at Bush House in 1948. Was a BBC Foreign Correspondent for 27 years successively in Berlin, East Africa, Far East, Balkans, Central Europe, Bonn, Brussels and Paris. Has contributed to most of the major news and current affairs programmes over the past 30 years including *From Our Own Correspondent, International Assignment* on Radio 4. Is editor and presenter of *Six Continents*, a review of foreign broadcasts monitored by the BBC Monitoring Service, on Radio 3. Is also the author of many books, 'German Notebook', 'African Turmoil' and 'Foreign Correspondent' and has written seven novels under the pseudonym William Fennerton.

■ Most exciting moment of career: Being appointed a BBC Foreign Correspondent.
■ A moment to remember: 'I am one of the relatively few broadcasters who have been given a Rumanian Army Guard for protection against wild bears. It happened in Transylvania while I was accompanying former Soviet leader Kruschev on a train. In the middle of the night we came to a halt in the middle of a thick forest. I was ordered by guards to change my light coloured pyjamas for dark clothes and was then escorted to a signal box. I was quite convinced I was being arrested, but much to my surprise a telephone call had miraculously arrived from BBC News to pick up my report, and as I discovered later, the reason for the change of clothes was so as not to attract the attention of the wild bears!' ■ Likes writing books. Hates people who smoke pipes in crowded rooms and dogs in urban areas.
■ Married to Elizabeth Thornton, has three children and lives in Oxfordshire.

JIMMIE MacGREGOR
'A standing ovation. . .'

BORN: 10th March 1932. Father a steel worker.
EDUCATED: Albert Senior Secondary School,
Glasgow. Glasgow School of Art. FIRST JOB:
Engraver. Also worked as a navvy,
schoolteacher, hospital porter, mould maker,
potter, author and illustrator. FIRST BROADCAST:
TV series for Rediffusion in 1959. Over the past
twenty years has appeared on hundreds of
radio and television programmes as a folk
singer in the UK, Australia, New Zealand,
Canada, America, Israel, Middle East, Hong
Kong, Russia and Hungary. Became household
name along with Robin Hall on the BBC's
Tonight programme on which they appeared
nightly for 4 years. They appeared on BBC
Scotland television's *White Heather Club* for 5
years. In recent years has turned more to
presenting and in 1982 walked 100 miles
through the West Highlands with a tape
recorder, making eight half-hour programmes.
He hosts Scottish Television's *Talking Scots* and
has his own radio show on BBC Radio
Scotland, *Macgregor's Gathering.*

■ Most exciting moment of career: 'Getting a
standing ovation from the pit orchestra at the
Victoria Palace in London, during a
rehearsal.' ■ Likes the outdoors, wildlife,
socializing, drawing, vintage cars, and
collecting furniture and paintings. Dislikes
rules and regulations. ■ Lives in London and
Scotland.

SUE MacGREGOR
'Interviewing French sailors. . .'

BORN: In Oxford. Father a doctor. EDUCATED:
Herschel School, Cape Town, South Africa.
FIRST JOB: As a BBC secretary on the *In Town
Tonight* programme. Then returned to South
Africa and quite quickly managed to get in front
of a microphone after her boss (a charming
woman) got married and left. FIRST BROADCAST:
Calling to Youth, South African Broadcasting
Corporation . . . interviewing French sailors!

Subsequently took charge of *Woman's World,*
a daily radio programme which she presented
'live' on the SABC's English Service. On
returning to the UK worked steadily in radio,
contributing to such programmes as *South East
News, Radio Newsreel, The World at One, The
World this Weekend* and *PM.* Established
herself as one of Radio's top women when she
took over as presenter of Radio 4's *Woman's
Hour.* Also chairs *Tuesday Call* and the
interview series *Conversation Piece* on Radio 4.

■ Most exciting moment of career: Taking the
Woman's Hour microphone to China in 1977
on Margaret Thatcher's first visit, at a time
when few Western journalists were allowed in.
■ A moment to remember: 'Having to keep a
"live" interview going for twelve minutes when
all the interviewee would say was "yes" and
"no". He was much more interested in his
girlfriend in the cubicle next door. Running a
close second, when the Pope arrived twenty
minutes early outside Westminster Cathedral
and I had to verbally get him inside, for
technical reasons, in two minutes instead of the
much-prepared twenty. But that's
showbusiness!' ■ Likes being lazy, reading,
theatre and cinema. Dislikes getting up early
but has to for 'Tuesday Call'.

JIMMY MACK
'I'm an optimist. . .'

BORN: 26th June in Greenock, Scotland. Father
a bank manager. EDUCATED: Lenzis Academy,

Glasgow. Bathgate Academy, West Lothian. FIRST JOB: Insurance Company sales representative. FIRST BROADCAST: 1966 on 'pirate' Radio Scotland, having gained experience with Edinburgh Hospital Broadcasting Service. He then moved down South to join BBC Radio Medway 1970–'78. Programmes include *Radio 1 Club, Lunch Call* (Radio 4, Scotland), *Night Ride* (Radio 2), *You and Yours, In Britain Now, Woman's Hour* (Radio 4), *Play the Standards, Early Show, Treble Chance* (Radio 2), *Glen Miller Legend* (Radio Scotland). Presents *The Jimmy Mack Show* and *Jimmy Mack's Old Gold* on BBC Radio Scotland.

■ Most exciting moment of career: 'Still to happen, I'm an optimist!'   ■ Likes photography. Dislikes kippers and people who are not punctual.   ■ Married to Barbara, has two children and lives in Dumbartonshire.

KEITH MACKLIN
'The press weren't informed of the change...'
BORN: 19th January 1933 in Newton-Le-Willows, Lancashire. Father an engineering fitter. EDUCATED: Prescot Grammar School. Manchester Polytechnic. FIRST JOB: junior editorial assistant on 'Liverpool Evening Express'. Had a brief spell as a clerk in a Lancashire colliery when he was 18. FIRST BROADCAST: A Rugby League commentary. Leeds v Oldham in February 1956, having passed an audition held at a Rugby League game with six other would-be commentators. Although Keith has specialized in sports commentaries, he has been involved with all kinds of programmes. On television he has reported for *BBC News* and *Look North*. Has introduced *Songs of Praise* and *A Spoonful of Sugar* [with yours truly!] He covered the *1972 Olympics*, and *The World Cup* from Germany in 1974. He is now the Head of Programmes for Red Rose Radio in Preston and presents a daily programme.

■ Most exciting moment of career: 'Being chosen as a BBC commentator for the Wembley Rugby League Cup Final in 1956, only my third broadcast. Being chosen as an ITV World Cup commentator in 1974.'
■ A moment to remember: 'In the early years of my radio sports career I did a Rugby League commentary on Hull K.R. v Leigh at Hull. It was before the days of the M62 and travel from Leigh was difficult. The Leigh team arrived late due to fog. Because of the fog, I had difficulty in following the play. Indeed when the play disappeared into the fog I had to guess at identification using the printed programme for names and guessing which team had possession by crowd cheering (for Hull KR) or silence (for Leigh). One player, Brophy, a Leigh second row forward, got repeated mentions as I looked down at the programme. After the match I was told that Brophy hadn't played! He had been taken ill on the coach and replaced. As the coach arrived late and in the dark the press weren't informed of the change!'   ■ Likes writing and broadcasting. Dislikes extremes of noise.   ■ Married to Sheila, has two children and lives in Lancashire.

DON MACLEAN
'The longest "dry" in radio comedy...'
BORN: 11th March 1944 in Birmingham. Father a sheet metal worker. EDUCATED: St. Philip's Grammar School. Birmingham Theatre School. FIRST JOB: 2nd comic in *Follies on Parade*, Pier Theatre, Skegness in the summer of 1964. Has played in Summer Seasons in all the major resorts and appeared in Pantomime in all the major provincial theatres. Has also done three seasons at the London Palladium. FIRST BROADCAST: *Take a Bow* in 1966. 'Gagcrackers Bar used two teams of three comedians alternate weeks. One comedian dropped out and I stepped in at short notice with Frank Carson and Freddie Davis and that's how I started in radio.' Has been a member of the *Wit's End* panel since the pilot programme and also on Radio 2 has had his own series *Maclean*

up Britain followed by three series of *Keep it Maclean.*

■ Most exciting moment of career: 'My first television appearance in 1967 . . . an eight minute solo comedy spot on the *Billy Cotton Band Show.'* ■ A moment to remember: 'Participating in what must surely be the longest "dry" in radio comedy. During a recording of *Maclean up Britain.* Chris Emmett entered as a PC from the river police wearing a tricorn hat, a mask and snorkel with a parrot on his shoulder. As he only had one leg, he was walking with a crutch, attached to the end of which was a single flipper. Jan Hunt was unable to deliver her next line "Inspector why has your constable got a flipper on his crutch?" When she finally managed to say it, the audience were incapable with laughter and it was Bob Todd's turn. He had even more difficulty with "Lower your snorkel in front of the lady constable." Needless to say, this lack of professionalism was never transmitted but when we timed the "dry" afterwards, it lasted a total of 9 minutes!' ■ Likes squash and the study of World War 1 in the air. Dislikes meat and bad language. ■ Married to Toni, has a daughter Rachel and a son Rory and lives in the West Midlands.

LAURIE MACMILLAN
'I was accepted and he wasn't . . . embarrassing!'
BORN: 10th May 1947 in Aberdeen. EDUCATED: Haberdasher's Girls School, Monmouth, Gwent. University of Newcastle upon Tyne. FIRST JOB: Studio manager in BBC Radio. 'I had applied for the job with a friend from University who was much brighter than me. I was accepted as a trainee studio manager and he wasn't . . . embarrassing really.' FIRST BROADCAST: Reading letters on *PM* and *You and Yours* while still a studio manager. Joined Radio 4 as a newsreader/announcer and has presented *From Our Own Correspondent*, a schools radio series on industrial geography,

Up to the Hour and can be heard at 0745 on a Sunday introducing those famous church bells. She also presents Radio 4's 'live' concerts on Thursday evenings.

■ Likes yoga, classical music, opera and the sea. Dislikes flying, big spiders, meat and real fur coats. ■ Lives in London.

DINAH MAIDEN
'A sub-editor when women subs were a rarity. . .'
BORN: In Rotherham, Yorkshire. Father a glass worker. EDUCATED: Rotherham High School for Girls. FIRST JOB: Junior reporter with 'Rotherham Advertiser'. Became sub-editor with 'Sheffield Morning Telegraph' during the 60's when women subs were a rarity; also wrote a weekly current affairs column for the same paper for 17 years. FIRST BROADCAST: April Fools Day 1970! as a guest on a current affairs discussion on BBC Radio Sheffield. This led to her being asked to join Radio Sheffield by the then Station Manager Michael Barton (later Controller Local Radio). She established Radio Sheffield's first phone-in programme and was runner-up in 1978 in the NRRI awards for phone-in presenter. Now presents Radio Sheffield's *Breakfast Show.*

■ Likes learning to play the classical guitar and keeping her Boxer dog fit. ■ Married to Benny Hill, sports editor of the Sheffield Morning Telegraph, and lives in Yorkshire.

COLIN MAITLAND
'Won a hand of poker fom Telly Savalas. . .'
BORN: 12th August 1945 in Birmingham. Father a comedian/singer/dancer. EDUCATED: In Canada and the United States. FIRST JOB: At the age of 7, he joined the cast of *The Gillans*, a kind of Canadian Archers series, and stayed with it for several years. Has had many roles as an actor including one of *The Dirty Dozen.* Has

also been an ice-cream salesman, bingo caller, wages clerk, lorry driver and ice hockey player. FIRST BROADCAST: In *The Gillans*. He worked on various North American radio stations before returning to the UK where he has worked for Capital Radio, LBC, Radio Hallam and contributed to *Woman's Hour* on Radio 4. Joining BBC Radio London he presented their *Rush Hour* and *Weekly Echo*. He now presents *The Maitland Show* on Radio London.

■ Most exciting moment of career: 'There are three: The first time I heard my work on *Pick of the Week*; the first time I presented my own programme; the first (and only) time I won a hand of poker from Telly Savalas!' ■ A moment to remember: 'Ever since that famous Orson Welles "Martians have Landed" broadcast, I've wondered just how much the public really do believe what they hear on radio. Well in 1981 I found out. The BBC and ITV had just announced their commitment to Breakfast telly, so the producer of Radio London's early morning *Rush Hour* programme which I was co-presenting, decided on a spoof. The next morning we announced that *Rush Hour* was on television with cameras in the studio. Many of our items were "visual" and we commented on colours, dress etc. which would only be valid in vision. I even confessed how nervous I was to be on telly at that time of the morning,! As you'd expect, many people phoned in to say they couldn't find us on any channel, but almost as many called to say how good we looked on screen and how much they were enjoying the show! Now were they conning *us*? And if not, just what *were* they watching. . .' ■ Likes motoring, sport, travel and music. Dislikes rush hour driving, and un-professionalism. ■ Married to . . . No! Number of children . . . Well . . .

JOHN MARSH
'Hasn't blown anything up for years. . .'
BORN: 28th July 1947 in Bournemouth. Father Congregational Church Minister. EDUCATED: Not much . . . Wallington Grammar School.

FIRST JOB: Television cameraman. He then became a Technical Operator for the BBC, moving into Studio Management and finally to announcing on the BBC World Service. 'I was always interested in electronics, I still am, but haven't blown anything up for years.' FIRST BROADCAST: 1970 on the World Service. In 1973 he joined Radio 4 as a newsreader/announcer. He transferred to Radio 2 in 1982 as a newsreader/announcer and introduces *Marching and Waltzing* on Radio 2.

■ A moment to remember: 'The day I was driving a motorized TV camera platform and I managed to smash into the audience stand and ran over the power cable cutting it and nearly electrocuting the cameraman. Roads in Sussex are dangerous places these days!' ■ Likes playing the organ and piano and kicking the dog. Dislikes people who kick dogs. ■ Married to a speech therapist, has two children and lives in Sussex.

DAVE MARSHALL
'Founder member of hospital radio in Paisley. . .'
BORN: 2nd December 1945 in Edinburgh. Father a shipping accountant. EDUCATED: Carolside Primary School and Eastwood Senior Secondary School, Clarkston, Glasgow. FIRST JOB: Export clerk in a shipping company. Was a sales rep for United Biscuits from 1967–'71, and a senior salesman for Rank Xerox from

1971–'73. FIRST BROADCAST: 1st January 1974, having sent a demo tape to Radio Clyde in Glasgow in October 1973 and been offered a job. Had gained broadcasting experience by working in Hospital Radio in Glasgow and Paisley where he was a founder member. Has presented Radio Clyde's Saturday *Children's Choice* programme and presents their *Breakfast Show* Monday to Friday.

■ Most exciting moment of career: First day on Radio Clyde. ■ Likes work and gets little time for much else. Dislikes insincerity in people. ■ Married to Barbara, has two children and lives in Scotland.

Medical photographer and in 1956 was awarded Associateship of Institute of British Photographers and Royal Photographic Society. FIRST BROADCAST: On *Children's Hour* in 1946. He joined the BBC staff in 1957 as a studio manager in the General Overseas Service. He then did holiday relief announcing for the Overseas Service, Home, Light and Third programmes and was eventually taken on full time in Presentation by John Snagge. He is the senior newsreader on Radio 4. ■ Likes photography, food and drink and his cottage in Suffolk. Dislikes piped music in pubs and writing autobiographies! ■ Lives in London and Suffolk.

PETER MARSHALL
'An actor in Bournemouth Rep. . .'
BORN: 11th April 1945 in Londonderry, Northern Ireland. Father a headmaster. EDUCATED: St. Columb's College, Londonderry. St. Jude's Teachers Training College, Belfast. The Open University B.A. Psychology. (1976–'80). FIRST JOB: As an actor in Bournemouth Rep after being turned down by RADA. FIRST BROADCAST: newsreading for Ulster Television in 1968. Since coming to London has hosted many network television programmes, including *Miss World, Miss UK* and *Come Dancing*. Has presented the *Late Show* at the weekends on Radio 2 and has also presented the *Early Show*.

■ Most exciting moment of career: The night there was a demonstration at the televising of the Miss UK contest in 1982. ■ Likes writing, cycling and weight training. ■ Married to Brenda, has two children and lives in Berkshire.

BRYAN MARTIN
'Associate of Institute of British Photographers. . .'
BORN: 29th May 1934 in Ulverston, Cumbria. Trained as a medical photographer. FIRST JOB:

CHRISTOPHER MARTIN-JENKINS
'The situation is looking blacker and blacker. . .'
BORN: 20th January 1945 in Peterborough. Father a Lt. Col. in the Army. EDUCATED: Marlborough, Cambridge. (M.A. Modern History). FIRST JOB: Deputy editor the 'Cricketer' in 1967. Has written nine books on cricket including 'The Complete Who's Who of Test Cricketers' and 'Bedside Cricket'. (Both supposed to be 'best sellers' according to 'The Sunday Times' list!) FIRST BROADCAST: *Sports Session* in 1968. He started as a freelance reporter mainly on football for BBC Radio Sport. Joined the staff of the BBC in 1970 and was the BBC's Cricket Correspondent from 1974–'80. Is now a freelance commentator and

reporter on *Test Match Specials*, *Sport on 2*, *Sport on 4*, etc: He is also commentator and editor of 'The Cricketer International'.

■ Most exciting moment of career: 'Commentating when England regained the Ashes in 1977. ■ A moment to remember: 'When Asif Iqbal (Kent and Pakistan) was out in the 1977 Benson and Hedges Cup Final, he was succeeded at the wicket by John Shepherd (Kent and Barbados). I remarked to Radio 3 listeners that the "situation for Kent is looking blacker and blacker".' ■ Likes playing cricket, golf, tennis, fives, squash and going to the theatre. Dislikes litter, coconut, garlic, bad grammar and some ugly dialects on radio. ■ Married to Judy, has three children and lives in West Sussex.

BRIAN MATTHEW
'Started it all with Saturday Club. . .'
BORN: 17th September 1928 in Coventry. Father a mechanic, but brilliant amateur musician. EDUCATED: Bablare School, Coventry. Royal Academy of Dramatic Art. FIRST JOB: Joined the army straight from school. After leaving RADA played bit parts and understudied at the Old Vic. Played in Repertory and toured. FIRST BROADCAST: In 1948 for BFN in Hamburg while in the army, after pestering his CO to let him have a go. He also broadcast on the Dutch Overseas Service in Hilversum, did a spell on Radio Luxembourg and made his first broadcast for the BBC in 1954. In the 50's presented the Light Programme's tremendously popular pop music programme *Saturday Club*. Other radio shows include *Easy Beat, Roundabout, Late Night Extra, After Seven, Album Time, My Top Twelve* and *Be My Guest*. Presents Radio 2's nightly arts magazine *Round Midnight* and since 1963 has been presenting *Top of the Pops* for the Transcription Service on the BBC.

■ Most exciting moment of career: 'November 1982 when I introduced an "all live" *Round Midnight* from Queen's University, Belfast. Students queued to thank me. The courage was theirs, the privilege mine. I cried.'

■ A moment to remember: 'Princess Margaret was asked to invite six broadcasters to tea in the Governor's Suite at Broadcasting House, I was one. "Of course", she said, "you started all this didn't you?" (meaning the "pop DJ lark") Inaccurate but flattering, and the moment I began to feel really old.' ■ Likes sailing, travel and DIY. Dislikes mediocrity. ■ Married to Pamela, has one son, Christopher and lives in Kent.

PETER MATTHEWS
'Give this boy a go, and then get rid of him. . .'
BORN: 27th November 1957 in Lytham St Annes, Lancashire of Scottish parents. Father a marine engineer. EDUCATED: Junior School in Hong Kong. Boarding schools in England. Marine College of Further Education. ('I needed it'). FIRST JOB: Navigating cadet in the Merchant Navy. Has also been a car salesman, an assistant hotel manager, a chauffeur and a night club DJ. 'I'll do anything so long as they pay me. I always wanted to be a pilot but have never got around to it'. FIRST BROADCAST: On Hospital Radio. 'I progressed to local radio by continuously knocking on Programme Controller's doors until one day someone decided that perhaps "we should give this boy a go then get rid of him", but they never did.' 'I've presented just about every kind of programme apart from Heavy Rock (it's too noisy) and classical (which I don't understand). I concentrate mainly on nostalgia and oldies, current pop and meaningful speech programmes.' Is producer/presenter of weekly *Nostalgia Show* and the daily *Lunchtime Shows* on Radio Tees.

■ Most exciting moment of career: 'It hasn't happened yet'. ■ A moment to remember: 'On my very first radio programme my first words were "Thanks to IRN Radio 1 for the news", which completely sent me into nervous convulsions for the rest of the show. I thought my career in Radio had finished before it had even started. Oh, and I once had three blondes banging on the studio door for two hours . . . but I still didn't let them out!' ■ Likes girls, travelling and meaningful speech (in no particular order). Dislikes people without a sense of humour, punk rockers and men in drag. ■ Married to . . . 'You're kidding'. Number of children. 'No comment'.

RICHARD MAYNE
'Expert on European affairs. . .'
BORN: 1926 in London. Father a businessman. EDUCATED: St. Paul's School and Trinity College Cambridge. M.A and Ph.D. FIRST JOB: Film critic for the 'Cambridge Review' and Rome Correspondent for the 'New Statesman'. Other posts held, Assistant tutor Cambridge Institute of Education; Official of the European Communities (Luxembourg and Brussels); Assistant to Jean Monet (Paris); Paris correspondent of 'Encounter'; Visiting Professor University of Chicago; Director, Federal Trust for Education and Research; Head of UK Offices of European Community; Special Adviser European Community. FIRST BROADCAST: In 1958 as member of *The Critics* panel having been invited to join them after a talk on movies given to a student society in Cambridge. Since then has contributed to numerous programmes on Radio 4 including *Critics Forum, The World Tonight, Stop the Week,* compiled and presented *French Sunday, German Weekend, Italian Weekend.* Has presented *Not Now I'm Listening, Now Read On* and is one of the regular team of *Kaleidoscope* presenters. Has written several books on European affairs . . . *The Community of Europe* (1962), *The Recovery of Europe* (1970), *The Europeans* (1972), *Postwar* (1983). Has edited *Europe Tomorrow* (1972) *The New Atlantic Challenge* (1975). Has translated *The Memoirs of Jean Monet* (Scott-Moncrieff Prize 1978).

■ Most exciting moment of career: The 1975 Referendum on British membership of the European Community. ■ A moment to remember: 'Saying in a recorded talk on Petain and De Gaulle, "Now the two voices are stilled" – thinking "I must get the producer to re-record that since De Gaulle's still alive – and getting home to hear that he had actually died that same day".' ■ Likes sailing, fell-walking. Dislikes bullying and muzak. ■ Married to former BBC producer Jocelyn Ferguson, has two daughters and lives in London.

MICHAEL MEECH
'From pulpit to microphone. . .'
BORN: 29th September 1932 in East Coker, Nr. Yeovil, Somerset. Father a farm worker. EDUCATED: Yeovil School, Wesley College, Headingley. FIRST JOB: Methodist Minister. While doing National Service in the RAF, was a nursing assistant. FIRST BROADCAST: News report in August 1958. 'I was dared to 'phone a story to the BBC newsroom in Bristol! Subsequently I auditioned successfully for television newsreading in Bristol.' Television credits include *Points West* and *Songs of Praise.* Became Radio 2 newsreader/presenter before going freelance. Programmes include *Sunday on Radio 4; In Conversation* and *A Little Light Music* on BBC Radio London; *The Late Show* on Radio 2; various sports programmes for the World Service. Is a regular contributor to Radio 2's *You and the Night and the Music* and can also be heard reporting for Radio London, and on LBC's *AM* programme.

■ Most exciting moment of career: 'There's a new one every day!' ■ Likes cricket, after dinner speaking, listening to Mozart and gardening. Dislikes artificial flowers, pheasant and people who never listen! ■ Married to Wendy Draper, has two children and lives in Surrey.

CLIFF MICHELMORE
'Broadcasting led to romance...'

BORN: 11th December 1919 in Cowes, Isle of Wight. EDUCATED: Cowes High School. Loughborough College. Leicester College of Technology and Art. RAF College and RAF School of Technical Training. FIRST JOB: Royal Air Force in 1935. FIRST BROADCAST: 1946 for British Forces Network in Hamburg, having been appointed RAF Officer Commanding RAF Element BFN. He became a household name presenting the German end of *Two Way Family Favourites* which also led to one of Radio's most famous romances! He married the voice on the other end of the line . . . Jean Metcalf who introduced the London end of *Family Favourites*. Was a commentator for BBC Outside Broadcasts from 1950 and was the front man of one of the most successful television news magazines ever . . . *Tonight*. Has presented many features and documentaries for Radio 4 including *Choice of Paperbacks, Whatever You Think, Sacred Cowes* and the *Story of Gleneagles*. Has also presented the *Jimmy Young Show* on Radio 2. Television credits include BBC 1's Holiday programme. Was awarded the CBE in 1969.

■ Likes golf, reading and doing nothing.
■ Married to Jean Metcalf, has one son, Guy and one daughter, Jenny, and lives in Surrey.

PHIL MILES
'A "live" OB from H.M.S. Cardiff...'

BORN: 29th June 1953 in Newport, Gwent. Father a Sub-postmaster/travel agent. EDUCATED: St. Julian's High School, Newport. FIRST JOB: Helping to run the family businesses. Ran a mobile disco and worked as a club DJ/compère as well as working in Hospital Radio. Was a sales rep for a record wholesaler. FIRST BROADCAST: 12th April 1980 'Dancing in the Streets' for CBC Radio Cardiff. 'After ten years with Hospital Radio I sent a demo tape to CBC a couple of weeks before they went on air. At the same time a gap appeared in the

programme schedule and I was offered the job. A case of being in the right place at the right time!' Other CBC Shows include *Countdown, Factory Call, Welshwise, Happy Health* and a two year stint on the *Breakfast Show*. In April 1983 moved to the newly opened County Sound in Guildford to present their *Breakfast Show* and their *Chart Show*.

■ Most exciting moment of career: Doing a 'live' Outside Broadcast from HMS Cardiff as she sailed home towards the port she was named after, on her return from the Falklands campaign. ■ Likes vegetarian cookery, photography and wine making. Dislikes posers, prunes and cold weather. ■ Married to Barbara, has one son and lives in Surrey.

JACKIE MONKMAN
'Helped to set up BBC Radio Jersey...'

BORN: 25th March 1956 in Jersey, Channel Islands. Father Managing Director of family jewellery business. EDUCATED: Harlow College, Essex. FIRST JOB: Reporter on the 'Jersey Evening Post'. Also worked as a reporter on the London 'Evening News' and the 'Daily Mail'. FIRST BROADCAST: December 1981 on BBC Radio Solent. Is one of a team of four who set up BBC Radio Jersey in March 1982. Contributes to most of the station's output and presents *Jersey Today* and *Jersey at Five*. As management assistant is responsible for researching and presenting entertainment in the island.

Likes dinghy sailing, tennis and figure drawing. Dislikes dishonesty. ■ Lives in St. Helier, Jersey.

church music and going out to dinner. Dislikes Cruise Missiles and the Common Market. ■ Married to Alma and lives in London.

RAY MOORE
'Muttering behind the undergrowth at beauty competitions. . .'

BORN: 2nd January 1942 in Liverpool. Father a cabinet maker with funeral directors. EDUCATED: Waterloo Grammar School. FIRST JOB: Unloading cotton at Liverpool Docks. Also delivered wages to dock workers. From the dockyard to the stage as an ASM and bad actor with repertory companies in Oldham, Swansea, Sidmouth and Lyme Regis. FIRST BROADCAST: As a continuity relief announcer for Granada Television in Manchester. 'I wrote to Granada saying I wanted to be an announcer. The following week they were desperate and employed me on a weekly contract. I started in radio in 1967 doing *Breakfast Special* and sixteen years later I'm still doing the same thing. Some progress!' Has also presented the *Late Show* on Radio 2 and is the regular stand-in for Terry Wogan. He has done several extended interviews for Radio 2 with such stars as The Carpenters, Abba and Tom Jones. Over the past decade his name has become synonymous with that of Radio 2, he is very rarely off it! His voice is also heard regularly on BBC Television promoting programmes. His television credits as commentator/presenter include *Miss World, Horizon* and the *Variety Club Awards.* 'I seem to specialize in doing the muttering behind the undergrowth at beauty competitions!'

■ Most exciting moment of career: 'Several . . . interviewing the Carpenters in Hollywood; presenting the Eurovision Song Contest from Jerusalem; commentating on the Royal River progress in Jubilee year.' ■ A moment to remember: 'Once booked to do the commentary for a special Boat Race edition of *Crackerjack*, I ended up being flung in the river fully clothed.' ■ Likes the theatre, early

JOHNNY MORAN
'Broadcasting looked like a fun thing to do. . .'

BORN: 18th September in Melbourne, Australia. EDUCATED: Melbourne High School, Australia. FIRST JOB AND FIRST BROADCAST: Radio Station 3AW in Melbourne, Australia. 'Having visited some radio and television studios while still at school, and not having any firm vocational plans, it flashed into my head that broadcasting looked like a fun thing to do.' On arriving in the UK he worked for BBC Radio 1 for several years before joining Radio Hallam in Sheffield when it opened in 1974. As well as presenting a daily show on Radio Hallam he also appears on Yorkshire Television.

■ Most exciting moment of career: 'Lots of them, but opening up Radio Hallam in October 1974 with it's first ever programme was probably the most highly charged moment of them all.' ■ A moment to remember: 'In one memorable radio show a few years ago, it was announced that I was to ride a horse called "Hallam Rock" in the Aintree Grand National. Radio Hallam was flooded with calls for details of the horse, it's form and it's prices. My colleague Roger Moffat went to Liverpool and broadcast interviews with BBC sports commentators David Coleman and Peter O'Sullevan as to my chances as a (disc) jockey on "Hallam Rock" and they both concluded we were a good outside bet. More 'phone calls came to the station from people wanting to know why the betting shops had no information on this fancied dark horse. By midday all became apparent: The National that year was run on April 1st. However as a foot (or even four foot) note, shortly thereafter "Hallam Rock" did become familiar as a winner to punters and bookmakers. Not a horse at all, but someone with a sense of humour christened a greyhound by that name.' ■ Likes motoring, squash and horse riding. Dislikes people with small minds and small pockets. ■ Married to Susan and lives in Derbyshire.

GUY MORRIS
'Did audio presentations. . .'
BORN: 12th January 1956 in Wythall, Warwickshire. Father a sales executive EDUCATED: King's School, Macclesfield, Cheshire. Art College (two years). FIRST JOB: ICI pharmaceuticals. Also worked as an installer of sound and light equipment and did audio presentations in a store. FIRST BROADCAST: July 1975 on Radio Trent, Nottingham, having sent in a demo tape. After leaving Radio Trent he moved to BRMB and from there to Radio Victory in Portsmouth where he presents the *Afternoon Drive Time* and also their *Top 40*.

■ Most exciting moment of career: 'Being offered a job for the first time in radio'.
■ A moment to remember: 'While driving to an interview I took the Motorway which was very busy. Lorries hemming me in on either side. All of a sudden I felt one of my wheels bumping and realized that the securing nuts were coming adrift. The radio was on at the time and the record being played? Kenny Rogers "You Picked a Fine Time to Leave me Loose Wheel"!' ■ Likes sub aqua. Dislikes passport photographs. ■ Married to Caz and lives in Hampshire.

JOHNNY MORRIS
'One of the West Country's best loved broadcasters. . .' d. 1999
BORN: 20th June 1916 in Newport, Monmouthshire. Father a postmaster. EDUCATED: Hatherleigh School, Newport. FIRST JOB: Solicitor's clerk. Has also worked as a timekeeper on a building site, a salesman and been the farm manager of a 2,000 acre farm in Wiltshire. FIRST BROADCAST: April 1st, 1946. Since then has become one of the West Country's best loved broadcasters both on

D. May 1999

Radio and Television. Programmes include *Pass the Salt, Journeyman Johnny, Johnny Comes to Town, Johnny's Jaunts* and *Around the World in 25 years.* Plus of course numerous series on television.

■ Most exciting moment of career: 'Getting arrested in Hungary.' ■ A moment to remember: 'In the days when all broadcasts were "live", I used to do a weekly programme from Bristol that went out from 6.45pm to 7pm. Although the studio was meant to be sound proof, one could always hear noises from outside and that included Big George, the clock at the University. My programme was timed to finish at 7 o'clock and with one page of script left to read, that clock would strike seven as it was always one and a half minutes fast. It was a very un-nerving experience, which used to happen quite frequently and I never got used to it'. ■ Likes music, watching animals and people. Dislikes muzac, badly behaved dogs and their owners. ■ Married to Eileen, has two step children and lives in Berkshire.

MARTIN MUNCASTER
'Practically my whole career has been exciting. . .'
BORN: 17th July 1934. Father the landscape and marine painter Claude Muncaster, who was President of the Royal Society of Marine Artists. EDUCATED: Fernden School, Haslemere and Stowe School, Buckingham. FIRST JOB: Announcer for the General Overseas Service of

the BBC. 'I attended a Board for Studio Managers, didn't get that job but was invited to work as an announcer by the Head of Presentation, General Overseas Services who was sitting on the Board.' Prior to joining G.O.S. he made his first broadcast on Radio Luxembourg presenting a series of programmes on famous American composers. He spent three years National Service as a Signalman and then a Sub Lieutenant in the Royal Navy. Has worked extensively in television as well as radio and was the first presenter of BBC 1's *South Today*, the regional news magazine from Southampton. Has also worked as a newsreader/reporter/announcer for Southern Television and has been a presentation announcer for BBC 1. Spent several years as a newsreader/announcer on the BBC Home Service then Radio 4. Is now a freelance broadcaster and radio programmes include *An Evening in Old Vienna, Strings by Starlight, Family Fare, Today For All Seasons, Morning Story, Storytime, Countryside, Seaside, Breakaway, You and Yours, Sunday Half Hour* and he also makes regular contributions to *You and the Night and the Music*. Has written two books, 'The Wind in the Oak', about the life, work and philosophy of his father, 'The Yachtman's Quiz Book'; and 'A History of the International Engineering Consultancy'.

■ Most exciting moment of career: 'Practically my whole career has been exciting!' ■ A moment to remember: 'Just before presenting *South Today* one evening, I was kidnapped by Southampton students as a Rag Week stunt and carted off to be locked up for ransom in the University. It took a lot of persuasion to get them to let me go free and I only got back to introduce the programme in the nick of time after having parted with ten shillings towards Rag funds. The producer of the programme that night was furious and the BBC didn't stand me the ten shillings!' ■ Likes sailing, fly fishing, photographing wildlife and bird watching. Dislikes cigarette and tobacco smoke, pop music at high volume and plastic cups. ■ Married to Iona, has two sons and one daughter and lives in Surrey.

Robinson Family for the BBC World Service in April 1943. Pete, or Peter as he likes to be called when in serious frame of mind, had established himself as a stage actor before becoming a household name in radio. It all started when he went to Radio Luxembourg as a three months replacement DJ and stayed 5 years! Since then he has presented many hit shows on BBC Radio . . . *Pete's Party, Open House*, which ran from 1969 until 1980 on Radio 2. He also hosted the first late night show on Radio 2 to go until 2am, in 1965 and they've got him burning the midnight oil again with the *Pete Murray Late Shows* on Saturday and Sunday nights. Not that he has given up acting. I seem to remember him appearing in a straight play at Guildford with another radio personality Mike Aspel, not so long ago and his 1982 appearance in pantomime at Lewisham broke all box office records! Was awarded the OBE in 1970.

■ Most exciting moment of career: Being nominated ATV Actor of the Year in the Rediffusion production of Richard Hilary's *The Last Enemy* in 1959, and being awarded the OBE in March 1970. ■ A moment to remember: 'The day we had Burt Lancaster as a guest on *Open House*. There were about twenty photographers milling around and he really didn't want to know. The record came to an end rather suddenly and I uttered the immortal words, "And now I'd like to welcome my guest Burt Bacharach", to which Mr Lancaster replied "I haven't written too many good tunes recently!"' ■ Likes tennis and cricket. ■ Married to barrister and authoress Patricia Murray and lives in South London.

PETE MURRAY
'The first late night show through till 2 and he's still at it!'
BORN: 19th September 1928 in London. Father an electrical engineer. EDUCATED: St. Paul's School. Royal Academy of Dramatic Art. FIRST JOB: With Jean Cadell in *Miss Marigold* at the Q Theatre, Kew. FIRST BROADCAST: In the

BARBARA MYERS
'Unscheduled interview with Prince Charles. . .'
BORN: 27th February 1948 in Leeds, Yorkshire. Father an engine driver turned businessman. EDUCATED: Retford High School for Girls, Nottinghamshire. Sussex University, (Hon

Degree in Sociology). FIRST JOB: Paid her way at University as a part time waitress/shop assistant/market researcher for a baked beans company/research assistant to Tom Harrison at the Mass Observation Archive. FIRST BROADCAST: 'As a contestant in a radio quiz show. I was 12 years old and I won! First television was at University for a student programme when I interviewed Godfrey Winn and that gave me my taste for interviewing and presenting. I then offered student type stories to BBC Radio Brighton and when I graduated, they took me on as a freelance reporter/presenter.' Since then Barbara has spent seven years with the *World at One* and *P.M. Reports*. Has presented 2 series of *Inside Medicine* for BBC Television, *Science in Action* for the BBC World Service and several Further Education series. She was a guest presenter on Radio 4 and contributes regularly to *Woman's Hour* and also presents *Tuesday Call*. Major radio features have included *Pain – A Way of Life* and *The Dietary Fibre Story*, which won the Medical Journalists Association Prize for the best medical radio programme of 1982.

■ Most exciting moment of career: Recording the birth of a baby, in every last detail, for the final programme in a 9 month series on *Having a Baby*. Mother, baby and series all did well! ■ A moment to remember: 'The day I "scooped" an interview with Prince Charles. Such things usually have to be arranged through the Palace Press Office, but on this occasion HRH was giving a Press Conference about his work for young people. I asked the first question from the floor, and before he started to answer, bounded up on to the platform with my tape recorder running. Not being one to miss an opportunity, I then asked half a dozen more questions and ended up with a 5 minute interview for the *World at One*. The Police bodyguards and the Palace press officials were so taken aback, they didn't know what to do. Prince Charles was surprised but responded admirably and even the *World at One* team were impressed!' ■ Likes sport

including squash and golf. Dislikes getting up in the morning. ■ Married to Paul Loman, has one son and lives in Sussex.

ANNE NIGHTINGALE
'The first female DJ on Radio 1 . . .'

BORN: 1st April (really!) in Osterley, Middlesex. Father a textile designer/wallpaper manufacturer/electronics administrator. Mother was an assistant to Dr. Scholl. EDUCATED: St. Catherine's Convent, Twickenham. Lady Eleanor Holles School, Hampton, Middlesex. Polytechnic of Central London School of Journalism. FIRST JOB: General reporter on 'Brighton and Hove Gazette'. Has also been the Rock columnist for 'Cosmopolitan' and the Rock/Pop columnist for the 'Daily Express'. FIRST BROADCAST: *Today* in the South and West. As a freelance interviewer she worked for *Woman's Hour* as well as *Today* before joining Radio Brighton and from there becoming the first woman DJ on Radio 1 in 1970. Programmes since then have included *What's New*, the *Anne Nightingale Request Show* 1974–'79; *Anne After Dark* 1980–'81. She has been presenting the Radio 1 *Mailbag* since 1977 and the *Annie After Dark Sunday Request Show* since 1982.

■ Most exciting moment of career: 'Presenting "The Who, The Final Concert" for the USA and Canada and a "live" satellite transmission from Toronto in December 1982.' ■ A moment to remember: 'Presenting a Rock and Pop Award to the "Police" in Hong Kong working with a Chinese crew! . . . for further details of this amazing incident, you might like to read my book "Chase the Fade".'[Nice plug Anne!] ■ Likes photography. Dislikes scallops, spiders, being asked what it's like being the first female DJ on Radio 1, and not being able to play all the requests one gets asked to play.' ■ Married to Binky Baker, has two children and lives in Sussex.

CHARLES NOVE
'A childhood dream come true. . .'

BORN: 29th June 1960 in London. Father a university professor. EDUCATED: Kelvinside Academy, Glasgow. FIRST JOB: 'I don't wish to go into that, but I did have a short spell assisting in an electronics factory.' FIRST BROADCAST: 1976 on Glasgow Hospital Broadcasting service. 'Being a broadcaster had been a childhood dream and after early experiments with tapes and records at home I started for real in hospital radio.' He then joined BBC Radio Scotland presenting *Nightbeat* and their *Top 40* show. He moved South in 1981 and is a Radio 2 newsreader/presenter. He is one of the regular presenters of *You and the Night and the Music.*

■ A moment to remember: 'Once during a late evening shift on Radio Scotland, I was reading out the nightly report on sales at Scotland's fish markets, when I came to a class of fish I'd never heard of before . . . "Jumbo Haddock". As I read the words my mind became full of pictures of ridiculous creatures . . . giant haddock with trunks and tusks, and elephants with fins . . . As any broadcaster knows, these pictures in the mind are highly dangerous, they certainly were in this case . . . I burst out laughing and proceeded to broadcast a rather giggly weather forecast to the Scottish nation!'   ■ Likes computing, driving (fast when possible) and hospital radio. Dislikes wife!, bad drivers, incompetence and dieting (but I have to). ■ Married to Anne and lives in London.

storekeeper's clerk, Bible publisher's clerk, technical editor, conference organizer, bookseller etc! FIRST BROADCAST: BBC Radio London *In Concert* in 1970. Having been writing programme notes for concerts, his name was suggested by a mutual friend when Radio London were looking for a presenter. Since then has presented *Record Review, Your Concert Choice* and *Music Weekly* for Radio 3 and *Kaleidoscope* for Radio 4. Has also done several one-off radio documentaries . . . *David Munrow, Many a Beautiful Thing Had the People Who are Gone', The Larks of Dean.* Is also a regular reviewer for 'Gramophone' magazine.

■ Most exciting moment of career: Too many to single out one! [Being a mortuary attendant must have provided quite a few!]   ■ Dislikes politics and politicians, wearing a tie, aubergines and 'gosh do you want *names?*' ■ Married to nobody and lives in London.

MICHAEL OLIVER
'A whole host of fascinating jobs. . .'

BORN: 20th July 1937 in London. Father a postman. EDUCATED: St. Clement Dane's Grammar School. Sundry polytechnics and schools of printing and librarianship. FIRST JOB: Hammersmith Public Library as the most lowly of library assistants. But even more fascinating jobs were in store, a mortuary attendant, kitchen porter, clerk to a music publisher,

DAVID OLVER
'Northern Ireland end of Family Favourites. . .'

BORN: 26th April 1959 in Belfast. Father a chartered architect. EDUCATED: Royal Belfast Academical Institution. Belfast College of Business Studies. FIRST JOB: Part-time newsreader with Radio Ulster while still at college. FIRST BROADCAST: January 1978, the late night *Radio Ulster News.* He applied to the

BBC for a voice test and was appointed as a staff announcer on Radio Ulster. 1979–'81 he was the Northern Ireland presenter for *Family Favourites* on Radio 2. Has presented a late night record show and presents *Early Call* on Radio Ulster. As a newsreader/presenter, he reads news on both radio and television and is responsible for both radio and television continuity.

■ Most exciting moment of career: 'Being asked to become the regular Northern Ireland presenter of *Family Favourites*. This was my first experience of network radio and afforded me the opportunity of working with such broadcasters as Pete Murray, Jean Challis and Steve Jones.' ■ A moment to remember: 'In an unattended news studio it's usual for the camera to be lined up about ten minutes before we go on the air. This particular night, nobody had turned up to do it, but as the newsreader and myself (duty continuity announcer) were satisfied with the studio conditions, the news went ahead on schedule. Imagine our horror when half way through the bulletin, the engineer, unaware of the time and thinking we were rehearsing, started to line up the camera. Viewers at home were treated to shots of the studio ceiling, floor and walls. Fortunately not a word was spoken, but the look of horror and total disbelief on my colleague's face, had to be seen to be believed.' ■ Likes cooking, listening to music, swimming and driving. Dislikes cigarettes, opera, driving on icy roads and rats. ■ Is a bachelor and lives in Antrim, Northern Ireland.

JOHN OSMAN
'From the Kremlin to Buckingham Palace. . .'
BORN: 3rd July 1929 in Worthing, Sussex. Father a gardener, ex-Army. EDUCATED: Worthing High School for Boys. FIRST JOB: Junior reporter on the 'Brighton Evening Argus' and the 'Sussex Daily News'. Has also been a reporter for 'Worthing Herald', 'Bristol Evening Post', Press Association, and Foreign

Correspondent of the 'Daily Telegraph'. FIRST BROADCAST: 'On Kenyan Radio in the 1960's when I was still with the "Daily Telegraph".' Joined the BBC in 1965 as the Commonwealth Correspondent on the Foreign News staff. Since then has worked in some 90 different countries as a foreign correspondent and has contributed to every BBC Radio, Television and World Service news and current affairs programme. Is now back in the UK as the BBC's Diplomatic and Court Correspondent for Radio News. 'It was quite a change to be posted from Africa in 1980 to Moscow, and perhaps even more of a change to be switched in 1983 from covering the Kremlin to covering Buckingham Palace and the Foreign and Commonwealth Office!'

■ Likes skiing, squash, mountain walking, reading, swimming and listening to music. ■ Married to Virginia Waite, has three children and lives in London.

BILL PADLEY
Musician/singer/songwriter/DJ. . .'
BORN: 5th March 1961 in Paisley, Scotland. Father education welfare officer/entrepreneur! EDUCATED: Scotland and the Isle of Wight. FIRST JOB: Part time engineer at Radio Victory. Also a musician/singer/songwriter and played in various rock groups in clubs, pubs and holiday camps throughout the South for the best part of fourteen years. The last band he was with was Fury who've now landed a recording contract. FIRST BROADCAST: 1977 in *New Faces* on Radio Victory. 'I had a foot in the door and that's all I needed to show the people who mattered, what I could do'. Has presented various programmes for Radio Victory including their *Top 40*, the *Late Show* and the *Rock Show*. Presents the *Breakfast Show* Monday to Friday and *Saturday Sport*. Is also a regular session singer on *Jingles* and he writes them too.

■ Most exciting moment of career: 'Being given the challenge of the *Breakfast Show* at 19. I'm still there!' ■ Likes flying light aircraft, women and music (playing and songwriting). Dislikes inefficient people and apathy (in myself as well as others). ■ Lives in Hampshire.

KENNY PAGE
'Hands that wash records. . .'

BORN: 13th April 1955 in Stirling, Scotland. Father a security guard. EDUCATED: Bellahouston Academy, Glasgow. FIRST JOB: Clerk/typist in the BBC buying department in London. (Yuk). FIRST BROADCAST: January 1974 *Ken's Korner* on Radio Clyde. 'Having worked in Hospital broadcasting, I pestered the living daylight out of Andy Park, Head of Entertainment at Clyde.' After a couple of years with Radio Clyde he joined Radio Caroline in the summer of '76 and then became Programme Director with the *Voice of Peace* ship anchored six miles of Tel-Aviv. Moving back to dry land and his native Scotland, he joined Radio Tay and presented their *Heading Home* and their *Breakfast Beat*. Is now music controller at Radio Tay and presents *The Lunchbreak* and *7 O'clock Rock*.

■ Most exciting moment of career: 'Yet to happen, but up to now, receiving the letter confirming my appointment with Radio Tay'. ■ A moment to remember: 'When I joined Radio Tay, one of my duties was to wash the oldies collection which had just been purchased. There wasn't really anywhere suitable so I ended up washing over 2,000 singles in the ladies loo (which I had to vacate every time someone wanted to use it). Furtunately there were only 5 people employed at the time and traffic was light. One thing I did find out was . . . "Hands that wash records *can* feel as soft as your face!" . . . with apologies to Fairy.' ■ Likes travel and relaxation. Dislikes bad manners, inconsiderate people and curries. ■ Lives in Tayside.

MARK PAGE
'An early starter. . .'

BORN: 13th October 1958 in Middlesbrough. Father a brain surgeon. EDUCATED: At school! FIRST JOB: As a dustbin man but the pay was rubbish. FIRST BROADCAST: Hospital Radio at 14, sports programme on Radio Clyde at 15 and his own Sunday lunchtime show on Radio Tees at 16. Has been presenting the *Breakfast Show* at Radio Tees since 1977. Also presents their *Holiday* programme and is their Head of Presentation. Writes two local newspaper columns and does a weekly *Pop Spot* on Tyne Tees Television. Has also appeared in pantomime.

■ Most exciting moment of career: 'Numerous'. ■ Likes supporting Middlesbrough F.C. Dislikes bland DJ's and people who crash records. ■ Lives in Cleveland.

NICK PAGE
'Carved a niche for himself on Sunday mornings. . .'

BORN: 27th November 1943 in Doncaster. Father a doctor. EDUCATED: Dulwich College. St. Mary's Hospital Medical School. Ealing Technical College. FIRST JOB: As a trainee for the Metal Box Co. Ltd. But then went on to import and export wax and vanilla beans [this is getting curiouser and curiouser!] FIRST BROADCAST: Reporting a meeting on Radio Medway. A toe in the door, or maybe it was a vanilla bean, was all he needed. More work for

Radio Medway followed and then came a move to LBC in London with contributions to such shows as *Nightline, Sunday Supplement, Weekend AM*. From LBC, he moved to the BBC presenting the *Sunday Breakfast Show* for BBC Radio Wales, *Banners and Bonnets* for the World Service and *European Pop Jury, String Sound* and the *Early Show* for Radio 2. Carved something of a niche for himself with his Sunday morning *Nick Page Show* on Radio 2.

■ Most exciting moment of career: Presenting 'live' Outside Broadcasts from places such as Belfast, California, Jerusalem and Rome.
■ A moment to remember: 'Late night broadcasting on LBC could be fraught . . . one night a cleaner, ignoring the red light, pushed the studio door open with a vacuum cleaner. Another time the telephone switchboard jammed with an hour to go on my 'phone-in programme which ended with close down at 1am. Fortunately my pre-midnight guest, Ned Sherrin, hadn't left so *we* enjoyed an hour's impromptu conversation.' [Talking about those vanilla beans?] ■ Likes theatre, cinema and church activities. Dislikes marzipan, tea and cigarette smoke. ■ Married to Margaret, keeps twenty hens and lives in Kent.

BARRY PAINE
'Never try to cope with all the beverages. . .'
BORN: 20th October 1937 in Woodford Essex. Father a pharmacist. EDUCATED: Wanstead County High School. University College of North Wales, Bangor. FIRST JOB: Trainee laboratory technician in Rodenside Colour Film Research Laboratory, before going to University. After University joined the BBC as a trainee studio manager in Radio Drama and as a SM/Announcer at Bush House. Transferred to BBC Bristol and trained as a film technician, film cameraman and film sound recordist. Entered television production in 1965. 'When local radio was first mooted in 1961, I was recruited from University, but then the government changed and local radio didn't

happen so I became an SM.' FIRST BROADCAST: As a studio manager, 'This is London Calling. . .' etc. Or a one minute comedy insert to *Good Morning* on the BBC West Home Service in 1962 as Senor Manuel Dexterite . . . the character became a regular programme feature. Television credits as a producer and producer/narrator include *Life – in the Animal World* with Desmond Morris, *Great Zoos of the World* and *The World About Us*. Radio programmes include *From the 50's*, (Drama). *Round Up, At the Luscombes*, and *Good Morning* for BBC West Region; *Nature News* for Radio 3 and *Nature Notebook* for the World Service. Makes various contributions to Radio 4's wildlife programmes. Is a freelance presenter/writer/narrator/producer for *The World About Us* and presents BBC West's *Day Out* series.

■ Most exciting moment of career: 'Leaving the BBC to go freelance as a broadcaster after 21 full, varied and exciting years in radio and television all over the world.' ■ A moment to remember: 'Having survived severe electrical storms on a jungle mountain and being swept off in flooded forest at night as well as being used as a punch-bag on radio by a heavyweight champion, I discovered the most dangerous hazard to broadcasting . . . hospitality, especially with Royalty present. Only meticulous rehearsal beforehand, and a sober vision mixer afterwards, can save the director who tries to cope with all the beverages served at lunch on a Grade 1 broadcast!' ■ Likes acting with the Mercury Players, Bristol (Little Theatre), and sleeping. Dislikes liquorice and environmental apathy. ■ Is a bachelor and lives in that part of Somerset they now call Avon!

JOE PALEY
'Every broadcaster leaves the pause button down once. . .'
BORN: 13th April 1948 in Blackpool,

Lancashire. Father and mother solicitors. EDUCATED: Sedbergh School, Yorkshire. Liverpool University. FIRST JOB: Reporter on the 'Birkenhead News'. Also worked for a news agency in Liverpool and as a reporter on 'The Journal' newspaper in Newcastle. FIRST BROADCAST: 1973 on BBC Radio Merseyside. In 1976 left 'The Journal' in Newcastle to join BBC Radio Newcastle. Is now a reporter for BBC Radio News based in London.

■ A moment to remember: 'Every broadcaster leaves his "pause" button down just once in his life. I hope others don't choose such an important interview in which to do it. (In my case the first!)' ■ Likes most music and cricket. Dislikes meat, fizzy beer and opera. ■ Married to Carol Anne and lives in London.

Father an accountant. EDUCATED: Skinners School, Tunbridge Wells. London College of Printing. FIRST JOB: Scriptwriter for Radio Luxembourg. FIRST BROADCAST: Radio 210, Thames Valley in 1977. Worked for various commercial stations as a freelance reporter and then joined BBC Radio London. Is a freelance reporter and presenter on Radio 1's *Newsbeat*.

■ Likes anything to do with cars and is an amateur racing driver. ■ Is a bachelor and lives in London.

RICHARD PARK
'The first broadcast is the most exciting. . .'
BORN: 10th March 1948 in Kirkaldy, Fife. Father a factory general manager. EDUCATED: Kirkaldy High School. FIRST JOB: Reporter for the Fife Free Dress Newspaper Group. FIRST BROADCAST: August 1966 on BBC Radio Scotland, having previously worked on a Pirate Station. Programmes on Radio Scotland include *Radio One Club* and *Roundtable* between 1969 and '73. He then joined Radio Clyde to present the *Lunchtime Show* and a sports programme. Is Music Controller at Radio Clyde.

■ Most exciting moment of career: 'The first broadcast with each of the three organizations I've worked for.' ■ Likes squash, football and golf. Dislikes smoking. ■ Married to Brenda, has two children, Paul and Jennifer and lives in Scotland.

IAN PARKINSON
'Amateur racing driver. . .'
BORN: 12th September 1958 in South London.

JOHN PARRY
'From television to radio. . .'
BORN: 28th August 1936 in York. Father an optician. EDUCATED: 'Yes'. FIRST JOB: Reporter on the 'Blackburn Evening Telegraph'. Has also worked for the 'Daily Express' as a reporter on the William Hickey column. FIRST BROADCAST: 1973 on radio but before that was a reporter for BBC 1's *Tomorrow's World*. Is the Arts Correspondent for BBC Radio and is heard regularly on all the news and current affairs programmes.

■ Likes the theatre, music, reading and cooking. Dislikes parsnips. ■ Married to actress Judy Cornwell, has one son and lives in Sussex.

ALEX PASCALL
'Specialist knowledge of Afro/Caribbean cultures. . .'

BORN: 21st November 1936 in Grenada, West Indies. Father estate owner/dealer in agricultural produce. EDUCATED: G.B.S.S. (Grenada Boys Secondary School). FIRST JOB: Folklore researcher/insurance salesman. Add to that percussionist/singer/songwriter/humourist/recording artiste/producer and storyteller. FIRST BROADCAST: November 1974 having been invited to take part in a programme because of his specialist knowledge of Afro/Caribbean Cultures and experience in Showbiz. Has contributed to a wide variety of programmes across the networks. Radio 4 Schools programmes *Folkstories and Songs* and *Faraway Foods*. *Black and Blue*, documentary about Police and Black Youth. 18 Hour Radio Marathon *Caribbean Disaster Fund* in 1979. Radio 2 *Brian Matthew's Tribute to Bob Marley*. *Black Londoners* on BBC Radio London. Has also contributed to many television programmes including a dramatized version of the *Lord Scarman Enquiry on the Brixton Riots in 1981* on BBC Television. Is a producer and presenter with BBC Radio London.

■ Most exciting moment of career: 'My first visit to Africa to "Festac '77" the second black and African Festival of Art and Culture (a breathtaking spectacle). ■ Likes cricket, table tennis and meeting people. Dislikes soppy handshakes. ■ Married to Joyce (S.R.N/Painter), has two children, and lives in London.

ANDY PEEBLES
'The final interview with John Lennon. . .'

BORN: 13th December 1948 in Hampstead, London. Father a head postmaster G.P.O. EDUCATED: Bishop's Stortford College, Hertfordshire. FIRST JOB: Barman for one year, prior to one year of 4-year hotel management course in Bournemouth. Worked in discos from 1967 to '72. Opened 'The Hardrock' concert venue in Manchester in 1972 and worked as compère with David Bowie, Rod Stewart, Elton John, Led Zeppelin etc., FIRST BROADCAST: Hospital Radio (Radio Cavell, Oldham, Lancashire) late 1972, then BBC Radio Manchester the following year. 'The late Dave Kaye of the pirate station Radio London lived in the flat above when I was at school and he was a great influence. I did the usual auditions, but Radio 1 approached me while I was at Piccadilly Radio.' His Radio 1 programmes include *Stayin Alive, My Top Twelve* and the regular Friday night slot 7–10pm. *Peebles Choice* for the BBC World Service; *On Another Track* for BFBS; *Wavelength* for BBC Schools Radio.

■ Most exciting moment of career: '(And the saddest) Interviewing John Lennon in New York two days prior to his senseless murder.'
■ A moment to remember: 'Prior to joining Radio 1 I had never been out of the country, so you can imagine the amusement at the Corporation when my first trip out of England was to Moscow to compère Elton John's concert at the Rossya Hall in Moscow . . . a trip I shall never forget. I even managed to hit the G.T.S. on the nose "live" from Moscow and I claim that as a first (and totally irrelevant achievement) in British broadcasting!' ■ Likes sport, the cinema and photography. Dislikes false people and rice pudding. ■ Married to . . . 'No luck as yet'. Children? . . . 'How dare you!' ■ Lives in Hertfordshire.

JOHN PEEL
'Mobbed in downtown Dallas. . .'

BORN: 30th August 1939 in Heswall, Wirral, Cheshire as John Robert Parker Ravenscroft. Father a cotton broker. EDUCATED: Miss Jones' Kindergarten, Neston. Woodlands School, Deganwy. Shrewsbury School. (Too dumb to get any further). FIRST JOB: Office boy in Cotton Exchange, Liverpool. 'Father shrewdly sent me to work for one of his competitors. After National Service (never rose above the rank of

gunner) I worked at a cotton mill in Rochdale and in 1960 went to live in Dallas, Texas. Sold crop-hail insurance in West Texas before going to work (as an office boy again) for the Republic National Life Insurance Co. Became a reluctant computer programmer before getting into radio full time in Oklahoma City, KOMA. FIRST BROADCAST: 1961 in Dallas, station WRR, a Rhythm and Blues programme called *Kats Karavan*. 'It all came about because I had some records the radio station didn't have which had sleeve notes in French, which they couldn't read. I eventually got work because of vague associations with Liverpool, Americans assuming that this meant I was a good pal of the Beatles. I used to get mobbed in downtown Dallas on the strength of this rather tenuous connection. Rather enjoyed being mobbed.' Back in the UK John hosted a late night show *The Perfumed Garden* on the pirate station Radio London. Then to Radio 1 for *Top Gear*, *Night Ride* on Radio 2 and Radio 1's *Sounds of the Seventies*. Since 1977 has been presenting the Monday to Thursday late night programme on Radio 1 cleverly entitled *The John Peel Show*. Also presents a weekly programme for the World Service and for BFBS. Regularly presents *Top of the Pops* on BBC 1 in his own inimitable style!

■ Most exciting moment of career: 'Meeting Kenny Dalglish and seeing Liverpool win the European Cup in Paris. (Bet this isn't what you had in mind.) Otherwise hearing my name mentioned in the *Truckers Hour*.' [Not half as exciting as being mentioned on the *John Peel Show*!] ■ A moment to remember: 'Making love to my wife during a long record whilst theoretically on the air.' ■ Likes football, although that's more of a religion, and collecting old magazines, books and papers. Dislikes being tired, broadcasters who talk down to their audience and flies. ■ Married to Sheila Gilhooly, has two sons and two daughters and lives in Suffolk.

MARGARET PERCY
'The power of radio to change lives. . .'
BORN: 2nd May 1944 in Belfast. Father a medical practitioner. EDUCATED: Richmond Lodge, Belfast. Belfast College of Technology. FIRST JOB: 'Belfast Telegraph'. Then became a research assistant in economics at Queen's University into government and local government housing. 1966–'69 a Research Associate with town planning group of a building design partnership. FIRST BROADCAST: 1973 as a newsreader on Ulster Television. 'I had been invited to audition in 1968, but the day I was told the job was mine, I had to accept another more demanding role . . . Motherhood. 4 years of that and reading Paddington Bear convinced me I was a star.' Has contributed to many news and current affairs programmes on both television and radio including *Today*, *Woman's Hour*, *Sunday*, *You and Yours*, *Victims* (series), *Poor Britain* (series) and Northern Irish documentaries *Landscape and Bandits*, *Townscape with Brits* and *Heartland*. As a freelance reporter/presenter she presents *File on Four* and *Feedback* for Radio 4 and *Network UK* and *Outlook* for the BBC World Service.

■ Most exciting moment of career: 'I'm not being facetious when I say I'm still planning it!' ■ A moment to remember: 'Very early on in my broadcasting life, when the first two or three fan letters dropped onto my desk, I vowed I would always send a handwritten reply, but inevitably, I suppose, I had to renegue otherwise no one would ever have got an acknowledgement. But one day, a letter arrived from the Chief of a village in North Island, New Zealand. He had heard a documentary I had made concerning the problems of the fishing communities who depended on the dwindling stocks of herring in the Irish Sea. This man, headmaster of the school and chairman of the Village Council, said there were plentiful supplies of fish and not enough men to catch them. So he'd been empowered to issue an invitation to the fishermen who'd taken part in the programme, to bring their boats and their families to where the fishing was easy. Needless to say, I was so overwhelmed by the power of radio to change lives, I sat down and wrote letters to everyone concerned. But I have my suspicions that the fishermen concerned are still lamenting their poor catches in the same pubs in the Northern Hemisphere!' ■ Likes the theatre, films, hill walking and food. Dislikes blinkers and hidden agendas. ■ Married to Norman Percy, has one son and lives in London.

BRIAN PERKINS
'Played Double Bass with the New Zealand Symphony Orchestra. . .'
BORN: Wanganui, New Zealand. Father Senior Manager of Dalgety & Co: Ltd. EDUCATED: Wanganui Technical College. Wellington Boys College. N.Z. FIRST JOB: Clerk in an electrical engineering firm. As a professional musician played Double Bass in the New Zealand Symphony Orchestra. FIRST BROADCAST: May 1962 on the New Zealand Broadcasting Service. May 1965 for the BBC. 'Having lived through the golden days of radio as well as being steeped in those golden programmes, I was very aware of voices and always admired immensely the newsreaders on the BBC World Service. I never thought for one moment I would be accepted by the BBC, but I was.' As a newsreader was heard on all the BBC Domestic Services and introduced music shows on the Light Programme. He returned to New Zealand for a period during the seventies but rejoined the BBC in 1978 as a newsreader/announcer for Radio 4. He is also featured on the *Noel Edmunds Show* on Radio 1 each week.

■ A moment to remember: 'There have been countless occasions when I have been in the embarrasing position of desperately trying to continue talking on the air, while someone has been doing their best to make me laugh. I'm glad to say that those days are well in the past and don't happen a lot on the BBC. But I have been guilty many times of "corpsing" while in the employ of the New Zealand Broadcasting Corporation.' ■ Likes music, photography, Jaguar cars, things nostalgic and gardening. Dislikes Muzak, digital displays, canned beer and talking about myself. ■ Married to Joan, has three children and lives in Surrey.

JOHN PETERS
'You're only as good as your last effort . . . (see**)'
BORN: 22nd November 1949 in Ashford, Middlesex. Father an engineer. EDUCATED: Kenyngton Manor School, Sunbury-on-Thames, Middlesex. FIRST JOB: On the record counter at Woolworth's in Hounslow. Has also worked in catering at Heathrow and spent eight years as a Post Office Telecom engineer. FIRST BROADCAST: Officially on the United Biscuits Network. UBN, in 1974. 'Having built a DJ set up at a Youth Club, and being told "You made it, you do it", it became a hobby. I made a demo tape for Radio 1 in 1971 and was told "You're up to standard", but then, nothing. I joined UBN in 1974 and the following year when Radio Trent opened, joined them to present the *Breakfast Show*.' Now presents the *Afternoon Show* on weekdays and Radio Trent's *Top 30* on Sundays.

■ Most exciting moment of career: 'We've had some near misses! I think starting up Radio Trent, so far. You get that wonderful feeling of being first man on and anything could happen!' ■ Likes old cars (Austin Healey's a favourite), and 'hooottt' curries. ■ Married to Christine, has twin girls** and lives in Leicestershire.

IAN PHILLIPS
'Went for secure job as a teacher. . .'
BORN: 16th November 1953 in Plymouth, Devon. Father a builder and decorator.

EDUCATED: Oxford Street Primary School, and Tamar Secondary School, Plymouth. University of London Goldsmith's College. **FIRST JOB:** Teaching drama at Burrington Secondary School, Plymouth. Also worked as a stagehand and a ticket tearer. **FIRST BROADCAST:** 1971. 'I had always wanted to work in radio, but went for a secure job as a teacher. I enjoyed it but I started freelancing for BBC Plymouth and was eventually offered a job with the last regional Radio 4 programme *Morning Sou'West.'* Was with *Morning Sou'West* for just over two years and during that time presented *Bank Holiday Specials* for BBC South West and also some educational programmes for the Devon Educational Television Service. Has now joined BBC Radio Devon as a producer/presenter.

■ Most exciting moment of career: 'Getting my first full time broadcasting job.' ■ A moment to remember: 'The day I set a "Where Am I Now!" competition and decided to do it from the top of the North Hessary Tor transmitter mast. I was taken up a cable in a tiny basket and had to climb from the basket to the mast 500 feet up . . . very frightening! Having got there, the tape recorder wouldn't work because of radiating aerials, so it was all to no avail, I had to do it from the bottom.' ■ Likes the theatre, old railways and musicals. Dislikes intolerant people. ■ Married to Val, has two daughters and lives in Devon.

ROY PLOMLEY
'On a desert island since 1942. . .'
BORN: Kingston-upon-Thames. Father a pharmacist. **EDUCATED:** King's College School. **FIRST JOB:** Copywriter in West End advertising agency. Then became an actor working in theatre and films, playing in everything from opera to pantomime. **FIRST BROADCAST:** April 1936 as resident announcer at Radio Normandy, 'As a young actor, I was usually out of work and I had an idea for a commercial radio programme, so I went to see the man in charge of the London office of Radio Normandy. He thought it was a marvellous idea, but there was one snag, he said he hadn't got the technical resources to do it and it was too expensive. But as he had a few minutes to spare, we got talking and he told me that his main problem was keeping English announcers on Radio Normandy, because the station was in a small fishing port on the north coast of France and there were always problems with homesickness or alcohol and announcers were always quitting, and he was short of one right now, did I happen to know of anyone. Well there's me, was my reply, and within a couple of days I was on the air and I've been on it ever since.' After six months he transferred to Poste Parisien and from there to London to work in the studios of the International Broadcasting Company producing programmes for commercial stations. In 1938 he returned to France and Radio International. When he was chased out in June 1940 he started freelancing for the BBC. He devised *Desert Island Discs* and in January 1942 the BBC booked him for eight programmes. His contract has been renewed quarterly ever since, and *Desert Island Discs* now qualifies as the longest-running radio programme. He also devised the series *Hurrah for Hollywood* and is heard on many panel games and quiz shows including *One Minute Please, Round Britain Quiz* and *Many a Slip.* He was awarded the OBE in 1975, the Variety Club Radio Personality of the Year award in 1979, and in 1981 the Radio Programme of the Year award by the Television and Radio Industries Club and the Broadcasting Press Guild Radio award. He has written many plays and one novel.

■ A moment to remember: 'I saw Alistair Maclean being interviewed on television, quite an occasion, because he rarely gives interviews and what he had to say was fascinating. He didn't consider himself to be a writer, but he wrote a film script every year, turned it into a novel and then flew around the world in his private jet selling it. There were lots of questions I wanted to ask him about this, so I asked my producer to see if he could be persuaded to do a *Desert Island Discs*. A couple of days later he rang to say he had got Alistair Maclean and he would be delighted to do the programme. The appointed day arrived, and I met him for lunch at my club prior to the recording. He looked much as I remembered him from the television programme although he seemed to have a little more hair. Having a drink before lunch, I asked him which time of year he put aside for writing, to which he replied "Och, I get no time for writing, I wish I did." It turned out that who I had got was the · man who was in charge of Canadian Tourism in Europe who's name was Alistair Maclean. But in my pocket was a BBC contract to record *Desert Island Discs* with Alistair Maclean and I wanted the money. So into the studio we went, he was a delightful man and the interview was going very well when my producer called me out of the studio on the pretext of an urgent telephone call. "What's all this about Canada, ask him about his books" said my producer. "He hasn't written any" I replied. We finished the interview which was very successful as he was a first rate broadcaster, but the programme was never transmitted because he was the wrong Alistair Maclean.' ■ Likes French, travel, and English history. Dislikes getting up in the morning, going to bed at night, tidying up and cutting the hedge. ■ Married to Diana Wong, has one daughter and lives in London.

PETER POWELL
'If it looks good, feels good, sounds good, go for it...'
BORN; 24th March 1951 in Stourbridge, West Midlands. Father in agriculture. EDUCATED: Uppingham School, Rutland. FIRST JOB AND FIRST BROADCAST: As a DJ on BBC WM in Birmingham at the age of 17. He also worked for a while in his father's agricultural business and ran a mobile disco. Three and a half years with Radio Luxembourg consolidated his

broadcasting career and in 1977 he joined BBC Radio 1. He hosted a number of weekend shows before getting his daily show. In 1981 he won the Carl Alan Award for 'live' entertainment's best disc jockey. He's a regular presenter of BBC 1's *Top of the Pops* and has hosted *Seaside Special* and *Get Set* for BBC Television. Introduces new talent on BBC 2's *Oxford Road Show*.

■ Most exciting moment of career: 'When I was working on Radio Luxembourg, I knew Radio 1 were going to sign up a new DJ and I thought I was on the short list, but nobody had said anything. It was a Sunday night and I was about to catch the plane back to Luxembourg feeling a bit despondent, when the 'phone rang. A friend of mine answered it and I heard him saying, yes, yes, I'll tell him. I walked into the room as he hung up and said "Who was that?". "Oh someone I don't think you know, called Doreen (Doreen Davies, Radio 1 Executive Producer) and I told her you weren't in". "What do you mean, I'm not in" I almost shouted! I rang back and was told I had the job on Radio 1. I was very controlled on the 'phone, but when I put it down, I hit the ceiling, but literally, I still have the marks to prove it!' ■ A moment to remember: 'My initiation to Radio Luxembourg where we had to read the news as well a present programmes. We used to rip it off the telex and on my very first news, I was trembling so much it must have sounded like an earthquake at the other end of the radio, with the paper crackling. A couple of the DJ's were leading me through my first night and one of them came up to help me, I thought, but he put a cigarette lighter underneath the telex, and the news went up in flames . . . I never finished it!' ■ Likes photography, driving his Porsche, Range Rover and powerboat. 'My philosophy has always been, if it looks good, feels good, sounds good, go for it!'

TONY PRINCE
'Stand-in DJ for £2.00. . .'
BORN: 1944 in Oldham, Lancashire. Father a scrap metal merchant. EDUCATED: Oldham Municipal Art School. FIRST JOB: Apprentice jockey, along with Willie Carson! After taking part in a talent contest at Butlin's, where he met Ringo Starr, he joined a semi-pro group in Oldham called the Jasons. In the early 60's he turned pro singing and playing guitar with a Top Rank Dance Band. 'One night the resident DJ failed to turn up and the manager asked me to stand in for an extra two pounds, and there I

was a DJ.' FIRST BROADCAST: As a DJ compèring *Disco-A-Go-Go* on TWW, a show on which Tony Blackburn made his debut as a singer! It was Tony B who gave Tony P the telephone number of Radio Caroline and at the end of the TV series he joined them for two years. In April 1968 he joined Radio Luxembourg as part of the first ever 'live' team of DJs with Paul Burnett and Kid Jensen. He became Radio Luxembourg's Director of Programmes and Promotions, a job he held until February 1983 when he resigned to go freelance and form his own company, The Disco Mix Club, which provides DJ's with all the new records on cassettes before they appear in the shops. He is still heard three times a week on Radio Luxembourg, presenting *Disco Music Express* on Thursdays, *Top 30 Disco* on Fridays and the *Top 30* on Sundays.

■ Most exciting moment of career: Introducing Elvis Presley on stage at the Las Vegas Hilton in 1973. ■ A moment to remember: In 1979 Tony Prince was given the Royal Humane Society Award for saving a man from drowning in the Thames at Eton. His comment afterwards was . . . 'I just made an immediate reaction, there was no time for fear. Heroes are those who have time to consider the risks, I didn't.' The pay off to the story was that when the man appeared in court for being drunk and disorderly, (that's how he came to fall in the river in the first place), the press asked him if he had any message for Tony Prince. His reply was 'Yes, could you ask him to play *Bridge Over Troubled Water* for me on his radio programme.'! ■ Likes sub-aqua diving and horse racing. Dislikes liars and prejudice. ■ Married to Christine, has two children, Daniel and Gabrielle, and lives in Buckinghamshire.

ROBIN PULFORD
'*Wogan comes second up here. . .*'
BORN: In Cottingham, East Yorkshire. Father a quantity surveyor. EDUCATED: The Grammar

School, Kingston-upon-Hull. FIRST JOB: A laboratory assistant. 'As I hated science I soon joined the BBC on the very first intake of junior probationary Technical Assistants. Six days in the job and I was a nervous TV cameraman at Lime Grove studios in London. Over several years, I changed fom TV operations to General Production and on an attachment to Aberdeen discovered local radio, liked it and stayed. FIRST BROADCAST: Aberdeen in 1964. 'The radio service in Aberdeen in those days was a form of local radio and that convinced me that National Radio was an "also ran" and the future lay in local radio.' Is now the producer and presenter of one of the country's most successful radio phone-ins, serving the East of England . . . *Countywide* on BBC Radio Humberside.

■ Most exciting moment of career: 'Reporting from the centre of a mass meeting of angry dockers who were venting their fury at recent media coverage!' ■ Likes drinking wine, watching Eastern European steam engines. Dislikes Scottish food (with the exception of haggis) and devious spokesmen. ■ Married to Muriel Innes, has two daughters, Andrea and Beverley, and lives in East Yorkshire/North Humberside.

STEVE RACE
'*My Music led to other things. . .*'
BORN: 1st April 1921 in Lincoln. Father a solicitor. EDUCATED: Lincoln School. Royal

Academy of Music. FIRST JOB: Pianist with Harry Leader's Band. Also played with the bands of Lew Stone and Cyril Stapleton. Arranged for Ted Heath Band and for Judy Garland. FIRST BROADCAST: April 1941 while in the RAF. A well respected musician, Steve has used his musical talent to provide himself with an extremely lucrative alternate string to his bow as Chairman and the compiler of questions of the very popular panel game *My Music* which Radio 4 pioneered and television has borrowed. This in turn led to him appearing on such programmes as *Any Questions* and *Many a Slip*. He also presents *Musician at Large* for the World Service.

■ Most exciting moment of career: Hearing Dennis Norden's singing voice for the first time. ■ A moment to remember: 'I was playing the Warsaw Concerto in a Birmingham radio studio when the leg fell off the grand piano. At the moment the keyboard descended firmly on to my right knee, I happened to have the sustaining pedal down. It stayed down until the end of the piece, when the studio manager thrust a chair under the treble end of the piano, and about time too. Two days later, I had a letter from a listener, which read: "Dear Mr Race I was sorry to note that you were guilty of over-pedalling. It is all the more to be regretted in an Academy-trained musician such as yourself, and sets a poor example to impressive students." (So did my language after reading the letter).' ■ Likes antiquarian pursuits, looking at paintings, the open air. Dislikes cigarette smokers, cinemagoing and chatty taxi drivers. ■ Married to former BBC producer Lonny Mather, has one daughter, Nicola, and lives in Buckinghamshire.

CHRIS REA
'Nicklaus has gone for a pee. . .'
BORN: 22nd October 1943 in Dundee, Scotland. Father a banker. EDUCATED: High School of Dundee. University of St. Andrews. FIRST JOB: In hospital administration. Is now the

Rugby and Golf Correspondent of the 'Scotsman'. FIRST BROADCAST: On the BBC World Service in September 1971. 'I had applied for a job as administrator of *Look North* based in Leeds in 1970 but was then selected for the British Lions Rugby party to tour New Zealand. On my return I was appointed admin man of the French, German and African Services at Bush House, but two months later joined the Sports Department.' Is now a freelance reporter and commentator on rugby and golf for BBC Radio and television in Scotland.

■ Most exciting moment of career: 'Doing the commentary at Cardiff in March 1982, when Scotland beat Wales by a record margin 34–18.' ■ A moment to remember: 'During the 1975 Open Golf Championship at Carnoustie, I was the on-course commentator following Jack Nicklaus. Just before I was due to go on air, Nicklaus disappeared from the fairway to answer a call of nature. In my haste to ascertain what had happened to the great man, I failed to hear my cue from the studio and screamed into the mike. . . "For God's sake don't come over yet, Nicklaus has gone for a pee!". It was alas, too late. The nation heard every word.' ■ Likes reading and golf. Dislikes work and the smell of stale cigarette smoke. ■ Married to Terry, has one daughter and lives in Edinburgh.

MIKE READ
'You were marvellous, you're going to be a star. . .'
BORN: 1st March 1951 in Manchester. Father a publican. EDUCATED: Brooklands School, Weybridge. FIRST JOB: Singing in local pubs. His grandfather bought him his first guitar which he taught himself to play. FIRST BROADCAST: March 1976 on Thames Valley Radio, having spent a year doing Hospital Radio in Weybridge, Radio Wey. 'Thames Valley wanted me for their cricket team, so they had to give me a programme.' He joined Radio

Luxembourg in 1978 and also got his first TV show, a four month series of *Pop Quest* for ITV. He joined Radio 1 at the end of 1978 presenting a Saturday night show from Manchester and started to present BBC 1's *Top of the Pops*. A regular evening slot on Radio 1 followed and since 1981 he's been presenting the *Breakfast Show*. He also chairs BBC 1's *Pop Quiz* and hosts what is the longest 'live' TV show in the world . . . *Saturday Super Store*. Is the co-author of the Guiness Book of Hit Singles, The Guinness Book of Hits of the 70's and the Guiness Book of 500 No. 1's, not to mention the Guinness Book of British Hit Albums [and that's a lot of Guinness!] He has also written a biography of the Shadows.

■ Most exciting moment of career: 'My first day in local radio and the opening day for Thames Valley when there was a crowd of two or three thousand people in Reading town centre waiting for the visiting celebrities. Somebody had to go and talk to them, and as nobody else wanted to, they sent me. I was mobbed . . . the police had to get me out, but my feet were six inches off the ground. When I got back to the station, the boss Neil ffrench Blake said "You were marvellous, you're going to be a star".' ■ A moment to remember: 'Steve Wright and I were both with Thames Valley at the start and they gave us a two handed show *Read and Wright* (well it's obvious when you think about it). We got in early the first morning to have a practise. What we didn't know was that the engineers, who were as green as we were, had left the line switched through so everything we said was going out on the air . . . like "You read the list of bus cancellations Steve, I'll do this next bit and then you can" etc: It wasn't long before the telephones started to ring . . . "What's going on, there are two blokes on Thames Valley sounding like Bill and Ben the Flower pot men!" Then all hell broke loose. A message came from Neil ffrench Blake "I want to see the two of you in my office". This is the end of the road, we thought, and do you know what he said? "I'm proud of you two, you didn't swear, you weren't rude to anyone apart from mentioning the colour of my pyjamas and you didn't know you were on the air".' [Neither of them ever looked back]. ■ Likes pretty girls, chili con carne, The Graduate, the Beatles and juke boxes. Dislikes prunes and 'my untidy bedroom'. ■ Is a bachelor and lives in Surrey.

BRIAN REDHEAD
'Getting a word in edgeways since 1965. . .'
BORN; 28th December 1929 in Newcastle

upon Tyne. Father a silk screen printer. EDUCATED: Royal Grammar School, Newcastle upon Tyne. Downing College, Cambridge. FIRST JOB: Reporter on the 'Whitley Bay Seaside Chronicle'. Was Northern Editor of 'The Guardian' 1965–'69, and editor of the 'Manchester Evening News' 1969–'75. FIRST BROADCAST: Playing the clarinet on *Children's Hour* in 1941. Apart from that, he got his first break as a broadcaster when he stood in for someone who had lost her voice. Has been the Chairman of Radio 4's *A Word in Edgeways* since it began in 1965. Has been presenting the *Today* programme on Radio 4 since 1975.

■ Most exciting moment of career: Presenting the Radio 4 General Election Results programme in 1979. ■ A moment to remember: 'In 1963 I interviewed a man, "live", and he never spoke. So I asked the questions and answered them. It made for brevity.' ■ Likes cats. Dislikes dogs. ■ Married to Jenni, has three children and lives in Cheshire.

RICHARD REES
'First broadcast on Friday 13th. . .'
BORN: 17th April 1955 in Llanelli, South Wales. Father a retail shop manager. EDUCATED: Llanelli Boy's Grammar School. Trinity College, Carmarthen. FIRST JOB: Physical education teacher. FIRST BROADCAST: Friday 13th December 1974 on commercial radio, having gained experience in hospital

radio. Joined BBC Radio Wales and has presented a wide variety of programmes in both English and Welsh. Presents their *Rockpile* rock music show twice a week, their *Top 40* show, *Sospan*, a Welsh language music/chat show and two outdoor pursuit programmes. Also does announcing for television.

■ Most exciting moment of career: 'My first ever "live" television transmission, taking part in an RAF Air/Sea rescue mock-up.' ■ Likes walking on mountains, shooting, reading and outdoor pursuits generally. Dislikes paperwork, car maintenance and decorating. ■ Married to Judith and lives in Dyfed.

on the 'Kentish Gazette'. Also worked as a reporter on the 'Kentish Observer', the 'North East Times', chief reporter on the 'Eastbourne Gazette', and the 'Oxford Mail'. In 1970 joined the newsroom team at BBC Radio Oxford. FIRST BROADCAST: August 1970 on BBC Radio Nottingham (while on attachment from Radio Oxford) 'From working in the newsroom, I slowly wormed my way into presenting general and music programmes.' In 1978 he joined BBC Radio 2 as a newsreader/announcer and has presented *Band Parade, Two's Best, Radio 2 Top Tunes, Brass and Strings, Music From the Movies*, and has sat in at short notice on *Much More Music*. Has also presented *Sounds of Jazz* for Radio 1. Is one of the regular presenters of *You and the Night and the Music*.

JACK REGAN
'Gave chase to Hercules the bear. . .'
BORN: 10th January 1942 in Edinburgh. EDUCATED: Scotus Academy, Edinburgh. Edinburgh University. (M.A. Hons History). FIRST JOB: Copy boy on 'The Scotsman' in Edinburgh. Has also worked in journalism in Africa and was Chief Sub-editor on 'Daily Nation' in Nairobi. FIRST BROADCAST: April 1971, *Reporting Scotland* on BBC Television. Has contributed to almost all the news and current affairs programmes for both television and radio, ranging from *John Craven's Newsround* to Radio 1's *Newsbeat*. Is the Scottish Affairs Correspondent for BBC News.

■ Most exciting moment of career: Chasing Hercules the bear through the Western Isles. ■ Likes Heart of Midlothian FC and Whisky. Dislikes Glasgow Rangers and real ale. ■ Married to Katrina Thewlis, has five children and lives in Glasgow.

BILL RENNELLS
'Putting out a programme on all four networks at once. . .'
BORN: 25th July 1931 in Canterbury, Kent. Father was a publican. EDUCATED: Bridge School, Canterbury. FIRST JOB: Pupil reporter

■ Most exciting moment of career: 'Scarcely exciting, but memorable . . . I put out a programme on all four BBC Radio networks from 10pm to 2am in December 1978 in the aftermath of a strike.' ■ A moment to remember: 'One day in the Spring of 1979 I was covering cricket results and local election nominations on the same day. I ended up confusing runs with votes and Councillor Roger Liddle won Quarry Ward by 342 runs.' ■ Likes playing and watching cricket. Dislikes the pop music of the 50's and curry. ■ Has two daughters and lives in Hampshire.

PAUL REYNOLDS
'From New York to Brussels. . .'
BORN: 23rd February 1946 in Southend. Father an overseas civil servant. EDUCATED: Ardingly College, Sussex. Worcester College, Oxford. FIRST JOB: Reporter on the 'Hertfordshire Pictorial', Hitchin. FIRST BROADCAST: 1968 on BBC Radio Norwich when Harold Wilson visited Norwich. From being a news assistant at Radio Norwich he moved to London as a Sub-editor for Radio News. Became a reporter for Radio News and was appointed as their

1967. ■ A moment to remember: 'Working as a studio manager on Radio 4's *Today* programme, I was making fun of the piping voice of interviewer Wendy Jones when the producer introduced me to a lady sitting in the studio . . . it was Wendy Jones. Was my face red! Yes, it was!' ■ Likes restoring two elderly cars and a bus, reading, gardening, cooking. Dislikes people who talk down to children and decimal coinage. ■ Lives in East Sussex.

New York Correspondent. Is now the Brussels Correspondent and contributes to all the news and current affairs programmes.

■ Married to Louise, has two children and lives in Brussels.

CORMAC RIGBY
'Answered an advert in the "New Musical Express". . .'
BORN: May 1939 in Watford, Hertfordshire. Father a pattern-maker, mother a teacher. EDUCATED: Merchant Taylor's School. St. Johns' College, Oxford. (M.A., D.Phil.) FIRST JOB AND FIRST BROADCAST: 1965, when he joined the BBC as an announcer, after answering an advertisement in the 'New Musical Express'. Since then has presented many programmes including *Ballet in Britain*, and *The Royal Ballet at 50* for the BBC World Service. *Royal Repertoire* for Radio 3. Is the Presentation Editor of Radio 3 and also a newsreader/announcer for the network.

■ Most exciting moment of career: Overseas tours with the BBC Symphony Orchestra.

DAVID RIDER
'Was my face red. . .'
BORN: 9th December 1940 in Dibden Purlieu, Hampshire. Father a clerk. EDUCATED: Primary schools in Southampton and New Milton. Brockenhurst Grammar School. FIRST JOB: A audit clerk in an accountant's office. He then joined the BBC as a clerk working in the Tape Library, and from there went on to become a studio manager. FIRST BROADCAST: 9th February 1966 for the BBC European English Service, after a friend in the European Service had suggested me as a presenter to a producer. Since then has worked regularly for BBC Radio . . . *Rider's Record Ride* and *Playground* for Radio 1. *After Seven Roundabout, You and the Night and the Music* (his *Radio Yesteryear* feature is a big hit with the overnight audience) *Movie Go Round* for Radio 2. *Signing on* for Radio 4. And for the World Service, *Brass of Britain, Music on the March, Theme and Variations.* He also contributes to *In the News* and *Wavelength* for schools radio and to Tony Blackburn's *Sunday Show* on Radio 1.

■ Most exciting moment of career: Being chosen as one of the original Radio 1 team in

ALAN ROBERTS
'Finding out I had listeners who enjoy my company means a lot. . .'
BORN: 19th July 1946 in Maidenhead, Berkshire. Father a blacksmith and wrought-iron worker. EDUCATED: Grammar School, Stage School and Art College. FIRST JOB: A waiter in High Wycombe. Has also been a croupier, an actor, antique dealer, a photographer and a few other things besides . . . FIRST BROADCAST: Radio England in 1965. 'I survived one week of American arrogance'. He then worked in Scandinavia and became a part

time producer with Denmark Radio before joining Gavin McCoy (Radio 210) and the team on the Voice of Peace ship anchored off Tel Aviv, in 1976. Back in the UK, he joined BBC Radio Oxford presenting in turn the weekend *Morning Show*, the *Evening Show*, the *Drive Show* and the *Lunchtime Show*. In 1979 joined Swansea Sound for a year as Head of Music, doing the weekend, morning and late shows. In 1980 moved to Severn Sound where he is Head of Music and presents *Home to Severn* weekdays and Sunday's *Top 40 Countdown*.

■ Most exciting moment of career: 'Never being approached by Radio 1 (what does one do after!) and finding out I had listeners who enjoy my company which means an awful lot to a broadcaster.' ■ A moment to remember: 'One day at Radio Oxford, the station assistant persuaded me to do my somewhat under par David Bellamy impersonation "on air", only unbeknown to myself, the said celebrity was in the next studio listening in, waiting to be interviewed by one of my colleagues. Half way through my programme, *The Flora and Fauna of Oxfordshire's Countryside,* in burst Mr Bellamy, looking somewhat irate. I was agasp and almost speechless but managed to mutter "Well it's a bit like Alladin's Lamp this studio if you rub somebody up the wrong way, they suddenly make an appearance'. Of course it turned out that it had all been set up, and the programme concluded with a marvellous interview.' ■ Likes painting, driving, antiquities, photography and art. Dislikes football hooligans, rude people, tapioca, being sick, bad weather. ■ Married to Lori and has one son Nicholas.

prospector in Papua, New Guinea. He also spent one term as a Prep School master in Sydney, Australia. FIRST BROADCAST: April 1936 on ABC, Sydney. 'I started doing freelance talks in New Guinea and after nine months and several auditions, I joined ABC as an announcer.' Back in the UK, he became a sports commentator for BBC television and radio. He covered both the Summer and Winter Olympics between 1948 and 1968. He was the chairman of the original *Panorama* in 1954 and of *Going for a Song* from 1964 to 1977. He has been one of the radio commentary team at Wimbledon since 1946 and also commentates on all the Davis Cup and Wightman Cup matches.

■ Most exciting moment of career: 'Too many to identify, but perhaps the first commentary ever from a bobsleigh at the Olympic Games in 1948.' ■ A moment to remember: 'Wimbledon 1949 when a squirrel came onto the Centre Court during a match between the blonde Dutch giant, Hans Van Scooll and the diminutive Frenchman Robert Abdessaleau. It gave Van Scooll who was sinking fast in the fifth set, a breather of three minutes. He went on to win. I was off the air at the time, but yelled to the engineers to start recording, and I did a commentary on the squirrels antics, marred alas by the raucous laughter of a producer sitting beside me. The recording has often been used in "look back" programmes.' ■ Likes collecting antiques, especially Chinese porcelain. Dislikes abuse of the English language, noise and pop music. ■ Married to Elisabeth Beresford, has four children and lives in the Channel Islands.

MAX ROBERTSON
'First commentary ever from a bobsleigh. . .'
BORN: 28th August 1915 in Dacca, Bengal. Father an engineer for Indian railways. Later became an apple farmer. EDUCATED: Haileybury College. FIRST JOB: A gold

MICHAEL ROBINSON
'Instrumental in "uncovering" Signal Life Insurance. . .'
BORN: 1st January 1948 in Capetown, S. Africa. Father an advertising executive. EDUCATED: Diocesan College, Capetown. University of

Radio Tees from Hard Rock to MOR to Classical. He originated the Arts programme *Spectrum* and the FM style rock show *Rock me Gently*. He is the presenter/producer of the weekday morning show *Morning Call*, on Radio Tees.

■ Most exciting moment of career: 'Getting into broadcasting'. ■ Likes working and enjoying life. Dislikes the lazy or sloppy. ■ Married to Gill and lives in Cleveland.

York. FIRST JOB: Self employed musician. Has also worked in an iron foundry in Slough and as a picture framer. FIRST BROADCAST: Reporting on the more worthwhile aspects of Pop Festivals for *Nationwide*. Worked as a researcher for *The Money Programme*. Then went on to report for *Moneybox, The Financial World Tonight, The World Tonight, Profile,* and most recently *File on 4* for Radio 4.

■ Most exciting moment of career: 'There have been many, mostly to do with discovering something new or getting a scoop. The biggest was the uncovering of *Signal Life*, an insurance company which misappropriated some six and a half million pounds.' ■ Likes friends and listening to what they have to say. Dislikes people who think they know more than they do.

ROBERT ROBINSON
'The man who sat next to the man who said ---- on TV. . .'
BORN: 17th December 1927 in Liverpool. Father an accountant. EDUCATED: Raynes Park Grammar School. Exeter College Oxford. FIRST JOB: A journalist right from the start. TV Columnist for the 'Sunday Chronicle' 1952; film and theatre columnist 'Sunday Graphic' and radio critic the 'Sunday Times' 1956; editor *Atticus* 'Sunday Times' 1960; weekly column Private View, 'Sunday Times' 1962; film critic 'Sunday Telegraph' 1965. FIRST BROADCAST: As a journalist in 1955. Worked in television regularly from 1959 beginning with *Picture Parade* and *Points of View. Call My Bluff* and *Ask the Family* started in 1967 and are still running. *The Book Programme* dates from 1974. Has also made many documentary films for television and is the author of numerous books. In 1971 he took over as presenter of Radio 4's *Today* programme from Jack de Manio, about the only person who could have stepped into that august and well loved broadcaster's shoes. He remained with the *Today* programme for three years, receiving the Radio Industries Club's Radio Personality of the Year Award in 1973. He was also named as Radio Personality of the Year in 1980 by the Variety Club. Since 1973 he has chaired Radio 4's *Brain of Britain* and also on Radio 4 has presented *Stop the Week* since 1974.

■ 'A highlight of my broadcasting career, if you

PAUL ROBINSON
'I don't know how I got away with it. . .'
BORN: 31st December 1956 in Farnborough, Hampshire. Father an electronic engineer. EDUCATED: Camberley Grammar School. Manchester University. FIRST JOB: Paper boy. FIRST BROADCAST: November 1977 in hospital radio . . . Radio St. Stephens, Chelsea. 'I don't know how I got away with it, it was dreadful.' Then by sheer persistence, I eventually persuaded ex Strawb Dave Cousins, Programme Controller for Radio Tees, to give me a show.' Has done almost everything on

can call it that, was when I appeared with the late Kenneth Tynan on a programme called *BBC 3*, during which he uttered "THE" word for the first time on television. I thought I shall go down in history as the man who sat next to the man who said ---- on TV.' ■ Another moment to remember: 'The occasion I spat my two false teeth out on *Call My Bluff*. With a gesture reminiscent of Henry Irving, I caught them before they reached the ground. Milton Shulman said afterwards "I thought you were chewing a fruit gum!"' ■ Likes playing tennis. ■ Married to Josephine Richard, has three children and lives in London.

Home) and weekend feature programmes. Is co-presenter with Glyn Freeman of *206 Team* weekdays on Radio WM which he describes as 'current affairs, phone-ins and a good laugh'.

■ Most exciting moment of career: 'In a hot air balloon, a sewer, a submarine, a parachute jump, a Good Year air ship, up the side of a chimney stack and 7 minutes on Radio 1.' ■ A moment to remember: 'A young lady wandered into the studio one morning in a fur coat which she proceeded to remove. I then got an eyeful of bra and panties "live" on air.' [Then what happened?] ■ Likes photography, swimming, motor cars. Dislikes expensive beer. ■ Is a bachelor and lives in the West Midlands.

DAVID RODIGAN
'Actor/DJ...'

BORN: 24th June 1951 in the British Military Hospital, Hanover, West Germany. Father in management training. EDUCATED: Gosford Hill School, Kidlington, Oxford. FIRST JOB: Actor. FIRST BROADCAST: BBC Radio London's *Reggae Show*. Also presented their *Reggae Rockers*. He moved to Capital Radio and is the producer and presenter of *Roots Rockers*.

■ Most exciting moment of career: 'Being employed either as an actor or a disc jockey.' ■ Likes music, the theatre and the cinema. ■ Is a bachelor and lives in London.

STUART ROPER
'Current affairs, phone-ins and a good laugh...'

BORN: 26th January 1948 in Birmingham. Father a tailor. EDUCATED: Bourneville Boys Technical School. FIRST JOB: Press photographer. Has also been a film cameraman. FIRST BROADCAST: March 1974, having gained experience with the Birmingham Hospital Broadcasting Network, as a part time hobby. Started with BBC Radio WM as a technical operator before presenting the 5am–7am show, *Home James* (now *Coming*

LES ROSS
'Calling up friends and relatives Round the World...'

BORN: 7th February 1949 in Birmingham. EDUCATED: King Edward's Grammar School, Aston, Birmingham. FIRST JOB: Office worker for IBM. Also worked at Witton Cemetery, Birmingham, (in the office!) FIRST BROADCAST: November 1970 on BBC Radio Birmingham. 'Hearing that Radio Birmingham were opening, I auditioned and they said "OK, have a programme!"' Since then has always worked on *Breakfast Shows*. BBC Radio Birmingham 1970–'75; Radio Tees 1975–'76; BRMB

Breakfast Show since 1976. He also presents their Sunday morning show which connects listeners to friends and relatives *Round the World.*

■ Most exciting moment of career: 'Yet to happen'. ■ Is too lazy for hobbies. Dislikes being too lazy to have hobbies! ■ Lives in Warwickshire.

Orchestra and the Ulster Orchestra. FIRST BROADCAST: September 1972 on BBC Radio 4 in Northern Ireland, reading the *News* and the *Fatstock Prices.* Is a Radio 3 newsreader/announcer and has presented Radio 3's *Playbill.* ■ Likes music, animal welfare, gardening and DIY. ■ Lives in London.

KEVIN RUANE
'On the streets of Warsaw in 1982. . .'

BORN: 20th May 1932 in Woolton, Liverpool. Father a gardener. EDUCATED: St. Francis Xavier's College, Liverpool. Peterhouse, Cambridge. National Service Russian Interpreter's Course. FIRST JOB: Eight months at GCHQ. Cheltenham. 1957–'60 Russian Monitor for the BBC's Monitoring Service. FIRST BROADCAST: In *From Our Own Correspondent* in December 1970 on Radio 4. Was appointed Foreign Duty Editor, BBC Radio News in 1971. Programmes have included *International Assignment* and *Six Continents* which he produced and presented. He was appointed the BBC's Moscow Correspondent 1977. Is now the BBC's Eastern Europe Correspondent.

■ Most exciting moment of career: 'Not so much exciting as physically exhausting . . . covering the pro-Solidarity demonstrations and subsequent riots on the streets of Warsaw on 31st August 1982.' ■ Likes golf. Dislikes getting out of bed. ■ Married to Beryl, has two children and lives in Berkshire when not abroad.

MALCOLM RUTHVEN
'An extremely small entry, but I'm an extremely small person!'

BORN: 4th February 1943 in Hertfordshire. EDUCATED: In Canterbury. Worked in orchestral management with the London Symphony Orchestra, The Royal Philharmonic

JOCELYN RYDER-SMITH
'A most important voice test. . .'

BORN: 14th March 1940 in Nottingham. Father a doctor. EDUCATED: King Alfred School, Hampstead. Keele University. FIRST JOB: A BBC General Trainee. [A word of explanation re the term general trainee. As a BBC General Trainee you learn about all aspects of broadcasting, working in many different departments both in radio and television. The BBC invites applications for this scheme and literally thousands of young people, mostly University graduates, apply to be admitted. Very few are chosen and those who are, are considered to be the 'creme de la creme'. Several Director Generals of the BBC have started as general trainees.] FIRST BROADCAST: 'While I was at University I took part in a programme with Wilfred Pickles, but my first broadcast after joining the BBC was when I presented a magazine programme for the European English Service just two weeks after joining!' Since then, programmes have included *Woman's*

Hour, In Touch, Home This Afternoon, You and Yours, and *Enterprise*. Nowadays a freelance interviewer and presenter and occasionally a producer.

■ Most exciting moment of career: 'I think anyone doing a job like this would find it difficult to pick one special event, but perhaps for me it was meeting Mother Theresa of Calcutta; and later interviewing His Holiness The Dalai Lama. . . (there, I've cheated by choosing two events!)' ■ A moment to remember: 'I once voice tested someone who had sent me a script, to see if she had a good broadcasting voice. She had a frog in her throat so I got her some cough sweets and she tried to clear it, but with no success, I suggested she get in touch with me again when her voice was back to normal. I didn't hear for a year, when I received a letter to say, that because of the voice test, she had gone to her doctor. The very early stages of cancer were diagnosed, she was quickly operated on and was told that because it had been caught so quickly, she would have no further trouble. It must have been the most important voice test I ever took part in.'
■ Likes reading and walking. ■ Married to Bob Dearden, has three children and lives in Hereford.

JIMMY SAVILE
'It's a great life. . .'
BORN: In Leeds. Father was a bookies clerk. EDUCATED: St. Anne's Elementary School, Leeds. FIRST JOB: Down the pit. FIRST BROADCAST: In the 50's after someone had heard him as a dance hall DJ. [Around 1959 Jimmy was the manager of a ballroom in Manchester which was near to the Cabaret Club. My partner and I as the Tracy Sisters made many appearances at the Cabaret Club which was run by an ex-wrestler Bill Benny, and after the show each night when the customers had all gone home, Jimmy would come over the road, and join Bill for a couple of hours of what I can only describe as

side-splitting entertainment. Those two would have made a great double act. Sadly Bill Benny died many years ago, but I often wonder what he would have said if he had seen Jim introducing *Top of the Pops* and fixing it for the kids in *Jim'll Fix It*. He would have loved every minute of it and died laughing!] Jim does more television than DJ work these days but currently presents Radio 1's *Old Record Club*. Much of his time is taken up with voluntary work in and for hospitals especially Stoke Mandeville for which he has succeeded in raising an enormous amount of money. He was awarded the OBE in 1971. His reward in heaven will be infinitely greater. He is a marvellous person. ■ Most exciting moment of career: Too many to choose. ■ Likes running, cycling, helping in hospitals. Hates cold water. ■ Is a bachelor and lives in Yorkshire.

GRAHAM SEAMAN
'Thames Valley listeners well amused. . .'
BORN: 26th January 1959 in Tadley, Hampshire. Father a photographer. EDUCATED: Sixth Form College, Queen Mary's Basingstoke. FIRST JOB: Electronic test technician. FIRST BROADCAST: Summer of 1980 on Radio 210 (Thames Valley), having sent in an audition tape. A spot of journalism and news reading to begin with then he had to do an emergency take over when an Outside Broadcast went down. . . 'My big break'! Has since done the *Morning Show, Drive Time, Late Show* and 210's Holiday/Travel programme. Is producer/presenter of *Daybreak*, Monday to Friday, Kids Stuff and *On the Move* on Saturdays. All on Radio 210.

■ Most exciting moment of career: Producing and reporting a documentary made on a submarine trip with the Royal Navy, networked to other ILR stations. ■ A moment to remember: 'Jean Challis in studio, me on an Outside Broadcast at Henley-on-Thames. Jean handed over to me . . . me not wearing headphones, so I didn't hear her cue and promptly said, talking to my interviewee about our engineer, "I wish they'd pull their fingers out"! Thames Valley listeners well amused.' ■ Likes watching video and reading (occasionally radio books!) Dislikes spiders and millipedes! ■ Lives in Hampshire.

JOHN SERGEANT
'Alan Bennett's straight man. . .'

BORN: 14th April 1944 in Oxford. Father a teacher. EDUCATED: Millfield School, Street, Somerset. Magdalen College, Oxford. FIRST JOB: Reporter on the 'Liverpool Daily Post' and the 'Liverpool Echo'. FIRST BROADCAST: As an actor! 'I had been spotted by Alan Bennett in an Oxford Revue at the Edinburgh Festival in 1966, and the following year I appeared with him in his TV series *On the Margin* which won the Comedy Award of the year. I played a series of parts including a boy scout (to Alan Bennett's scoutmaster) a city gent, a literary critic and a trendy in the NW1 series which inspired the cartoonist Marc. Four years later I applied for a job in Radio News which I got.' He was a radio reporter from 1970 to 1980 and during that period was acting correspondent in Dublin, Washington, Saigon, Israel, Paris, Cairo, Cyprus and Rhodesia. Has presented *Today*, *PM*, and *The World This Weekend* for Radio 4 and has also made two documentaries for BBC 1 called *The Europe we Joined*. Is now one of the BBC's political correspondents at Westminster and contributes to all news and current affairs programmes on both radio and television.

■ Most exciting moment of career: 'Being hijacked with John Simpson, by the IRA in Londonderry in 1973. We were driven at breakneck speed into the Bogside. Our car was stolen, but mercifully we were allowed to go free.' ■ A moment to remember: 'The day I joined Radio News, the Editor told the staff that he had taken on Alan Bennett's straight man. A deeply unimpressed senior reporter said "Why didn't we take on Alan Bennett?".' ■ Likes sailing. Dislikes shop assistants who seem pleased when they tell you that something you want isn't in stock. ■ Married to Mary, has two children and lives in London.

PAT SHARP
'Is there really anybody out there. . .'

BORN: 25th October 1961 in London. Father a marketing consultant. EDUCATED: Merchant Taylor's School, Northwood. FIRST JOB: Trainee sales assistant in a large department store. Has also been a motor cycle courier. Worked as a club DJ in Europe. FIRST BROADCAST: September 1982 on Radio 1's *The Steve Wright Show*. 'I sent a short demo tape to a top agent who knew the ropes of radio and he advised me accordingly'. Has deputized for other DJ's on Radio 1 and done children's interviews for Tony Blackburn's Weekend Shows. Presents the Radio 1 *Sunday Early Show*.

■ Most exciting moment of career: Monday 6th September 1982, 2pm (first broadcast on Radio 1). ■ A moment to remember: 'After completing one of the "Earthlink" shows on Radio Luxembourg during my short stay there in November 1982, the feeling of amazement at getting up and turning off the whole radio station by pushing up three buttons, turning off the lights, shutting the door and going home. It leaves you wondering about the old space message "Is there really anybody out there?"!' ■ Likes trail bikes, car maintenance, and sport. Dislikes smoking and drinking. ■ Lives in Middlesex.

ROBBIE SHEPHERD
'Accountant turned broadcaster. . .'

BORN: April 30th, 1936 in Dunecht, Aberdeenshire. Father a shoemaker. EDUCATED: Dunecht School. Robert Gordon's College, Aberdeen. FIRST JOB: Audit clerk for a

chartered accountant. Qualified as a chartered accountant and has always worked in accountancy. FIRST BROADCAST: 1978 on BBC Radio Aberdeen. 'Because of stage work as a character/comedian specializing in the humour of the North East of Scotland, and work associated with Accordian and Fiddle Clubs, I was approached by a BBC producer to present some programmes on Radio Aberdeen.' Programmes include *Take the Floor* and *Reel Blend* on BBC Radio Scotland; *Meet Ye Monday* and *Shepherds Tartan* on BBC Radio Aberdeen and on television, *Beechgrove Garden Roadshow* for BBC Scotland.

■ Most exciting moment of career: 'Each programme brings it's own pleasures.' ■ Likes gardening, and following the fortunes of Aberdeen F.C. Dislikes those who turn up their noses at the music and song of Scotland as though it were inferior which it is not.
■ Married to Esma, has one son Gordon and lives in Aberdeen.

PHILIP SHORT
'Excitement is not a criterion. . .'
BORN: 17th April 1945 in Bristol. Father a schoolmaster. EDUCATED: Sherborne School. Queens' College, Cambridge. FIRST JOB: As a journalist on 'Drum Magazine' in Johannesburg in 1966. Worked as a freelance journalist in Blantyre, Malawi 1967–'70, and in Uganda 1971–'73. Joined the BBC in 1974. FIRST

BROADCAST: 'By cable . . . from Malawi in 1967 on President Banda's decision to establish diplomatic relations with South Africa. By voice . . . from Uganda in 1971. 'As a freelance journalist in Africa, I worked first for the written press and then progressively for more and more radio outlets, the BBC, CBC in Canada, ABC in the USA and Radio Australia.' Was the BBC's Moscow Correspondent 1974–'76 and their Peking Correspondent 1977–'81. Is now the BBC's Chief of Bureau in Paris and contributes to all the news and current affairs programmes.

■ Most exciting moment of career: 'The question is wrongly expressed. [Sorry Sir] Excitement is not a criterion. If the word is memorable, the answer would be: Watching Israeli planes bomb Damascus in 1973; Attending a public execution in Amin's Uganda; Travelling through Tibet; and being the first to report Chairman Hua's fall from power.' ■ Likes Song and Yuan dynasty porcelain. Dislikes brassières. ■ Married to Christine, has one child and lives in Paris.

PETE SIMPKIN
'I helped John Boorman . . . look at him now!. . .'
BORN: In 1942 in England . . . the tide was turning! Father a lifeguard. EDUCATED: Yes . . . Taunton's School, Southampton, before they turned it into a comprehensive. FIRST JOB: Trainee film editor for Southern Television in Southampton 'I helped John Boorman . . . look at him now!' Went on to work as an engineer for ATV and for BBC South as a cameraman and sound man on *South Today*. 'Entirely unaided I stuck a microphone with twinstick to Valerie Pitt's chest'. [See what I missed!] FIRST BROADCAST: 'My left hand in vision on *South Today*, handing the telephone to presenters'. For real . . . Radio Solent 1970. 'I discovered I couldn't get on with mending TV studio equipment, so I broadcast on Southampton Hospital Radio, learned about radio from Radios Solent, and Leeds, also BBC Bristol

where I was a studio manager. I also sent blank cheques to high officials.' Has been connected with almost every type of programme in local radio. At one time specialized in complicated Outside Broadcasts and church services, including the first Sikh 'live' broadcast in UK. Is the regular presenter/producer of Radio WM's mid-afternoon show *Good Company*, also presents the *Breakfast Show*.

■ Most exciting moment of career: 'One or two occasions being left alone "on air" with no other programme source available . . . most recently talking continuously for 45 minutes "live" at the Birmingham Falklands homecoming. Also being allowed to present a programme on station KVIL in Dallas, Texas.'
■ A moment to remember: 'I confidently did a full station identification for BBC Radio Solent on my first day on Radio Birmingham!' ■ Likes walking about the Lake District, eating and cutting bottles to make ornaments. Dislikes inconsideration, curry and loud noise. ■ Married to a reflexologist, has three children and lives in West Midlands ('but I wish they'd call it Warwickshire').

BOB SINKINSON
'Covered the Iranian Embassy siege. . .'
BORN: 3rd January 1947 in Stafford. Father a photographer. EDUCATED: Ellesmere College, Shropshire. FIRST JOB: Reporter on the 'Cannock Advertiser' in Staffordshire. Also worked as a reporter on the 'Birmingham Post'. FIRST BROADCAST: On an American radio station in New York. But in the UK, January 1972 on BBC Radio Birmingham. Is now the Midlands Correspondent for BBC Radio News based at Pebble Mill in Birmingham and contributes to all the news and current affairs programmes.

■ Most exciting moment of career: 'Sailing strapped to the side of a yacht in the Round Britain Race in a force 9 gale. Also covering the siege of the Iranian Embassy.' ■ Likes

gardening, listening to music, reading and walking. Dislikes faulty telephones and cars that won't start. ■ Married to Janet and lives in Warwickshire.

RICHARD SKINNER
'Hosts BBC Rock Line, syndicated world wide. . .'
BORN: 26th December 1951 in Portsmouth. Father a Civil Servant. EDUCATED: Portsmouth Grammar School. Highbury Technical College, Portsmouth. FIRST JOB: Reporter on the 'Portsmouth News'. FIRST BROADCAST: 1st April 1970 on Portsmouth Hospital Broadcasting which he set up with Paul Robbins, now a station engineer at Radio 210 in Reading. He joined Radio Solent and made his first broadcast for them in October 1971. In 1973 joined Radio 1's *Newsbeat* team and in 1980 presented the Radio 1 *Rock Show* for a year. Other Radio 1 programmes include *Roundtable* and *Rock On*. He also presents the BBC *Rock Hour* for the USA and BBC *Rock Line* which is syndicated world wide. Television credits include *Top of the Pops*.

■ Most exciting moment of career: 'Learning I'd been accepted as a DJ on Radio 1.' ■ Likes listening to music of all kinds (really!) and sketching. Dislikes people who think they are clever.

KEITH SKIPPER
'Specializes in local dialect. . .'
BORN: 11th March 1944 in Beeston, King's Lynn, Norfolk. Father a farm labourer. EDUCATED: Beeston Primary School. Hamond's Grammar School, Swaffham, Norfolk. FIRST JOB: Junior reporter for Eastern Counties Newspapers at Thetford in 1962. Then became the football correspondent for the 'Eastern Daily Press', 'Eastern Evening News' and the 'Eastern Football News'. FIRST BROADCAST: September 1980 with BBC Radio Norfolk. 'I left the local paper and joined the new local

station, so I could stay in Norfolk!' Has contributed to all the programmes on Radio Norfolk and specializes in local dialect. Presents the *Dinner Time Show* Monday to Friday on Radio Norfolk.

■ Most exciting moment of career: 'Conducting a 40-minute interview with Spike Milligan, and not losing track!' ■ A moment to remember: 'Being offered a cameo role as "Norfolk Compo" in Mother Goose at the Norwich Theatre Royal 1982/83, playing opposite Kathy Staff, alias Nora Batty (Last of the Summer Wine)!' ■ Likes cricket, reading, writing, after-dinner speaking. Dislikes big cities, traffic and snobs. ■ Married to Diane and lives in Norfolk.

KEITH SKUES
'Alias Beef Stews or Keef Screws...'

BORN: 4th March 1939 in Timperley Lodge, Cheshire. Father a director of furnituring company. EDUCATED: County Grammar School, Altrincham. FIRST JOB: Clerk in an insurance office until called up for National Service in RAF in 1958. FIRST BROADCAST: Announcer for British Forces Network in Cologne, Germany in 1958, while in the RAF attached to BFN. Started as a presentation assistant, progressed to announcing and then became a producer. Has been associated with numerous programmes over the years including *Saturday Club* on the Light Programme, *Radio 1*

Club and *What's New.* He joined Radio 1 when it opened in 1967 and just before he left in 1974 was responsible for the Radio 1 documentary, *The Story of Pop.* In May 1974 he became Programme Director of the new ILR station in Sheffield, Radio Hallam, and is heard regularly on that station.

■ Most exciting moment of career: 'Reaching the summit of Mount Kilimanjaro 19,340 feet for a radio documentary in 1962.'
■ A moment to remember: 'Having an unusual surname Skues (which is Cornish meaning "A shade or shadow") I do tend to receive some pretty unusual spellings. When working on the BBC World Service I received a letter from Singapore addressed to Beef Stews, another from India to Cheese Skewers and from Australia, Keef Screws.' ■ Likes flying (holds a pilot's licence and is a member of the Aircraft Owner's and Pilot's Association), genealogy, photography and writing books (latest, 'Cornish Heritage' 1983). Dislikes 'people who ring me up at 3am and ask me if I want to buy a battle ship.' ■ Is a bachelor and lives in Yorkshire.

COLIN SLADE
'Thank you valve...'

BORN: 11th May 1953 in Dartford, Kent. Father a sales manager. EDUCATED: King's School, Rochester, Kent. Medway and Maidstone College of Technology. FIRST JOB: Freelance presenter/ops clerk with BBC Radio Medway. Also worked as a freelance station assistant for BBC Radio Blackburn. FIRST BROADCAST: Rock Show BBC Radio Medway in 1971. 'After some hospital radio I got into Radio Medway by "hanging around" and doing odd jobs, eg: making tea and tape reclamation. It was a combination of good luck and persistence.' Has presented all types of daily programmes from *Breakfast* to *Late Night.* Specializes in Rock. Is Presentation Controller at Radio Hallam and presents their daily early evening news magazine *Dateline,* also *Hallam Rock* (Heavy Rock) and *Sunday Soundsation.*

■ Most exciting moment of career: Joining Radio Hallam on 1st September 1974.
■ A moment to remember: 'My first broadcast came about because of a duff transmitter valve which put Radio Medway off the air, resulting in an hour's precious needletime in hand. I asked to do a "one off" *Rock Show* to use up the needletime. That one show became a series which ran for over three years and was really responsible for my broadcasting career. Thank you valve!' ■ Likes music, musical instruments, sea fishing and reading. Dislikes ... 'None really, although I'm not too keen on carrots.' ■ Married to a choreographer, Marie, has one son and one daughter and lives in South Yorkshire.

CLIVE SMALL
'An old fashioned scoop...'
BORN: 22nd, September 1925 in Manchester. Father a teacher. EDUCATED: Diocesan College, Cape Town, South Africa. University of Cape Town. FIRST JOB: Reporter on the 'Cape Times' in Cape Town, 1948/49. Back in the UK became sub-editor of 'The Times' in 1950. Then joined the 'News Chronicle' as reporter and sub-editor. FIRST BROADCAST: Presenting a Jazz programme on SABC in Cape Town in 1949, having been writing a Jazz column for a Cape Town paper. Joined the BBC in September 1951. Is the Washington Correspondent for BBC Radio News and contributes to all the news and current affairs programmes.

■ Most exciting moment of career: 'Being summoned to Idi Amin's command post in Kampala for an interview and a few days later getting a further summons, this time to be expelled from Uganda.' ■ A moment to remember: 'Early in the morning of 24th April 1979, I was woken by the telephone next to my bed. It was the White House press officer, telling me of the failure of the rescue mission to free the American hostages in Iran. The tip-off

coincided with the *Today* programme in London. I quickly called the programme and went on "live" with the first report of the abortive mission. An old fashioned "scoop".' ■ Likes collecting stamps. Dislikes exotic foods like liver, kidneys, brains and oysters. ■ Married to Monica, has three children and when in the UK lives in Middlesex.

DAVID SMEETON
'I've acquired the nickname of Tiger...'
BORN: 16th September 1936 in Gillingham, Kent. Father in the Royal Navy. EDUCATED: St. Christopher's School, Bath. Malvern College, Worcestershire. FIRST JOB: Reporter on the 'Western Morning News', Plymouth. FIRST BROADCAST: Interviewing Francis Chichester in 1959. In 1960, he successfully applied for the post of Regional Reporter for the BBC in Plymouth, and was a regular contributor to their nightly television news magazine *Spotlight South West*. Moved to London where he was a general reporter before being appointed Education Correspondent and then Home Affairs Correspondent. His first overseas posting came as the BBC's Tokyo Correspondent. Back in the UK he was the Local Government and Education Correspondent. Is now the BBC's Bonn Correspondent and contributes to all news and current affairs programmes.

■ Most exciting moment of career: 'Successfully meeting new impossible News deadlines!' ■ 'I appear to have acquired the nickname of "Tiger" over the years ... quite why has been lost in the mists of time!'
■ Likes family life. Dislikes beetroot.
■ Married to Diana Pitts, has two children and lives in Bonn, West Germany.

ERIC SMITH
'Tumbling out of an aeroplane, frightened out of my mind...'

BORN: 30th October 1951 in Barnsley, Yorkshire. Father a machine fitter. EDUCATED: Barnsley Broadway Grammar School. Richmond College, Sheffield. FIRST JOB: Junior clerk in a firm of solicitors in Barnsley. FIRST BROADCAST: 'A phone-in "instant" request programme on BBC Radio Sheffield in 1973. I was the one making the excuses when I couldn't find the record. I had answered an advertisement for a Record Librarian at Radio Sheffield in the local evening paper after many unsuccessful applications to the BBC. Has presented the *Breakfast* and the *Mid-Morning* shows on BBC Radio Sheffield and BBC Radio Stoke-on-Trent. Moved across to the "other side" and is now the senior announcer and presents the *Breakfast Show* on Radio Aire in Leeds.

■ Most exciting moment of career: 'My first Royal visit commentary in Jubilee Year 1977 when the Queen and the Duke of Edinburgh visited Sheffield.' ■ A moment to remember: 'The day when I wished I had kept my mouth shut. I was doing an interview on Radio Aire's mid-morning show with a representative from Help the Aged and I found myself being persuaded to do a parachute jump. The next thing I knew I was tumbling out of an aeroplane frightened out of my mind. But what an experience!' ■ Likes work. Dislikes smoking and the smell of cigarette smoke. ■ Married to Linda and lives in West Yorkshire.

MIKE SMITH
'Never hit the alarm snooze button in the dark...'

BORN: 23rd April 1955 in Hornchurch, Essex. Father a motor industry executive. EDUCATED: King Edward VI School, Chelmsford. Bangor Grammar School, N. Ireland. FIRST JOB: Noel Edmond's chauffeur and then a language laboratory technician! Has also worked in

Public Relations, and been a racing driver. FIRST BROADCAST: May 1975 on a recorded promotion for BBC Radio 1. First programme was *Nightflight* 2am on Capital Radio in 1978. ' I worked in hospital radio in Chelmsford before sending a demo tape to Radio 1. As a result I joined them as a promotions voice and copywriter for £12 per week. In 1978 I joined Capital Radio as a holiday relief presenter and progressed to the *Breakfast Show* in 2 years.' Shows for Capital included *UK Top 30, London Tonight*, news reporting and many outside broadcasts ranging from the Arctic Circle to the top of a London bus. In 1982 it was back to Radio 1 as an established DJ where he presents the *Mike Smith Early Show* Monday to Friday and the *Mike Smith Saturday Show*.

■ Most exciting moment of career: 'Just about every time the red light goes on! Most exciting broadcasts were a series of "live" breakfast shows for Capital Radio from the Arctic Circle, minus 26 degrees centigrade plus reindeers.' ■ A moment to remember: 'The biggest shock of my life was waking up one morning at one minute to six and I was due on the air at six!! The moral of that little tale is never hit the alarm snooze button in the dark ... it may just be the wrong one.' ■ Likes motor racing, the theatre and films and hot holidays. Dislikes late nights, Volvo drivers and DJ's who shout. ■ Is a bachelor and lives in London.

PETER SMITH
'A review of Jimmy Young at the Nottingham Empire...'

DATE OF BIRTH: 'When this crept into a Who's Who in Financial Journalism, I found myself repeatedly stopped in corridors by colleagues disbelieving my great age. Since I don't want to upset the distinguished elderly gentleman below (see Most Exciting Moment) by rumbling him, let's be vague and merely say "approaching a time of actuarial misgivings."' EDUCATED: Very little, mostly at Hurworth

Evening News' and Nottingham Empire both
long since defunct, which ought to be a
warning to the BBC in general and Radio News
and Terry Wogan in particular.' ■ Likes
tennis, golf, music, eating good food, and
slimming. Dislikes slimming. ■ Married to
Dorothy, has one daughter and lives in Essex.

Council School, near Darlington, Co. Durham;
and Clacton County High School, Essex. FIRST
JOB: Student apprentice, Marconi Wireless
Telegraph Co. Has been a reporter on 'East
Essex Gazette', 'Nottingham Evening News',
'The Star', 'Sunday Graphic', 'Daily Express',
'Sunday Telegraph', 'Daily Mail' (London and
Manchester). Served National Service in Royal
Navy; reached rank of Electrician's Mate,
Grade One (promotion from Grade Two
automatic after six months), spent most of
service overseas (Isle of Wight and Northern
Ireland) and witnessed much front-line, hand to
hand fighting (mostly Royal Marines versus US
Navy). Working in Fleet Street and suffering
from Drowning Rat Syndrome, he made his
FIRST BROADCAST: On the BBC Overseas
Service to Rhodesia, on the subject of
Scientology. 'I had written exposés of this in the
'Daily Mail', and located and interviewed the
founder L. Ron Hubbard on his 'yacht' . . . a
converted steamer . . . in the Mediterranean;
subsequently he lived in Rhodesia for a while.'
As the Industrial and Business Correspondent
for BBC Radio News, he is heard on all news
bulletins and current affairs programmes such
as *Today, World at One, PM, Financial World
Tonight, Newsbeat* and the *Jimmy Young
Show.*

■ Most exciting moment of career: 'As a young
reporter and embryo Kenneth Tynan on the
'Nottingham Evening News', reviewing Jimmy
Young when he topped the bill at the
Nottingham Empire, in the golden days of
variety when most acts involved topless young
ladies obliged to stand absolutely still for fear of
offending the Lord Chamberlain. Mr Young was
wearing, I recall, a smart blue suit (probably his
demob suit from the RAF which he still wears
on special occasions I believe) for which the
Lord Chamberlain and P. Smith were duly
grateful. Review was quite complimentary, but
unfortunately printed in $5\frac{1}{2}$ point type which
requires an electron microscope to be legible,
and regrettably no cutting has been preserved
(by me; I can't speak for J. Young). 'Nottingham

PHIL SMITH
*'I've hacked my way through many
programmes. . .'*
BORN: 24th June 1941 in Colne, Lancashire.
EDUCATED: The gang hut on the railway sidings
followed by the Finishing Department of the
Endurance Cotton Mill Company. (More
formally and less usefully – Nelson Sec. Tech.
and night school). FIRST JOB: Cleaning out the
roof gutters of the above premises, an activity
which nearly resulted in loss of life and an
unimaginable loss to broadcasting. Other jobs
include weeding the long border in the
Corporation Park, an occupation more taxing
and solitary than clearing an Amazon rain
forest. Teaching in a London school full of
psychopaths. Running an Italian restaurant in
the heart of the Lancashire fish and chip belt.
One day he hopes to become the world's first
geriatric astronaut, but he does suffer from car
sickness. FIRST BROADCAST: A taut piece of
string stretched between two cocoa tins by
which a message was sent across the back
street to Michael Plews, aged 8. Contents of
message obscure. From a small satellite studio
in Burnley (Third Division Champions
1981–'82), I delivered my first tirade against
the Establishment via BBC Radio Blackburn.
This resulted in a torrent of abusive mail from
deaf listeners. I've since hacked my way
through many programmes too numerous to
mention. I have not yet hosted *Desert Island
Discs* nor been invited to Ambridge, but if the
money's right . . . I seem to spend most of my
time prostrate, or at least on my knees, begging
for work, like all hard-done-by freelancers, or

'Free-lances' as my Manchester identity card has it. [I can see I'll have to tell you what he really does . . .] A series of talks *The Smith Series*, reports for *Woman's Hour, You and Yours, The Food Programme, In Britain Now* and two off-beat documentaries, *The Haunting of Hobstones* and *The Battle of Brunnenborough*, for Radio 4.

■ Most exciting moment of career: 'As a passenger in a low flying training exercise in an RAF jet, every exhilarating moment of which, I spent with my head between my legs, being sick!' ■ A moment to remember: 'I once had to interview an exorcist sitting in a garden in one of those ridiculous enclosed hammocks. As we swung together trussed up in saggy canvas, he revealed he had the power to read minds. That mad parrot which inhabits the less congenial corners of my mind began to screech abuse, willing him to reveal that he knew what I was really thinking. He never did, thank God, but it was the most uncomfortable half-hour of my life.' ■ Likes riding horses and walking in high windy places. Dislikes Home Counties patronage. ■ Married to 'My wife' and lives in Lancashire.

Cornwall as presenter and producer of their mid-morning show *Ken Snowdon – Nine till Noon.*

■ Most exciting moment of career: 'After giving up regular employment, chancing everything on a period of freelance work for Radio Cleveland to give me work experience, and then getting a staff job at Radio Blackburn.' ■ A moment to remember: 'I agreed to host a series of 'It's a Knock Out' events for Pendle Leisure Services in Lancashire. There was a lot of water about and the last game involved a large swimming pool and of course everyone fell in. I was the only dry one left until the end when the contestants grabbed me and threw me in. I can't swim. They thought I was waving at them until I went down for the third time. The sequel to this story was even more embarrassing . . . I hadn't brought along any spare clothes. It was a long walk back to my car in my underpants and an even longer drive back home.' ■ Likes home computers, photography and bird watching.
■ Married to Jude Bunker and lives in Cornwall.

KEN SNOWDON
'Thrown in at the deep end. . .'

BORN: 22nd May 1953 in Stockton-on-Tees. Father a driver. **EDUCATED:** Stockton Church of England Grammar School. **FIRST JOB:** Selling car parts. Has also erected tents in the South of France; run a building and property repair company; and formed the Govey Botch Group (management/building/agency). **FIRST BROADCAST:** September 1978 on BBC Radio Cleveland. 'After the 100th letter to Radio Cleveland management, citing hospital radio experience as qualification for the job, they let me make tea for the sport's producer.' Presented *Success to the Weavers* and then became one of the main presenters of the *Morning Show* on Radio Cleveland. In 1983 moved to the newly opened BBC Radio

JULIA SOMERVILLE
'First girl to be appointed Labour Affairs Correspondent. . .'

BORN: in Somerset. **EDUCATED:** Headington School, Oxford. Sussex University. Joined the BBC as a sub-editor in the Radio Newsroom in 1973. 1979 was appointed a reporter for Radio News. 1981 was appointed Labour Affairs Correspondent for Radio News.

SAMMY SOUTHALL
'Opening up Radio Wyvern, a memory I'll cherish for ever. . .'

BORN: 15th June 1955 in Worcestershire. Father in middle management in the carpet industry. **EDUCATED:** Yes! Primary, Secondary, Further and Self. **FIRST JOB:** Salesman. Spent two seasons as a DJ at Butlins. Worked as a

Club DJ in most of central Europe and also in Iceland. Was a hotel DJ/Compère and part time Bingo Caller in Jersey, Channel Islands for 6 years, and started the cable station in Jersey for Hotels 'MHG Radio'. FIRST BROADCAST: 15th June 1980, opening the new cable station MHG Radio in Jersey. Presented their evening show and then sent an audition tape to Radio Wyvern in his home county. Is now Head of Music and the breakfast show presenter on Radio Wyvern for Hereford and Worcester.

■ Most exciting moment of career: 'Opening up Radio Wyvern at 7am on October 4th, 1982, a moment I'd been nervous about for months but a memory and experience I'll cherish for ever.' ■ Likes video, collecting post cards, good food and reading. Dislikes getting up at 4 in the morning. ■ Is a bachelor and lives in Worcestershire.

my own self-op radio studio and after a holiday in America where I visited US radio stations, I began to present a pre-recorded chart programme which was aired on six local radio stations. I then met the Radio 1 DJ "Emperor Rosko" who introduced me to BBC producers. In 1979 I moved to Guernsey and left the radio scene, but when the BBC set up a local radio station in Guernsey I successfully applied for a freelance post. I still have my own studio and make programmes and trails at home.' Produces and presents BBC Radio Guernsey's *Sounds Like Saturday* and *Island's Sundae.*

■ Most exciting moment of career: 'Apart from my first "live" show, the 12-hour marathon broadcast which raised £12,000 for charity, must be to date, if not the most exciting, the most tiring!' ■ A moment to remember: 'Radio Guernsey had been on the air for four days and I was presenting my first and the station's first Sunday programme. This coincided with Mother's Day and like a fool I suggested that listeners ring in with dedications. In 2 hours nearly 200 people rang in and Guernsey names are notoriously difficult to pronounce. I ended up with all sorts of problems! However I'm pleased to say I can now handle the local pronunciations reasonably well.' ■ Likes flying, recording local groups and radio! Dislikes smoking. ■ Married to Ita and lives in Guernsey, Channel Islands.

SAM SPINDLOW
'Built his own self-op radio studio. . .'
BORN: 31st August 1950 in London. Father a company director. EDUCATED: Private School in Romford, Essex. College of Further Education, Loughton, Essex. North East London Polytechnic. FIRST JOB: Working in Merchant Bank in the City of London. Has also worked as a flying instructor at the local Aero Club. FIRST BROADCAST: March 1982 although his voice had been heard on air on 'voice overs' before that. 'It all started as a hobby. I eventually built

PAM SPRIGGS
'Her own mobile roadshow. . .'
BORN: 6th May 1955 in Beaconsfield. Father the owner of a furniture business. EDUCATED: St. Bernard's Convent, High Wycombe. High Wycombe College of Further Education. FIRST JOB: My own mobile roadshow. Also worked as a hairdresser. FIRST BROADCAST: 1979. Worked in hospital radio in Ealing and Southall before joining Radio 210, Thames Valley in Reading. Has presented all the shows on

Thames Valley including the *Soul Show* and *Off the Wall*.

■ Most exciting moment of career: Being accepted by Radio 210 ■ Likes sport. Dislikes boring people, being short of cash and anything fried. ■ Lives in Berkshire.

ROBERT SPROUL-CRAN
'The excitement of meeting someone who had heard of me. . .'

BORN: 14th August 1950 in Halifax although he *is* Scottish! Father a pension scheme manager. EDUCATED: Daniel Stewart's College, Edinburgh. Pembroke College, Cambridge (M.A.) Edinburgh University. (PlD) FIRST JOB: freelance graphic designer. Has also worked as an underwater photographer. FIRST BROADCAST: 1977, having talked his way into a Book Review team with Radio Forth. He subsequently did several Arts reviews, particularly during the Edinburgh Festivals. Programmes on BBC Radio Scotland include *Leisure Trail, Portrait, Beneath the Surface* (Scottish Shipwrecks), *A Pastoral View of Scotland in the 1790's, Summer Sportsound, The Morning Tale*, and on Radio 4, *Origins*. He is the Head of Presentation Radio Scotland and presents and produces their Archaeology programme *Foundations*. He also produces *The Light Programme*.

■ Most exciting moment of career: 'Meeting someone who had heard of me!' ■ A moment to remember: 'When my non-coverage of a regal non-event made the papers from Perth, Scotland to Perth, Australia.' ■ Likes skin diving, sailing, cooking, brewing and wine making and computing. Dislikes cheap imitations and 'Jobsworths' (couldn't do that pal, it's more than my job's worth). ■ Married to Lizzy, has one child and lives in Lanarkshire.

MARTIN STANFORD
'I learnt the business the best way. . .'

BORN: 2nd May 1958 in Didcot, Berkshire.

Father a Methodist Minister. EDUCATED: Ingsham County Primary School, Chichester. Chichester High School for Boys. Wood Green School, Witney Oxon. FIRST JOB: BBC Transcription Recording Unit in London. Then became a station assistant at BBC Radio Oxford. FIRST BROADCAST: August 1975 as summer relief on a music show on BBC Radio Oxford. 'As a fifth former I had been invited to take part in a schools discussion programme at Radio Oxford. This led to my being allowed to "goffer" (coffee, answer phones etc:) on Saturday mornings. I learnt the business the best way! Announcing and presentation followed.' Shows at Radio Oxford included *It's Saturday, The Late Breakfast Show, Home Choice, Afternoon Delight, Sport on Saturday, Swap Shop* and *Countywide*. Moved to BBC Radio Northampton where he is a staff producer and presents the *County Show*.

■ Most exciting moment of career: 'Interviewing the Duke of Gloucester "live" for the opening of BBC Radio Northampton and being filmed for TV at the same time. Also the 75-hour marathon broadcast which I co-presented and which raised £18,000 for the Year of the Disabled.' ■ A moment to remember: 'Covering a colleague's descent from an aircraft, parachuting to earth with a radio mic attached. I had to do a commentary from the roof of a car doing 50mph over a rough field with a mic in one hand and holding on to the aerial mast with the other!' ■ Likes keeping fit, squash, hi-fi, video and computers. Dislikes coleslaw, cigarettes, booze (I'm teetotal) and unprofessionalism. ■ Is a bachelor and lives in Northamptonshire.

CELIA STEVENSON
'I told them they'd be mad to start without me. . .'

BORN: 22nd September 1943 in Ballantrae, Ayrshire, Scotland. Father a farmer. EDUCATED: Wellington School for Girls, Ayr. Edinburgh College of Art. Macadam's Secretarial College,

Edinburgh. FIRST JOB: Assistant to a fashion photographer. Also worked as a freelance interior designer in between having three kids and being a farmer's wife. FIRST BROADCAST: October 1981, a half hour news bulletin on West Sound. 'I had persuaded West Sound that they would be mad to start without me!' Handles a lot of the station's news and current affairs output including *Open to Question*. Produces and presents a daily current affairs phone-in *Open Air* and also reports for *West Sound News*.

■ Most exciting moment of career: 'I think I would probably categorize it as the most terrifying . . . going down an old coal mine under threat of closure, in Ayrshire.'
■ A moment to remember: 'Just after West Sound went on the air, I was sent to do a Vox Pop at a small town which had just been spared the horrors of nuclear dumping. The locals had organized petitions and there had been great concern that the area should not be used for this type of dumping. On the great day of the ''reprieve'' I was transmitting from our outside broadcast van direct onto the air and as I thrust my mike under one elderly gentleman's nose, I noticed too late that he was wearing a hearing aid. "How do you feel now you've heard there's to be no test boring at Dalmellington?" I asked. He looked at me with his head on one side "eh?" I repeated the question. Then came the answer . . . "Ah hen, I'm no interested in cricket". That went straight out on air and I gather the assembled experts in the studio, fell about!' ■ Dislikes stuffy officialdom and red tape. ■ Married to Bill Judge, has two sons and a daughter and lives in Ayrshire.

BOB STEWART
'Europe's best known Country music DJ. . .'
BORN: 1939 in Liverpool. FIRST JOB: Army. On returning to civvy street in 1962 he sold household appliances . . . 'I was supposed to guide customers to the more expensive items, but because I couldn't bring myself to do it, I never made much money.' FIRST BROADCAST:

1963 on Radio Caroline, where his mild Liverpool accent was replaced by a mid-Atlantic one. 'The programme director there took the view that it you had a dialect, it could cause offence in various parts of the country, and as seventy five per cent of the staff were Americans or Canadians, I paid a great deal of attention to their pronunciation, enunciation and everything else.' From Radio Caroline he joined Radio Luxembourg and in the mid-70's found himself sharing an apartment with an American Army master sergeant by the name of Roxy who was mad about Country music. As he weighed 22½ stones and was 6'5" tall, Bob decided he had better like Country music too. And when Radio Luxembourg ran a survey to find out what people wanted to hear, and the answer was more Country music, he was chosen to do the programme. Now his late night *Big L Marlboro Country Show* attracts several million listeners and once a month he presents it 'live' by satellite from America. He has been made an Honorary Citizen of Nashville and of Tennessee for his services to Country music.

■ Most exciting moment of career: Broadcasting by satellite from Nashville on the world's longest running radio show, the *Grand Ole Opry*, the first occasion it had ever been broadcast outside the United States.
■ A 'monthly' moment to remember: 'Arriving in Nashville on a Thursday night after a nineteen hour journey from Luxembourg and promptly crashing out in bed. Rehearsing on Friday, doing the show on Saturday and on Sunday morning flying back to Luxembourg!' ■ Likes Country music ('it tells a story and it has melody'). ■ Married to Texas born Cynthia and lives in Luxembourg.

ED STEWART
'His stomach muscles got him the nickname of Stewpot. . .'
BORN: 23rd April 1941 in Exmouth, Devon. Father a solicitor. EDUCATED: Eagle House, Sandhurst. St. Edward's, Oxford. FIRST JOB:

Retail assistant in a record store. FIRST BROADCAST: At the age of 9 on the BBC World Service broadcasting to North America. 'My father was a Newfoundlander and we used to broadcast messages to relatives twice a year'. Started broadcasting for real in Hong Kong in 1961 having gone out to join a band (he plays double bass) and the job fell through so he became a film critic and a rugby reporter. Returned to the UK and joined the pirate station Radio London in 1965 where he got the nickname of Stewpot. 'I have this talent for isolating my stomach muscles and it was Dave Cash who called me Stewpot and it sort of stuck because the kids liked it'. In 1967 he went 'legit' joining the BBC for the opening of Radio 1. Programmes include *Junior Choice* on both Radios 1 and 2 and *Family Favourites* on Radio 2. Has had his own daily show *The Ed Stewart Show* on Radio 2 since 1980.

■ Most exciting moment of career: 'Flying to the Falklands to record requests for my programme Christmas 1982. The flight involved two re-fuellings in mid air at 25,000 feet.' ■ A moment to remember: 'As a DJ on the pirate station Radio London, I was advertising our Tee shirts . . .' 3 different sizes, only 12/6 including Pastage and Poking . . . to cover my confusion I pressed the weather jingle and read . . . there'll be shattered scowers over East Anglia . . . two spoonerisms in 10 seconds must be something of a record.' ■ Likes golf, tennis and snooker. ■ Married to Chiara, has two children and lives in Surrey.

IAN STRACHAN
'I like radio because it's so personal. . .'
BORN: 8th June 1938 in Altrincham, Cheshire. Father a newsagent. EDUCATED: Navigation Road Primary School. Altrincham Grammar School. Central School of Speech and Drama. FIRST JOB: ASM at Manchester Library Theatre. Later became stage director of the Playhouse, Sheffield. Joined the BBC as an assistant floor manager, moving up the ladder to Production Assistant and Associate Producer for BBC

Television drama. FIRST BROADCAST: 1950, a very small part in a Margaret Potter play for Children's Hour produced in the North region by Trevor Hill. 'I was eleven when I first wrote to the BBC for an audition. They told me I must wait for my twelfth birthday. On my next birthday I wrote again, got an audition and soon after, my first job for which I was paid the princely sum of half a guinea. Much later I wrote a play for *Children's Hour*, then they took the programme off.' From Television drama department, Ian joined BBC Radio Stoke where he has presented their breakfast show *First Edition*, a quiz programme *What Comes Next* and several documentaries. Is the co-producer and presenter of Radio Stoke's mid-morning magazine programme *Here and Now*. 'I like radio because it's so personal and I like it best when I convince an interviewee we're having an ordinary conversation to the point at which I ask an unexpected question which produces a totally honest but unexpected answer which in turn convinces the listener that the whole thing isn't set up, then they become involved too.'

■ Likes gardening, beekeeping, washing up and writing. (His first book for teenagers 'Moses Beech' won the Young Observer Rank Organization Fiction prize for 1981). ■ Married to Jo, has two children and lives in Staffordshire.

CHRIS STUART
'Professional musician and DJ. . .'
BORN: 19th February 1949 in Durham City. EDUCATED: Longslade School, Birstall, Leicester. New College Oxford. FIRST JOB: Journalist with 'Western Mail'. FIRST BROADCAST: Reporter piece on children's play scheme for *Good Morning Wales* (BBC Wales) having been working as a freelance researcher. Is also a professional musician playing keyboards for the group Baby Grand who have had two series on BBC 2 and one on Radio 2. He also writes many of the groups songs. Was researcher, producer and presenter for *Good*

Morning Wales and has presented *Home Run* both for BBC Wales. He has also done several documentaries for Radio 4. Presents BBC Radio Wales breakfast show *A.M.*

■ Most exciting moment of career: Doing the television commentary on the Pope's visit to Wales. ■ Likes sport, particularly soccer and music of all kinds. Dislikes are few and far between. ■ Lives in Gwent.

JOHN TERRETT
'Turned down the theatre for broadcasting. . .'

BORN: 23rd July 1963 in Portsmouth. Father sales executive for a Brewery. EDUCATED: Oaklands Road Comprehensive, Waterlooville, Hampshire. FIRST JOB: Trainee journalist/newsreader. He trained for the Theatre at Highbury College of Technology in Portsmouth and gained a place at the Bristol Old Vic Theatre School, but turned it down in favour of broadcasting. FIRST BROADCAST: February 1975 in *The Choice is Yours* on Portsmouth Hospital Broadcasting. Having gained experience in hospital radio, he started to help out at weekends at his local ILR station, Radio Victory in Portsmouth. He then moved to Two Counties Radio in Bournemouth where he did a nightly current affairs programme. Is the producer/presenter of the *Breakfast Show* on Two Counties Radio.

■ Most exciting moment of career: 'All of it!'

■ A moment to remember: 'Mis-pronouncing the word "Diarrhoea" during a programme feature on guinea pigs. I pronounced it as Di-a-roe-a, no less than five times. The switch board was jammed!'
■ Likes theatre and travelling. Dislikes over-confident people. ■ Lives in Dorset.

NORMAN THOMAS
'The broadcasting publican. . .'

BORN: 10th September in St. Helens Merseyside. EDUCATED: Cowley Grammar School, St. Helens. Carnegie College Leeds. FIRST JOB: Teacher of physical education. Also worked as a promotion manager with Thomson Holidays. FIRST BROADCAST: October 1974 when Radio City in Liverpool, went on the air. Radio City shows include *Venue*, the *Lunchtime Show*, the *Breakfast Show* and their *Sunday Quiz* show. Also manages to run his own Travel Agency and his own pub!

■ 'The "highlight" of my career was meeting the Prince and Princess of Wales.' ■ Likes cooking, golf, and running his Travel Agency and Pub. Dislikes objectionable people, rudeness, bothersome drunks, bores and *Crossroads*. ■ Married to Allison and lives in Merseyside.

JOHN THURSTON
'A lifetime's ambition. . .'

BORN: 28th June 1937 in London. FIRST JOB: A Shipping clerk. Also worked as a sales representative. FIRST BROADCAST: November 1976 on BBC Radio Medway. 'After doing hospital radio for many years I was given a one-off request programme on Radio Medway which started a chain of events which soon led to my turning professional . . . a lifetime's ambition.' Has presented a wide variety of programmes on Radio Medway and is the producer/presenter of the daily afternoon sequence programme and their Saturday morning show.

■ A moment to remember: '(Several!) Being "live" on air with a lion in a cage; having a ten-foot crocodile in the studio; having a cigarette knocked out of my mouth by six-inch nails being thrown from ten feet away. [That is taking the campaign against smoking too far!]; and being kidnapped in mid programme by the Fire Brigade and held to ransom for charity, with the £500 demanded being exceeded within half an hour.' ■ Likes squash and playing football for the Showbiz Eleven. ■ Married to Christine, has three children and lives in Kent.

JOHN TIMPSON
'Hates waking up at 4am . . .'
BORN: 2nd July 1928 in Kenton, Middlesex. Father a banker. EDUCATED: Merchant Taylors' School. FIRST JOB: Junior reporter on 'Wembley News' in 1945. Was district reporter for 'Eastern Daily Press' in Norfolk from 1951–'59. FIRST BROADCAST: Report on Margate Ship Spotters Club for S.E. Regional News in March 1959, having successfully applied for a job as Radio and Television reporter in News Division of the BBC. Remained with News until 1970, during which time he spent five years as Deputy Court Correspondent covering Royal Tours, State Occasions etc. Has also worked for Radio Newsreel, and on television for *Newsroom* BBC 2, *Tonight* BBC 1. Chaired *Mastermind of Gardening Finals* for Radio 2 in

1981/82/83. Is co-presenter of Radio 4's *Today* programme.

■ Most exciting moment of career: Being invited to appear in 'Who's Who on Radio' [very funny!] ■ A moment to remember: My only conversation with Prince Philip during Royal reporting. On board Royal Yacht Britannia in Auckland harbour when arriving for reception.
Prince Philip: Who are you?
Timpson: Timpson, sir, of the BBC.
Prince Philip: Oh. ■ Likes sleeping and avoiding gardening. Dislikes waking up at 4am and gardening. ■ Married to Pat, has two boys and lives in Hertfordshire.

STEVE TONGUE
'A strange whirring noise behind me. . .'
BORN: 1st January 1951 in London. Father a librarian. EDUCATED: Leyton County High School. Selwyn College, Cambridge. FIRST JOB: Sports reporter on the 'Waltham Forest Guardian'. Also worked for Hayter's Sports Agency. FIRST BROADCAST: Reporting on the Spurs v Arsenal match in October 1973 for LBC. 'I had auditioned for LBC as a football reporter before they went on the air. I was offered a staff job when the two sports presenters realized they'd each be working a 70 hour week.' Is now the football correspondent for LBC/IRN.

■ Most exciting moment of career: 'Covering the World Cup Final in Madrid. I got so excited that I left a rather expensive lip microphone in the press box.' ■ A moment to remember: 'The day I was reading the racing results when a strange whirring noise began behind me. The cleaner, who didn't understand what the red light over the studio meant, had come in to do the hoovering!' ■ Likes football and family (though not necessarily in that order).
■ Married to Catherine, has three children and lives in London.

FRANK TOPPING
'Pause for Thought...'

BORN: 30th March 1937 in Birkenhead, Merseyside (then Cheshire). Father a shipyard caulker. EDUCATED: St. Annes R.C. Junior School. St. Anselm's College. North West School of Speech and Drama. Wesley College of Theology, Bristol. FIRST JOB: 'Office boy in a shipping office in Liverpool who's duties included baling out drunken whalers from Water Street clink.' Has also worked as a market gardener, a dustman and assistant manager of a pin factory. Has been electrician/stage manager/actor for both the Leatherhead Repertory Company and Wolverhampton Rep:, and a studio floor manager in television. FIRST BROADCAST: In Regional Round Quiz on Children's Hour, about 1952. Worked as a local radio freelance in Brighton and then joined the production staff of BBC Radio Bristol when it opened. Produced music, farming and religious programmes. Has been presenting *Pause For Thought* on Radio 2 since 1970. Radio 4 religious programmes include *Thought for the Day, Prayer for the Day, Lighten Our Darkness* and the *Daily Service*. At the time of going to press, he is working on two documentaries for Radio 4.

■ Most exciting moment of career: 'Winning the Grace Wyndham Goldie Award in 1975 for the Best Production in the UNDA Saville Radio Festival: a play I had written, produced and performed in. Secondly, when Donald Swann and I were invited to perform at the Opera House, Jersey on the strength of our radio partnership. The biggest event in my career was starring in the West End show, *Swann with Topping*. It was only because of the encouragement of the BBC that our songwriting partnership developed, and in the West End, at the Ambassadors Theatre, we were singing songs and performing sketches, 95% of which had been written for radio.' ■ A moment to remember: 'In Bristol, I presented a programme in which all the guests were fictional characters I had invented. There was nobody else in the studio, just me. After the programme, the producer received a letter from a listener, complaining that I had hogged the air and not given enough time to my guests!' ■ Likes sailing. Dislikes people who work to the exact letter of the law. ■ Married to June Berry, has three children and lives in Kent.

NORMAN TOZER
'A wide ranging career...'

BORN: 13th July 1934 in London. Father a haulage contractor. EDUCATED: Latymer's School, North London. Royal Academy of Dramatic Art. FIRST JOB: Television floor manager. Became interested in working in radio and television by deputizing for a fellow student, who through illness, was unable to work on a television programme. FIRST BROADCAST: 15th June 1952 in *Home at Eight* on the BBC Home Service. Programmes include *A Fine Blue Day* (Drama feature about the Battle of Britain) *Weekend* (Co-presenter of series) *Woman's Hour*, and others from Current Affairs to Drama and Variety back into the mists of time. Presents *It's a Bargain* on Radio 4.

■ Most exciting moment of career: Getting a definite go-ahead for the next programme or series I want to do. ■ A moment to remember: 'I once travelled to Greece to collect material for a programme. The only certain arrangement was to interview a world famous artist. It was to be an important and even topical interview. Due to transport difficulties just a few hours before the appointment, the only item of equipment which I did *not* have was the microphone. Have you ever glared in frustration at a recording machine which cannot be used! I always double check all portable equipment (almost hourly) nowadays.' ■ Likes photography and cooking. Dislikes trying to make a wide ranging career fit into pigeon-holing 'forms' like this. [You haven't done too badly!] ■ Lives in London.

SHEILA TRACY
'First woman to read the news on Radio 4. . .'

BORN: 10th January 1934 in Helston, Cornwall. Father a grocer. EDUCATED: Truro High School, Cornwall. Royal Academy of Music, studying piano (LRAM), trombone and violin. FIRST JOB: Trombonist with the Ivy Benson Band, 1956–'57. Formed the Tracy Sisters with another girl trombonist, Phyl Brown. FIRST BROADCAST: 24th May 1958, *In Town Tonight* (Tracy Sisters). Other programmes included *Workers Playtime, Mid-Day Music Hall* and *Saturday Club.* She joined BBC Television as an announcer in February 1961. First radio show *Late Choice* for the Light Programme in February 1963. 'It went out at 11pm on a Sunday evening and I wasn't allowed to play anything loud or fast!' Other programmes include *Melody Fair, Anything Goes* and *Music for Late Night People.* Television credits, *Spotlight S.W., South Today, Spoonful of Sugar, Call My Bluff, Holiday* BBC 1, *Music From Great Houses, The Sunday Prom.* October 1973 joined Radio 4 as an announcer and in July 1974 was the first woman to read the news. Took part in the Broadcasting from Parliament Experiment in 1975. In 1977 she joined Radio 2 presenting the *Late Show*, the *Early Show* and *You and the Night and the Music.* She went freelance in May 1981 devising and presenting the *Truckers Hour* for Radio 2. She presents *Big Band Special, Trucking with Tracy* and the *Weekend Early Show* on Radio 2.

■ Most exciting moment of career: '16th July 1974, reading my first news bulletin on Radio 4. I had joined Radio 4 with the express purpose of doing the breakthrough in News . . . it was an ambition achieved. Also getting the *Truckers Hour* on the air and meeting many of the drivers . . . super people.' ■ A moment to remember: '*Spoonful of Sugar*, was a TV series we did from hospitals where we often surprised patients with stars they wanted to meet. We had fixed for Mike Yarwood to be hidden in the corner of the ward while I was talking to the patient. The cameras started to roll and I go into my spiel about how much red tape we've had to cut to get this special guest on the programme. Mike then does his impersonation of Harold Wilson. "And who do you think that is?" I ask the patient. Obviously very excited she goes . . ." Ooh Ooh, . . . it's . . . Freddite Frinton" (*Meet the Wife* fame). Poor Mike Yarwood was absolutely devastated, Harold Wilson was his favourite impersonation. However it was all quite hilarious and all went out just as it happened!' ■ Likes playing bass trombone, golf, Arizona and Jack Daniels. Dislikes drivers who drive in the outside lane and force you to break the law. ■ Married to actor John Arnatt, has one son, Richard and lives in Surrey.

DAVE LEE TRAVIS
'In the middle of the North Sea clad only in his underpants. . .'

BORN: 25th May 1945 in Buxton, Derbyshire. Father a stage manager. EDUCATED: Central Grammar School, Manchester. FIRST JOB: Graphic designer. FIRST BROADCAST: 1964 on Radio Caroline (South). 'I'd been doing some DJ work around the clubs in Manchester so I came down to London to see the Programme Controller of Radio Caroline. When I walked into his office, the whole of one wall was covered with shelves full of audition tapes and I knew that if I walked out of that office without a job, no way was I going to get one by sending in a tape. So when he said "Send us a tape and we'll give you a call", I replied "Look, I know I've got what it takes, you've got a studio here, just give me ten minutes and it will save both of us a lot of time". He was so taken aback he agreed. That was Thursday, the following Monday I was on the ship.' He spent the next two years on Radio Caroline South and then six months on their Northern ship off the Isle of Man. When the pirates were made illegal, he returned to Manchester and it was BBC producer John Wilcox who gave him his break on network radio, as the host of the lunchtime show *Pop North*. He joined Radio 1 just after it opened and from 1971 to 1983 had his own daily show. He now has the Saturday morning slot from 10–1pm, *Talkabout*.

■ Most exciting moment of career: 'Exhilarating would be a better word to describe how I felt at the end of my first *Pop North*, knowing that it had gone well . . . the horror and the joy all rolled into one.' ■ A moment to remember: 'My first night on Radio Caroline. At dinner the Captain had gone through the safety regulations for my benefit, emphasising that if the fire bells went we all had to go up on deck to our lifeboat stations and to wait until the Dutch crew told us what to do next. That night we had a lot to drink and I rolled into my top bunk clad only in my brief underpants, at 3am very much the worse for wear. At 4am the fire bells sounded. Half awake I tried to grab a pair of trousers. "No time for that said the other occupant of my cabin" as he half carried me up the stairs. Everybody was making for the deck, and I stumbled up to my position on the uppermost deck and there I stood by the lifeboat in sub zero temperatures in the middle of the North Sea, clad only in my underpants, for a full five minutes before I realized that everything had gone suspiciously quiet. Of course everyone was back in bed asleep after a very successful joke played on the new boy!' ■ Likes specialized cars (drives a Thunderbird), photography, is compiling a book of his own work. Dislikes people who stick an autograph book in your hand without saying anything, and people who blow hot and cold.
■ Married to Marianne and lives in Buckinghamshire.

School, Bristol. Bristol Polytechnic, (B.A. in Law). FIRST JOB: (Part time) Bar maid, sales assistant on cheese counter at British Home Stores, and right-hand girl in solicitor's office to gain experience of law before deciding to go into broadcasting. FIRST BROADCAST: On BBC Radio Bristol, presenting *I-Level Student*, a programme by students for students . . . 'I should be surprised if even they listened. "I had bumped into a friend who was already working in *I-level* and he suggested I join in. From the moment I put £300 worth of BBC tape recorder over my shoulder, I was hooked!"' Has reported for *Woman's Hour, You and Yours, The Food Programme* and *Staying Alive*. Is now a reporter/presenter/newsreader for Radio 1's *Newsbeat*.

■ Most exciting moment of career: 'The most terrifying was probably presenting *Newsbeat* for the first time. There have been lots of exciting times, mostly getting sent out on big stories, like my first experience of reporting terrorist activity at the Hammersmith bombings in 1980.' ■ A moment to remember: 'My most memorable achievement in television was breaking the world record for the number of cub scouts you could get in a Mini. It was the anniversary of the car, so we filmed this great idea of mine using scouts from all over the West Country. They had to be measured for size, and when graded, they started squashing in . . . more than 80 of them. The tyres of the Mini were in tatters!' ■ Likes DIY (rebuilding a wrecked house in sunny Cricklewood), and walking mad, yellow, labrador bitch who when it comes to carrying sticks, thinks she's a lumberjack. Dislikes driving and liver. ■ Lives in London.

JANET TREWIN
'80 scouts in one Mini, a world record. . .'
BORN: 19th March 1957 in Bristol. Father, Harbour Master of the Port of Bristol.
EDUCATED: Amberly House School, Redmaids

FREDDIE TRUEMAN
'A natural step from bowling to broadcasting. . .'
BORN: 6th February 1931 in Stainton, South Yorkshire. Father a national hunt jockey who

later became a miner. EDUCATED: Stainton Council School. Maltby Hall Modern School. FIRST JOB: Apprentice bricklayer. In 1949 he played cricket for Yorkshire for the first time against Cambridge University. FIRST BROADCAST: Being interviewed as a professional cricketer in 1949; as a member of the *Test Match Special* commentary team, in 1976. Has appeared on numerous radio and television programmes over the years. For 'Firey Fred', it was a natural step from professional cricketer to professional broadcaster. Is heard regularly on Radio 3's *Test Match Special*. Has written many books on cricket including 'My Yorkshire' which he has written in collaboration with Don Mosey, published in 1983.

■ Most exciting moment of career: 'Whenever I've walked onto a cricket pitch with a Yorkshire or England cap on my head.'
■ A moment to remember: 'It was my first season with the *Test Match Special* commentary team when John Arlott and I were doing the lunchtime summarizing. As I was talking into the microphone I caught sight of John lying back in his chair with his head lolling to one side. I thought he was dead and was terrified, but somehow I managed to carry on talking. Don Mosey, who was at the other end of the commentary box, saw what had happened and came to my rescue. Twice, John Arlott fell asleep on me in the commentary box, but just think what a story that would have made if he really had passed out beside me!' ■ Likes bird watching; 'I'm always looking for new species.' Dislikes . . . 'Strange people coming up to me and making personal comments like "Are you dyeing your hair? . . . it shouldn't be that dark at your age".' ■ Married to Veronica . . . 'she's a super girl', has two daughters and one son, and one stepson and one step daughter. Lives in Yorkshire.

MARK TULLY
'Likes India and all things Indian. . .'

BORN: 24th October 1935 in Calcutta, India. Father a chartered accountant. EDUCATED: Marlborough College. Trinity Hall, Cambridge. FIRST JOB: Teacher. Has also been the assistant director of the Abbeyfield Society. FIRST BROADCAST: In 1966, reporting on the Delhi Veteran Car Rally for *Woman's Hour*. He joined the BBC in the Personnel Department but transferred to the New Delhi office in 1965 where he started broadcasting. Has made two full length film documentaries a) *Morarji Desai, Prime Minister of India* and b) *From our Delhi Correspondent*. As the BBC's Delhi Correspondent he contributes to all news and current affairs programmes for both radio and television.

■ Most exciting moment of career: 'The day I was allowed to return to India after being expelled during the emergency.' ■ Likes India and all things Indian. ■ Married to Margaret, has four children and lives in India.

COLIN TURNER
'264 winners in 64 days. . .'

BORN: 6th February 1945 in Dublin. Father a company official/writer & broadcaster. EDUCATED: High School in N. Ireland, Boston, USA and Boston University. Did a Radio/TV and journalistic course at University. FIRST BROADCAST: Junior Sports programme on Irish radio. 'I wrote to RTE who had a programme for young listeners, and said I could do a better job than those who were on the air, so they gave me a spot.' He has presented Pop and all types of music programmes. Has covered news stories all over the world. Has worked in the USA on both radio and television. He is the Racing Consultant, Equestrian Commentator, Sports Commentator for LBC and IRN. He also presents *Sportswatch* for LBC.

■ Most exciting moment of career: 'Doing the greyhound commentary at Romford Stadium when my dog was favourite to win the race.

She lost by a short head in the final of the Essex Vase.' ■ A moment to remember: 'Setting the World record in the Guinness Book of Records by breaking the 22 year old Tipping Record. I selected 264 winners in 64 days and the company director wasn't pleased because LBC's wavelength is 261 and he thought I should have stopped at that.' [Eat your heart out Wogan]. ■ Likes playing golf, tennis, horse riding and the cinema. Dislikes people who have no time to help the handicapped. ■ Is a bachelor and lives in Spain, Ireland and England (in that order).

JOHN TURNER
'A musician who became "hooked" on radio. . .'

BORN: 2nd January 1947 in Bristol. EDUCATED: Cotham Grammar School, Bristol. FIRST JOB: Professional musician and songwriter. Has written music for BBC Radio and Television Drama. FIRST BROADCAST: '1968 as a guest musician on a radio show after which I was invited to do a regular review of new records for a programme. I was consequently hooked.' Has done freelance reporting for *Today, PM, Woman's Hour* and *You and Yours* on Radio 4. Has produced and presented BBC Radio Bristol's daily four hour *Compass* since 1979. Also presents a regular Folk and Blues show and a Sunday morning record dedication show.

■ Most exciting moment of career: 'Flying upside down at 400mph at a height of 250 feet, towards a 600 foot high hill in an RAF Hawk whilst recording. P.S. I was sick!' ■ Likes walking, music, and French cooking. Dislikes musak, bad restaurants and unsolicited mail. ■ Married to Pat Vedmore and lives in Avon.

CHRIS UNDERWOOD
'I managed to fix the set and get the interview. . .'

BORN: 22nd November 1937 in Weybridge,

Surrey. Father an aircraft engineer. EDUCATED: Hinchley Wood Commercial College. FIRST JOB: Reporter on the 'Surrey Herald'. Has also been a reporter for the 'Extel' News Agency; a feature writer for the 'Daily Herald'; and handled special investigations for the 'Daily Mail'. FIRST BROADCAST: October 1966, a piece of local government reorganization for Radio Newsreel. 'I applied to the BBC for a job as a reporter, knowing that the incoming editor of the 'Daily Mail' wouldn't like me as much as his predecessor.' Is now the BBC's Home Affairs Correspondent and contributes to all the news and current affairs programmes.

■ Most exciting moment of career: 'Escaping unscathed from any number of riots in Northern Ireland.' ■ A moment to remember: 'Having arranged to interview Sir Alan (A.P.) Herbert on one of his hobby horses, Greenwich Mean Time, I drove to his home in Chiswick Mall. Lady Herbert answered the door and I announced myself as the BBC. "Ah", said Lady Herbert, "it's out the back". What a strange way to refer to such a worthy knight, I thought. Her Ladyship led me through to the parlour and indicated the television set. "Every time I switch on, the picture flickers", she said. I finally managed to fix the set and get the interview back in time for transmission!' ■ Likes cricket, crosswords and beer. Dislikes dancing, computers and tea. ■ Married to Jenny, has two children and lives in Surrey.

TOMMY VANCE
'Just happy to keep on broadcasting. . .'

BORN: 11th July in Eynsham, Oxon. Father an electronics engineer. EDUCATED: St. Mary's Convent, Abingdon, Berkshire. Sir William Collins, London. FIRST JOB: A trainee hotel manager. Has also been a cabin boy, a juke box mechanic, an actor and a waiter. Is now the producer and director of a recording studio complex called 'Silk Sound' in London. FIRST BROADCAST: In the UK for BBC Schools Television in 1953, having been to America

and bombarded radio stations with demo tapes until one said 'yes'. Has worked on Radio Caroline, Radio Luxembourg, Radio Monte Carlo, BBC Radio 1, BFBS Radio and the BBC World Service. BBC Television credits include *Top of the Pops* and *Disco Two*. Does a lot of voice overs for commercials. Presents the *Friday Rock Show* on Radio 1 also the *Top Forty*. Presents a daily two hour music and chat show for BFBS which is broadcast around the world. 'I'm just happy to keep on going, doing something in broadcasting until I drop.'

■ Likes doing 'voice overs', watching the Silk Sound Studios grow into a large company, and loves good beer, also enjoys watching films on video. Dislikes being tired. ■ Married to 'my wife', has one child.

PAUL VAUGHAN
'They thought I was someone more influential. . .'
BORN: 24th October 1925. Father an association secretary. EDUCATED: Raynes Park School. Wadham College, Oxford. FIRST JOB: Assistant Export Manager of a small drug company in London. Became Chief Press Officer of British Medical Association (1959–'64) Deputy Editor of 'World Medicine' (1970–'73). FIRST BROADCAST: 1956 or thereabouts . . . 'It was probably a mistake, as they thought I was someone more influential'. Since then programmes have included *Science*

and *Industry, New Ideas, Science in Action, Discovery*, all for the World Service. *Horizon* (BBC 2), *Today, New Worlds* on Radio 4. Is a regular presenter of Radio 4's *Kaleidoscope* and *Record Review* on Radio 3.

■ Likes playing the clarinet. Dislikes clichés. ■ Has four children and lives in London.

WYNFORD VAUGHAN-THOMAS
'Running commentary from a bomber over Berlin. . .'
EDUCATED: Swansea Grammar School. Exeter College, Oxford. FIRST BROADCAST: 12th May 1937 commentating on the coronation of George VI along with Tommy Woodruffe (of *The Fleet's Lit Up* fame), having just joined the BBC. Throughout his long broadcasting career he has commentated on many Royal occasions including the Royal Commonwealth tours. He was a BBC War Correspondent 1942–'45. He was awarded the OBE in 1974 and the Croix de Guerre in 1982. He has written many books including *The Royal Tour 1953–'54, Anzio, Madly in All Directions, Trust to Talk* (his autobiography) and in 1982 *The Princes of Wales*.

■ Most exciting moment of career: '5th September 1943 when I gave a running commentary from a bomber on a raid over Berlin.' ■ A moment to remember: 'The launching of the Ark Royal at Birkenhead by the Queen Mother which was being televised and I was doing the commentary. My producer Ray Lakeland told me to start talking, without waiting for a cue, as soon as the ship hit the water. Unfortunately in the excitement of the moment he forgot about this and noticing that one camera had a marvellous shot of the Queen Mother, he punched it up on the screen just as the Ark Royal hit the water and I cried out "There she is, the whole vast bulk of her"!' ■ Likes playing the piano incompetently, rock climbing and messing about in boats. Dislikes people who are indifferent to the beauty of the countryside. ■ Married to Charlotte, has one son and lives in Dyfed.

MICHAEL VESTEY
'Hey what's all this about you being a colonel?. . .'

BORN: 7th March 1945 in Bournemouth. EDUCATED: In London. FIRST JOB: Reporter on the 'South London Advertiser'. In 1966 he was feature writer and occasional drama critic on the now defunct 'London Life Magazine'. 1967–'70 gossip columnist and feature writer for the 'Sunday Express'. Was also a reporter for 'Newsweek' magazine, London Bureau for a short period in the 60's and a reporter on the 'Daily Sketch'. FIRST BROADCAST: 1970, a short piece on a demonstration in London for Radio 4's *South East News*. 'Along with hundreds of others, I had applied for a post at BBC Radio London when it opened in 1970.' 1970–'72 reporter and presenter for Radio London. He is a reporter for BBC Radio News based in London with Special Correspondent status when abroad and contributes to all the news and current affairs programmes.

■ Most exciting moment of career: 'Flying from Southern Chile across Cape Horn and Drake's Passage to Antarctica to produce a radio report for the *World at One* and film for BBC's 9 o'clock news during the Falklands conflict. Other exciting moments . . . being shot at during various wars, including Iran-Iraq, El Salvador, Rhodesia and Northern Ireland.' ■ A moment to remember: 'My nickname, unfortunately given to me during my broadcasting career because of my abrupt manner with News Editors, is "Colonel". It can have it's disadvantages. Once, when reporting on the Northern Ireland hunger strikes in 1981, I was standing at the graveside of a hunger striker in Londonderry as IRA men fired a volley in salute, when an American cameraman

turned to me and said: "Hey, what's all this about you being a colonel?" I shivered with apprehension as I was surrounded by IRA men. "It's a joke", I said hurriedly, "I'll tell you later".' ■ Likes reading, cricket and women. Dislikes pseuds, frozen food and Nigerian Airways. ■ Has three children and lives in London.

ROBBIE VINCENT
'Tea boy on the "Sunday People". . .'

BORN: In Felixstowe. EDUCATED: 'At skool'. FIRST JOB: Tea boy on the 'Sunday People'. Graduated to becoming a reporter on the 'London Evening Standard'. FIRST BROADCAST: On Radio North Sea International. Joined the BBC as a reporter. Presents *Robbie Vincent's Saturday Show* on BBC Radio London, and *Robbie Vincent's Talk Programme* on Radio 1. Has also presented their *Black Music Show*.

■ Most exciting moment of career: 'Meeting Tony Blackburn and giving him *MY* autograph.' ■ Likes greyhound racing. Dislikes losing greyhounds. ■ Lives in London.

JOHN WAITE
'A Hollywood extra in Alias Smith and Jones. . .'

BORN: 26th February 1951 in Stafford. Father a

shopkeeper. EDUCATED: In UK, America and Australia. FIRST JOB: BBC News Trainee. In 1970 was a Hollywood extra in several television shows including *Alias Smith and Jones*. FIRST BROADCAST: Westward TV in Plymouth in 1969 when he won National Student TV Award for the best amateur TV production. Has worked on such television shows as *Pebble Mill, Spotlight SW, Look North*. Radio programmes include *Today, Start the Week* and *You and Yours*. Does a weekly book programme and presents BBC Radio London's early morning current affairs programme *Rush Hour*.

■ Most exciting moment of career: 'Interviewing Fiona Richmond in her (un)dressing room at the Whitehall Theatre as she disrobed to go on stage in *Let's Get Laid*. ■ A moment to remember: 'The day I had a touch of the verbals in a news bulletin with a story of a dentist who was a "pioneer in 'Cowning and Crapping'." But it got me into the 'Evening Standard' Diary!' ■ Likes reading voraciously for his weekly book programme. Dislikes the 'Sunday Express' and southern beer.

■ Most exciting moment of career: 'When the Programme Controller at CBC told me he was going to give me a daily daytime programme.' ■ A moment to remember: 'My mother, who was never entirely convinced of the virtues of my becoming a broadcaster, decided on a whim to enquire after my state of repair from the Managing Director at CBC. After a glorious conversation, the content of which both parties refused to disclose, it came to light that my mother's parting shot had been to say "And by the way can you make sure he's wearing his vest". It not only came to my attention but the whole staff and half of South Wales . . . some sons do 'ave 'em.' ■ Likes playing acoustic guitars, football (supports Everton), sailing and golf (after a fashion). Dislikes snakes, marzipan and people leaving the top off the toothpaste. ■ Lives in South Glamorgan.

PETER WALKER
'Three caps for England. . .'
BORN: 17th February 1936 in Bristol. Father a journalist. EDUCATED: Highlands North High School, Johannesburg, S. Africa. FIRST JOB: Professional cricketer for Glamorgan County Cricket Club. Three caps for England v South Africa in 1960. Worked in the travel trade for four years and as a freelance journalist for overseas newspapers and periodicals. FIRST BROADCAST: In 1962, having been invited to audition for new BBC Wales Television programme *Sports Roundup*. This led to a gradual increase of work in the region on both television and radio. Programmes include *Good Morning Wales, Sportstime, A.M., Just for You, Dateline, Roundup, Today*. Makes regular contributions to BBC World Service, Also Forces Broadcasting and South African Broadcasting Corporation. As well as presenting *Sportstime, A.M.*, and *Just for You*, he's also a lecturer in Practical Broadcasting to post graduate students at College of Journalism Studies, U.C. Cardiff.

WILL WALDRON
'Make sure he's wearing his vest. . .'
BORN: 27th October 1957 in Liverpool. Father a barrister. EDUCATED: St. Edward's Grammar School, Liverpool. University of Wales. FIRST JOB: Part time research for Radio City in Liverpool. 'I did plenty of voluntary work, decorating old people's homes (even when they didn't want it), play schemes etc. and consequently met some amazing people.' FIRST BROADCAST: September 1979 doing the *Rock Review* on Radio City. Joined CBC in Cardiff and produced a weekly programme for the disabled which won a local award during the International Year of the Disabled. Is the Senior Presenter at CBC and presents their *Mid-Morning Show* Monday to Friday.

■ Most exciting moment of career: Making 'live' contributions into local and network programmes during General Elections. ■ Likes golf, squash, classical and jazz music, historical research. Dislikes amateur producers. ■ Married to Susan, has three children and lives in South Glamorgan.

GEOFFREY WAREHAM
'A meeting with rebels in the North Zambian bush. . .'
BORN: 22nd November 1929 in Newton Abbot, Devon. Father a commercial traveller. EDUCATED: Hele's School, Exeter. FIRST JOB: Reporter in the Exeter district office of 'The Western Morning News'. Moved to London as reporter/feature writer on the 'London Evening News'. Also worked on the 'Daily Express' and the 'Daily Mail'. FIRST BROADCAST: 1966 on BBC World Service. Joined the BBC staff in 1968 at a time when News division was expanding and needed people with journalistic experience rather than impressive academic qualifications. Has worked for television news and *Town and Around*. Is a reporter with BBC Radio news based in London and contributes to all the news and current affairs programmes.

■ Most exciting moment of career: 'The Kowezi massacre when I met the retreating rebels in the North Zambian bush after they'd massacred the whites in the Zaire copper mining community.' ■ A moment to remember: 'It was at the time when hostilities were about to break out between the Greeks and the Turks over Cyprus. I was on call at home, waiting for the word to fly out at a moment's notice. I listened to the one o'clock news on Radio 4 announcing that things had started and that Athens airport had been closed. My call came and I was told to catch the next plane to Athens. "Wait a minute, you've just said on your one o'clock news that Athens airport is closed" . . . "Oh did we?, then you'd better go to. . ."!' ■ Likes sailing, skiing and fishing. ■ Has two children and lives in London.

PETER WEST
'Rugby, tennis and cricket. . .'
BORN: 12th August 1920 in Addiscombe, Surrey. EDUCATED: Cranbrook School. FIRST JOB: On HM's Service in the Duke of Wellington's Regiment. From 1971–'82 was Rugby Football Correspondent of 'The Times'. FIRST BROADCAST: In 1947 which came about through an introduction from C.B. Fry. Between 1950 and 1983 worked regularly in television as a host for such programmes as *Come Dancing* and as a sports commentator, concentrating mainly on Rugby Union Football tennis and cricket. Has presented many programmes on radio over the years including *Housewives Choice*. Is now one of the commentary team at Wimbledon and is one of the BBC's commentators on Rugby Union.

■ Most exciting moment of career: 'England regaining the Ashes in 1953.' ■ Likes gardening. ■ Married to Pauline, has three children and lives in Devon.

WALLY WHYTON
'Skiffle, Folk and Country, hand in hand. . .'
BORN: 23rd September in London Father in building trade. EDUCATED: Regent Street

Polytechnic and Soho. FIRST JOB: Testing electric flying suits. Then progressed to more artistic pursuits . . . as a commercial artist, an advertising executive, a busker which led to him joining a skiffle group. Turning his attention to folk music, he became a folk singer and for a while a puppeteer. FIRST BROADCAST: As a member of a skiffle group in 1957. Skiffle, folk and country, they all go hand in hand and Wally has been associated with them all presenting such programmes as *Folk Room, Skiffle Club, Guitar Club, Country Meets Folk, Both Sides Now, Strings and Things*. Presents *Country Club* and *Folk Review* on Radio 2.

■ Most exciting moment of career: 'Broadcasting "live" from London to America on the occasion of the 50th birthday of the Grand Ole Opry on Station WSM in Nashville Tennessee. We were heard from Coast to Coast and it was exciting!' ■ A moment to remember: 'On my first ever compère job on *Folk Room*, which was "live", the main studio fuse blew putting us off the air. The talkback to the Producer also broke down. The main guests got the time wrong and turned up after we had started the programme. I swore it would be my first and last radio show!' ■ Likes photography, music and travel. ■ Married to Mary Christopher, has three children and lives in Middlesex.

JAMES WILKINSON
'I'm basically a shy, retiring bloke. . .'
BORN: 19th September 1941 in Winchester. Father a company director. EDUCATED: Westminster Abbey Choir School. Grammar School. King's College, London University and Churchill College Cambridge. FIRST JOB: Science Correspondent of the 'Daily Express'. FIRST BROADCAST: 1973 when he joined the BBC. Is now the BBC's Science and Air Correspondent and contributes to all the news and current affairs programmes. (As a choirboy at Westminster Abbey, he sang at the Coronation of Queen Elizabeth II.)

■ Married to Elisabeth Morse, has two sons and lives in London.

ALUN WILLIAMS
'Seen on the wireless many times. . .'
BORN: 26th August 1920 in Port Talbot, South Wales. Father a Presbyterian minister. EDUCATED: Llandeilo and Pontypridd Grammar Schools. University College, Cardiff. FIRST JOB: Ordinary Seaman in the Royal Navy. Later became an RNVR Intelligence Officer in the Far East. FIRST BROADCAST: In 1938 Children's Hour from Cardiff while a student at the University. After the war he applied for a job with the BBC as an Outside Broadcast Assistant, before being demobilized from the Navy. From there it was but a short step to the other side of the microphone and over the years he has become one of Wales' best known voices. He has commentated on the Queen's Coronation and other Royal occasions. Has covered the Olympic and Empire Games since 1956. Has done rugby and sporting commentaries all over the world, as well as introducing such programmes as *Forces Chance, Housewives' Choice* and *Worker's Playtime*. Apart from Saturday sporting commentaries, he has two weekly programmes on BBC Radio Wales, *Monday Morning Miscellany* and *On the Road*. On Radio Cymru the weekly programmes *Dewch am Dro* (Down Your Way) and *Alun Yn Galw*, in which he speaks to Welsh people all over the world.

■ Most exciting moment of career: 'Either the Submarine Escape Hatch outside broadcast at Gosport, or the day at Port Elizabeth in 1974 when the British Lions won the series against South Africa.' ■ A moment to remember: Man in Llanelli Street, 'Good morning, you are Alun Williams aren't you? . . . I thought so, I've seen you on my wireless many times'. (I do a bit of tele too.) ■ Likes golf, music and walking. Dislikes people who say 'You don't remember me do you' and champagne which hasn't been

on ice for at least one and a half hours.
■ Married to Perrie Hopkin-Morris, has three children and lives in South Glamorgan.

GERALD WILLIAMS
'BBC's first full time tennis correspondent. . .'

BORN: 24th June 1929 in London. Father a banker. EDUCATED: Queen Elizabeth Grammar School, Carmarthen. Croydon High School for Boys. FIRST JOB: Junior reporter on the 'Croydon Advertiser'. Later became Sports Reporter on the 'Leicester Mercury', 'The South Wales Echo', and the 'Daily Mail' where he also specialized as Tennis Correspondent. Has been Promotions Officer for the Lawn Tennis Association. FIRST BROADCAST: He can't remember, but was appointed by Cliff Morgan and Bob Burrows as the BBC's first full time Tennis Correspondent. Contributes to *Sport on 2* and *Sport on 4* and is responsible for the BBC's coverage of Wimbledon for both radio and television.

■ Most exciting moment of career: 'Covering the 1982 Commonwealth Games in Brisbane.' ■ Likes not answering the 'phone. Dislikes bigots. ■ Lives in Surrey.

MARK WILLIAMS
'Programmes on many of the local stations. . .'

BORN: 26th February 1954 in Maesteg, Glamorgan. Father an engineer. EDUCATED: Local Welsh School in Maesteg, Glamorgan. FIRST JOB: In a tyre warehouse. FIRST BROADCAST: November 1974 in Newcasle-upon-Tyne. 'My first break in radio was thanks to Peter Lewis who was then programme director of Metro Radio. ' Has worked for many of the local radio stations throughout the country, Radio City, Beacon Radio, Centre Radio Leicester and CBC Radio

in Cardiff. Has also, presented Rock programmes for CFNY in Toronto, and has broadcast on ABC Radio in Australia and Blue Danube Radio in Vienna.

■ Most exciting moment of career: 'Opening CBC Radio in Cardiff which was very moving!' ■ Likes travel, women, radio and people (but not in that order!) Dislikes big heads and Women's Lib. ■ Is a bachelor and lives in Leicestershire.

MARTYN WILLIAMS
'Where's the turkey then?. . .'

BORN: Pontyberem, Llanelli, Dyfed. Father a University Reader. EDUCATED: Atlantic College St. Donats. Trinity College, Hartford, USA. FIRST JOB: Television news presenter for HTV. Cardiff. Has produced *Good Morning Wales* for radio and took part in the Broadcasting from Parliament experiment in 1975. Has been the Welsh Rugby Correspondent for both the 'Sunday Telegraph' and the 'Guardian'. FIRST BROADCAST: A Welsh Schools broadcast when he was eight years old. He became a teenage actor in America and then a news presenter for WRTC/FM Connecticut. Returning to the UK, he met an editor in a pub who made him an offer he couldn't refuse and joined BBC Wales. Has contributed to and presented almost all of Radio Wales' output including sports programmes over the years. Is now the rugby commentator for Radio Wales and the regional reporter and presenter for *Breakfast Television*.

He also presents a *News Quiz* on Radio Wales.

■ Most exciting moment of career: 'Being the only man on the spot giving exclusive coverage when a Greek tanker, the 'Christos Bitas', already holed, started giving out a May-Day call.' ■ A moment to remember: 'After three years of doing rugby commentaries in Wales, I was asked to cover my first international at Cardiff Arms Park. Quite clearly an important occasion and naturally I spent the previous week mugging up all kinds of facts and figures. The match was between Wales and a visiting Australian team. The Australians had a hooker called Chris Carberry in their side. Whether it was nervousness or a complete mental blackout, I don't know, but for the first ten minutes I kept calling him Chris Cranberry, until my colleague and co-commentator Alun Williams whispered in my ear "Where's the turkey then?"'. ■ Likes reading and writing. Dislikes car mechanics, pineapple, liver and 'do it yourself' enthusiasts. ■ Married to Delyth, has two children and lives in Wales.

ROBERT WILLIAMS
'Shot down in Vietnam. . .'

BORN: 11th April in Cardiff. Father a factory manager. EDUCATED: Howard Garden's High School for Boys, Cardiff. FIRST JOB: Steelworker. Spent four years in the Army where he got a taste for journalism, editing several army magazines. On leaving the Army, he worked on several newspapers including the 'Daily Mail,' 'The Times,' and 'Daily Sketch'. Was also Parliamentary reporter for the Press Association. FIRST BROADCAST: On Radio Hong Kong in the late 50's while in the army. He worked as a television reporter for *Newsroom 2* on BBC 2 before joining the *World at One* team in 1972. Is a reporter and presenter for the *World at One* and *PM* on Radio 4, and has reported from many of the world's trouble spots . . . Vietnam, the Middle East, Northern Ireland and the Paris riots.

■ Most exciting moment of career: 'When the helicopter in which I was flying, was shot down in Vietnam. Luckily they missed the rotors, so we floated gently to earth.' ■ A moment to remember: 'When I was working on the 'Mansfield Reporter', I was sent to cover a concert given by a very famous pianist who shall be nameless. I knew nothing about piano music, and at the end of the recital, the whole audience, all six of them in Mansfield Towh Hall rose and applauded this chap, who then said "As you've given me such a warm reception and I have never played in Mansfield before, I'll play you a little piece of my own composition which some of you will think is a shocking mess." This was a good news peg, so I wrote a story about this internationally famous pianist who modestly described his own work as a shocking mess. Many years later, I was at Heathrow Airport working for BBC television, when I was asked to attend an impromptu press conference that was being given by this world famous pianist who was pasing through London. The conference was very boring until someone asked for his most amusing moment in England, at which point he pulled a press cutting from his wallet and proceeded to read my piece from the 'Mansfield Reporter'. "What I actually said" he explained, "was, some of you may find it a little Chopinesque." I did not reveal my identity!' ■ Likes farming (he runs a small farm) and photography. Dislikes everything . . . 'depending on my mood!'
■ Married to BBC producer Helen Wilson, has two sons and two daughters and lives in Norfolk.

ROY WILLIAMSON
'Dubbed "Raceaway Roy". . .'

BORN: August 1929 in London. Father a teacher. EDUCATED: Surbiton County Grammar School. FIRST JOB: In Hospital Administration. National Service 1947–1949. In 1956 joined the BBC as a studio manager. FIRST BROADCAST: Autumn 1957, the closing announcement for the *Reginald Leopold Orchestra* at the Palm Court of Grand Hotel on the BBC Light Programme. Other programmes include *London Lights with Tommy Trinder; My Song Goes Round the World; Saturday Concert Hall with Vilem Tausky and the BBC Concert Orchestra* and many *Light Music Festivals*. For many years was a newsreader on Radio 4. Has presented *Town and Around* for BBC Television. Is now a Radio 3 newsreader/announcer and presents a whole range of Radio 3 programmes including the *Bristol Lunchtime Concerts*.

■ A couple of moments to remember: 'At a refreshment trolley in the thick of a General Election night, mouth full, sandwich in one hand, tea in the other, being introduced by the DG to the Chairman of the Governors! I also recall the day I launched into a reading of *Today's Papers* having run with a script from the far end of Broadcasting House after a mix up with Ronald Fletcher and his copy of *Yesterday in Parliament*. After a couple of tries, I abandoned the attempt to read without breath and handed over to the *Today* presenter, John Timpson. The Corporation doctor chided my boss John Snagge for overworking his staff and a friend I hadn't seen for years wrote in asking if he should subscribe to a wreath. Finally the 'Daily Mail' dubbed me "Raceaway Roy".' ■ Likes sailing, (racing an 18 foot catamaran), woodwork and anything outdoors. Dislikes Radio 1, crab and lobster. ■ Married to Leila, has three sons and lives in Surrey.

while in the army and this led to a job as a studio manager with the BBC in June 1953. Over the years he has worked in both television and radio. He was Presentation Organizer for BBC Television, BBC North, television adviser in Benghazi, Libya, newsreader on Dubai Television, BBC Television drama director, producer of *Points of View*. He has written and read the *Morning Story* on Radio 4 and as an announcer has been associated with such programmes as *Stop the Week, All Gas and Gaiters, Morcambe and Wise, Hall of Fame*. Is now a newsreader/presenter on Radio 3 and is heard introducing the *Promenade Concerts*, the *Robert Mayer Concerts* and the *Morning Concert*.

■ Most exciting moment of career: 'There have been too many to pick one. . . Bringing together all the BBC and ITV television and radio networks for the Prime Minister's speech after the assassination of President Kennedy; working with Ingrid Bergman on *Hedda Gabler*; reading the news on Radio 2 with a story that didn't end, and having to make it up!' ■ A moment to remember: 'Being warned by personnel department when I joined the BBC in 1953 as a contract studio manager on *The Archers*, that the job would last only as long as the programme! Also giving Ray Moore his first job in radio . . . did I do the right thing?' ■ Likes writing, photography and listening to music. Dislikes yoghurt and people who aren't straightforward. ■ Married to Kate Willmott, has two sons and lives in Middlesex.

DAVID WILLMOTT
'Gave Ray Moore his first job in radio. . .'
BORN: 15th September 1931 in Windsor.
Father a master coach painter. EDUCATED:
Windsor County Boys School. FIRST JOB:
Assistant stage manager/actor with the Windsor Repertory Company. FIRST BROADCAST: 1950 on Forces Broadcasting Service Middle East. (Egypt). He applied to Forces Broadcasting

KATE WILLMOTT
'The sound man was praying in the corner of the studio. . .'
BORN: 7th October 1943 in Worthing, Sussex.
Father a company director. EDUCATED: St. Paul's Girls' School, Hammersmith. FIRST JOB:
Secretary to the managing director of a firm of industrial caterers. Has also been the fashion page assistant with the 'Daily Express' in

Manchester. FIRST BROADCAST: 1969 on Libyan Broadcasting Service. 'I became a radio announcer and programme maker in Benghazi, Libya during the 1969 revolution.' Now provides clips, interviews and trails for the promotion of all television programmes on both Network and Local radio. Has contributed to such programmes as BBC 2's *Late Night Line Up*, Radio 4's *Breakaway* and *Kaleidoscope* and Radio 2's *You and the Night and the Music.*

■ Most exciting moment of career: 'During Ramadan in Dubai when with five seconds to go to the programme junction, the sound man was still praying in the corner. Should I disturb him? ■ A moment to remember: 'I spent an evening with Dominick Beehan (brother of Brendan) having had strict instructions to keep him sober for a broadcast. I was only partly successful!' ■ Likes gardening, aerobics and the theatre. Dislikes tripe and men in flat hats who smoke pipes. ■ Married to David Willmott (qv), has two sons, Benjamin and Simon, and lives in Middlesex.

TERRY WOGAN
'A Gi-normous success. . .'

BORN: 3rd August 1938 in Limerick, Ireland. Father managing director of grocery and wine chain. EDUCATED: Well beyond his intelligence at Crescent College, Limerick. Belvedere, Dublin. [His words, not mine]. FIRST JOB: Bank clerk for five years . . . probably the best soiled-note sorter in the history of banking. He left under a cloud which has followed him ever since even to Barbados on holiday. FIRST BROADCAST: The *Cattle Market Report* on RTE Dublin, sometime in 1961, having answered an 'ad' for announcer/newsreader in an Irish newspaper. Since that auspicious occasion has gone on to become probably the biggest star radio has ever produced and as there is a limit to the size a book can be, I'm not going to try and list the programmes he has contributed to

over the years. Enough to say he has been a 'Gi-normous' success [Is that how you spell it?] and has become something of a national institution. He has been helping the nation to digest it's breakfast on Radio 2 for many years and will hopefully continue to do so until he runs out of steam. His face, not to mention his figure, adorns our television screens and his greatest asset is that Terry is Terry on or off air, success hasn't changed him.

■ Most exciting moment of career: 'Doing my first popular music programme *Hospital's Requests* on Irish Radio in 1961 when I was a mere boy broadcaster'. ■ A moment to remember: (Several) 'My very first ad lib when a record stuck on Irish Radio "I seem to be stuck in the middle of the Spanish Lady." "Announcing on Irish Television one Friday night when to fill in the gap between two programmes, we had a girl playing a guitar 'live' in the studio. I even remember her name Amanda Douglas. Me . . . 'And now let's meet Amanda" . . . CRASH . . . all the viewers can see are Amanda's two legs up in the air, she'd fallen off her stool. The floor manager holds up 4 fingers [I'm glad it was 4] which means 'talk for four minutes, and all I had prepared was 'Thank you Amanda'!" More recently on the first of the Wogan series on television I interviewed Marvin Hamlisch and told him how much I had enjoyed seeing his marvellous show *Company* to which he replied "Would you like me to impersonate Stephen Sondheim?"!'
■ Likes sitting, sleeping, reading, tennis and golf. Dislikes work. ■ Married to Helen, has three children and lives in Buckinghamshire.

PHIL WOOD
'Starring with Basil Brush. . .'

BORN: 9th April 1951 in Manchester. Father a representative. EDUCATED: Secondary Modern School. FIRST JOB: Assistant to production manager in an advertising agency. Rose to be a production manager, print buyer and account executive in several advertising agencies. FIRST BROADCAST: April 1974. Has presented just about all the daytime and night time shows on Piccadilly Radio. Also their *Rock Show* and the *USA Top 50* show. Is the presenter of Piccadilly Radio's *Afternoon/Drivetime* programme.

■ Most exciting moments of career: 'Appearing in two top pantomines . . . Aladdin with Russ Abbot, and Dick Whittington with Basil Brush. Practically doubling the *Breakfast Show* audience figures. Entertaining the European celebrities after the 1982 *Eurovision Song Contest* and interviewing my personal hero Alan Whicker.' ■ A moment to remember: 'I was the first to interview Julio Iglesias in the UK after his very first performance before an English audience. At the concert he sang 99% of his repertoire in Spanish and French, and only occasionally spoke a few words in broken English. The realization slowly dawned on me . . . he couldn't speak English. I went cold at the thought of my "live" interview the next day. I had a mental picture of Mr Iglesias sitting opposite me in the studio, taking an envelope out of his pocket and reading the script . . . it read "Hello Phil, you unshaven yob, and knickers to all your listeners." The floor opened, it swallowed me, it was all over. It was then the applause woke me from my torment. I was still at the concert. The next day on air arrived, his English was perfect, my Spanish was lousy, it went like clockwork. What a gentleman!' ■ Likes the cinema, video and eating at home with friends. Dislikes being unwell, the dentist and the day of the appointment. ■ Married to Lorraine, has two daughters and lives in Cheshire.

MIKE WOOLDRIDGE
'To Africa and back . . . again . . .'
BORN: 24th July 1947 in Surbiton, Surrey. Father a legal executive. EDUCATED: Bournemouth School for Boys. FIRST JOB: Reporter in the Lowestoft office of Eastern Counties Newspapers. (1965) In 1968 went to Uganda for two years as a volunteer with Voluntary Service Overseas, helping with the production of newspapers and other information material for the Ministry of Co-operatives. FIRST BROADCAST: A programme about International Co-operative Day on Radio Uganda in 1969. On his return from Uganda, he applied to the BBC for a job and from 1970–'78 worked in the BBC's External Services newsroom. Was a reporter for Radio News from 1978–'82 when he was appointed the BBC East Africa Correspondent.

■ Most exciting moment of career: 'Doing my first newspaper story in Lowestoft and taking up the post in East Africa.' ■ Married to Ruth, has three children and lives in Kenya.

STEVE WRIGHT
'The correct time but not the correct sponsor. . .'
BORN: 26th August 1954 in Greenwich, London. Father a company director. EDUCATED: Eastwood High School, Leigh, Essex. FIRST JOB: Telephone engineer. Has also been a singer. (Still is with a record to prove it!) Has worked as a production manager making radio ads: a shelf stacker and a journalist on local papers. From journalism he started to work for local radio news programmes. FIRST BROADCAST: Radio Atlantis in Belgium in 1975. He was in at the 'off' on Thames Valley Radio (see Mike Read's entry) where he presented various shows during his three-year stay. In 1979 he joined Radio Luxembourg presenting a nightly show and in January 1980 joined Radio 1. He does movie reviews and hosts his own daily show *Steve Wright in the Afternoon*. He is also one of the regular presenters of BBC 1's *Top of the Pops*.

■ A moment to remember: His first week at Radio Luxembourg and a time check . . . 'The correct time by my H. Samuel Ever-right watch is . . .' Only one thing wrong with that . . . the programme was being sponsored by Seiko Quartz Watches! Mike Read takes up the tale . . . 'One of the Luxembourg bosses Richard Swainson and myself had been out for a meal, and we tuned in to hear Steve's first show. I persuaded Richard to get on the telephone and play the heavy. . . ''There's a plane leaving first thing in the morning and you're going to be on it, etc.'' Poor Steve was horrified. Then I rang up and said ''Hugo Green of Seiko Quartz here . . .'' and suddenly Steve realized what was going on. ''You . . . . . Read, I'll get you for this if it takes for ever!''' ■ Likes photography, travel and the movies. Dislikes people who wear cravats. ■ Is a bachelor and lives in Oxon.

Radio Birmingham on the day of the Queen's Jubilee, I got into trouble with the management for gargling the National Anthem over the air. At Beacon Radio I fell off the studio chair, damaged my coccyx and couldn't sit down for a week. And finally after doing a two-way hand-over from the all speech breakfast programme on BBC Radio Oxford, I came to open up my Housewives programme with the first record to find that both Gram decks had blown a fuse and so i had to talk for ten minutes while the engineer repaired them. Things don't always go wrong for me, but when they do, they go very wrong!' ■ Likes motorbikes (owns a Kawasaki 400) and speedway cars. Dislikes Dallas, time wasting, wallies and Yorkie Bars. ■ Married to Diana, who works for BBC Radio 2, has two children and lives in Oxfordshire/Warwickshire.

PETER YORK
'When things go wrong, they go very wrong. . .'

BORN: 2nd May 1948 in Stoke-on-Trent. Father a works manager for Grosvenor China. EDUCATED: Lawton Hall, Cheshire. FIRST JOB: Disc jockey at the Embassy Club, Stoke-on-Trent for £1.00 per night. (1964). Has also been a Speedway Track announcer and commentator. FIRST BROADCAST: 1966 on the pirate station Radio City. That year he won the South Coast Disc Jockey of the Year award in the Melody Maker. Between 1968 and '71 presented the BBC *Radio 1 Club* and also had his own show on Saturday evenings on Radio 1. *The Album Show* for the BBC World Service in 1970. BBC Radio Birmingham (WM Radio now) breakfast show plus a weekly Sunday show from 1975–'79. Joined Beacon Radio in 1980, then moved back to the BBC and presents and produces the morning show for Radio Oxford.

■ Most exciting moment of career: 'Being asked to do a television Speedway commentary for ATV, three minutes before the first race at Birmingham and having to sprint from one side of the stadium to the other.' ■ A moment to remember: '(Many and all disastrous!) On BBC

JIMMY YOUNG
'They try to tell me I'm too young. . .'

BORN: 21st September. Christened Leslie Ronald. EDUCATED: East Dean Grammar School, Anderford, Gloucestershire. Was in the RAF 1939–'46. FIRST BROADCAST: *Songs at the Piano* on BBC Light Programme in 1949. Was a pianist/singer/bandleader in London's West End 1950–'51, the year he had his first hit record 'Too Young' which went to Number 1. His first broadcast as a DJ was in 1953 on *Flat Spin*. He presented *Housewife's Choice* in 1955, and that same year had two Number 1 records, *Unchained Melody* and *The Man From Laramie*, becoming the first British singer to have two consecutive Number 1's. He hosted several radio shows in the late 50's and early 60's . . . *The Night is Young, 12 o'clock Spin, Younger than Springtime, Keep Young.* [In the summer of '56 or '57 he was the star of a Sunday concert in the Villa Marina, Douglas, Isle of Man. He was backed on that occasion by the Ivy Benson Band with yours truly in the trombone section]. His last chart entry was *Miss You* in 1963. He joined Radio 1 when it opened in 1967 and in 1968 was named Radio Personality of the Year by the Variety Club of Great Britain. In 1973 he transferred to Radio 2 with a show each weekday morning. He became known for his highly individual presentation . . . the JY prog . . . BFN, bye for now, which drove some people to distraction but which gained him quite a reputation. There was the daily recipe from Raymondo . . . 'and this is what you do'! Who could have forseen how the *JY prog* would develop over the next decade? Raymondo has been banished to make way for Prime Ministers and Presidents. The *Jimmy Young Show* has travelled the world bringing current affairs to the masses who would never dream of tuning in to Radio 4's *The World at One*. In 1977 it came 'live' from the Soviet Union; in 1978 from Israel; in 1979 from Zimbabwe; in 1981 from Tokyo and in 1982 from Australia. In what has been a most extraordinary career, Mr Young OBE, (he received it in 1979) has come a long way from the hit parade.

■ Likes worrying. Dislikes being asked to fill in forms! ■ Lives in London.

MUSICIANS

CLIFF ADAMS
'Sing Something Simple. . .'
BORN: 1923 in Southwark. EDUCATED: Was a choirboy at St. Mary-le-Bow, the city church of Bow Bells fame, Studied piano and organ. FIRST JOB: Dance band pianist and then joined the RAF for the duration of the Second World War. After the war he established himself as an arranger working for Ted Heath, Cyril Stapleton, Eric Winstone and Stanley Black among others. In 1949 he formed the Stargazers who became the top vocal group of the 50s. Record hits included *I See the Moon, Broken Wings, Twenty Tiny Fingers* and *Close the Door.* They appeared in three Royal Command performances. In 1954 he formed the Adam Singers for the BBC *Show Band.* Television credits include *The Val Doonican Show, Something Old Something New,* and *Singalong Saturday. Sing Something Simple* was first broadcast on BBC Radio in 1959 and has been running continuously ever since on Radio 2. The Cliff Adam Singers have had several albums in the charts and have won a gold record. Cliff himself writes for television commercials and has won many international awards.

■ Most exciting moment of career: 'When I appeared with Duke Ellington and his Orchestra at Coventry Cathedral in 1966 and had the accolade of being invited by Ellington to a repeat performance in Oxford two years later.' ■ Is married with two daughters, one son and two grandsons, and lives in London.

RONNIE ALDRICH
'And The Squadronaires. . . one of the finest bands this country ever produced'.
BORN: 15th February 1916 in Erith, Kent. Father a shop manager. EDUCATED: Harvey Grammar School, Folkestone. Guildhall School of Music. Studied piano, also violin, clarinet and saxophone. FIRST JOB: Playing violin in the Folkestone Municipal Orchestra and playing saxophone in Phil Cozzi's Jazz Club. During the war joined the RAF and became pianist and arranger for what has been described as the finest swing band ever to be heard outside America – The Squadronaires. After the war he took over the leadership of the band which became known as Ronnie Aldrich and the Squadronaires. Has conducted and played with most of the Radio Orchestras over the years and has recorded and broadcast with his own orchestra as well as his own Continental Sextet. Now works as a freelance conductor, solo pianist and arranger with the strings of the BBC Radio Orchestra and is heard on just about all of Radio 2's music programmes including *You and the Night and the Music.*

■ Most exciting moment of career: 'For me, every time the red light goes on.'' ■ Likes music, sailing, good food and wine. Dislikes pretension. ■ Married to his business manager! Has one child and lives in the Isle of Man.

PETE ALLEN
'The Pete Allen Jazz Band, a family affair. . .'
BORN: 23rd November, 1954 in Newbury, Berkshire. Father a musician. EDUCATED:

Downs School, Compton, Nr. Newbury. He had music lessons at school but is also self taught. Plays the clarinet, alto and baritone saxophones. FIRST JOB: Selling musical instruments in a small music shop in Newbury. Then spent nearly three years as a Police Constable in the Thames Valley Force. In 1976 he left the police force to join the Rod Mason Jazz band and made his first broadcast with the band that year. Two years later he decided to take over the semi-pro jazz band that had been formed by his father Bernie Allen in 1971. Bernie remained with the band on banjo and vocals and since then they have appeared on numerous radio and television programmes, as well as working extensively on the Continent. They were the first ever jazz band to broadcast on Radio 2's *Friday Night is Music Night* and the first jazz band to be booked for the new series of *Music While You Work* on Radio 2. In fact they're probably the most played Dixieland Band on Radio 2! Programmes include the *Truckers Hour, Weekend Early Show, Weekend Late Show, Gloria Hunniford Show, Music Round Midnight* and *You and the Night and the Music.*

■ Most exciting moment of career: 'Being invited to the Greatest Dixieland Jazz Festival in the World, the tenth anniversary of the Sacramento Dixieland Jubilee, California, USA in May 1983. Playing with over 90 other bands from around the world in front of an audience around the 200,000 mark.' Peter Clayton once said of the band 'The Pete Allen band is totally useless if all you want to do is be miserable.' ■ Likes all types of sport, television and radio and Indian cooking. Dislikes cooked cheese and warm beer. ■ Married to Trish and lives in Wiltshire.

CAROLE ALLUM
'Began singing in pubs. . .

BORN: 21st October 1941. Father an insurance broker. EDUCATED: Brentwood County High School for Girls. Took piano lessons at school and gained an 'O' level in music. 'I'm the worst

pianist in the world.' FIRST JOB: At 17, modelling coats and suits in a Bond Street fashion house. Made her first broadcast in February 1980. Has sung with the Dave Shepherd Quintet, Brian Lemon Trio, Keith Smith's Hefty Jazz and the Mike Sammes Singers. Is heard on Radio 2's *You and the Night and the Music*, the *Weekend Late Show* and the *Early Show.*

■ Most exciting moment of career; 'My first broadcast.' 'I didn't take up singing professionally until September 1978, after many years as a housewife and mother. I began singing in pubs with trumpeter Freddie Randall, and made a demo tape which I sent to the BBC in December 1979. A couple of months later I got a trial broadcast and I've been broadcasting ever since.' ■ Likes sewing and knitting. ■ Has three children and lives in Essex.

KENNETH ALWYN
'Over 30 years of broadcasting. . .'

BORN: 28th July 1927, in London. Father a Civil Servant. EDUCATED: John Ruskin School, Croydon. Royal Academy of Music, London. He plays piano, organ, viola and trombone. FIRST JOB: Announcer and Conductor of the Radio Orchestra on Radio Malaya in Singapore. He made his first broadcast on BBC Radio in 1952 and since then has conducted all the BBC Orchestras apart from the Symphony Orchestra. He was principal conductor for the

Royal Ballet at Covent Garden for seven and a half years, and has also conducted such successful West End Musicals as *Camelot, Half a Sixpence* and *My Fair Lady*. He is probably best known for his frequent appearances on *Friday Night is Music Night* but contributes to many other radio programmes, such as *Melodies for You* and *Lights of London*.

■ Most exciting moment of career: 'My first pay cheque'. ■ A moment to remember: 'During a short spell in New Zealand as conductor of the New Zealand Choral Society, someone in New Zealand Broadcasting thought I was an actor! When I presented myself for an audition, he handed me a radio script of Anouilh's play *Point of Departure* (A modern Orpheus) I read 'Death', got the part and a few others as well! I must have been terrible but at least I was terribly "French"!' ■ Likes flying and jogging. Dislikes people who say they're going to do something, and don't. ■ Married to actress Mary Law, has two children and lives in Sussex.

COLIN ANTHONY
'There was this 'bird' with big. . .'

BORN: Bath, Somerset. Father a fire/ambulance man. EDUCATED: Moorfields Junior School. Bath Art School. West of England College of Art. Private tuition piano and singing. Guildhall School of Music. FIRST JOB: Fronting his own band at the Storyville Club, Cologne and Frankfurt, Germany. In 1979 sang the lead role in the rock musical *Rock-a-bye Becket* at the Cockpit Theatre in London. He made his first broadcast many moons ago on the Dave Lee Travis Show on Radio 1 with Colin Anthony's Cycles. Since then has sung with all the BBC Orchestras in London and the regions and can be heard regularly on just about every music programme broadcast on BBC Radio 2. Has also sung extensively on the Continent, including the British entries in the Nordring Radio competitions. Is one of the regular guest vocalists on Radio 2's Big Band Special. As well

as doing a lot of radio, he finds time to run his own small band which plays for dances and parties. He's also a talented songwriter and has had many songs published, several of which he has sung himself on the air.

■ Most exciting moment of career: 'There was this 'bird' with big. . . Oh, sorry, do you mean professionally? . . . well, working with the Beatles.' ■ A moment to remember: 'Well, there was this "bird" with the big . . . sorry! I walked on the stage in Malmo, Sweden, facing an audience to perform a new song. The programme was going out "live" to eight countries. When I put the ear-phones on they immediately fell apart around my head – the sound-pieces around my chest. I couldn't hear a thing! Ahhh!' ■ Likes music and sailboarding. ■ Lives in Surrey.

JOHNNY ARTHEY
'A collection of almost 50 gold discs. . .'

BORN: 24th September, in London. Father an engineer. EDUCATED: Royal Liberty School, Essex. Is a self taught pianist. FIRST JOB: Pianist with a Military Band Concert Orchestra during National Service. His first broadcast was with his own orchestra on the BBC Light programme in 1962. Has worked for record companies as a musical director/arranger, and has provided the backing for many a hit record both in this country and on the Continent. For BBC he conducted The Soul Train Orchestra 1972-76; The Softly Sentimental orchestra 1975-78 and since then has been a regular conductor of the BBC Radio Orchestra. He also broadcasts with the Johnny Arthey Orchestra and can be heard on just about every music programme on Radio 2.

■ Most exciting moment of career: 'Conducting at the "Olympia" in Paris'. ■ Likes ufology. Dislikes junk food. ■ Married to Sylvia, has two children and lives in Surrey.

VIC ASH
'Enjoys the late night broadcasts. . .'

BORN: 9th March 1930, in London. EDUCATED: London. Originally a self taught musician but then took private lessons. Plays all the saxes, clarinets and flutes. FIRST JOB: With the Kenny Baker Sextet 1950-53. During the 60s and 70s he toured with his own group on the modern jazz circuit. Made his first broadcast in 1951. He has played with Vic Lewis and Johnny Dankworth among others. Now does a lot of freelance session work and records with his own quartet for Radio 2's *Early Show, Round Midnight, Jazz Club* and *You and the Night and the Music.*

■ Most exciting moment of career: 'Playing in the orchestras that have backed Frank Sinatra on all his UK, European and Middle East tours since 1970.' 'I particularly enjoy late night broadcasts with my quartet as these are the rare times I can play the standard tunes of the great composers like Gershwin, Porter and Kern.' ■ Likes listening to records, seeing shows and watching TV. Dislikes onions. ■ Married to Helen, has two step children and lives in London.

KENNY BAKER
'Plays and sings at the same time. . . well almost!'

BORN: 1st March 1921, in Withernsea, East Yorkshire. Father a shoemaker. EDUCATED: Local primary school. Had music lessons from his mother. Plays trumpet, cornet and flugel horn. FIRST JOB: Playing at local gigs. In 1939 he joined the Lew Stone Orchestra, appeared at the Palace Theatre in *Under Your Hat* with Jack Hulbert and Cicely Courtneidge and on the *Road Show* with Sandy Powell. Made his first broadcast with Lew Stone in 1940. Has played with Ambrose, Jack Hylton, Geraldo, Syd Milward, Maurice Winnick, Ted Heath, Ken Johnson, George Shearing and Robert Farnon. 1951-58 had his own show on radio, *Listen to My Music* with Kenny Baker's Dozen. Can be heard on most of Radio 2's music programmes including *You and the Night and the Music* with this own quartet. Has the astonishing ability to sing and play at the same time – well almost!

■ Most exciting moment of career: 'All of it! But especially being demobbed at the end of the war after six years in the RAF and joining the newly formed Ted Heath Orchestra on lead trumpet.'' ■ Likes gardening and DIY. Dislikes bad cooking. ■ Married to Susan, has one daughter and lives in Hertfordshire.

CHRIS BARBER
'1959 was a great year. . .'

BORN: 17th April 1930, in Welwyn, Hertfordshire. Father a statistician. EDUCATED: King Alfred School and St Paul's School, London. Guildhall School of Music. He plays double bass, trombone, trumpet and baritone horn. FIRST JOB: before becoming a musician, he worked as a life assurance clerk. He thinks his first paid job as a professional musician was probably with Beryl Bryden. Has also played with George Webb and Ken Colyer, before forming the Chris Barber Jazz Band. Made his first broadcast in 1950 on a BBC *Jazz Club.* Has had several radio series – *Chris Barber's Bandbox* in 1958; *Trad Tavern* in 1961. Was the castaway on *Desert Island Discs* in 1959, the same year that he had a hit record with *Petit Fleur*. Makes regular *Jazz Club* appearances on Radio 2.

■ Most exciting moment of career: 'My first concert in New Orleans in 1959.' ■ Likes motor racing, record collecting and snooker. ■ Lives in London.

MADELEINE BELL
'A tap on her shoulder...'

BORN: 23rd July 1942, in Newark, New Jersey, USA. Father a floral decorator. EDUCATED: Miller Street School, Newark, South Side High School, Newark, N.J. FIRST JOB: A meat wrapper in a supermarket at 16. 'The day I left school I got a job''. She started singing in churches and on street corners. Joined her first gospel group at 14 and did gospel gigs at weekends. Made her first broadcast with a gospel group in a church where there was a radio broadcast every Sunday night. She came to the UK in 1962 in a musical called *Black Nativity*. Made her first broadcast here on *Saturday Club* with Brian Matthew in 1964. Joined the vocal group Blue Mink in October 1969 and stayed with them for almost five years. Is now one of this country's top session singers and broadcasts regularly with the BBC Radio Orchestra/Radio Big Band. Programmes include the *Joe Loss Show, Nordring Radio Festival 1981*, and she is heard on many of Radio 2's music programmes including *Big Band Special*.

■ Most exciting moment of career: 'I was appearing in a charity show at the Theatre Royal, Windsor and after the first half I had changed ready for the finale and was standing side stage watching Morecambe and Wise when somebody came through the door behind me and tapped me on the shoulder. It was Prince Charles and he said how pleased he was to meet me. That for me, being an American, was a very exciting moment.' ■ A moment to remember: 'In 1981 I did a thirteen week series on Radio 1 on Sundays from 10am to 12 noon.

I was also appearing at the Talk of the Town which meant that I didn't get home until 4am on a Sunday morning, so I gave up all idea of going to bed and sat up answering my fan mail, then took a long bath and left for the studio at 7.30am. One Sunday, Paul Williams said to me "You're sounding really tired, what you should do is to smile when you talk into the microphone." So, there I was with a big grin prancing around the studio to make myself sound awake ... and it worked!' ■ Likes eating, cooking and watching television. Dislikes getting up in the morning and phoney people who are always posing. 'I don't like to be seen too much, maybe that's why I've never become a big star.' ■ Lives in Middlesex.

ACKER BILK
'Bowler hat and waistcoat still very much in evidence...'

BORN: 28th January 1929 in Pensford, Avon. (It was Somerset then!) Father a cabinet maker. EDUCATED: Local school in Pensford, where he had piano and recorder lessons. He had heard a visiting preacher (his family were Methodists) playing the recorder when he was 4 years old and from then on he pestered his mother until she bought him one. Later he taught himself to play the clarinet. FIRST JOB: Working in Wills Tobacco factory in Bristol for 24/- a week. Has also worked as a blacksmith and a builder's labourer. As a member of the village boxing team, he never lost a bout but did lose his two front teeth. This and the loss of a finger in a snow sledging accident accounts for his instantly recognizable style of clarinet playing according to Acker! It was in 1948, with the Royal Engineers in the Canal Zone, that he borrowed a clarinet and started copying the sounds he heard on records. A spell in the Glasshouse for sleeping on guard duty, gave him lots of time to practise. When he was demobbed he joined Ken Colyer's Band in London, but hated London so much that he returned to Bristol and formed his first

Paramount Jazz Band. FIRST BROADCAST: In 1954 for producer Brian Patten in Bristol. Since then has been heard on just about every music programme on the Light Programme and then Radio 2: *Pop Score, Jazz Score, Music While you Work, You and the Night and the Music, Late Show, Early Show* etc. His own show *Acker's 'Alf 'Our* has proved to be one of the most popular of the evening music programmes on Radio 2. His own original hit *Stranger on the Shore* which in 1961 was the first ever record to be Number 1 simultaneously in the UK and the USA, wrote him a meal ticket for life. It remained in the charts for over a year.

■ Most exciting moment of career: 'Certainly my most satisfying moment was when Duke Ellington recorded *Stranger on the Shore*. "Acker", by the way, means "mate" or "friend" in the Somerset dialect which is a pretty good summing up of Mr Bernard Stanley Bilk! ■ Likes playing darts, fishing and snooker. Dislikes pain! ■ Married to Jean Hawkins, has a son and a daughter, Peter and Jenny, and lives in Hertfordshire.

more than 95 films. 'It's all music, music to be studied and digested and made available for others to enjoy, and I deplore the closed minds and musical bigotry which exists in many quarters. Naturally, there are many different levels and only a fool would suggest that there is the same emotional intellectual depth in a popular movie score as there is in a Brahms symphony, but this doesn't mean that the movie score is valueless and shouldn't be enjoyed on its own level. Why not learn to appreciate and enjoy both?'

GERRY BOYCE
'The excitement of the next gig. . .'
BORN: 6th July 1933 in Peterborough. Father an engineer. EDUCATED: Kings College, Peterborough. Studied the piano from 10 to 15 and from then on was self taught, which included teaching himself to play the drums. FIRST JOB: 1959 at the American Club, Lancaster Gate having spent eight years as a semi-pro in Peterborough. At the local jazz club there, had backed all the well known British stars including Tubby Hayes, Don Rendell, Vic Ash, Joe Harriot etc. Made his first broadcast around 1966 as a Nigel Brooks Singer(!) in *Fanfare*, a 'live' show from the Camden Theatre. Has played drums with Ted Taylor, Bob Miller, Don Lang, Pete Winslow, Ian Cameron and Gordon Langford. Has contributed to most of Radio 2's music programmes over the years not only as a drummer and leader of his own group but also as an arranger.

■ Most exciting moment of career: 'The next gig'. ■ Likes reading, writing, boozing and collecting jazz tapes. Dislikes synthesized theme tunes. ■ Married to singer Lee Gibson (qv), has one daughter Claire and lives in Hertfordshire.

STANLEY BLACK
'I deplore the musical bigotry that exists in some quarters. . .'
BORN: In London. Started piano lessons at the age of seven and at the age of 12 had one of his compositions broadcast by the BBC Symphony Orchestra. In 1944, on being demobbed from the RAF, he was appointed conductor of the BBC Dance Orchestra and over the next nine years notched up some 3,000 broadcasts. Has also composed many theme tunes and incidental music for various radio series. He is now a regular guest conductor of the BBC Concert Orchestra and also records with his quartet for many of Radio 2's music programmes. He is one of those rare musicians who enjoys playing all kinds of music whether it be playing jazz piano, conducting a symphony orchestra or composing the scores of

BRIAN BROCKLEHURST
'Have bike, will travel. . .'

BORN: 16th August in Buxton Derbyshire. Father a musician. EDUCATED: 'Yes!' Born into a musical family, he learnt to play piano, guitar and drums. Now plays double bass. FIRST JOB: Playing guitar and piano in a dance band at the Pavilion Gardens, Buxton at the age of 12. Joined the Merchant Navy as a Radio Officer. Made his first broadcast playing guitar with his own group around 1947. Has played with Ken Mackintosh, Jack Parnell, Humphrey Lyttleton and Ted Heath. As a session musician has backed Marlene Dietrich on her last tour of the UK, Shirley Bassey, Tommy Steele, Petula Clark, Simon and Garfunkel. Has played with many of the jazz greats including Jack Teagarden, Willie 'the Lion' Smith, Pee Wee Russell, Kai Winding and Buck Clayton. Has appeared on literally hundreds of radio shows over the years such as *Country Meets Folk* (seven years), *Round the Horne* (all of them), *I'm Sorry I'll Read That Again*, *Jazz Club*, *Music While You Work* and all of Radio 2's music programmes. Fronts his own line-up, Brian Brocklehurst and Brocade, which is heard regularly on *You and the Night and the Music*, the *Early Show* on Radio 2, and on Capital Radio. Other programmes include *Friday Night is Music Night* on Radio 2 and *Play School* on BBC 1. Has made something of a name for himself by cycling around London with his double bass slung on his back! Runs his own music company, Brock Music.

■ Most exciting moment of career: 'Working with Mel Torme, Lena Horne, Josh White, José Feliciano, Marlene Dietrich and the Jazz Greats was extremely stimulating to say the least!'
■ A moment to remember: 'Programme. . . *Pebble Mill at One*, "live". My brief: to cycle down Pebble Mill Road with my bass and into the studio, dismount, unzip (the bass cover) and join the group already playing, then launch into the following dialogue. . ., Leader to me "Where have you been, we're 'live' you know". "Ah", I replied, "it was very foggy on the M1 this morning and then I got lost on the one-way system here in Brimingham, Bi-sically speaking, that's my explanation." And then we all finished the number together. Later that week, in a hostelry near Maida Vale Studios in London, a chap who had seen the show said to me "I've seen you charging around town on your bike with your bass, but I never realized you pedalled up to Birmingham with it." "Ah, yes." I replied; "but I always check with Michael Fish at the wet [Met.] office to see if there's a following wind before I go!" Which explanation seemed to satisfy him!' ■ Likes photography, planes n' playing n' phood! Dislikes — 'don't like to mention them.' ■ Married to music! and lives in London.

BOB BURNS
'I'm really serious about my quartet. . .'

BORN: 16th May 1923 in Toronto, Canada. Father a jeweller/musician. EDUCATED: P.C.I. Ontario. Royal Academy of Music and Royal College of Music. FIRST JOB: In his father's orchestra, playing second alto to his sister and doubling on violin for solos. His father had taught him to play the saxophone which he also played with Pop Brownlee's Circus. He came to Britain in 1942 and studied clarinet at the Royal College of Music, achieving his ARCM. He broadcast regularly in Canada, but first broadcast for the BBC was with the Royal Canadian Airforce Band in 1942. After the war he played with Ambrose, Ted Heath, Geraldo and George Melachrino as well as performing with the London Symphony Orchestra, the Royal Philharmonic Orchestra and Sinfonia of London. Plays with Benny Goodman on his continental Big Band tours and also does chamber music tours with John White and Gavin Bryars. He played on all the *Goon Shows* and many other light entertainment shows on radio including *Hancock's Half Hour*. Has also made many chamber music broadcasts. Has been leading his own quartet since 1951 and can be heard regularly on all the Radio 2 music shows such as *You and the Night and the Music,*

■ Most exciting moment of career: 'Walking onto the platform of the Royal Festival Hall and performing a concerto which had been written for me by Robert Farnon, accompanied by 85 members of the Royal Philharmonic Orchestra.' ■ A moment to remember: 'When a producer advanced to a bandleader who had just played a solo on the rehearsal, "You are flat" which drew the reply . . . "OK, I'll stand back a little!"'. ■ Likes his quartet. Dislikes snobs, bigots, hypocrites and anyone who doesn't like his quartet! ■ Has one son and two daughters and lives in London.

COLIN CAMPBELL
'A musical family. . .'

BORN: 3rd May 1940 in Birmingham. Father a foreman metalworker. EDUCATED: Moseley School of Art, Birmingham. He studied the piano privately from the age of 8 to 16 and studied the clarinet from 12 to 16 at the Birmingham School of Music. Plays the piano, synthesizer, organ, sax and clarinet. FIRST JOB: As part of a multi-instrumental group known as the Merry Macs, playing throughout the Midlands 1952-56. After leaving school he formed a double act with a girl called Christine (she later became his wife) and they toured in variety shows as Christine and Colin Campbell. Made his first broadcast on the Welsh Home Service in *Seaside Nights* in 1958. Spent four years as pianist/arranger for television's *New Faces.* Has made numerous broadcasts as the conductor of the Midland Radio Orchestra. Radio series include *Keep it Maclean* with his own group, The Colin Campbell Clan. Records with his own orchestra for such programmes as the *Early Show* on Radio 2 and was the Musical Director of the BBC's 1982 pantomime, *Dick Whittington.* As a freelance MD/arranger/ pianist, backs many stars on the air in a wide variety of programmes.

■ Most exciting moment of career: 'When I was MD for Vera Lynn at the Bluejays Baseball Ground in Toronto in 1980 and 18,000 people stood up at the end of her act and sang *Land of Hope and Glory.*' ■ The Campbell family are all musical – wife Christine had a record in the charts in 1962 and son Kevin was a drummer with the musical *Call Me Madam* starring Noele Gordon. ■ Likes skiing, sea fishing and golf. Dislikes punk music. ■ Married to Christine, has one son, Kevin.

ELAINE CAROLE
'It was so thrilling. . .'

BORN: 5th March in Havering-atte-Bower, Essex. Father a managing mechanical engineer. EDUCATED: Chase Cross Girls School, Essex. Voice training at the Bush Davies Stage School. She plays the piano and gained an 'O' level in music at school. FIRST JOB: 'At the age of 14 when I sang *Charmaine* and *Doh-ray-me* for the local old-age pensioners' Christmas party.' Made her first broadcast on Radio 2's *Round Midnight* in 1978. Since then has recorded regularly with the BBC Radio Orchestra, the Brian Dee Trio, the Frank Stafford Trio/Quartet and is heard on such programmes as *Round Midnight, You and the Night and the Music* and *Variety Club,* all on Radio 2. Television credits include *Opportunity Knocks, Seaside Special* and *Starburst.* Has also played most of the major entertainment venues in the country.

■ Most exciting moment of career: 'My very first performance with a large orchestra. As a singer who up until then had appeared only with small groups and bands, it was so thrilling.' ■ Likes tennis, crochet and music. Dislikes incompetence, unprofessionalism and uninteresting conversation.
■ Married to Ateyan and lives in Essex.

RONNIE CARROLL
'A very long three minutes. . .'

BORN: 18th August 1934 in Belfast, Northern

Ireland. Father a plumber. EDUCATED: Elementary School in Belfast. Also took singing lessons. FIRST JOB: Machine operator. He also worked as an auctioneer's assistant, a job that lasted one hour because he lost his voice! Made his first broadcast in 1956 he thinks! Since then has made hundreds on both radio and television.

■ Most exciting moment of career: 'Hasn't arrived yet, although the Royal Command was good and my first date at the London Palladium.' ■ A moment to remember: 'It was a "live" outside broadcast from a theatre. I was singing a song which had a lot of verses and I hadn't bothered to learn the words. Someone opened a side door and the music flew from my hands and disappeared down a crack in the stage. I spent the next three minutes singing any words that came to mind. It was a *very long* three minutes.' ■ Likes writing children's stories, golf and poodling around. Dislikes politicians, VAT and noise. ■ Has two sons and lives in London.

FRANK CHACKSFIELD
'The most promising new orchestra of 1953...'
BORN: 9th May 1914 in Battle, Sussex. Father an engineer. EDUCATED: Battle and Langton Schools, Sussex. Studied organ under the late J.R. Sheehan-Dare. Plays both piano and organ. FIRST JOB: Gigs with various bands in Sussex and Kent. Has had a resident band at Hilden Manor Road House, Tonbridge, Kent and L'Etacq Hotel, Jersey. His first broadcast was *Original songs at the Piano* from Glasgow. He conducted both Henry Hall's Orchestra and the Geraldo Orchestra. When he formed his own line up in 1953 it won an award as the most promising new orchestra. He was awarded two Gold Discs for his recording of *Limelight* and a Gold Disc and Baton d'Honneur for *Ebb Tide*. Has recorded over 100 LPs and numerous singles. Has also conducted the music for several films. his orchestra can be heard on *The Splendour of Strings*, on Radio 2.

■ Most exciting moment of career: 'My first trip to America with *Limelight* and *Ebb Tide* in the Top 10.' ■ Likes music. Dislikes curry and Chinese food. ■ Married to Jeanne Lehmann and lives in Kent.

GEORGE CHISHOLM
'Not to be confused with GC the trombonist...'
BORN: 19th January 1947 in Newcastle-upon-Tyne. Father a telephonist. EDUCATED: St. Mary's Technical School. Plays trumpet, flugel horn, piano. Self taught. FIRST JOB: With Val Marral at Butlins. Has also played with Maynard Ferguson, Thad Jones, Bert Kaempfert, John Dankworth, EBU Big Band and many others. Made his first broadcast in 1970 with John Williams Octet in Jazz in Britain. Has played on many of the radio variety shows, Morecambe & Wise, Arthur Askey etc. Makes regular appearances on *Jazz Club* and can be heard on just about every music programme on Radio 2.

■ Most exciting moment of career: Representing the UK in Oslo in 1974 in the EBU Big Band. ■ Likes swimming, and reading. Dislikes shopping. ■ Married to Irene and has one son.

GEORGE CHISHOLM
'The best broadcast we'd ever done. . .'

BORN: 29th March 1915 Glasgow. Father an engineer. EDUCATED: ? Glasgow! Plays trombone, euphonium, baritone, piano, vibes and xylophone etc; 'I'm mostly self taught, with some lessons from the local LRAM on piano, and trombone lessons from Jimmy Chalmers who was the solo trombonist with the SCWS Band in Glasgow.' FIRST JOB: 'Playing the piano in a Glasgow cinema at the age of 14, for silent films . . . fitting the appropriate music to the action on the screen.' He played in Greens Playhouse ballroom in Glasgow, West End Cafe, Edinburgh and the Tower Ballroom in Glasgow, before moving to London in 1936 and getting a job in the Nest Club (naughty West End). Made his first broadcast from Glasgow in approximately 1932. Has played with Ambrose, Lew Stone, Harry Roy, Jack Harris, Benny Carter (in Holland), Fats Waller and Louis Armstrong. From 1939-50 was a member of the famous Squadronaires Dance Band along with several other ex-Ambrose sidemen. He played with the BBC Showband 1950-55. Has made valuable contributions to many famous radio series, including *Band Wagon, It's That Man Again* (ITMA) *Much Binding in the Marsh, The Goon Show* etc: Unfortunately for jazz lovers, his great talent for comedy has somewhat overshadowed his even greater musical talent, because he is probably the best jazz trombonist this country has ever produced. He is heard with his Gentlemen of Jazz on many of the music programmes on Radio 2, including *You and the Night and the Music.*

■ Most exciting moment of career: 'Playing and recording with Benny Carter and Coleman Hawkins in Holland; recording with Fats Waller; and playing with Louis Armstrong at the Royal Festival Hall during the 1950s.'
■ A moment to remember: 'Doing a broadcast with the Squads from Aberdeen on New Year's Eve 1947 . . . much whisky flowing. We were "issued" with an OB announcer and balance engineer, both of whom passed out before the transmission. We took over the announcements as it was a "live" broadcast and afterwards went round to the side room to ask the balancer how it had gone, only to find him slumped over the controls fast asleep. We were told later that it was the best broadcast we'd ever done and that the balance was excellent! (He'd obviously switched the controls to "George"!)' ■ Likes arranging, orchestrating and has a vague leaning towards DIY. Dislikes intolerance and impatience. ■ Married to Etta, has three children and lives in Bedfordshire.

ANGELA CHRISTIAN
'Please say hello to the ansaphone. . .'

BORN: 20th April 1948 in Edgware, Middlesex. Father a caterer. EDUCATED: Grammar School, Twickenham. Secretarial College in Kingston, Surrey and Torquay, Devon. Had no formal musical training but sang in local choirs. Taught herself to play the guitar. FIRST JOB: Resident singer/guitarist with a trio at the Imperial Hotel, Torquay in 1965. Also spent a year singing at the New Stanley Hotel in Nairobi and six months in a hotel in Bahrain. Toured with the Syd Lawrence Orchestra for a year and has also appeared with the Don Lusher Big Band. Made her first broadcast, she thinks, in March 1966 in an OB from the Imperial Hotel, Torquay with the Steve Evans Trio for *Swingalong* on the BBC Light Programme. Broadcasts regularly with the BBC Radio Orchestra, and the Brian Dee Trio, and can be heard on most of Radio 2's music programmes, including *String Sound* and *You and the Night and the Music.*

■ Most exciting moment of career: 'My first "live" concert for radio, part of the BBC Festival of Light Music from the Royal Festival Hall in June 1979, with the Syd Lawrence Orchestra. Also my trip to Nairobi.' ■ Likes reading, sewing and dressmaking. Dislikes housework, tripe and onions, and people who hang up without saying anything when her Ansaphone answers the telephone. ■ Is single and lives in Avon.

ALAN CLARE
'Played in clubs around the world. . .'

BORN: Walthamstow, London. Father a clerk.
EDUCATED: Roger Asham School and Eliot
Wittingham School, Walthamstow. Plays
piano, piano accordion and organ. Had piano
lessons but is mostly self taught. FIRST JOB:
Playing piano in the Orford Social Club at the
age of 11. Has played in many clubs around the
world including the Coconut Grove in Palm
Beach, California, and the Cotton Club. While
in the army appeared in *Stars in Battledress*.
Has also worked for Leeds Music Publishers.
Made his first broadcast in *Piano Playtime* and
has been heard on *Variety Bandbox, Ignorance
is Bliss* and *Kings of the Keyboard*. Has played
with Cab Calloway, Sid Millward and the
Nitwits, Stephane Grappelli, Maurice Winnick,
Jack Payne, Ted Heath, Harry Parry and Sid
Phillips. Now has his own group The Alan
Clare Trio which broadcasts regularly and can
be heard on Radio 2's *You and the Night and
the Music*.

■ Most exciting moment of career: 'Getting to
know Billy Strayhorn and hearing my own
compositions sung and played on the radio by
such stars as Eartha Kitt, Cleo Laine, John
Williams and Peter Sellers.' ■ A moment to
remember: 'Five minutes to go before a "live"
broadcast when the pedal fell off the piano. The
producer and the balancer pushed a piano from
an adjoining studio and got it to me with 20
seconds to go!' ■ Likes music, fishing and
reading. Dislikes snobs, bigots, drunks,
parsnips and getting old. ■ Married to Bloom,
has a daughter and a son and lives in London.

LORNA DALLAS
'Commended by the Queen Mother. . .'

BORN: Illinois, USA. Father a lumber dealer.
EDUCATED: Voice and Opera Major at Indiana
University School of Music, Honours Graduate
Advanced Degree. Also plays piano, violin,
percussion. FIRST JOB: Singing ambassadress for
Coca-Cola after winning their national talent
contest, 'Talentsville USA'. Has been a
campaign worker in the election of the
Governor of Indiana and was the principal
artiste with Metropolitan Opera National
Company singing at Lyndon Johnson's
inauguration ball in Washington DC. Her first
broadcast in the USA was on The Baptist Hour;
in the UK it was for the BBC World Service in
June 1972. Has sung with the Stanley Black
Quartet, BBC Radio Orchestra, BBC Concert
Orchestra, Stan Kenton, Peter Knight
Orchestra, Iain Sutherland Orchestra, Norrie
Paramor, NBC TV Orchestra and John
Dankworth. Radio 2 programmes include the
Festival of Light Music from the Royal Festival
Hall, *Friday Night is Music Night, Among Your
Souvenirs, Variety Club, Charlie Chester,
Round Midnight* and the *Weekend Early Show*.
Recent television credits include *Star Brass* and
the *Good Old Days*.

■ Most exciting moment of career: 'Being
commended by the Queen Mother after singing
for her in the 1982 Royal Variety
Performance.' ■ A moment to remember:
'Minutes before I was to make my début at the
Royal Festival Hall, I found one false eyelash
hanging precariously and my adhesive dried
out. In a mad panic I accepted the only
substitute to be found – UHU glue. Needless to
say the standing ovation was not the only
lasting impression of that eventful evening.
That slang expression "give me some skin!"
took on a new meaning!' ■ Likes
photography, shopping for clothes in New
York, and reading 'Time' and 'Newsweek' from
cover to cover. Dislikes early mornings, the
colour green, tasteless lyrics, self service petrol
stations, cooking eggs and bacon first thing in
the morning, white linen, Renaissance Art,
liver, kidneys, kippers, and/or sardines (not
separately and most definitely not together!
[Sure there's nothing else Lorna?] ■ Married
to Garry Brown, has two step children and lives
in Surrey.

RAY DAVIES

'Has written the ident music for several ILR stations. . .'

BORN: 7th October 1927 in Wales. EDUCATED: Swansea. Royal College of Music, London, where he studied the trumpet. FIRST JOB: The Teddy Foster Band in Birmingham. Has also played with Oscar Rabin, Geraldo, Melachrino, Henry Mancini, Quincy Jones, Ambrose, Carol Gibbons, Burt Bacharach, Billy Cotton and Frank Chacksfield. As an arranger/composer/lyricist/conductor has worked with many star names including Frank Sinatra, Ella Fitzgerald, Bing Crosby, Judy Garland and Bob Hope. Has MD'd at many music festivals all over the world. Made his first broadcast with Teddy Foster in 1943 in *Saturday Night at the Palais.* Conducts and arranges for the various BBC Orchestras and also broadcasts with his own line-ups, The Button Down Brass and The Ray Davies Orchestra. Can be heard on most of Radio 2's music programmes including *Music While You Work* and *You and the Night and the Music.* Has composed the ident music for several ILR stations; Radio City, Beacon Radio, Radio Orwell, Swansea Sound, Pennine Radio and Metro Radio.

■ Most exciting moment of career: 'Just being part of the musical profession means every day something exciting happens!' ■ Likes skiing, golf, swimming, music and travel. ■ Married to Diane, has three children.

JIM DAVIS

'Lead violin and now conductor. . .'

BORN: 16th September 1920 in Birmingham. Father an engineer. EDUCATED: Sladefield Road School, Birmingham School of Music. 1934-38. Plays the violin also the oboe, flute clarinet and percussion. FIRST JOB: Violinist with the City of Birmingham Symphony Orchestra after six and a half years in the army 1940-46. He then joined the BBC Northern Orchestra for a year and from there went to the Royal Opera House at Covent Garden. He

returned to the BBC in 1969 as Leader of the BBC Midland Light Orchestra/Midland Radio Orchestra. Has also played with Herman Darewski, The Army Radio Orchestra, Geoff Love, Joe Loss, The Liverpool Philharmonic Orchestra, The London Symphony Orchestra, Ad Socem String Quartet, Palm Court Trio, London Festival Ballet and spent two years with the Band of the Royal Regiment. Made his first broadcast on a Carrol Levis programme in October 1937, and in over 45 years of broadcasting has been heard across the networks, Radios 1, 2 and 3, in a wide range of music from chamber and symphonic to light and popular. Is lead violin for Stanley Black, Frank Chacksfield, John Fox, John Gregory Orchestras. Is also the leader of the Vivaldi Chamber Ensemble and the Hepplewhite String Quartet and he conducts his own orchestra.

■ Most exciting moment of career: 'Turning up for a rehearsal of the Mid-Day Prom at Manchester Town Hall to find the leader of the BBC Northern Orchestra taken ill and having to take on *Scheherazade* for a "live" public broadcast.' ■ A moment to remember: 'The late Gordon Franks, composer, conductor and brilliant jazz pianist was instrumental in my performing one of Stephane Grappelli's own compositions. Imagine the shock when the great man himself walked into the studio during the recording session. I also remember the time during the late 50s when immediately after the musician's strike, I organized the BBC Orchestra's committee and as secretary eventually succeeded in getting management, Musicians Union and players' representatives around one table, which resulted in over 20 years free from industrial trouble!' ■ Likes fly fishing, philately and gardening. Dislikes carrots. ■ Married to Sylvia Knussen, has two step children and three grandchildren and lives in Herefordshire.

BRIAN DEE

'Broadcasting is the most enjoyable of all session work. . .'

BORN: 21st March 1936 in London. Father a

professional musician (arranger and saxophonist). EDUCATED: Minchenden Grammar School, Southgate. At the age of 10 went to a local piano teacher but in five years, only reached Grade 4! It was while doing National Service in the RAF that he began to take his piano playing seriously. Plays piano and organ. FIRST JOB: Playing at a jazz club in Southall. Joined the Lennie Best Quartet and turned professional in 1960. Has played with Eric Winstone, Frank Weir, Ken MacIntosh, Vic Ash, Harry Klein and Barry Forgie's Thames Eight. His first broadcast was backing singer Danny Street ('I can't remember the year') Now broadcasts regularly with his own trio, The Brian Dee Trio and can be heard on just about every music programme on Radio 2 including *You the Night and the Music*, The *Late Show* and *Music While You Work*. ■ Most exciting moment of career: 'No one moment – just being lucky enough to enjoy 95 per cent of what I do and being healthy. Broadcasting is the most enjoyable of all session work because it is the nearest thing to a spontaneous "live" performance.' ■ Likes watching speedway and owning an old London bus. Dislikes getting up early. Has two children and lives in Surrey.

studied piano, viola and composition at the Royal Academy of Music in London. Also plays the organ, harpsichord and the violin. FIRST JOB: 'Accompanying a Working Men's Club concert for 12/6 at the age of 14. Very good experience!' Had his first arrangement broadcast in 1936 and made hs début on the air as a pianist some ten years later. Formed a well known two-piano partnership with Edward Rubach which lasted for 15 years. Has been heard on numerous programmes both as a soloist and an accompanist over the years. Appears regularly on *Friday Night is Music Night, Melodies for You, Among Your Souvenirs* and *Grand Hotel*, all on Radio 2.

■ Most exciting moment of career: 'Receiving the Gold Medal for the best pupil at school during the final five years. This was undoubtedly due to the fact that I was the first and only pupil ever to win a music scholarship in the history of the school.' ■ A moment to remember: 'Accompanying Pat Whitmore in a *Melodies for You* broadcast, we decided to improvise a piano part as the existing arrangement wasn't in the right key or suitable (I seem to remember the song was *Ye Banks and Ye Braes*) Unfortunately I thought Pat asked for it to be played in E Major and we performed it only to find that she had asked for A Major, a fourth higher! Needless to say she sang it beautifully, if in the lower key, somewhat sexily!' ■ Likes bowls, indoors and outdoors. Dislikes unpunctuality, dirty shoes and bad music copying. ■ Married to Meryl Unsworth, has two children and lives in Suffolk.

ROBERT DOCKER
. . .at the piano'
BORN: 5th June 1918 in London. Father a gas worker. EDUCATED: North Paddington Central School. Had private musical tuition and then

JACK DORSEY
'I have the scars still. . .'
BORN: 1929 in Wrexham, North Wales. Father a musician. EDUCATED: Hammersmith Central School. The Song School, Westminster Abbey. Royal College of Music where he studied trumpet under Ernest Hall and composition and orchestration under Gordon Jacob. FIRST JOB:

As a boy chorister at Westminster Abbey. On leaving school he played trumpet in the Grenadier Guards. Spent five years playing, arranging and conducting for the Crazy Gang and was in the orchestra for the West End musicals, *Kismet* and the *King and I*. Has been MD for the Rank Organisation and A & R Manager for EMI and Pye. Played trumpet with Ambrose, but since then has worked as an MD. Made his first broadcast about 1961/62. Fronts his own line-up, The Jack Dorsey Orchestra, and is heard on many of Radio 2's music programmes including *Music While You Work*. 'Looking back over the years, *Music While You Work* immediately springs to mind, I have the scars still to prove it but there have been other programmes with lesser scars!'

■ Most exciting moment of career: 'Is yet to come.' ■ A moment to remember: 'Some years ago BBC Radio commissioned a major audience research survey. It revealed the startling fact that the highest audience was achieved during the two minutes silence prior to the Remembrance Service at the Cenotaph on Armistice Sunday, My suggestion of extending the two minutes silence to thirty minutes, in order to achieve an even bigger audience was turned down. In my view it is still a good idea!' ■ Likes photography.
■ Married to Hazel (the light of my life), has one son, Martin and lives in Sussex.

CRAIG DOUGLAS
'Number 1 with Only Sixteen *at just 18. . .'*
BORN: 13th August 1941 in Newport, Isle of Wight. EDUCATED: Newport Secondary School, where he sang in the school choir. Taught himself to play piano and guitar. FIRST JOB: Milkman (on leaving school). Has sung with many bands including Eric Winstone, Bob Miller, Ted Heath, Billy Cotton, Tito Burns, Harry Robinson, the Northern Dance Orchestra, The Midland Radio Orchestra and the Scottish Radio Orchestra. Made his first broadcast on the BBC's *Saturday Club* in 1959 he thinks. That was the year that at just 18, his

record of *Only Sixteen* made the Number 1 spot in the charts. Many more hits were to follow over the next three years. He appeared at the Liverpool Empire with the Beatles in 1962, and in that same year had his own radio series *On the Scene*. Other radio programmes include *Parade of the Pops, Easy Beat, Late Night Extra, the Billy Cotton Band Show*. He now broadcasts regularly on such Radio 2 programmes as the *John Dunn Show* and the weekend *Early Shows*.

■ Most exciting moment of career: 'Hearing that *Only Sixteen* had reached the Number 1 position in the charts in 1959.' ■ Likes golf and tennis. ■ Is a bachelor and lives in London and Hampshire.

ALAN DOWNEY
'In trouble with the BBC top brass who dared to watch ITV. . .'
BORN: 11th February 1944 in Liverpool. Father an insurance agent. EDUCATED: St. Margaret's Commercial Grammar School, Anfield, Liverpool. Had trumpet lessons but learnt mostly from tutor books and locking himself up. He also half finished a postal arranging course! Plays trumpet, flugel horn, even worse drums and piano. FIRST JOB: Ivor Kirchin Band, Sale Locarno in Cheshire, Made his first broadcast with the Dennis Mann Seven in Bristol in 1964. ('I was scared to death'!) Has played with Maynard Ferguson, Louis Bellson, Ronnie Scott, John Dankworth, P. Herbolzheimer, Norwegian Radio Orchestra, Finnish Radio Orchestra, Metropole Orchestra in Holland, SFB, NDR, SWF and James Last in Germany. The London Symphony Orchestra, The Royal Philharmonic Orchestra, the Bournemouth Symphony Orchestra, Bob Sharples, the Midland Light Orchestra and also had a spell with the BBC Radio Orchestra on lead trumpet. Now composes and arranges for the BBC Radio Orchestra, both the strings and the Radio Big Band and is one of the orchestra's

regular conductors, and as such contributes to most of Radio 2's music programmes including *You and the Night and the Music, Music While You Work, Round Midnight* and *Big Band Special.*

■ Most exciting moment of career: 'Working with Maynard Ferguson and Frank Sinatra . . . oh, and "opening time"!' ■ A moment to remember: 'When I was on the BBC staff playing in the Radio Orchestra, I got into trouble for working on ITV playing with Maynard Ferguson on the *Simon Dee Show.* When confronted by a few BBC chiefs (they thought) in an office, I just couldn't resist asking them, "How dare you watch ITV!"' ■ Likes playing the trumpet. Dislikes Hitler, scotch and gin. ■ Has two children (I've seen!) and lives in Surrey.

ADRIAN DROVER
'Worked his way down from cornet to bass trombone. . .'

BORN: 19th May 1940 in London. Father a professional musician. EDUCATED: Duke of York's Royal Military School, Dover. Is a 90 per cent self-taught musician although he learnt the basics from his father. Started on cornet, then trumpet, saxes, clarinet, oboe, vibraphone and finally bass trombone and tuba. Made his first broadcast on Granada Television round about 1955 playing solo clarinet. As a professional musician, *Music While You Work* with the Colin Hulme Orchestra in 1962. Has also played with the Maynard Ferguson Orchestra 1969-73 including three tours of the USA. Played bass trombone with Scottish Radio Orchestra from 1974 to 1981 during which time he did a lot of writing and arranging for the orchestra. Now fronts his own line-ups, The Adrian Drover Orchestra and the Adrian Drover Big Band, and can be heard on most of Radio 2's music programmes, including *You and the Night and the Music, Strings and Things, Slide Rule*, John Dunn Show, the *Early*

and *Late Shows* and *Gerry Davis Show* (Radio Scotland).

■ Most exciting moment of career: 'Probably playing with Maynard Ferguson.' ■ A moment to remember: 'While playing once on a recording session that was going rather slowly, the trombonist next to me leaned over and said "Why don't they just start at Take Ten, the first nine takes are always rotten".' ■ Likes music, cookery and brain surgery. Dislikes wallpaper music, cheap and shoddy work and discotheques. ■ Married to Louise Tobias (daughter of bandleader Bert Tobias), has one child and lives in Scotland.

GEOFF EALES
(Dr.) B.Mus., M.Mus., Ph.D., LRAM and all that jazz. . .'

BORN: 13th March 1951 in Aberbargoed, Gwent, S. Wales. Father a church organist. EDUCATED: Lewis School for Boys, Dengam, Monmouth. University College, Cardiff. At university studied composition under Professor Alun Hoddinott and piano under the concert pianist Martin Jones. Obtained his B.Mus., M.Mus., LRAM. In 1980 was awarded a doctorate, Ph.D, for his work on a thesis on Aaron Copeland, and for composition. Plays all the keyboards and French Horn. FIRST JOB: Playing piano for variety shows in South Wales social clubs at the age of 13, Made his first broadcast in 1961 at the age of 10 accompanying a local choir conducted by the tenor Stuart Burrows, on BBC Radio Wales. After leaving University, he toured the world for a year on a Greek liner as the only British member of an all Greek band . . . a trip on which he met many famous film names, Rita Hayworth, June Allyson, Glen Ford and Cornel Wilde. Has played with Joe Loss, Chico Arnez and the BBC Radio Orchestra/Radio Big Band. Now fronts his own line-up Electric Eales and can be heard on most of Radio 2's music shows including *Night Owls, Round Midnight, You and the Night and the Music* and the *Early Show.*

■ Most exciting moment of career: 'Being taken to dinner by Rosemary Clooney at the Beverley Wilshire Hotel, Beverley Hills, California in August 1982. I was part of the orchestra that backed her for a concert in London and she told me to look her up when I went to California on holiday, so I did!' ■ Likes swimming and tennis. Dislikes gardening and decorating. ■ Is a bachelor and lives in Hertfordshire.

JOHNNY EDWARDS
'Slightly Latin. . .'
BORN: 16th September 1927 in Plymouth, Devon. Father a painter/signwriter and also keen semi-pro musician. EDUCATED: Public Central School, Plymouth. St. George's Selective Central School, Ramsgate. Learnt to play drums in school band. Played string bass while doing National Service with the RAF in Singapore, where he was in a CSE unit band. Started to play the trombone in 1949 at the age of 22, what you might call a late starter! Mostly self taught, but spent 18 months studying with the principal trombone with the Royal Marines Band in Plymouth. Plays tenor trombone, occasionally bass and valve trombone. FIRST JOB: George Evans Band at the Oxford Galleries in Newcastle. Made his first broadcast with the George Evans Orchestra from the BBC's Newcastle studios in 1951. Has also played with the Squadronaires, Joe Loss, Jack Parnell, Cyril Stapleton, Geraldo, Ted Heath. Has been a freelance session musician since 1967 but fronts his own group called Slightly Latin which is heard on many of Radio 2's music programmes including *You and the Night and the Music*.

■ Most exciting moment of career: 'Many, over thirty years as a professional trombonist, but I would single out working with Judy Garland and Liza Minelli at the London Palladium; working with Frank Sinatra and of course with the great Ted Heath Band.' ■ Likes golf and DIY. Dislikes mechanical musicians.
■ Married to Sylvia, has three children, Peter, Elaine and Martin, and lives in Surrey.

BERNARD EBBINGHOUSE
'Plays bass trombone as a hobby. . .'
BORN: 18th March 1927 in Dusseldorf, Germany. Father a playwright/drama critic. EDUCATED: Kings Mill School, Cromer, Norfolk. Gresham School, Holt, Norfolk. King Edward VI Grammar School, Stratford-on-Avon. Taught himself to play the trumpet, but at the age of 20 switched to trombone after hearing Bill Harris of the Woody Herman Band playing *Bijou*. Studied composition at Guildhall School of Music and with Matyas Seiber. FIRST JOB: Trombonist with Joe Daniel's Hot Shots, replacing Don Lusher. Was a Dixielander with Freddie Randall, a bebopper with Ralph Sharon. He played with Teddy Foster (who didn't) and Oscar Rabin. Made his first broadcast with Teddy Foster in the early 50s. He did arrangements for all the bands he played with. Also arranged for Geraldo & Edmundo Ross. He arranges for and frequently conducts the BBC Radio Orchestra and also fronts his own line-up for many of Radio 2's music programmes including *Music While You Work*. Has been MD for the BBC Festival of Light Music, Nordring Radio Prize and Top Tunes. Has composed and conducted scores for over 50 films.

■ Most exciting moment of career: 'Probably scoring my first major film, although a six-month TV series with Mel Torme didn't hurt either.' ■ Likes music! and playing the bass trombone and tuba. Dislikes bigotry, especially perhaps in music. ■ Lives in Surrey.

FRANK EVANS
'As a musician I have a dual role to play. . .'
BORN: 1st October 1936 in Bristol. Father a carpenter. EDUCATED: Bristol Technical School. Plays the guitar and is mainly self taught. FIRST JOB: As a guitarist, backing Tessie O'Shea in variety theatres. Has played in nightclubs and ballrooms all over the country with Tubby Hayes Quartet, Alex Welsh Band, Ike Isaacs

Duo, Russ Conway, Ron Goodwin, Dartington String Quartet and has duetted with George Benson. Is MD, arranger and composer for his own group Nova. Made his first broadcast on *Guitar Club* in 1955. Since then has been heard on *Jazz Club, Strictly Instrumental, Round Midnight, Capital Jazz, Sounds Interesting*, the *Late Show*, and *You and the Night and the Music*. He is also composing the music for a drama series.

■ Most exciting moment of career: 'Hearing the Dartington String Quartet playing my compositions; and watching my solo record *Noctuary* climb up the jazz best sellers. ■ As a guitar soloist it took me many years to discover that to give a relaxed performance on radio, I had to play the way I would in a small nightclub. In other words I play best in a darkened studio performing music from the top of my head, not using any written solos. My best records and broadcasts have been produced in this way. BBC producer Brian Patten discovered it for me when I used to get very nervous with red lights and all the usual studio situations. When directing an orchestra, the reverse situation applies – I get excited about recording film music to a split second and enjoy the tension of the situation – so as a musician I have a dual role to play.' ■ Likes good draught beer. Dislikes avant garde jazz. ■ Married to Mary, has two sons and lives In Avon.

BRIAN FAHEY
'Organizing the entertainment in POW camps...'
BORN: 25th April 1919 in Margate, Kent. Father a professional musician. EDUCATED: Colfe's Grammar School, Lewisham. His father taught him to play the piano and cello. FIRST JOB: A clerk in a leather factory. He joined the Territorial Army in 1938, was called up in 1939 and joined REME. He was wounded and captured by the Germans during the retreat to Dunkirk. He spent the next five years as a prisoner of war organizing entertainment in

POW camps. When he was demobbed at the end of the war he was determined to make it as an arranger. First job as a musician was with Rudi Starita's Band on piano. Started to arrange for Geraldo, Harry Roy and Ken MacIntosh. In the early 50s joined Chappell's as a staff arranger. Was Musical Director for Shirley Bassey 1966-72. He made his first broadcast with his own orchestra on the BBC Light Programme around 1960. In 1971 he appeared in the Royal Variety Show. Was conductor of the Scottish Radio Orchestra from 1972 to 1981 when it was disbanded. He now fronts his own line-up, the Brian Fahey Orchestra and is heard regularly on most of Radio 2's music programmes including *You and the Night and the Music*, the weekend *Early Show* and the weekend *Late Show*. His best known compositions are *Fanfare Boogie* for which he won an Ivor Novello award, and *The Creep* which he wrote with Ken MacIntosh.

■ Most exciting moment of career: 'Conducting the Woody Herman Band during a tour of the USA' 'I think, probably my proudest moment was being appointed a senior Examiner at the Leeds College of Music, never having had any formal musical training.' ■ Likes golf, gardening and reading. Dislikes wastage of food, and hypocrisy. ■ Married to Audrey Laurie (who sang with Rudy Starita's Band), has three sons and three daughters and lives in Ayrshire.

ROBERT FARNON
'Lethal with a baton...!'
BORN: 24th July 1917 in Toronto, Canada. Father a clothier EDUCATED: Our Lady of Lourdes Private School. Humberside College. Studied composition with Louis Waizman and was a student at the Broadus Farmer School of Music, Toronto. Plays percussion, piano, trumpet and trombone. FIRST JOB: Brian Farnon Orchestra (percussion) in 1932. Was principal trumpet with the CBC Concert Orchestra; also played with the Toronto Symphony Orchestra and played trumpet and arranged for the Percy

Faith Orchestra. Made his first broadcast with the CBC Radio Orchestra in 1935. Came to Britain with the Canadian AEF Band during the Second World War. After the war established himself as one of our most popular composer/conductor/arrangers. Is a prolific composer, his first published composition being *Jumping Bean.* His most popular are probably *Portrait of a Flirt* and *Westminster Waltz.* He broadcasts regularly with his own orchestra and also conducts the BBC Radio Orchestra and the BBC Concert Orchestra on numerous occasions. Programmes include *Melody Hour, Melodies for You, Robert Farnon in Concert, Vera Lynn Sings* and *Friday Night is Music Night.*

■ Most exciting moment of career: 'The performance of my first symphony by Eugene Ormandy and the Philadelphia Symphony Orchestra in 1941.' ■ A moment to remember: 'During the Vera Lynn Radio series, we were rehearsing an arrangement by Bruce Campbell. While he was peering into the score at close range checking some doubtful notes I accidentally caught him full force under the chin with the back of my hand during a sweeping up-beat, knocking him unconscious. We remained the best of friends, but he never again came within five feet if I had a baton in my hand and frequently referred to me as "Henry the Hammer of Harmony".' ■ Likes photography, golf and the Sport of Kings. Dislikes temperamental singers and drum solos. ■ Married to Patricia, has five children and lives in Guernsey, Channel Islands.

BRIAN FITZGERALD
'Has accompanied many stars. . .'
BORN: 9th February 1932, in Manchester. Father a sports journalist. EDUCATED: Xaverian Catholic Grammar School, Manchester. Learnt elementary piano while at school. FIRST JOB: At the age of 15, playing the piano in a dance band at the Casino Ballroom, Warrington. Has toured the UK and abroad as accompanist to

many stars including Malcolm Roberts (South America), Gladys Knight, Russ Abbott and Andy Williams. Made his first broadcast around 1955 as deputy pianist with Alyn Ainsworth and the Northern Dance Orchestra. Has played with Bob Sharples ABC TV Orchestra and the Northern Radio Orchestra which he also conducted. As a freelance musical director and pianist he contributes to most of Radio 2's music programmes as well as many Light Entertainment programmes on the network including *Listen to Les, Castle's On the Air, The Grumbleweeds.* On Radio 4 in the north he provides the incidental music to drama productions and Richard Stilgoe's *Traffic Jam Show.*

■ Likes compulsory gardening. Dislikes presumptuousness and dirty ashtrays.
■ Married to Jean, has two sons and lives in Cheshire.

KEELEY FORD
'Fell asleep at rehearsal. . .'
BORN: 13th October 1948. EDUCATED: County High School, Redditch. Worcestershire. 'I took singing lessons at the age of nine, but didn't like it!' FIRST JOB: *For Teenagers Only* on ATV television at the age of 14 and under her real name, Mair Davies. At that time joined a group, The Mavericks, and later a Leicester based group called The Rockets. Made her first radio broadcast on the *Ken Dodd Show* from

the BBC's Manchester studios in July 1973. Has sung in top venues all over the world and in 1973 was the first girl to win the International song Festival in Almeria, Spain and later that year shared first place in the Yamaha World Song Contest in Japan. Sings regularly on Dutch and German Radio and in 1977 representing the BBC at the Nordring Radio Festival, she won the vocal prize. Took part in 1982 in Radio 2's tribute to Judy Garland and can be heard on most of Radio 2's music programmes.

■ Most exciting moment of career: 'Winning the Song Festivals in Spain and Japan and the Nordring Festival in Denmark for the BBC.' ■ A moment to remember: I was appearing in a summer season in 1977 when I was released to go to Denmark for the Nordring Festival. I got so tired travelling to and fro between Denmark and London that I literally fell asleep whilst rehearsing with Peter Knight and Nick Curtis!' ■ Likes knitting (a fanatic), crochet, embroidering and dressmaking. Dislikes creepy crawlies, liver and smoking. ■ Lives in Worcestershire.

BARRY FORGIE
'Making oneself understood, an occupational hazard. . .'

BORN: 28th May 1939, in Peterborough, Northamptonshire. Father an engineer.
EDUCATED: King's School, Peterborough. University of Wales, Cardiff. (B.Mus.) Plays trombone and piano. FIRST JOB: Teaching music at a school in Croydon. Did his first arranging for Ken Thorne on the first Val Doonican television series. Spent a year playing trombone with Syd Lawrence. Made his first broadcast with his own 13-piece band in September 1969. As a freelance MD/arranger/composer he fronts his own line-ups under various names; Thames 8, Swing Machine, Peter Dennis Boogie Woogie Band. Was the Festival conductor for the 1981 Nordring Radio Festival in Jersey. Has

conducted the Norwegian Radio, Dutch Metropole, Helsinki Light, Hamburg Radio and the Malmo Symphony Orchestras. He conducts the BBC Radio Orchestra and is the principal conductor of the BBC Radio Big Band. Is heard regularly on Radio 2's *Big Band Special, Round Midnight, Gloria Hunniford Show, Night Owls* and *You and the Night and the Music.* With his own Thames 8, Swing Machine etc. is heard on *Music While You Work* and *You and the Night and the Music.*

■ Most exciting moment of career: 'Conducting my own 50-minute work, *A Beatles Symphony*, written for the 1982 Nordring Festival held in Malmo, Sweden.' ■ A moment to remember: 'Making oneself understood is an occupational hazard when working with foreign orchestras despite the universality of the English language. On one occasion in Oslo, I had used a delicate 'water bell' effect and spent some time explaining to the percussionist the technique of hitting the tubular bell with a wooden mallet and dipping it up and down in a bucket of water, so changing the pitch of the sound. Imagine my consternation when on the rehearsal this moment of unparalleled subtlety arrived and amidst a texture of shimmering strings and undulating woodwind chords, the bell was struck and was immediately followed by a sickening "clunk" as it crunched into the bottom of the metal bucket. The orchestra collpased with laughter. "No". I said resignedly. "You dip it in the water, can't you see, the part says Dip in Water." "Ah, so sorry," came the bemused reply, "I thought it said "Deep in Water"!' ■ Likes chess, squash and opening time. Dislikes predictability in all things. ■ Married to Tesni, has two daughters and lives in Surrey.

JOHN FOX
'Musical ideas while walking the dog. . .'
BORN: 30th January 1926, in Sutton Surrey.
EDUCATED: Sutton West. 'I took piano lessons at

an early age at 2/- a time! After the war I studied very hard at the Royal College of Music (piano , which I loved, and violin, which I played rather badly) and gained my ARCM. I also studied at Fitzwells College where I won a composition scholarship.' FIRST JOB: At the age of 15 playing with a young drummer at the local hall for 15/-. Taught music for a short while at Wandsworth School and also ran a local amateur choir. Accompanied all sorts of talent competitions at local cinemas. Made his first broadcast in the early 50s playing piano with the Harold Turner Quartet. Conducted the BBC Radio Orchestra for the first time in the mid 60s. Has also played with Fred Hedley's Big Band, the Jack Newman Orchestra, Johnny Howard Band, Lennie Lewis Quintet and with Harold Turner's Quartet at the Grand Hotel, Eastbourne. Conducts the BBC Radio Orchestra regularly and records and broadcasts with his own orchestra, always with the accent on strings. Radio 2 programmes include *The Magic of John Fox, The Musical World of John Fox, John Fox Conducts The Romantic Strings* and *Music While You Work.* The John Fox Singers are frequently heard on *Friday Night is Music Night.*

■ Most exciting moment of career; 'Driving to Poland to conduct the Krakow Symphony Orchestra recording my own symphonic composition; and the launching of my Gershwin album at a special reception where the special guest was my mother!' 'Without a good deal of help throughout my career, perhaps my musical world might never have seen the light of day and many of my musical ideas have been thought up while walking my collie dog Taly. But the biggest thank you must go to my lovely wife Joy and my family who have put up with my artistic temperaments!' ■ Likes walking with his collie in the country, listening to and reading about medieval music and instruments. Dislikes interruptions when working, commercial holidays, adverts, bad drivers, bad manners, exotic foods and music in restaurants. ■ Married to Joy Devon (singer), has two sons and one daughter and lives in Surrey.

GEORGE FRENCH
'Played many times in the Palm Court. . .'
BORN: 13th July 1921, in Bentley, Yorkshire. Father a parks superintendent. EDUCATED: King Charles I Grammar School, Kidderminster. Midland Institute of Music, Birmingham where he studied the violin. FIRST JOB: Joined the London Philharmonic Orchestra as rank and file and left it as sub-leader to join the BBC's London Studio Players. Has been leader for Barry Gray (Thunderbirds etc), Mike Batt

(Wombles), Gordon Langford, Reg Leopold Orchestra (*Melodies for You*) and the John Fox Orchestra. He made his first broadcast at the age of 15 in *Young Artists* for the BBC Midland Region. Radio programmes include *Grand Hotel* with Tom Jenkins, Jean Pougnet, Reg Leopold and Max Jaffa. *Among Your Souvenirs, Much More Music, Thru' Midnight.* He has lead and directed The Spa Orchestra for the BBC. Now conducts the London Studio Players which are heard on the Jimmy Young programme on Radio 2; and conducts his own orchestra for Radio 2's *Music While You Work.*

■ Dislikes 'Bossy Boots' women, flying, and animal experiments. ■ Married to Marion, has three sons and lives in Middlesex.

ALLAN GANLEY
'Some pretty good drumming from Ronnie Verrall. . .!'
BORN: 11th March 1931, in Tolworth, Surrey. Father a bookmaker. EDUCATED: 'Not really!' Tolworth Secondary School. Plays the drums and enough piano to arrange and compose. Mostly self-taught, but in 1970 he studied arranging and composition at the Berklee School of Music in Boston, USA. FIRST JOB: Drummer with the Jimmy Walker Quintet, also made his first broadcast with them from the Aeolian Hall in Bond Street in 1952. Has recorded with Jim Hall, Ron Carter and Art Farmer. Has played with Jack Parnell, the first Johnny Dankworth Orchestra, Stan Getz,

Dizzy Gillespie, Al Cohn, Stephane Grappelli...' Perhaps I should list who I haven't played for!' 'I had my own jazz group for many years then with Ronnie Ross formed the Jazzmakers. I then spent two years with the Tubby Hayes Quintet and became resident drummer at Ronnie Scott's.' Broadcasts now with his own sextet and his own Big Band on *Jazz Club* and the late night music shows on Radio 2 such as *You and the Night and the Music.* But his radio programmes have included ('going back, and I can!') *Breakfast with Braden, Guitar Club, Variety Bandbox* ('I think'), even an interview with Peter Clayton on *Sounds of Jazz.* Does a lot of arranging and writing and his arrangements can often be heard on Radio 2's *Big Band Special.*

■ Most exciting moment of career: 'Hearing my Big Band arrangements for the first time.'
■ A moment to remember: 'I did a "dep" for Ronnie Verrall on a Bob Farnon broadcast and one of the numbers featured the drums (and during the solo catching the brass accents, not easy). I thought I did a good job. I listened to the show only to hear Radio 2 announcer Colin Berry say, "... and some pretty good drumming there from Ronnie Verrall." UGH!'
■ Likes tennis. Dislikes musicians who can't keep time. ■ Married to June, has one daughter, Allison, and lives in Berkshire.

Stapleton, Eric Winstone and Johnny Howard. Formed his own line-ups, the Bill Geldard Tentette in 1972 and the Bill Geldard Big Band in 1978 and has been guest conductor of the BBC Radio Big Band since 1978. Is heard regularly on most of Radio 2's music programmes including *You and the Night and the Music* and *Music While You Work.*

■ Most exciting moment of career: 'Being the featured bass trombonist with a specially written solo, *Nelson's Blues*, on *Nelson Riddle conducts the 101 Strings.*' ■ A moment to remember: 'In the days of 'live' broadcasting, round about 1953, I was with the Rabin Band and we were doing a series of late night programmes going out about 11pm. Every week we played a tribute to a famous American band, and on this particular night I was to play *Getting Sentimental Over You.* We also played a Latin number and as usual the trombone section were the ones that played the LA toys. Anyway during the rehearsal, about 9pm, disaster struck. I'd put my trombone on my chair during the LA number and before I could retrieve it, one of my section colleagues sat down rather quickly and it didn't do my slide any good at all. With a lot of tugging and pulling and lots of water, I managed to get it working in a fashion. The night was saved for me, but it was an experience I wouldn't care to repeat.' ■ Likes golf and swimming.
■ Married to trumpeter Gracie Cole, has two children and lives in Surrey.

BILL GELDARD
'An experience I wouldn't care to repeat...'
BORN: 27th September 1929, in Spennymoor, Co. Durham. Father a school keeper.
EDUCATED: Spennymoor. Studied trombone with J. Armstrong, T. Collinson and Geo. Maxted. Also plays violin and viola. FIRST JOB: Playing trombone at the Eden Theatre, Bishop Auckland, January 1945. Made his first broadcast on 9th October 1945 on *Children's Hour.* Has played with Charles Amer, George Evans, the Squadronaires, Ted Heath, Oscar Rabin, Johnny Dankworth and Jack Parnell. Has also freelanced with Geraldo, Cyril

LEE GIBSON
'Dancer turned singer...'
BORN: 5th March 1950, in Watford, Herts. Father a butcher. EDUCATED: Watford Girl's Grammar School. Took piano and singing lessons at school. Now plays the piano for her own amazement! FIRST JOB: As a dancer in The Black and White Minstrel Show. Spent a year as the lead in a reveue at London's Talk of the Town, where she sort of got pushed into singing. She made her first broadcast with the

Phil Phillips Quartet in 1971 and has been a backing singer for Barbra Streisand, David Essex, Gerard Kenny and Marti Webb. Has sung with Skymasters and Metropole Orchestra (Holland) and had a continental Top Ten hit with *Chorale.* Has also sung with Bob Miller, Pete Winslow, Peter Knight Orchestra and for MDs Ronnie Hazlehurst, Alyn Ainsworth, Ken Moule and Neil Richardson. Broadcasts regularly with the BBC Radio Orchestra/Radio Big Band. Radio programmes include *Tribute to Judy Garland, Tribute to Gershwin* and *Bing Crosby Tribute.* She has also sung at the Nordring Radio Festival for the Dutch and the Monte Carlo Producers Prize and the Knokke Competition which the BBC won. She is heard on most of Radio 2's music programmes including *You and the Night and the Music, Night Owls* and *Big Band Special.*

■ Most exciting moment of career: 'I'm not sure whether it was working in Los Angeles or meeting Terry Wogan or taking part in *Ring a Song*!' ■ A moment to remember: 'In 1981 I was asked to represent the Dutch team in the Nordring Festival which was being hosted by the British. At the rehearsals in London with the BBC Radio Orchestra, one of the brass section was off sick and a "dep" unknown to me was in his place. During the inevitable exodus to the pub at lunchtime. I was talking to several members of the orchestra, when the "dep", thinking I was Dutch, complimented me on my "incredibly good English", and couldn't understand the hilarity which greeted this remark! Since then I've been known to the orchestra as Lee Van Der Gibson.' ■ Likes swimming, reading, good food and wine. Dislikes doing the accounts. ■ Married to drummer/arranger Gerry Boyce, qv, has one daughter and lives in Hertfordshire.

LORNE GIBSON
'Over 5,000 broadcasts. . .'
BORN: 20th August 1940. Father a RSM in the

Black Watch. EDUCATED: Tyne Castle Technical College. Taught himself to play the guitar. FIRST JOB: Baker. Made his first broadcast singing on *Commonwealth of Song* in 1960. Has been associated mostly with Country Music and has made over 5,000 broadcasts on such Radio 2 programmes as *Country Club,* The *Early Show, Truckers Hour* and *You and the Night and the Music.*

■ Most exciting moment of career: 'Appearing with the Beatles and the Rolling Stones in the *Radio Pops Proms* at the Royal Albert Hall.' ■ Likes DIY and cooking. Dislikes people who add 'Western' to Country Music. ■ Married to Maggie Gibbs and lives in Middlesex.

RON GOODWIN
'Over 60 film scores. . .'
BORN: 17th February 1925, in Plymouth, Devon. Father a policeman. EDUCATED: Willesden County School. Pinner County School. Took piano and trumpet lessons at school, but mainly self taught. FIRST JOB: Music copyist at Campbell, Connelly & Co. (Music Publishers). Made his first broadcast on *Morning Music* in 1951 with Ron Goodwin and his Concert Orchestra. Played trumpet with Harry Gold and his Pieces of Eight. Became Musical Director for Parlophone Record Co. Has been the guest conductor of the Royal Philharmonic Orchestra, The Bournemouth Symphony, the London Symphony, Royal Liverpool Philharmonic, Ulster Orchestra, Gothenburg Symphony, Toronto Symphony, New Zealand Symphony, Sydney Symphony, BBC Concert and BBC Radio Orchestras. Broadcasts regularly with the BBC Concert, City of Birmingham Symphony, Bournemouth Symphony and the Ulster Orchestras on such programmes as *Friday Night is Music Night, BBC's Festival of Light Music, Gala Concerts* and Ron Goodwin's *World of Music.* Has also been heard on *Funny You Should Say That.* Has composed more than 60 scores for feature films and been the MD for many of them.

■ Most exciting moment of career: 'Working with Paul Whiteman on the *Patti Page Show* on American TV in 1957; and scoring *Frenzy* for Alfred Hitchock and meeting him in 1972.' ■ Likes reading and walking the dog. Dislikes yoghourt. ■ Married to Heather, has one child.

ALEC GOULD
'Mad about railways. . .'
BORN: 21st January 1930 in Northampton. Father a driver. EDUCATED: 'Slightly'. Plays the trombone. 'Self taught at the expense of the bands I've worked with over the last 30 years.' FIRST JOB: Trombonist and arranger, with the Oscar Rabin Band in 1953. Also played with the Vic Lewis Band and spent four years as a BBC Staff arranger. Made his first broadcast with the Vic Lewis Band in 1954. He now frequently conducts and arranges for the BBC Radio Orchestra/Radio Big Band and also fronts his own line up on such programmes as *You and the Night and the Music, the Jimmy Young Show* and *Music While You Work*.

■ Most exciting moment of career: 'Being asked to be in this book!' ■ Likes model railways, collecting railway books, food, booze and good cigars. Dislikes people who think they are important. ■ Is married, has one daughter and lives in Middlesex.

STEVE GRAY
'Exploring the fantastic world of music. . .'
BORN: 18th April 1944, in Billingham, Co: Durham. Father a steelworker. EDUCATED: Acklam Hall Grammar School, Middlesbrough. Took piano lessons from the age of 10 and obtained a GCE 'O' level in music. Plays piano plus electric keyboards plus synthesizer etc. FIRST JOB: 'I formed my own band while still at school playing gigs in Working Men's Clubs around Teeside. We were eventually resident at a local Country Club.' In 1962 was pianist with The Phil Seamen Quintet; 1964 Eric Delaney;

1965 Mike Cotton. Eventually settled in London with the Johnny Howard Band and became full-time session musician in 1968. Made his first broadcast with the Eric Delaney Band on 27th April 1964 in *Top Beat* on the BBC Light Programme. 'As a session musician I've played with virtually everyone from Quincy Jones and Buddy Rich through to Neil Diamond and Paul McCartney (pretty big time, huh?).' Is currently the keyboard player with Sky. 'Between 1968 and '77 I worked on nearly all of the non classical music programmes from *Jazz Club* to the *Jimmy Young Show* (I preferred *Jazz Club*).' His arrangements are heard frequently on Radio 2's *Big Band Special* and the Steve Gray Trio is heard on *You and the Night and the Music*. Although he is still a working musician, he has become one of the country's foremost arrangers over the past few years.

■ Most exciting moment of career: 'Pretentious answer: Discovering the chord of D 7th, on the piano I had only been playing a few days and it marked the realization that I could explore the fantastic world of music by myself' ■ A moment to remember: 'When I formed my first band, it was a three piece. Eventually we added a couple more members, but for some reason never changed the name, so there used to be a quintet going around Teesside called The Steve Gray Trio. This anomaly has followed me to the BBC. The first broadcast I ever did as a leader was with a trio, and although I've since conducted 40-piece orchestras on the radio, whenever the Beeb writes to me it addresses me as "Mr Steve Gray Trio."'

■ Likes cycling, beer-drinking and reading time-tables. Dislikes nothing in particular – cabbage maybe. ■ Married to Heather, has one daughter, Suzanne and lives in Somerset.

DAVE HANCOCK
'The best broadcast I nearly never did. . .'
BORN: 30th November 1937, in Wembley, Middlesex. Father a carpenter. EDUCATED:

Acton Country Grammar School. Taught himself to play the trumpet, piano and vibraphone. FIRST JOB: Playing at a holiday camp on the Isle of Wight. Made his first broadcast with the Ronnie Pleydell Band on *Music While You Work*, but he can't remember when! Has also played with Ken MacIntosh, Teddy Foster, Ronnie Scott, Maynard Ferguson, Johnny Howard, BBC Radio Orchestra, Peter Knight, London Philharmonic and Royal Philharmonic Orchestras. Toured Europe 1960-61 as pianist/accompanist to the singer Myra de Groot. Was Musical Director for Anita Harris 1970-72. He now arranges for and conducts the BBC Radio Orchestra/Radio Big Band and also fronts his own line-up Hancock's Junk Band and is heard on most of Radio 2's music programmes.

■ Most exciting moment of career: 'Hearing Segovia in person.' ■ A moment to remember: 'The best broadcast I nearly never did! Returning from the pub to perform "live" on BBC *Radio One O'clock* show in the late 60s, the BBC comissionaire didn't believe I was in the band and refused me entry. Standing there arguing I heard the signature tune being played with no melody (that was my part) . . . nobody noticed!' ■ Likes semi-pro football in which he is deeply involved! Dislikes Scott Joplin's music! ■ Married to Marlene and lives in Kent.

MAX HARRIS
'Musicmaker for radio's top comedy shows. . .'
BORN: 15th September 1918, in Bournemouth. Father a master tailor. EDUCATED: Lylaph Central School. Private tuition on piano up to the final grade RAM. Plays piano and keyboards. FIRST JOB: Playing at the Paramount Dance Palais in London. He also gave piano lessons as a teenager. Made his first broadcast on *Jazz Club* in 1950. Has played with Tommy Whittle, George Chisholm, and Jack Parnell. Has arranged for the BBC Show Band, Ted

Heath, Ella Fitzgerald, Stephane Grappelli and Yehudi Menuhin. The Max Harris Orchestra has provided the incidental music of many of Radio's top comedy shows over the years, including *Round the Horne, Stop Messing About, Sketch Book, Peter Goodwright Show, Frankie Howerd's One Man Show,* Windsor Davies and Arthur Askey. And is also heard on most of Radio 2's music programmes. Has written numerous television themes.

■ Most exciting moment of career: 'Writing and directing Yehudi Menuhin and Stephane Grappelli's joint LPs; Hearing my first *Art Tatum* record; the chart success of the Gurney Slade Theme.' ■ A moment to remember: 'Having been introduced as a Pianist, Musical Director, Composer on a quiz programme, I was struck dumb on one particular question, which prompted chairman Cardew Robinson to comment that I was obviously decomposing!: ■ Likes golf and wine. Dislikes indifferent Chinese cooking. ■ Married to Nanette, has one son and one daughter and lives in Surrey.

BOBBY HARRISON
'Over 2,000 broadcasts as soloist. . .'
BORN: 1st December 1933, in Brixton, London. Father an office worker. EDUCATED: Varndean Grammar School, Brighton. Played the trumpet in the RAF Fighter Command Band during National Service and then studied at the Trinity College of Music, London. Plays trumpet,

flugel and drums. FIRST JOB: With Syd Dean at the Regent Ballroom, Brighton in 1954. Spent 15 years at the Talk of the Town in London and played solos on 'live' albums recorded there by Tom Jones and Shirley Bassey. Made his first broadcast with the Les Watson Orchestra in Jersey in 1954. Has played with Eric Winstone, Frank Weir, Phil Tate, Frank Chacksfield. On television has been the featured soloist on Miss World since 1965. And since 1973 has made over 2,000 broadcasts as a freelance soloist with the BBC Radio Orchestra, on such programmes as Radio 2's *String Sound.* The Bobby Harrison Quartet is heard on many of Radio 2's music programmes including The *Late Show, Round Midnight, Jimmy Young Show* and *You and the Night and the Music.*

■ Most exciting moment of career: 'Having my youngest son, Gavin, playing drums on my quartet broadcast.' ■ A moment to remember: 'Talk about the show must go on – I went up north to do a 'live' broadcast with the Northern Dance Orchestra on sticks, due to a dislocated hip, only to find one of the other trumpet players swathed in bandages after a firework accident. As we staggered on before the audience, we were announced as the Walking Wounded.' ■ Likes motoring and boating. Dislikes loud bass players. ■ Married to Audrey, has three sons and lives in Hertfordshire.

GUNTHER HERBIG
'Conducted around the world. . .'
BORN: 30th November 1931, In Aussig. Father an architect. EDUCATED: Abitur. Franz-Lizt Hochschule, Weimar. Plays piano, cello, flute, french horn, percussion. FIRST JOB: Conductor Deutsches National Theater Weimar 1956-'62. 1962-'66 Principal conductor Potsdam. 1966-72 conductor Berliner Sinfornie Orchester. 1972–'77 principal conductor Dresdner Philharmonic. Since 1977 has been principal conductor and Generalmusikdirektor of Berliner Sinfonie Orchester. Occasionally conducts the BBC Symphony Orchestra. Made his first broadcast in 1960 and has conducted over 70 orchestras in Europe, America and Japan. In 1980, appointed Chief Guest Conductor of the BBC Philharmonic Orchestra.

■ Married to Jutta, has two children and lives in East Germany.

RONNIE HILTON
No. 1 with 'No Other Love'. . .'
BORN: 26th January 1926 in Hull, Humberside. Father a regular soldier and seaman. EDUCATED: Hull, Humberside. FIRST JOB: Began singing while in the Army. Made his first broadcast in April 1954. Has sung with all the BBC Orchestras over the years including several radio series with the Northern Dance Orchestra. Has sung with Ted Heath, Cyril Stapleton, Ken MacIntosh, Frank Cordell, Jack Payne and Harry Robinson. Had many hit records in the mid 50's and a Number 1 with *No Other Love.* Is heard on many of Radio 2's music programmes.

■ Most exciting moment of career: 'Three Royal Command Performances and singing in cabaret at Windsor Castle.' ■ A moment to remember: 'In my early days I was doing a 'live' broadcast when my pianist gave me an arpeggio intro about a tone and half too high causing rupture!' ■ Likes golf, most sports and being at home. Dislikes little people with big chips! ■ Married to Joan, has three grown up children and lives in Yorkshire.

LAURIE HOLLOWAY
'The things that happen on Music While You Work. . .'
BORN: 31st March 1938 in Oldham, Lancashire. Father a french polisher. EDUCATED: Greenhill Grammar School. Private tuition on piano. FIRST JOB: Playing piano at Billington's Dance Hall, Oldham on Saturday nights while still at school. Amongst his first broadcasts were *Workers Playtime, Music*

While You Work and the Rolf Harris Show, 1959. Mostly fronts his own bands but has played for Englebert Humperdinck, Cleo Laine, Stephane Grappelli, Bing Crosby, Robert White, Nelson Riddle, Sammy Davis and Sammy Cahn. Now runs a group called 'Prism' as well as his own band who are heard on many of Radio 2's music programmes including Jazz Club, You and the Night and the Music.

■ Most exciting moment of career: 'Playing for singer Marion Montgomery.' [The excitement proved too much, he married her!] ■ A moment to remember: 'I think my most amazed moment was during a "live" Music While You Work, when I saw a trumpet player strike a match on the microphone! On another "live" show, Friday Night is Music Night, I was accompanying a lady singer. I played the introduction and she started to sing the wrong song. It all finished well as we turned it into a medley.' ■ Likes golf, music and sport. Dislikes cold soup. ■ Married to Marion Montgomery, qv, has two daughters and lives in Berkshire.

ANTHONY HOPKINS see Presenters

JOHNNY HOWARD
'Has always fronted his own band. . .'
BORN: 5th February 1931, in Croydon, Surrey. Father a dancing teacher. EDUCATED: John Ruskin Grammar School, Croydon. Learnt to play the saxophone at school and later studied with Leslie Evans. FIRST JOB: Semi-pro gigs around Croydon but turned professional at the Orchid Ballroom, Purley on 26th August 1959. In 1961 he took over from Lou Praeger as resident leader at the London Lyceum and between 1962 and 1967 played at most of the major London ballrooms on a resident basis. Made his first broadcast on the Mid-Day Bandshow in July 1960 and from 1962-67 was the resident band on BBC's Easy Beat every Sunday morning. Other programmes during the 60s included Jimmy Young Show, Saturday

Club and Radio One O'clock. He has always fronted his own band and is heard on most of Radio 2's music programmes. He also formed and fronts the Capital Radio Big Band.

■ Most exciting moment of career: 'When my orchestra accompanied Miss Peggy Lee in concert, at the Royal Albert Hall, a memorable night.' ■ A moment to remember: 'Trying to conduct an interview with Tommy Trinder on a "live" outside broadcast from the Pavilion Ballroom, Weymouth, when the PA system went dead and both of us tried to continue above the noise of a very rowdy (and rather drunk) audience, mainly sailors! But the band played on!' ■ Likes music and spending time with his family. Dislikes the gullibility of the British public as far as music is concerned. ■ Married to Carole, has a son and a daughter and lives in Surrey.

NEVILLE HUGHES
'31 years as sub-leader of the BBC Radio Orchestra. . .'
BORN: 24th February 1918 in London. Father a tailor. EDUCATED: St. Dunstan's College, Catford. Trinity College of Music, London. Plays the violin and the saxophone. FIRST JOB: Playing at the Princes Restaurant, Piccadilly, London. Made his first broadcast playing a violin solo in the Navy Mixture in 1943. Has played with the BBC Revue Orchestra and was sub-leader of the BBC Radio Orchestra for 31

years. Was Musical Director of the Europa Hotel, London 1964-81. Has played with George Crow, Charlie Shadwell, Geoff Love, Frank Chacksfield, Malcolm Lockyer, Nat Temple, Bob Farnon, Neil Richardson, Dave Hancock, Roland Shaw and Peter Knight. Had his own twice weekly programme during the 60s with the Neville Hughes Septet, called *Just Seven*. Has fronted his own orchestra since 1978 and is heard on most of Radio 2's music programmes including the *Jimmy Young Show, You and the Night and the Music* and the *John Dunn Show* and was the first orchestra to broadcast *Music While You Work* when it was revived by the BBC on 4th January 1983. Has been seen in nine television plays as a 'Cafe' violinist!

■ Most exciting moment of career: 'Getting demobbed in 1946.' ■ Likes table tennis and wine. Dislikes unenthusiastic musicians.
■ Married to Joan, has two children and lives in Kent.

PETER HUGHES
'I have worked with many greats. . .'

BORN: At an early age in Rochdale, Lancashire. Father a commercial traveller. EDUCATED: King Edward School, St. Annes-on-Sea. Royal College of Music, Manchester and London's Archer Street! Plays all the saxophones, clarinets and flutes. FIRST JOB: Playing with the Bram Martin Orchestra in *On With the Show* at the North Pier, Blackpool. He also made his first broadcast from the North Pier, Blackpool in 1945. Has played with the RAF Band at Cranwell, Henry Mancini, Nelson Riddle, Benny Goodman, Ronnie Aldrich, Cyril Stapleton, Bob Farnon, Harry Stoneham, National Philharmonic Orchestra, Bill McGuffie, Jack Parnell, Bob Sharples, George Chisholm, Phil Tate, Syd Lawrence, Ray Charles and Peter Knight to mention but a few! Also occasionally plays with the BBC Concert Orchestra and the BBC Radio Orchestra. Fronts his own line-up, The Peter Hughes Quintet,

and is heard on *You and the Night and the Music*, the *Early Show* and *Music While You Work*.

■ Most exciting moment of career: 'Working "live" with Lena Horne. I have worked with many 'greats', but Lena, live, is the most exciting for me.' ■ A moment to remember: 'Two trumpet playing colleagues of mine were working with me on an out of town TV session, and each had identical trumpet cases. They also each had two pairs of false teeth, one for playing and one for everyday things like eating and smiling. After the session they decided to go for a blow at the local jazz club and try a glass or two of local beverage. After a splendid evening, they went their separate ways, one to continue the next day with the TV session and the other to London for a broadcast. Feeling a little the worse for wear, one duly opened his case in Maida Vale Studios at 10am ready for the broadcast and saw to his horror a strange trumpet and worse still, strange 'choppers'. his colleague was doing the same thing 80 miles away!' ■ Likes cricket and finding good reeds. Dislikes finding bad reeds. ■ Married to Mona, has one son Robert and lives in Middlesex.

DON INNES
'A lot of time listening to jazz records. . .'

BORN: 12th April 1928, in Aberdeen. Father a telephone engineer. Took piano lessons as a child and spent a lot of time listening to jazz and big band records. FIRST JOB: Playing piano in an Aberdeen ballroom at the age of 15. Made his first broadcast in 1950 on *Music While You Work*. Has played with George Evans, the Squadronaires, Eric Delaney, Billy Ternent and Cyril Stapleton. Is featured regularly with the strings of the BBC Radio Orchestra in many of Radio 2's music programmes including *String Sound*. ■ Likes walking and snooker. ■ Married to June, has two sons and lives in Middlesex.

MAX JAFFA
'Advice from Fritz Kreisler. . .'

BORN: 28th December 1912, in London. Father a tailor. **EDUCATED:** St. Marylebone Grammar School. Guildhall School of Music, London. Also studied violin under Sasha Lasserson. **FIRST JOB:** A concert appearance at the age of nine at the Palace Pier theatre, Brighton. At the age of 16, on leaving the Guildhall School of Music, he persuaded the Piccadilly Hotel in London to take him on a two week trial. He was given a contract and stayed five years. Made his first broadcast with the Max Jaffa Salon Orchestra from the Piccadilly Hotel in August 1929. That same year, he was released from the Piccadilly for a season to become the leader of the Scottish Symphony Orchestra, the youngest ever to hold such a post. After the war, his meeting with cellist Reginald Kilbey and pianist Jack Byfield, led to the formation of the famous Max Jaffa Trio. Since 1959 Max Jaffa has been Musical Director at Scarborough giving concerts with the Spa Orchestra for seventeen weeks every year. He has made several series of broadcasts from Scarborough and other programmes include *Melody on Strings, Music for Your Pleasure* and of course the very popular *Grand Hotel*. For over 50 years the music of Max Jaffa has been heard on the radio and in 1982 he was awarded the OBE for services to music.

■ Most exciting moment of career: 'Going to Buckingham Palace in February 1982, to receive the OBE.' ■ A moment to remember: 'I was 17 years old and playing in the Piccadilly Hotel when the great Fritz Kreisler walked into the restaurant to have lunch. I was seized with panic, how could I go on playing with the great man only a few yards away. To my surprise I was asked to join Mr Kreisler for a drink and I started to apologise for the kind of music I was playing. He stopped me in my tracks saying "You must never apologise for playing music, whatever sort it may be. I, too have played in cafés. Remember this advice. No matter what you play or where you play it, if you give a good performance of that particular piece, then your own playing will never suffer and the value of the music itself will be enhanced by your performance." I have heeded that advice all my musical life.'' ■ Likes golf and racing. ■ Married to Jean Grayston, the contralto, has three daughters and lives in Middlesex.

BARBARA JAY
'Featured with Benny Goodman. . .'

BORN: in Cardiff, Wales. Father played trumpet with Roy Fox, Billy Cotton and Joe Daniels Hot Shots. **EDUCATED:** All Saints School, Streatham, London. **FIRST JOB:** Singing with Geoff Love's eight-piece band. She made her first broadcast with the Billy Ternent Band. Has also sung with Ronnie Scott, Tito Burns, Harry Hayes, Bob Miller and in 1969 was chosen to sing with the Benny Goodman Orchestra on its tour of Europe. Radio programmes have included the *Arthur Askey Show* and the *Kenneth Williams Show*. She broadcasts with the BBC Radio Orchestra as well as with her husband's own group, The Tommy Whittle Quartet, and is heard on most of Radio 2's music programmes including Pete Murray's *Late Show*, the *John Dunn Show*, the *Gloria Hunniford Show*, the *David Hamilton Show* and *You and the Night and the Music*.

■ Most exciting moment of career: 'Being offered the postion as featured vocalist with the Benny Goodman Orchestra.' ■ A moment to remember: "During a "live" New Year's Eve broadcast with the Billy Ternent Orchestra from the Paris Cinema, I was getting into my strapless evening dress in the upstairs dressing-room when unexpectedly I heard the announcer introducing me over the intercom. Unbeknown to me the programme had been altered bringing my spot forward. I just made a mad dash down the stairs, through the curtain onto the stage as they were playing the intro to my song. But I didn't have time to do up my zip properly so when I started to sing, the zip started to come down. The only thing I could do was to stand with my arms pinned against my side through the whole song!' ■ Likes badminton, gardening and swimming. Dislikes British winters. ■ Married to Tommy Whittle, qv, and lives in Hertfordshire.

SALENA JONES
'Mad dash from snowbound Hilversum to snowbound London...'

BORN: 29th January 1946, in Newport News, Virginia, USA. Father a guitarist and folk singer. EDUCATED: High School and College in USA. Studied to be a teacher. FIRST JOB: Singing at the Apollo Theatre, New York. Made her first broadcast on station WNEW in New York. In the UK has sung with Jack Parnell, Roy Budd, Maynard Ferguson, Syd Lawrence and the BBC Radio Orchestra. The Skymasters Show Band in Holland and the Austrian Radio Orchestra. Is heard regularly on most of Radio 2's music programmes.

■ Most exciting moment of career: 'Several — winning a talent competition at the Apollo Theatre, New York; winning the Knocke Song Festival, Belgium; winning Gmunden Song Festival, Austria and being awarded a Gold Album in Japan in 1982' ■ A moment to remember: 'One Christmas I was invited to sing on a lunchtime radio show on Radio Hilversum in Holland. Having already been booked to do an evening show at the Café Royal in London, I was reluctant to accept, but was assured that I would be able to catch a plane by 3 o'clock to be back in England by 4 o'clock. I travelled to Holland on the evening of December 30th, with my husband and was booked into a beautiful small country hotel where we had a superb meal and a quiet drink. We remarked what a pleasant way it was to end the old year. The next morning when we awoke we found about two feet of snow and learnt that most Dutch and English airports were closed. All major airlines had cancelled their flights, but we managed to book a private jet that had to

come from Rotterdam to Amsterdam to collect us. The weather at Rotterdam closed in and at 7 o'clock in the evening a British Caledonian pilot decided to try for Gatwick although our luggage had already left for Heathrow. We landed at Gatwick at 8 o'clock, caught the last transfer helicopter to Heathrow to collect our luggage and arrived at the Café Royal at 10 o'clock to be on stage at 11. The booking agent greeted me with 'Well done Salena, you are the one artist I never have to worry about because you always give yourself plenty of time!' ■ Likes cooking and gardening. Dislikes liars. ■ Married to P.J. Rogers and lives in Hampshire.

ELEANOR KEENAN
'Fainted in the middle of a broadcast...'

BORN: January long ago in Belfast. Father was a British Army Captain. EDUCATED: In Africa and Northern Ireland. FIRST JOB: Appearing in a musical *Fancy Free* by Sam Cree at the Arts Theatre, Belfast. Made her first broadcast with the Johnny Joseph Five at the Playhouse in 1969. Has also sung with Ray McVay, Bob Miller, Johnny Howard, Christine Leer Set (all girls), Joe Loss and the Syd Lawrence Orchestra. Has travelled half-way round the world backing Roger Whittaker and cruised to the Bahamas for a month singing on the QE2, (fabulous!) She broadcasts with the Syd Lawrence Orchestra and with the BBC Radio Orchestra/Radio Big Band and is heard regularly on *You and the Night and the Music*, the *Gloria Hunniford Show*, the *Ed Stewart Show* and *Big Band Special*, all on Radio 2.

■ Most exciting moment of career: 'It hasn't happened yet!' ■ A moment to remember: 'I fainted during a "live" broadcast from the Royal Albert Hall, a concert given by the Syd Lawrence Orchestra and compèred by Alan Dell. I was singing with the group *Don't Sit Under the Apple Tree*, when I fell back into the middle of the sax section. Ug! The roadie carried me off and Syd said to the rest of the group, 'keep singing' . . . I had the lead line . . . can you imagine!' ■ Likes reading biographies, cooking and the theatre. Dislikes cold weather.

CAROL KIDD
'Likes laughing and sleeping . . . when she's not singing.'
BORN: 19th October 1947. **EDUCATED:** 'Not very.' **FIRST JOB:** Singing with a Trad Band in Glasgow at the age of 15. Made her first broadcast a year later on a show called *Come Thursday.* Had her own record and chat programme *Jazz 'n That* for two years on Radio Scotland. Made many broadcasts with the BBC Scottish Radio Orchestra before it was disbanded. Now broadcasts with her own trio and the BBC Radio Orchestra/Radio Big Band and is heard on many Radio 2 music programmes including *You and the Night and the Music.* With another singer, runs a hairdressing/beauty salon and Nearly New Clothes shop in Glasgow.

■ Most exciting moment of career: 'Working at Ronnie Scott's and making my very first broadcast with a whole orchestra backing me.' ■ A moment to remember: 'Being hi-jacked from a taxi en route to a recording session by a bunch of musicians because the producer had given them a break at 10.45 and the pubs didn't open until 11 and if the 'turn' isn't there, they can't start without her. Mind you it was Christmas!' ■ Likes laughing and sleeping. Dislikes getting up in the morning. ■ Married to trombonist George Kidd, has three children and lives in Glasgow.

SANDRA KING
'. . . that distinctive deep brown voice.'
BORN: 12th October 1953, in London. Father a postman. **EDUCATED:** Leiton Grammar School, London. The Peggy O'Farrell Stage School where she studied singing and dancing. **FIRST**

JOB: 1966, a modern Easter play on BBC Television. At 17, she toured Bulgaria with the National Youth Jazz Orchestra and at 17½ did an audition for Ronnie Scott's, sang there for three weeks and has made many return engagements. She makes many concert appearances on the Continent and has recently worked in the USA. Made her first broadcast on *Jazz Club* in 1968 with Pat Smythe Jazz Quartet. Has sung with Coe, Wheeler & Co: Danish Symphony Orchestra, Danish Big Band, The Metropole Orchestra of Holland, The Norwegian Symphony Orchestra, The BBC Radio Orchestra/Radio Big Band. Radio programmes include *Kaleidoscope* and *Midweek* for Radio 4 and all of Radio 2's music programmes at one time or another. Is heard regularly on *Big Band Special, Night Owls* and *You and the Night and the Music.* On BBC Radio Scotland, the *Gerry Davis Show* and the Radio Scotland *Road Show.*

■ Most exciting moment of career: 'Giving a concert in Washington DC in April 1982, a performance which was recorded as an LP. Before that, it was singing to a thousand people in Bulgaria when I was 17 with the National Youth Jazz Orchestra.' ■ A moment to remember: 'Arriving in the tiny *Midweek* studio at Broadcasting House, complete with shopping bags at eight o'clock in the morning to sing two songs and having Desmond Wilcox, who was practically sitting on top of the piano (there were four other guests) describing me singing with my shopping at my feet. Kenneth Robinson even described my shopping in his article in the Listener that week!' ■ Likes listening to music, collecting Victorian cards, yoga, reading anything from Eastern philosophy to thrillers. Dislikes ringing telephones in the early hours and cigarettes. ■ Is single and lives in London.

SARAH KING
'Broadcasting is my favourite occupation. . .'
BORN: 18th January 1948, in Barnsley, Yorkshire. Father a coal miner. **EDUCATED:**

Barnsley High School. Took singing and piano lessons. FIRST JOB: Backing singer for Tony Christie. Made her first broadcast on the *John Dunn Show* in 1978. Has sung with the Neil Richardson Orchestra, Ken Moule Orchestra, the Brian Fahey Orchestra, The Dutch Metropole Orchestra, the Finlandia Radio Light Orchestra, and the BBC Radio Orchestra/Radio Big Band. Represented the BBC on the Nordring Radio Festival in 1980 and sang on the BBC/Dutch co-production from Hilversum. Is heard on most of Radio 2's music programmes including *You and the Night and the Music, Round Midnight* and *Big Band Special.*

■ Most exciting moment of career: 'Representing the BBC on the Nordring 1980 Radio Prize in the Finlandia Hall, Helsinki and singing with the Finlandia Radio Light Orchestra conducted by Barry Forgie.'
■ 'Broadcasting, especially when it's for the BBC, is my favourite occupation. I always derive great professional satisfaction and pleasure when working with their tremendous producers, musicians and technical staff. My thanks to all concerned, long may it continue.' ■ Likes keep fit, music and cooking. Dislikes blood sports ■ Is single and lives in Staffordshire.

TONY KINSEY
'Studied in the USA. . .'
BORN: 11th October 1927, in Sutton Coldfield.

Father a manufacturing jeweller. EDUCATED: Greenmore College, Birmingham. Studied percussion with Bill West and Cozy Cole in the USA. Studied composition and orchestration with Bill Russo. Plays percussion and piano. FIRST JOB: Playing in a dance band in Newquay, Cornwall. Made his first broadcast from Birmingham in 1949. Has played with John Dankworth, Jack Nathan, Ronnie Aldrich, Oscar Peterson, Ella Fitzgerald, Lena Horne, Sarah Vaughan, Clark Terry. Fronts his own quartet, quintet and Big Band, and is heard regularly on *You and the Night and the Music, Night Owls* and *Jazz Club.* Has written several songs with singer Lois Lane.

■ Most exciting moment of career: 'Conducting my first large orchestral compositions and playing my own music with a big band.'
■ Likes reading and swimming.
■ Married to Patricia, has one child and lives in Surrey.

JEANIE LAMBE
'One broadcast changed her life. . .'
BORN: December 23rd, 1940 in Glasgow. Father a Music Hall artist. EDUCATED: In Inverness. FIRST JOB: Appearing with her mother and father on stage in their act at the Empire Theatre, Inverness at the age of 11. She went out on her own as a solo singer at the age of 15. Made her first broadcast for producer Ben Lyon on BBC Radio Scotland in 1957. Has sung with Clyde Valley Stompers, Kenny Ball, Acker Bilk, Chris Barber, Alex Welsh, Danny Moss Quartet, Eddie Thompson Trio, Dutch Swing College Band, Mike Cotton's Band, Pizza Express All Star Jazz Band, and most of the BBC Orchestras. Radio programmes include *Jazz Club, Workers Playtime*(!), the *Spike Milligan Show* and the *Rolf Harris Show.* Made many appearances with George Chisholm on the *Black and White Minstrel Show* on BBC Television during the 60s. Is heard regularly with the Danny Moss Quartet on most of Radio 2's music shows including

You and the Night and the Music, Sounds of Jazz, Night Owls, and is frequently the guest vocalist on Radio 2's *String Sound.*

■ Most exciting moment of career: 'Meeting Ella Fitzgerald and Duke Ellington.'
■ A moment to remember:' I had been working in London and touring with jazz bands all over Britain. I needed time to think about my next move, professionally and personally, so I went back home to Inverness. One week later, my agent, Jack Fallon, called me to say he had one broadcast, BBC *Jazz Club,* for me. I said "You've got to be joking, all the way from Inverness for one broadcast! Anyway who is it with?' – 'Danny Moss' he said – "I'll do it," I said. Can you imagine, I came all the way down from the Highlands of Scotland for that one broadcast but it changed my life. Danny proposed to me that week, I accepted and we have lived happily ever since. We now have two fine sons, Danny Junior and Robert.' ■ Likes golf and travelling the world. Dislikes injustice and bad manners.
■ Married to Danny Moss, qv, has two sons and lives in Sussex.

DUNCAN LAMONT
'From trumpet to tenor. . .'

BORN: 4th July 1931, in Greenock, Scotland. Father a professional musician. EDUCATED: St. Mary's High School, Greenock. Taught himself to play the trumpet while at school. Was 21 years old before he switched to saxophone, clarinet and flute. FIRST JOB: Playing gigs around Scotland when he was 13 years old. His first professional engagement was with Kenny Graham and the Afro Cubists in 1951 on trumpet. He also made his first broadcast with the Kenny Graham Band in *Jazz Club* that same year. Has played with Ted Heath, Geraldo, Jack Parnell, Malcolm Mitchell, Vic Lewis, Ken Macintosh, Benny Goodman; and has recorded with Nelson Riddle, John Williams, Paul McCartney, Peggy Lee, Sarah Vaughan, Tony Bennett, Bing Crosby, Fred Astaire and Gene

Kelly. Has had numerous *Jazz Club* broadcasts with his own small group and big band. Fronting his own small group he is heard regularly on many of Radio 2's music programmes including the *Late Show* and *You and the Night and the Music.* Has composed a number of suites for BBC Radio – *Young Persons's Guide to the Jazz Orchestra, Variations on the Carnival of the Animals, Cinderella* (a *Jazz Club* pantomime) and *A Christmas Carol.* He also composed the music for several children's television series – *King Rollo* and *Mr Benn, Victor and Maria* and *Towser.* One of the top session players, he manages to combine his playing with composing.

■ Most exciting moment of career: 'Recording with Crosby and Astaire; touring with the Benny Goodman Orchestra and a trip to Israel with Sinatra.' ■ 'There are many stories about musicians on broadcasts, this is my favourite. Musician to Conductor, "What a terrible arrangement". Conductor to Musician, "It's my arrangement". Musician to Conductor, "Well you can't do much with a tune like that". Conductor to Musician, "I wrote the tune". Musician (panicking) to Conductor, "Beautiful copying"!' ■ Likes music and travelling (with music). Dislikes celery, a reminder of digs and days touring! ■ Married to Bridget, has two sons Duncan and Ross, and lives in Surrey.

LOIS LANE
'Formed the Caravelles, a hit on both sides of the Atlantic. . .'

BORN: 3rd April 1944, in Sleaford, Lincolnshire. Father a salesman. EDUCATED: St. Martha's Convent, Barnet. Clarks College. Plays the guitar. FIRST JOB: Secretary/shorthand typist/receptionist. In 1963 formed The Caravelles and that same year their record *You Don't Have to be a Baby to Cry* reached Number 5 in the UK charts and Number 3 in the US charts. They toured the USA in 1964 appearing on the very first concert given by the

Beatles in America. Lois made her first broadcast with the Caravelles in *Mark Time* with Mark Wynter and the Les Reed Band. As a solo vocalist her first broadcast was on *Music Thru Midnight* with the Tony Osborne Four in 1967. She has sung with the Ted Heath band, Don Lusher Quartet, the Tony Kinsey Quartet and all the BBC popular music orchestras over the years. She broadcasts regularly with the BBC Radio Orchestra/Radio Big Band and the Tony Kinsey Quartet and is heard on most of Radio 2's music programmes including *Big Band Special* and all the daily shows known as the 'Strip' programmes (if you'll pardon the expression!) She is also a talented song writer and has written and broadcast many songs written in collaboration with Tony Kinsey qv.

■ Most exciting moment of career: 'Hearing that the Caravelles' first record had entered the charts: and the very first time I sang at Ronnie Scott's with Coleman Hawkins topping the bill. I had broken my leg and was in plaster and Ronnie Scott introduced me as the best one-legged singer in the business!'
■ A moment to remember: 'During a "take" at a recording session, at the end of my song, the entire trumpet section stood up and played as their trousers dropped to their knees (they were all wearing red underpants) and I was wearing a red face – (print that if you dare!)''
■ Likes 'our narrowboat' Melanie Anne. Dislikes cigarette ends in saucers, toilets or anywhere. ■ Married to 'Superman' of course! (better known as BBC producer Roger Pusey), has two children and lives in Surrey.

GORDON LANGFORD
'A deep involvement in the world of brass bands...'

BORN: 1930 in Edgware, Middlesex. Father a precision toolmaker. EDUCATED: Bedford Modern School. Royal Academy of Music, London. Private tuition in piano from the age of five. He won a Middlesex Scholarship to the Royal Academy of Music where he studied

piano, composition and trombone. Also plays the vibraphone. FIRST JOB: Playing trombone with a touring opera company. Made his first broadcast with the Royal Artillery Band in 1951, as a solo pianist. After National Service he played with Lew Stone, Billy Ternent, Henry Hall and countless radio and television orchestras. Programmes have included *A Man and his Music, Lines from Grandfather's Forehead, Music While You Work, Melodies for You.* He broadcasts as pianist/arranger/composer for *Friday Night is Music Night*, and as pianist/conductor/arranger with the BBC Radio Orchestra. He is also heard on many of Radio 2's music programmes fronting his own sextet. Accompanies Hubert Gregg for his song offering on *Thanks for the Memory.* He received the Ivor Novello Award in 1971 for his contribution to the world of Light Music. Composes a lot of music for Brass Bands and in 1980 was invited by the BBC to compose two pieces to represent its entry for the European Broadcasting Union's Competition for new music for bands. His march *Leviathan* and *A Foxtrot Between Friends* won first prize in both categories.

■ Most exciting moment of career: 'Winning the Ivor Novello Award and the European Broadcasting Union prize' ■ A moment to remember: 'Adjudicating a brass band competition for the Grand Shield at Manchester's Belle Vue, being shut up in a box and having to listen to the same piece of music twenty times. What a way to earn a living, I thought!' ■ Likes tramways and railways. Dislikes misuse of superlatives in radio programmes. ■ Lives in Devon and London (mostly Devon).

JIM LAWLESS
'The trumpet section were dying of thirst...'

BORN: 18th February 1935, in Woolwich. Father a Regimental Sergeant Major. EDUCATED: Isleworth Grammar School. Private piano lessons for three years, but apart from that, self taught. Plays vibraphone, xylophone, marimba, timpani and all Latin American instruments. FIRST JOB: Touring with the Eric Delaney Band for three years. Before becoming a professional musician he studied electronics and obtained his Higher National Certificate. Made his first broadcast with Eric Delaney at the Playhouse in 1960. Has also played with Ted Heath, Jack Parnell, Joe Loss, Johnny Howard, Ken MacIntosh, Eric Winstone, Denny Boyce, the Beatles, Brotherhood of Man, Blue Mink, The London Symphony Orchestra, the Philharmonic, The Royal Philharmonic Orchestra and the BBC Radio Orchestra/Radio Big Band. Has been broadcasting regularly since 1960. Everything from jazz to light music. He also fronts his own quintet and is heard on many of Radio 2's music programmes including *You and the Night and the Music.*

concert Orchestra in 1970. Since 1972 he has been Music Director to the Royal Ballet at Covent Garden and is also principal guest conductor to the ballet at the Paris Opera.

■ Most exciting moment of career: 'Becoming a professional musician and also playing jazz at Ronnie Scott's with members of the Count Basie Band.' ■ A moment to remember: 'It was a "live" broadcast with an audience, on a very hot day at the Playhouse. I had two tacet numbers followed by a timpani roll into an announcement introducing the guest on the show. The trumpet section were dying of thirst, so I volunteered to nip out the back door, go up to the Ship and Shovel and bring back some lagers, thereby quenching their thirst and enabling them to perform more efficiently. I had plenty of time in two tacets, but unfortunately, while I was out, someone locked the back door. The audience was treated to the sight of a panic stricken band leader glaring at an equally panic stricken percussionist running (with clinking bottles) the length of the Playhouse and making the timp roll with two seconds to spare.' ■ Likes squash, eating curries and drinking cider. Dislikes lack of professionalism, insincerity and undisciplined dogs and children. ■ Married to Carole, has three daughters and lives in Surrey.

ASHLEY LAWRENCE
'The Tagore Gold Medal in 1959. . .'
BORN: In New Zealand. EDUCATED: Schools in New Zealand. Auckland University. Royal College of Music, London where in 1959 he was awarded the Tagore Gold Medal for the most distinguished student. He studied conducting under Rafael Kubelik in Lucerne. FIRST JOB: Conductor for the Royal Ballet until 1967, when he became Musical Director of the Ballet of the Deutsche Oper in West Berlin. He was appointed conductor of the BBC

BRIAN LEMON
'Frequent appearances at Ronnie Scott's. . .'
BORN: 11th February 1937, in Nottingham. FIRST JOB: Playing in local bands in Nottingham while in his early teens. Joined Freddie Randall's Band in London 1956 and that year made his first broadcast with them. Has also recorded and broadcast with George Chisholm, Kenny Baker, Sandy Brown, Dave Shepherd, Danny Moss, Alex Welsh, Jack Emblow and John McLevy. Has worked at Ronnie Scott's many times playing with visiting jazz artists such as Ben Webster, Eddie Lockjaw Davis, Stephane Grappelli, Milt Jackson, Ray Brown, Ruby Braff and Benny Goodman. He did a broadcast with Benny Goodman on Radio 3. Broadcasts with the strings of the BBC Radio Orchestra playing his own arrangements and also fronts his own trio, quartet, quintet – Brian Lemon's Dixielanders who are heard on many of Radio 2's music programmes including *You and the Night and the Music.*

■ Likes golf.

REGINALD LEOPOLD
'The sound of Kreisler has stayed in my head. . .'
BORN: May 20th in London. Father an

advertising contractor. EDUCATED: Trinity College of Music, London, where he won a scholarship at the age of 11, to study the violin. FIRST JOB: Leader of the orchestra at the Trocadero Restaurant, London. Played with Carroll Gibbon's Savoy Orpheans along with Hugo Rignold, George Melachrino and Eugene Pini. In the early 30s led the Fred Hartley Sextet. Fronted his own orchestra at the Dorchester Hotel in 1932. Was with the famous Palm Court Trio from 1957 for 17 years. Was a session musician for many years, 'Three sessions a day, seven days a week. I don't know how I survived.' Made his first broadcast from Savoy Hill, 2LO, with Jack Payne around 1927. Fronts his own line-up, the Reginald Leopold Orchestra and is heard regularly on Radio 2's *Among Your Souvenirs* and *Melodies For You*.

■ Most exciting moment of career: 'The first time I went to a Yascha Heifitz concert; and hearing Fritz Kreisler play the Max Bruch G Minor Concerto at the Royal Albert Hall, the sound has stayed in my head ever since.' ■ A moment to remember: 'During the war, we were living at Stanmore which was very much in the doodle bug area. We had a Chow dog at the time, and whenever I started to practise my violin he always went straight to the air raid shelter, whereas a record of Heifitz playing, never worried him!' ■ Likes any form of music if it's well played; and eating – 'my wife's a magnificent cook, but I got the habit of eating well as a kid with the Savoy Orpheans when George Melachrino taught me to eat oysters and I used to eat next door at Simpsons in the Strand every night.' Dislikes driving ('but I do') ■ Married to Jeanne (who comes from Monte Carlo – they met while he was resident at the Dorchester). Lives in Sussex.

TERRY LIGHTFOOT
'Almost a very original first broadcast. . .'
BORN: 21st May 1935, in Potters Bar Middlesex. Father a greyhound trainer at White City Stadium. EDUCATED: Endfield Grammar School. Self-taught musician. Plays clarinet,

tenor, alto and soprano saxophones. FIRST JOB: Trainee newspaper reporter. Became a professional musician in 1956 when he formed his own band. Made his first broadcast that same year on BBC's *Jazz Club*. Has always led his own band apart from one year, 1967-68 when he played with Kenny Ball. Radio programmes include *Easy Beat, Sounds of Jazz*, the *Jimmy Young Show, Late Night Extra*. His band is heard regularly on Radio 2's *Round Midnight* and *You and the Night and the Music*. He and his wife also run a pub, 'The Three Horseshoes' in Harpenden, Hertfordshire.

■ Most exciting moment of career: 'Leading my own band at its debut concert at the Royal Festival Hall in 1956, shortly after my 21st birthday.' ■ A moment to remember: Having passed a BBC audition in 1956 and feeling like a nervous wreck in the studio on my first broadcast, I discovered I still had the mouthpiece cover on, about five seconds prior to the red light! Highly original, but difficult to blow' ■ Likes golf. Dislikes extremely cold weather and vandalism. ■ Married to Iris, has three daughters and lives in Hertfordshire.

JAMES LOCKHART
'Conducted practically all the major orchestras in the UK. . .'
BORN: 16th October 1930, in Edinburgh, Scotland. Father a weights and measures inspector. EDUCATED: George Watson's Boys

189

College. Edinburgh University. Royal College of Music, London. Plays the violin, piano, organ and harpsichord. FIRST JOB: Assistant conductor of the Yorkshire Symphony Orchestra in Leeds. Made his first broadcast as an organist in 1952, as a conductor in 1959 and as an accompanist with Margaret Price in 1962. Has conducted practically all the major orchestras in the UK. Musical Director, The Welsh National Opera; Generalmusikdirektor Staatstheater Kassel; Generalmusikdirektor Staatsorchester Rheinische Philharmonie and Koblenz Oper. Since 1982 has been the principal guest conductor of the BBC Concert Orchestra.

■ Most exciting moment of career: 'Conducting my first opera, *The Marriage of Figaro* with the Royal Opera House, Covent Garden. ■ Likes driving sports cars and hill walking. ■ Married to Sheila Grogan, has three children and lives in West Germany.

JOE LOSS
'Half a century of broadcasting and the first British Band to play in China. . .'

BORN: 22nd June, 1909 in London. Father a furniture maker. EDUCATED: Spitalfields. Trinity College of Music. London College of Music. Plays the violin. FIRST JOB: Playing violin at the Tower Ballroom, Blackpool. Played with Oscar Rabin but apart from that has always fronted his own band which he formed in 1931. A band that has played at such diverse engagements as Sandown Race Course, the circus, the boxing ring and for private dances at many of the Royal residences. Every year since 1973, the Joe Loss Band has entertained the customers on the QE2's world cruise. He has broadcast regularly since the 30s and remembers booking Vera Lynn to sing with the band. It was her first broadcast and she got 30/-. Was awarded the Queen's Silver Jubilee medal in 1977 and the OBE in 1978.

■ Most exciting moment of career: 'Being the first British musician to give a concert with my orchestra in China.' ■ A moment to remember: 'It was just after the Second World War and I'd arrived home just before breakfast time from playing at a dance in the provinces. I grabbed a quick cup of tea and was dressed in my pyjamas and dressing-gown when there was a loud knock at the front door. It was the late Billy Cotton, who was always a cheerful character. He'd treated himself to a new car and brought it round to show me! I was very tired and wanted to go to bed, but Billy was insistent that I go with him for a trial run. Even though the snow was thick on the ground he managed to persuade me, and I went with him still in my pyjamas and dressing-gown. Needless to say, he drove into the country and we ran out of petrol miles from anywhere! Petrol was rationed, but Billy was adamant that he could get some, and left me shivering in the car while he went to find a garage. I was sitting there with my teeth chattering when a local Bobby came along on his bike. I felt a proper fool when he asked me what I was doing there in my pyjamas. When I told him I was Joe Loss and that Billy Cotton had gone looking for petrol, I could see he was beginning to doubt my sanity! I was inwardly cursing Billy, but when he came back he did a much better job of explaining the circumstances than I did, and the young policeman went on his way with our autographs in his notebook. I doubt whether any of his colleagues believed how he got them, but I do know I've had many a chuckle thinking of that car ride with Billy.' ■ Likes motoring, walking and reading. Dislikes insincere people. ■ Married to Mildred, has two children and three grandchildren and lives in London.

DENNIS LOTIS
'Ten shillings for his first broadcast. . .'

BORN: 8th March 1925, in Johannesburg, South Africa, Father a restaurateur. EDUCATED: In South Africa. As a boy soprano took singing lessons for four years. Plays the piano. FIRST JOB: Singing at the Metro Cinema in

Johannesburg. Has also worked as a bus conductor and an electrician. He made his first broadcast in South Africa at the age of nine. On arriving in the UK in the early 50s he joined the Ted Heath Band and made numerous broadcasts with them. A hit record, *Cuddle Me*, prompted him to go solo. He was voted the country's Top Vocalist by the 'Melody Maker' and in 1957 appeared in his first Royal Command Performance. He rejoined the Ted Heath Band for their tour of the USA and an appearance at Carnegie Hall. He has appeared in many films, musicals and straight plays including John Neville's Playhouse production of Shakespeare's *Measure for Measure*. Has had his own radio show, worked as a DJ and made literally thousands of broadcasts. He is heard regularly on most of Radio 2's music programmes.

■ Most exciting moment of career: 'Playing Lucio in Shakespeare's Measure for Measure.' ■ A moment to remember: 'Receiving the princely sum of ten shillings for my first broadcast.' ■ Likes tennis and renovating old buildings. Dislikes philistines who rip down ancient buildings. ■ Married to Rena, has three children and lives in Norfolk.

GEOFF LOVE
'*Alias* Manuel of the Mountains. . .'

BORN: 4th September in Todmorden, Yorkshire. Father Kid Love, who came to the UK from the USA, was World Champion Sand dancer and met Geoff's mother who's family were all actors when they were playing the same town. EDUCATED: Roomfield Boy's School, Todmorden. Started to play the violin at the age of nine and hated it. The family doctor who was the President of the local amateur symphony orchestra and a trombone player, gave him a trombone and he learnt the rudiments of playing from the local brass band. The family doctor took trombone lessons at The Manchester College of Music and then came

home and taught Geoff what he'd been taught! FIRST JOB: Playing trombone at the Carlton Ballroom, Rochdale. Made his first broadcast on Radio Normandy in 1937. Came to London with the Jan Ralfini Orchestra and then joined the Alan Green Band on Hastings Pier. Spent six years in the Army where he had his first 'go' at arranging. In 1946 joined Harry Gold's Pieces of Eight for one week and stayed until New Years Eve 1949. Formed his own line-up for *On the Town*, a Saturday night show for commercial television in 1955. A recording contract followed and a hit record, *Patricia*. 'Manuel of the Mountains' came into being in 1960 so that another record could be released without clashing with the previous hit. That also got into the Top Ten and for four years Geoff kept the identity of Manuel secret! Used another pseudonym in 1971 when he formed Billy's Banjo Band, now known as Geoff Love's Banjo Band which is heard on *Music While You Work*. The Geoff Love Orchestra is heard on many of Radio 2's music shows including the *Weekend Early Shows*.

■ Most exciting moment of career: 'I've had so many and I've been so lucky, working with people like Judy Garland, Marlene Dietrich, Paul Robeson and Gracie Fields.'
■ A moment to remember: 'In 1981 I was conducting a concert at Golders Green Hippodrome which was being broadcast with an audience in the studio, when my trousers split up the back. I never sit down in my dress trousers as they're cut a bit on the snug side, but these were obviously just a little bit too snug! Have you ever tried conducting without moving your jacket!' ■ Likes water skiing or anything to do with water. Dislikes dishonesty and people who don't keep their word.
■ Married to Joy, has two sons, Adrian (qv) and Nigel, and lives in Middlesex.

DON LUSHER
'*With·Ted Heath at Carnegie Hall. . .*'
BORN: 6th November 1923, in Peterborough.

Father the manager of an ironmongers. **EDUCATED:** Deacons School, Peterborough. Taught himself to play the trombone but later studied with Will Bradley and Dick Nash. Plays trombone, euphonium, cornet and drums. **FIRST JOB:** Playing with Joe Daniels Hot Shots. Made his first broadcast with the Lou Praeger Band in 1948. Also played with Maurice Winnick, The Squadronaires, Jack Parnell, Geraldo and Ted Heath. Now one of the country's top session trombonists and as well as making many solo appearances also fronts his own big band, The Don Lusher Big Band, and conducts the Ted Heath Band. Is heard regularly on most of Radio 2's music programmes, including *You and the Night and the Music*, and *Music While You Work*.

■ Most exciting moment of career: 'Playing at Carnegie Hall with Ted Heath.' ■ A moment to remember: 'There were a couple of things the late Ted Heath could not stand, one was being late for rehearsals, the other was any member of the band being off sick. His maxim was 'death is the only excuse'. Rehearsals for the Sunday concerts at the Palladium were at 2pm and we always started on time. On one occasion a certain well-known trombone player was quite late. When he did appear it was obvious he was more than worried as to what Ted's reaction would be and was searching desperately for an excuse. Ted turned on him with the words "Well, what happened?" whereupon the poor trombonist blurted out "I knocked a man over and killed him!" "Well, that's OK, now let's get on with the rehearsal" said Ted, and we did just that. You see "death" was the only acceptable excuse!" ■ Likes golf, tennis, swimming. Dislikes poor quality in anything. Married to Diana, has two sons and one step son and lives in Surrey.

HUMPHREY LYTTELTON *see Presenters*

BILL McGUFFIE
'The nine fingered boy wonder...'
BORN: 11th December 1927 in Glasgow. Father a physiotherapist and teacher of anatomy and pathology. **EDUCATED:** Mount Vernon, Coatbridge. Royal College of Music. Victoria College. Atheneum, Glasgow. Plays piano (awarded Victoria Medal aged 11). Accordian (2nd in British Championships aged 10), trombone, alto sax and violin. **FIRST JOB:** Playing piano at the Carmyle Welfare Hall at the age of 9, when he earned five shillings. Lost one of his fingers in a childhood accident but

he still managed to do, with nine, more than most kids of his age could do with ten! He studied to be a Naval architect before becoming a professional musician. Made his first broadcast on *Children's Hour* on BBC Radio Scotland in 1939 and was broadcasting regularly with the BBC Scottish Variety Orchestra at the age of 14. Has played with Joe Loss, Phil Green, Robert Farnon, Nat Temple, Sydney Lipton, Frank Weir, Ambrose, Teddy Foster and was the featured soloist for 3 years with the BBC Showband when he became a household name. Also plays for Benny Goodman, British Band and American Sextet on his European tours. Has had his own Sunday radio programme alternating with Semprini. Other programmes include *Kings of the Keyboard, Piano Playtime, Baker's Dozen, Bedtime (and Breakfast) with Braden,* and *Round the Horne*. Fronts his own Big Band and the Bill McGuffie Quintet which is heard on many of Radio 2's music programmes including *You and the Night and the Music*.

■ Most exciting moment of career: (Three!) 'Meeting and marrying my wife through the profession. Being given my first break by Phil Green, from being a theatre rehearsal pianist to playing a concerto on a film he'd scored. Accompanying Sarah Vaughan singing 'Polka Dots and Moonbeams' on the *Show Band Show*.' ■ A moment to remember: 'When one of the Show Band trumpet section goofed during a "live" broadcast and with the mike still open, one of his colleagues in the section turned to him and said "What will you have, a lady's handbag or a box of chocolates?" . . . it was heard by all the listeners in the UK.' N.B. Bill is the founder President of the Niner Club which raises money for autistic children. So called because of his missing finger. Ostensibly all members have something missing! ■ Likes golf, reading non-fiction, crosswords and the study of anatomy and psychology. Dislikes self opinionated people who don't know anything and criticism of fellow musicians. ■ Married to Rosemary, has three children (by former marriage) and lives in Middlesex.

HENRY MACKENZIE
'An instantly recognizable sound. . .'
BORN: 15th February 1923, in Edinburgh.
Father a college caretaker. EDUCATED: James
Clark School. Edinburgh. Private tuition on the
clarinet and saxophone for three years. Plays
clarinet, saxophone and flute. FIRST JOB:
Playing at the Havana Club in Edinburgh.
Played in the R.A.S.C. Band for six months.
Made his first broadcast with the Al Bertino
Band in Edinburgh in 1942. Has played with
Tommy Sampson, Paul Fenhoulet, Ted Heath,
Eric Winstone, Billy Ternent, Henry Mancini,
Nelson Riddle, Billy May, Don Lusher and Max
Harris. Has many radio programmes to his
credit including *Jazz Club, Radio 2 Ballroom,
Friday Night is Music Night* and the *Open
House Variety Shows*. Fronts his own quintet
which is heard on Radio 2's *You and the Night
and the Music* and *Music While You Work*.

■ Most exciting moment of career: 'Playing
with Ted Heath at Carnegie Hall.' ■ Likes
watching sport, and music. Dislikes gardening
and DIY jobs! ■ Married to Barbara and lives
in Surrey.

JOHN McLEVY
*'A call from Benny Goodman in New
York. . .'*
BORN: 2nd January 1927, in Dundee. Father a
shipyard engineer and semi-pro drummer.
EDUCATED: Local schools in Dundee. Took
trumpet lessons with the trumpet player in his
father's band. FIRST JOB: Playing trumpet with
the George Elrick Band in 1941. Made his first
broadcast with George Elrick somewhere on
the West coast of Britain, because of the
bombing. Joined the army for the duration of
the Second World War. After his demob,
played with Les Ayling at the Lyceum
Ballroom, London and was then with the
resident band at London's Dorchester Hotel.
Spent two and a half years with Cyril Stapleton
and the BBC Showband and nine years with
Francisco Cavez at the Savoy Hotel. Now fronts
a small group with Jack Emblow and is heard
regularly on many of Radio 2's music
programmes including *You and the Night and
the Music*.

■ Most exciting moment of career: 'Being asked
to play with Benny Goodman. When he came
over here in the early 70s I joined his band for a
tour of Europe. About a year after that the
telephone went one day, and it was Benny
Goodman on the line from New York saying
"What are you doing in ten days' time – can
you meet me in Helsinki?" "Yes," I replied,
"whatever I'm doing in ten days' time I'll get rid
of!" And so I joined him in Helsinki and did
another tour of Europe." ■ Likes reading and
golf. Dislikes nothing – 'I like everything.'
■ Has two daughters and lives in London.

JANIE MARDEN
'A series on Cuban television. . .'
BORN: 23rd February 1934, Father a Boffin.
EDUCATED: Bristol and Littlehampton Girls
Schools. Took piano and singing lessons. Plays
'rotten ' piano! [but sings nicely!] FIRST JOB:
Singing at the Grand Spa Hotel Ballroom,
Bristol. Made her first broadcast from Bristol at
the age of 17. Has sung with Cyril Stapleton,
Jack Parnell, Geraldo, Don Lusher, Alan
Ainsworth, Johnny Arthey and Ted Heath. Was
the resident singer at the Tagomago Night Spot
in Majorca; starred in television series in Cuba,
Madrid and Berlin. Has made literally hundreds
of broadcasts and was with Radio 2's *Softly*

Sentimental for two and a half years. Is heard on many of Radio 2's music programmes including *You and the Night and the Music.*

■ Most exciting moment of career: 'Appearing on Cuban television before an audience of 20,000 people.' ■ Likes horse riding, the theatre, the cinema and dancing. Dislikes people who look at your left ear when they talk to you, insincerity, people who think they know it all, and moderationists in everything. ■ Married to composer Edward White and lives in Sussex.

JUNE MARLOW
'It's all been lovely. . .'

BORN: 15th January 1934, in Plymouth, Devon. Father a baker. EDUCATED: St. Andrew's Primary School. Coburg Street Secondary School. Took piano lessons at school. Plays one handed piano (the right hand) FIRST JOB: Singing with a local dance band in Plymouth. Also worked as a Post Office counter clerk. Spent several years out of the business bringing up her family. Since returning is working as an actress as well as a singer. Made her first broadcast at 13 years old on *Opportunity Knocks.* Was one of the Stargazers in the 50s. Has also sung with Eric Winstone, Bill McGuffie, Steve Race, Acker Bilk, BBC Radio Orchestra, Ronnie Price and Jack Emblow. Has made hundreds of broadcasts over the years on such programmes as the *Show Band Show,* the *Stargazer's Music Shop, Worker's Playtime, Mid-day Music Hall, Saturday Club, Educating Archie, Music Box, Sing it Again, Bernard Braden's Shows, Charlie Chester* and the *John Dunn Show.* Is heard regularly on Radio 2's Early and Late Shows and *Acker's Alf 'Our* with Acker Bilk. Television credits include *Horseman Riding By, Penmarric, Westward Ho, To Be a Farmer's Boy* and *Jamaica Inn.* She also appears on television commercials.

■ Most exciting moment of career: 'I cannot choose one exciting moment, I suppose it should be appearing at the London Palladium in the Royal Command Performance, but it's all been lovely.' ■ A moment to remember: 'It was a Sunday. I had a chicken cooking for lunch on a gadget in the oven and decided to wash my hair. The telephone rang – could I come at once to the BBC Paris Studio as the guest singer had failed to arrive for the Ted Ray comedy programme. Yes of course I could and I'll sing whatever she was going to sing if the orchestration is there, I said, my hair dripping into the receiver. One look at the clock. . . come in about half an hour the producer said and we should have time to rehearse the song. There was a steady klunk klunk from the kitchen as the chicken began falling from the spit. Ignoring that cry for help, I was hurrying off to the studio when my small son appeared from play proudly holding upside-down, a dislocated thumb, with my husband saying he would take him to casualty and not to worry. I left! Arriving for the broadcast I was told there was no vocal part with the orchestra. It was a new song but I'd heard it once or twice and recalled the lyric, so with Malcolm Lockyer giving me the routine "live" on the air, we did it. The song should have been *Cock Eyed Optimist!* To conclude – The thumb was fine, the chicken was not. The hair was still wet but the song went well.' ■ Likes reading, cooking and talking. Dislikes filling in forms. [She did pretty well.] ■ Married to Pete Van-Dike, has five children and lives in Devonshire.

PHILIP MARTIN
There is a ghost in Studio One, Maida Vale. . .'

BORN: 27th October 1947, in Dublin, Eire. Father a tobacconist. EDUCATED: St. Mary's college, Rathmines, Dublin. Learnt to play the piano at the Patricia Read Pianoforte School, Dublin. Studied piano with Mabel Swainson 1956-65. Studied piano and composition at the

Royal Academy of Music, London 1965-70. Also studied with Louis Kentner between 1971 and 79. FIRST JOB: Teaching the untalented son of a jeweller to play the piano! Made his first broadcast in 1953 on RTE Dublin in *Children at the Mike*. Broadcasts regularly with most of the BBC Orchestras and giving recitals solo and jointly with his wife, soprano Penelope Price Jones. Has played with the City of Birmingham Symphony Orchestra, the Royal Liverpool Philharmonic, the Bournemouth Sinfonietta and the Halle Orchestra. 1983, broadcast a series of American recitals using music found on UK/US Bicentennial Arts Fellowship 1981.

■ Most exciting moment of career: 'My first appearance at the Royal Festival Hall with a BBC Orchestra in 1977. ■ A moment to remember: 'There is a ghost in Studio One, Maida Vale! I was recording a programme there a few years ago and there were some very strange noises in the studio, which to this day are completely unexplained! Perhaps it was tummy rumbling!' ■ Likes pottery, walking and exploring places of interest. Dislikes hypocrites and petty bureaucracy. ■ Married to Penelope Price Jones, has one dog and lives in Wiltshire.

KIM MARTYN
'Such a friendly atmosphere at the BBC. . .'

BORN: 14th March in Dagenham, Essex. Father an engineer for Ford Motor Co. EDUCATED: Ripple Road Primary School, Barking. Downshall Secondary School, Seven Kings. Studied singing at the Eric Guilder School of Music. FIRST JOB: Singing with a local dance band. Made her first broadcast with Jimmy Young on the *Jack Dorsey Big Band Show*. Has appeared at several London night spots in cabaret including the Playboy Club and the Hilton Hotel where she was resident singer for 18 months. Has sung with the Tony Lee Trio, Harry Stoneham and the Pete Hughes Quintet. Television credits include the *Spytrap* series and the *David Nixon Show*. She broadcasts

regularly with the BBC Radio Orchestra/Radio Big Band and is heard on most of Radio 2's music shows including *Band Parade*, the *Late Show*, the *Early Show* and *You and the Night and the Music*.

■ Most exciting moment of career: 'The first time and every time I sing with a beautiful, large string orchestra.' ■ 'It is always such a pleasure to work with and meet so many lovely people connected with the BBC. The atmosphere is always so very friendly, whether you are having a coffee in the canteen or working in the studio with big personalities.' ■ Likes the theatre, gardening and DIY. Dislikes olives, blood sports, litter bugs and vandalism. ■ Married to TV producer David Clark, has one child and lives in Surrey.

VALERIE MASTERS
'Radio has an amazing advantage over television. . .

BORN: 24th April 1940, in London. EDUCATED: in London. Has studied the technique of singing and has learnt to sight read music. FIRST JOB: Singing with the Ray Ellington Quartet in 1957. Made her first broadcast in 1958 on *In Town Tonight*. Has sung with many different bands throughout her career and has had her own television and radio programmes. She broadcasts regularly with the BBC Radio Orchestra and is heard on most of Radio 2's daily music shows and on *You and the Night and the Music*.

■ Most exciting moment of career: 'When I had my hit record with Banjo Boy in 1959 and singing at the London Palladium.' ■ 'I have the greatest love for the BBC because through them, I have been able to keep singing and therefore keep in touch with all sorts of people, especially since the death of my husband. An amazing advantage radio has over television is that the artist can paint a picture of any type and try to get the listener to use his imagination, when in fact you are probably just sitting on a

stool in a studio in front of a microphone.'
■ Likes painting, sewing and collecting.
Dislikes smoking and arguing. Is the widow of
pianist Dick Katz, has two daughters, one of
whom Debbie Katz has made a name for
herself as a singer. Lives in Buckinghamshire.

MARYETTA MIDGLEY
'Our business is one long excitement. . .'

BORN: 27th May, in Edinburgh, Scotland.
Father the international tenor, Walter Midgley.
EDUCATED: Holy €ross Convent, New Malden,
Surrey. She won a music scholarship to the
Trinity College of Music, London where she
studied singing and the piano. FIRST JOB:
Soloist with the George Mitchell Singers. Made
her first broadcast as a child in Round the Horn.
Has appeared in the Fol-De-Rols at the
Congress Theatre, Eastbourne and in Camelot
at Drury Lane. She broadcasts regularly on
Radio 2 on such programmes as Friday Night is
Music Night, Melodies for You, Among Your
Souvenirs, Saturday Night is Gala Night and
Robert Farnon's World of Music. Radio 3
programmes include the Strauss opera Wiener
Blutt and the operetta les Cloches de Cornville.

■ Most exciting moment of career: 'Isn't our
business one long excitement?' ■ A moment
to remember: 'It didn't actually happen, as it
was a dream, but a very vivid one. I arrived at a
broadcasting stuido to meet everyone coming
out. The show was over and worst of all,
nobody had missed me!' ■ Likes driving,
embroidery, horseriding and gardening.
Dislikes packing and unpacking . . . ugh! Oh
yes, and spiders! ■ Is the sister of tenor
Vernon Midgley and lives in Surrey.

VERNON MIDGLEY
'On stage alone, singing a duet. . .'

BORN: 28th May in Worcester Park, Surrey.
Father, the international tenor, Walter Midgley.
EDUCATED: Bishop's Stortford College. Royal

Academy of Music where he studied singing
and the piano. (Sisselle Wray Scholar). FIRST
JOB: Entomologist with the Ministry of
Agriculture, Fisheries and Food, Pest Infestation
Headquarters at Tolworth, Surrey. 'At one time
I was offered the job of Assistant Pro to Vic
Saunders at Coombe Wood Golf Club, but I
turned it down.' Made his first broadcast in
Lights of London in 1971. Has sung with the
Ambrosian Opera Chorus and with most of the
military and brass bands in the country. Has
sung in many full-length operas and operettas
on Radio 3. Radio 2 programmes include
Grand Hotel, Ring Up the Curtain, Among
Your Souvenirs, Your Hundred Best Tunes,
Bakers Dozen, Glamorous Nights, and Walter
Midgley Remembers; and on Radio 4, Music to
Remember. Broadcasts regularly on Radio 2's
Friday Night is Music Night and Melodies for
You.

■ Most exciting moment of career: 'Whenever I
have been privileged to be presented to a
member of the Royal Family. In broadcasting, it
took place in Israel on Good Friday, 1981
when I sang in a Bach concert relayed by the
Israel Broadcasting Authority. The Old City was
the exciting place to be on a Good Friday and I
shall never forget the smell of orange blossom
in the evening. The Swedish conductor, Eric
Ericson and I, were the only non-Israelis taking
part.' ■ A moment to remember: 'During a
"live" public performance of Friday Night is
Music Night, at the Free Trade Hall,
Manchester in September 1978, I found myself
alone on stage, singing a duet! The soprano
was locked in the toilet of her dressing-room.
Happily I knew her lines, but the conductor
slowed the performance to a snail's pace in a
vain attempt to enable the unfortunate girl to
join us, which she eventually did as I was
singing the line, ''Tell me that where 'eer you
go. . .''!' ■ Likes golf, cricket, painting and
drawing. Dislikes tripe, bagpipes played too
near and discos. ■ Married to New Zealand
soprano Alexandra Gordon, has a son and a
daughter and lives in Surrey.

TRACY MILLER

'Nothing funny ever happens to me. . .'

BORN: in County Durham. Father a brick maker. EDUCATED: Fence Houses Secondary Modern School. Durham Technical College. Studied singing at the Guildhall School of Music London. FIRST JOB: Singing at the Continental Hotel, St. Helier, Jersey. Made her first broadcast as a backing singer with Clodagh Rogers in 1968. As a soloist in 1979. She has sung with many vocal groups – Sounds Bob Rogers, Polka Dots, Skylarks, Coffee Set, Neil Richardson Singers, Ladybirds, Breakaways, Ambrosian Singers, Charles Young Chorale, Cliff Adam Singers, Ray Charles Singers, Anita Kerr Singers. Has sung with the bands of Syd Lawrence and Jack Parnell. As a soloist she sang on the Monte Carlo Radio Prize entry in 1982 and the 1979 Nordring Radio Prize. She broadcasts regularly with the BBC Radio Orchestra and is heard on most of Radio 2's music programmes including *You and the Night and the Music*, and *String Sound*. Television credits include the Val Doonican series, *Helen McCarthy Show* for Scottish Television and *World of . . .* on BBC 2.

■ Most exciting moment of career: 'Appearing with Perry Como on the Royal Variety Show in 1976. ■ A moment to remember: 'Nothing funny ever happens to me on a broadcast – disastrous, yes; tragic, yes; hysterical, yes; horrendous, yes; funny? never. but I'm open to offers!' ■ Likes dancing, gardening, swimming and cooking. Dislikes the cold, noisy people, accountancy and bank managers. ■ Lives in Surrey.

MARIAN MONTGOMERY

'A confirmed Anglophile. . .'

BORN: Natchez, Mississippi, USA. Father a hotelier. EDUCATED: Gainesville, Georgia High School. Virginia Intermont College. Brenau College. FIRST JOB: Singing on television in Atlanta, Georgia while still in her teens. Was an established cabaret performer in the States before coming to the UK in 1965 and has a

thousand tales to tell . . . like driving along the Los Angeles freeway with Cy Coleman singing *You Are My Sunshine*, with the tears streaming down their faces from the smog and later at Coleman's house rehearsing songs for an album, the doorbell rings and it's Doris Day, more than a little annoyed that she hadn't been asked to do the album; and the time she, Nancy Wilson and Peggy Lee used to vie for the same material . . . Peggy always won! Being in Miami with Mel Torme, Jack Jones, Dave King, Joe Williams and Shirley and Gordon McCrea when they all used to wind up at an after hours club and sit in with the band . . . the club became the most popular rendezvous in town! Since living in the UK, Marian has presented her one-woman show and had a very successful collaboration with classical pianist/composer Richard Rodney Bennett. She broadcasts regularly with the BBC Radio Orchestra/Radio Big Band and is heard on many of Radio 2's music programmes including *You and the Night and the Music*, and *Big Band Special*.

■ Most exciting moment of career: 'Every time I go on stage.' ■ A moment to remember: 'I was working in Australia and on my return to the UK was due to sing at a Gershwin concert in London. My husband, Laurie Holloway telephoned me and said we were one number short, how about doing *Why do I love You*. "Fine" I said. So I get back from Australia and the next day is the day of the concert. Laurie's done a super arrangement but I rang Chappells, the music publishers just to check that I had remembered the lyrics as I hadn't got a song copy. Much to my surprise they said they hadn't got a copy and would have to telex New York. "Oh come off it", I said, "you must have a copy of *Why Do I Love You*. We have a copy of Jerome Kerns's *Why Do I Love You*, but not Gershwins.' Horror of horrors, we had made a dreadful mistake and how was I going to sing a Kern song in a Gershwin concert? No way could I drop it, because there was nothing else ready. So I came on stage and told the story of how George Gershwin and Jerome Kern were good friends and over diner one night, they got to discussing who could write the best song and they both said they would write *Why Do I Love You.* 'Ladies and gentlemen' I said, 'I will leave it to you to decide whether this was the best song', without saying which it was! I thought I had got away with it until someone in the audience came up to me after the concert and said 'That was a nice little story, I happen to know those two songs were written years apart. One day that's going to end up in a book.' [How right they were, it has!] ■ Likes reading and riding! Dislikes big parties, phoney people and loud places. Married to MD/pianist Laurie Holloway. (qv), has one daughter and lives in Berkshire.

DANNY MOSS
'From Saturday Night at the Palais to Sounds of Jazz. . .'
BORN: 16th August 1927, in Earlswood, Surrey. Father an engineer. EDUCATED: Steyning Grammar School, Sussex. Is a self taught musician (still learning!) Plays tenor saxophone, clarinet, bass clarinet and flutes. FIRST JOB: Playing at Sherry's Ballroom, Brighton at the age of 16. Made his first broadcast in September 1945 with the Wal Rodgers Quintet in *Saturday Night at the Palais.* Has played with Ted Heath, John Dankworth, Humphrey Lyttleton, Geraldo, Squadronaires, Oscar Rabin, Maynard Ferguson and Vic Lewis. Has fronted his own Quartet since 1963. In around 40 years (well almost) of broadcasting has been heard on just about every dance band and jazz programme from *Music While You Work* onwards! The Danny Moss Quartet is heard regularly on Radio 2's music programmes including *String Sound, You and the Night and the Music, Night Owls* and Radio 1's *Sounds of Jazz.*

■ Most exciting moment of career: 'So many, it's hard to select one, but recently, flying into Rio de Janeiro for a Jazz Festival.''
■ A moment to remember: 'One broadcast that changed my life (see Jeanie Lambe)!' (qv)

■ Likes golf. Dislikes bad music and cold climates. ■ Married to singer Jeanie Lambe, has two sons and lives in Sussex.

KEN MOULE
'Swinging Shepherd blues in a couple of hours. . .'
BORN: 26th June 1925, in Barking, Essex. Father a factory manager. EDUCATED: Chingford Boys School. Took piano lessons from local teachers at half a crown a time. FIRST JOB: Playing piano with Oscar Rabin's Band in 1945. Made his first broadcast in May 1945 on a solo spot for promising young players. (Still promising!) Took a job as pianist on the *Queen Mary* in 1947 doing the Atlantic run and when in New York heard everyone – Charlie Parker, Dizzy Gillespie etc: Has played with Frank Weir, Ambrose, Ted Heath, John Dankworth and in the mid 50s led his own modern jazz band. Was also an arranger for Ted Heath during the 50s and arranged *Swinging Shepherd Blues* which became a big hit for the band. 'My most successful arrangement ever and it took me a couple of hours.' He has also been Musical Director of several West End musicals – *Fings Ain't what They Used to Be, Cole* and *Oh Mr Porter.* Arranges for and conducts the BBC Radio Orchestra and is heard on many of Radio 2's music programmes including the *Gloria Hunniford Show* and the *John Dunn Show.*

■ Most exciting moment of career; 'Listening to Kenny Wheeler's contribution to a Suite which I was invited to write for him by the Hanover Radio Orchestra in 1979.' ■ Likes proper music. Dislikes exponents of the Three Chord Trick. ■ Married to Vera Baron, has two step children and lives in Surrey.

PAT O'HARE
'Bill Scott Coomber gave him his first break. . .'
BORN: 5th November 1931 in Manchester. Father a bus driver/crane driver. EDUCATED:

St. Dunstans Elementary, Moston, Manchester. St. Gregory's Secondary. FIRST JOB: Metal spinner. Spent seven years in the Royal Navy and was a motor mechanic/air mechanic in the Fleet Air Arm. Made his first broadcast on 3rd March 1959 in *Time to Celebrate* produced by Geoff Lawrence. Has sung with Eddie Shaw, Tommy Smith, Teddy Foster, Ambrose, Syd Lipton, Geraldo, Harry Roy, and Jack Parnell, and also done many broadcasts with the Northern Dance Orchestra and the Northern Radio Orchestra. Programmes include *Musical Merry Go Round, Mid-day Music Hall, Singin' and Swingin' Pat O'Hare* and the NDO (series), *Nice to Come Home To* (series), *In the Cool of the Evening* (series), *Workers Playtime, Melody on the Line, Teenagers Turn,* the *Beat Show, Linger Awhile, We'll Be Around, Blackpool Night.* Is heard regularly on Radio 2's *You and the Night and the Music,* the *John Dunn Show, David Hamilton Show, Stuart Hall Show, Round Midnight* and the *Early Show.* Was featured as Al Bowlly in the ATV series *And the Bands Played On.* Other television credits include *The Sounds of Pat O'Hare* for Border TV, *Stars on Sunday* for Yorkshire TV, followed by *Your Hundred Best Hymns.*

■ Most exciting moment of career: 'My first radio series in 1961.' 'It was Bill Scott Coomber who gave me my first break in broadcasting. I had no idea of his background until 20 years later when I was doing some research prior to playing Al Bowlly on television. I then discovered that Bill was a big name singer of that era, and I regret that I wasn't aware of it when I was working with him.' [N.B. Pat reminded me that we shared digs in Edinburgh when he was singing with Harry Roy at the Palace and the Tracy Sisters were on the bill at the Empire!] ■ Likes watching Manchester United and DIY. Dislikes watching Manchester City and too much DIY. ■ Married to Christine, has a son and a daughter and lives in Saddleworth.

NIGEL OGDEN
'An entertaining organist. . .'
BORN: 21st November 1954 in Manchester. Father an accountant. EDUCATED: Burnage Grammar School, Manchester. West Midlands College, Walsall. Didsbury Teacher Training College, Manchester. FIRST JOB: Electronic organ demonstrator. He also worked as a demonstrator/representative for Boosey and Hawkes Electrosonics Ltd. First broadcast: December 1970 as a guest artist on BBC 1's *Screen Test.* Made his first radio broadcast the following May, on BBC Radio Manchester, while resident weekend organist at the Gaumont Theatre, Manchester. Following this Robin Richmond recorded a public concert at the Gaumont for Radio 2's *The Organist Entertains* and Nigel has been a regular contributor to the programme ever since. He now presents *The Organist Entertains* and also is one of several organists featured on a rota basis on Charlie Chester's *Sunday Soapbox.*

■ Most exciting moment of career: 'Landing the job as presenter of *The Organist Entertains.*'
■ Likes keep fit/weight training, concert and theatre going. Dislikes water, apart from for washing and drinking, and British summers. ■ Lives in Lancashire.

ANGIE PAGE
'My father, Reg Conroy was a regular broadcaster in the 30s. . .'
BORN: 24th July 1944, in Nottingham. Father

musician/bandleader, Reg Conroy. EDUCATED: St. Catherine's Convent Grammar School, Nottingham. Her father taught her a lot about dance music. She also studied music as a main subject for three years at Nottingham College of Education, as part of a teacher training course. Plays the piano, electric piano and synthesizer. FIRST JOB: School teacher for three years while working with her own trio in Chinese and Italian Restaurants in Nottingham. With her trio has worked extensively on cruise ships, *Oriana* and *Canberra* 1974/75, the QE2 1976-79 including two world cruises. Also a six month spell on the Cunard *Countess* in the Caribbean. Has played the London hotel circuit and has been the resident pianist/vocalist at Morton's Restaurant, Berkeley Square, London. Made her first broadcast on 18th September 1980. Has always fronted her own trio or quartet and is heard regularly on the *Late Show* and *You and the Night and the Music* on Radio 2.

■ Most exciting moment of career: 'Being able to broadcast my own songs for the first time.' 'My father, Reg Conroy was a regular broadcaster in the 30s with his own band, The Harmo Knights. He often worked with George Shearing, Stephane Grappelli and Maurice Winnick. He played excellent vibes, piano and trumpet as well as violin, trombone, accordian and guitar. He was also a member of the Coconut Grove Quartet at the Coconut Grove in Regent Street, London, which included Ronnie Aldridge on tenor and Barney Gilbraith.' ■ Likes winemaking. Dislikes country and western music and garlic. ■ Lives in Nottinghamshire.

LEONI PAGE
'Discovered by Barney Colehan...'
BORN: 7th November 1936, in London. Father a salesman. EDUCATED: Aida Foster Stage School. FIRST JOB: 'On leaving school, I worked in a dress shop and then sold gramophone records, but my first big

professional job, at the age of 17 was in the original *King and I* at the Theatre Royal, Drury Lane when I played one of the King's wives, opposite Herbert Lom. Made her first broadcast on 23rd December 1957 with Morecambe and Wise and the Alyn Ainsworth Orchestra in a programme produced by Geoff Lawrence. That same year was 'discovered' by Barney Colehan and appeared in one of the first *Good Old Days* shows from the City of Varieties, Leeds. Many other television appearances followed. Has sung with the Royal Philharmonic Orchestra, Mantovani, Max Jaffa, Geoff Love, Frank Chacksfield, Kenneth Alwyn, the BBC Concert Orchestra, the Band of the Welsh Guards and the Scots Guards. Radio programmes include *Charlie Katz Music Box*, *Workers Playtime*, *Mid-day Music Hall*, *Strings by Starlight*, *Those Were the Days*, the *Sam Costa Show*, the *Charlie Chester Show*, *You and the Night and the Music*, *Round Midnight*, *Salute to Noël Coward*, *Music for Your Pleasure*, and *Among Your Souvenirs*. Is heard regularly as the 'star singer' on Radio 2's *Friday Night is Music Night*.

■ Most exciting moment of career: 'I have had several . . . appearing at the Persian Room in the Plaza Hotel, New York, only the second British girl to do so at that time; singing at the Royal Albert Hall; and last year, singing Land of Hope and Glory with the Band of the Scots Guards after the Falklands war had ended.' ■ A moment to remember: 'I was doing a "live" broadcast of *Grand Hotel* from the Aeolian Hall some years ago, and although children under the age of 10 weren't usually allowed into the studio, the producer had given permission for my young daughter to be there. As I walked on and started to sing she had a fit of coughing from nerves for me! It was so loud in the silence of the Concert Hall, that a very irate producer crept in and pulled her from her seat – I don't know how I carried on. I was warned afterwards to leave my family at home in future. Surprisingly the producer did book me again!' ■ Likes cooking, crochet and writing. Dislikes cruelty to children and animals. ■ Married to hairdresser, Colin Curtis, has two daughters and lives in London.

JOHN POOLE
'Directs the BBC Singers. . .'

BORN: 5th February 1934, in Birmingham.
EDUCATED: Balliol College, Oxford, where he took a degree in music. Plays the piano, cello and organ. ■ Is the Director of the BBC Singers. ■ Married to Anne Toler, has three children and lives in Hertfordshire.

SIR JOHN PRITCHARD
'My Father gave me my first musical grounding. . .'

BORN: 5th February 1921, in Woodford, near Epping Forest. Father an orchestral violinist. 'He would now be called a freelance and he was so freelance that he used to fall out with anyone he sat next to in the orchestra. He was difficult but a good player and he gave me my first musical grounding.' EDUCATED: Sir George Monoux School, London. Made his first broadcast as a conductor at Glyndebourne (see below). Was conductor of the Derby String Orchestra 1943-51; Royal Liverpool Philharmonic 1957-63; London Philharmonic 1962-66; Glyndebourne Opera 1962-77; Covent Garden Opera 1952-77; has been principal conductor of the BBC Symphony Orchestra since 1982. Was awarded the CBE in 1962 and was knighted in 1983.

■ A moment to remember: 'When I was a young assistant conductor to Fritz Busch at Glyndebourne, I had been working very hard taking all the rehearsals and one day the Maestro looked at me and said 'You are very pale, go and take a holiday.' I didn't know where to go so I went to Eastbourne, just a few miles from Glyndebourne. As I took my first swim in the sea, I couldn't stop thinking about the performance that night which was being broadcast to many countries in Europe. It was about 6.15pm and I thought I must get out of the sea as its getting late, when a man came along the shore with a loudhailer shouting "John Pritchard, John Pritchard". What had happened was Dr. Busch had started the Overture and then became terribly ill, but as the concert was being broadcast all over Europe he had to get through the first act, because once you start, you can't get out. All he could do was to whisper "get Pritchard, get Pritchard". So after my first few minutes of holiday, there I was mounting the rostrum at Glyndebourne for the first time in public. Then of course it had to be explained in 20 different languages . . . "due to the indisposition of Dr. Fritz Busch, his assistant Mr John Pritchard will take over the performance". I had to find some tails to wear and it was all very glamorous and romantic. The point was, if it had been an ordinary evening at Glyndebourne it would have been exciting, but the sudden illness made news and everybody in Denmark, Sweden, Italy and France etc were saying 'who is this John Pritchard?'. It was very good for my career of course and it was no problem to me to conduct the performance as I had done all the rehearsals, but I thought, that will teach me to take a holiday.' ■ Likes good food, wine and travelling the world. Dislikes muzak everywhere. 'I resent my thoughts being occupied by something that is essentially very second class; and seeing my compatriots behaving badly abroad.'

STEVE RACE *see Presenters*

MIKE REDWAY
'Likes the telephone to ring. . .'

BORN: 17th December 1939 in Leeds, Yorkshire. Father a baker. EDUCATED: All Saints School, Leeds. Plays piano and guitar as well as singing. FIRST JOB: Tailor. Has also worked as a baker, carpet salesman and song plugger. Made his first broadcast on the *Albert Modley Show* from BBC Manchester in 1958. Has sung with Oscar Rabin, Mike Sammes Singers, Cliff Adams Singers and Maggie Stredder Singers. Is a talented song writer who has yet to hit the jackpot. Has recorded many albums and

released a number of singles. Is heard regularly on many of Radio 2's music programmes including *You and the Night and the Music*.

■ Most exciting moment of career: 'When the telephone rings! Long live the BBC.' ■ Likes breeding canaries, parrots and kestrels. Dislikes not having the telephone ring. ■ Married to Marjorie, has three children and lives in Middlesex.

Director of BBC 1's *Pebble Mill at One*, and plays piano for Stanley Black, Frank Chacksfield, and Johnny Gregory Orchestras.

■ Most exciting moment of career: 'Receiving the Hopkinson Silver medal (1950) and the Hopkinson Gold Medal (1951) from Princess Elizabeth at the Royal College of Music. Also performing for the Queen Mother with the Palm Court Trio at an informal dinner party in Scotland.' ■ A moment to remember: 'Whilst giving a "live" afternoon recital of serious music from Birmingham, I was just about to begin Schubert's Impromptu in A flat (Op 90, No. 4) when I spotted a huge spider making its way across my foot and about to climb up my leg inside the trousers! The first few bars were spent in a vigorous shaking of same while trying to concentrate on the music!" ■ Likes walking, visiting places of historical interest, watching most kinds of sport and trying to play golf. Dislikes people who ring up and begin by saying 'Guess who this is'? ■ Lives in Warwickshire.

HAROLD RICH
'Almost an impromptu performance. . .'
BORN: 24th January 1927, in Wolverhampton. EDUCATED: Wednesbury Boys High School. Royal College of Music, London where he studied piano and organ. FIRST JOB: Music master at a secondary modern school at Old Hill, West Midlands. Made his first broadcast in March 1946, a 15-minute solo spot *At the Piano* from Bristol (he was in the Royal Navy at the time). Has been accompanist to the George Mitchell Choir and the Continental Ballet. Has played with the Palm Court Trio, BBC Midland Light Orchestra 1960-1973, the BBC Midland Radio Orchestra with Norrrie Paramor 1973-1980. In 1961 formed the Harold Rich Quartet, later to become known as the Easy Six, making numerous broadcasts. Programmes include *Friday Night is Music Night, Charlie Chester Show, Breakfast Special, Melody on the Move* and *Rich in Rhythm*. Is also Musical

GOFF RICHARDS
'Always exciting to work with top class performers. . .'
BORN: 18th August 1944, in St.Miniver, Cornwall. Father a builder. EDUCATED: Bodmin Grammar School. Royal College of Music, London. Reading University. Plays piano and trombone. FIRST JOB: Music teacher at Fowey School, Cornwall. Made his first broadcast in 1968 on BBC's *Morning Southwest* from Plymouth. Formed his own band in 1970 and played at the Sinbad Hotel, Malindi, Kenya and the Beach Hotel, Seychelles. Now fronts a 23-piece line-up, the Goff Richards Orchestra and is heard on many of Radio 2's music programmes including the *Jimmy Young Show*, the *David Hamilton Show, Charlie Chester Show, Round Midnight*, the *Late Show*, the *Early Show, You and the Night and the Music*, the *Stuart Hall Show* and *Listen to the Band*.

■ Most exciting moment of career: 'Too many to pick out one. It's always exciting to work with top class performers.' ■ A moment to remember: 'In helping to co-ordinate a "live" Radio 1 broadcast from the Salford College of Technology, it was my task to select suitable students to be interviewed by the DJ Kid Jensen. The principal of the College was naturally keen that the students should give a good account of themselves. The programme was going rather well and the moment for the first interview arrived. After answering several of Kid's questions with great clarity and distinction, the student was finally asked if he wished to send a message to any of his friends. I waited with apprehension. "Yes" said the student, his face beginning to beam at the thought of the whole nation waiting in anticipation. "I'd like to say hello to Nigel Thomas and hope his piles clear up soon." The audience broke into uproar, Kid Jensen for once was speechless and I hastened to make a discreet exit!' ■ Likes cricket, golf, crosswords, collecting wines and travel. Dislikes bad manners. ■ Married to Sue, has two sons, Matthew and Simon, and lives in Cheshire.

music programme on the Light Programme and Radio 2 since his first broadcast in 1957. Is now heard regularly on *String Sound, Round Midnight, You and the Night and the Music* and the weekend *Late Show*. His arrangements are played by all the BBC orchestras.

■ Most exciting moment of career: 'When I was Musical Director for the Thames TV Telethon in 1980, also doing a radio series with Neil Diamond.' ■ A moment to remember: 'Due to a mix-up of studios, we arrived very late for a morning *Music While You Work* being broadcast "live" from the Camden Theatre. The piano was facing down the raked stage. Several minutes into the broadcast, I realised that the piano was slowly rolling down the stage. Wild gestures to the "box" only elicited smiles and "thumbs up" signs from the producer for far, far too long and I was fascinated by watching the microphone rapidly approaching the frame of the piano! The situation was finally saved by three burly studio attendants holding on!' ■ Likes DIY. Dislikes pomposity and bigotry. ■ Married to Regine Launay, has three children and lives in Hertfordshire.

NEIL RICHARDSON
'A way with strings. . .'
BORN: 5th February 1930, in Stourport-on-Severn, Worcestershire. Father a clergyman. EDUCATED: Abberley Hall. Westminster Abbey Choir School. Lancing College. Royal College of Music, London. Plays the piano, clarinet and saxophone. FIRST JOB: Playing with the Chris Curtis Band at the Trocadero Restaurant, London. During National Service played with the RAF Band, Cranwell. Worked as a staff arranger for Chappells, Peter Maurice and Keith Prowse music publishing companies. Is noted for his fine string writing. Is a regular conductor of the strings of the BBC Radio Orchestra, but also fronts his own line-up of strings, brass and singers and has been heard on just about every

ROY SAINSBURY
'Trio augmented by the bass player's watch. . .'
BORN: 12th April 1942, in Birmingham. Father a legal executive and semi-pro bandleader. EDUCATED: Cotham Grammar School, Bristol. Took guitar lessons from Bristol guitarist, Jack Toogood. Plays electric and acoustic guitar. FIRST JOB: Playing with the Palais Band at the Locarno, Bristol in 1969, although he had been playing as a semi-pro several years prior to that. Made his first broadcast in 1973. Has played with the Midland Radio Orchestra, New Millionaires Orchestra, Midland All Stars Big Band and many small groups. Has his own trio and is heard on many of Radio 2's music programmes including the *Breakfast Show, Sounds of the Sun, Band Parade, Round*

Midnight and the *Early Show*. Is also heard as solo guitar accompaniment to vocalist Jane Christie.

■ A moment to remember: 'On a recent session with my trio we were recording a quiet number when the alarm suddenly sounded on the bass player's electronic watch. In the quiet of the studio it sounded more like a fire engine, but despite the three of us being struck with mirth, we somehow kept playing and completed the "take" which was subsequently broadcast, chimes and all!'
■ Likes swimming. ■ Married to Sylvia, has three children and lives in Shropshire..

MIKE SAMMES
'On stage with Judy Garland...'

BORN: 19th February in Reigate, Surrey. Father a photographic dealer. EDUCATED: Reigate Grammar School. Plays the piano and cello (which he played in the school orchestra!) FIRST JOB: In the professional department of Chappells music publishing co. under Teddy Holmes. His first professional performing job was with the top of the bill, on stage at the London Palladium! Has always fronted his own vocal group, The Mike Sammes Singers. Has had his own programme *Sammes Songs* on Radio 2 and has been heard on just about every musical programme going on the Light Programme followed by Radio 2. Is heard regularly on such Radio 2 programmes as *You and the Night and the Music* and any 'Special' that requires a vocal group.

■ Most exciting moment of career: 'Being on stage at the London Palladium with Judy Garland and to actually *feel* the electricity in the air and experience the tidal wave of emotion and affection that stopped her in her tracks when she made her first entrance. And

the day I was talking to Bob Farnon on the 'phone about something we were shortly to be doing together, when he said "Have you heard from Gene Peurling?" (the genius behind and the founder member of both the Hi-Lo's and Singers Unlimited) "Er, no", I said. "Why?" "Oh he's a great fan of yours. We exchange letters a couple of times a year and he always says; "What's Mike doing?" – I thought he was a friend of yours!" Astonished that he'd even heard of us, I remember commenting that if nothing else happened in the ensuing 364 days, it had been a pretty good year!' ■ A moment to remember: 'The night we tried to get a circus atmosphere into an Easter programme in the middle of Clapham Common. The bandstand was between where the animals go into and out of the ring, and we wound up just in front of it to one side on a little box about 4 feet square. All went surprisingly well 'till about half way through the show when I suddenly felt something like a king-size flexible hose probing about between my legs and looked around to see quite a large piece of my music about to disappear down the throat of a waiting elephant, bored with nothing to do and obviously peckish. I took a lunge at it, but noting the size of the beast, discretion took over and I'm afraid we found the next half chorus or so pretty hard to sing. Mercifully he'd chosen a piece we had already recorded, but the tears were streaming down our faces. To see this hulk cheerfully munching one bit of yer Best End of Irving Berlin was just hysterical. Then the lady in charge came round afterwards to collect the music. I told her it wasn't lost and I knew exactly where it was (give or take an elephant or two), but she was not amused and oddly enough we were never invited back again. This caused me no great grief, but I must confess it did put me off dialling trunk calls for quite a while afterwards.' ■ Likes pottering about in the garden and writing songs. ■ Lives in Surrey.

JOAN SAVAGE
'From the flying trapeze to Friday Night is Music Night...'

BORN: Blackpool. Father a comedian FIRST JOB: Singing and dancing in Tower Children's Revue in Blackpool at the age of twelve. Has also earned her living riding elephants and hanging upside-down on a trapeze. Made her first broadcast when she was fifteen in a 'live' series of the *Ken Platt Show*. Has sung with the BBC Concert, BBC Radio and Northern Dance Orchestras, Max Harris, Gordon Langford, Max Jaffa, Geoff Love, Billy Ternent, Jack Parnell,

Eric Robinson, Alyn Ainsworth, Dutch Metropole and Radio Orchestras, BRT Belgium, WDR Radio Orchestra, Bert Rhodes Band, Harry Rabinowitz and the Johnny Wiltshire Sound. Programmes include *Sweet and Savage*, Frankie Howard series, *Magic of the Musicals*, *The Pleasure of Your Company*, *Among Your Souvenirs*, *Charlie Chester Show*, *Round Midnight*. She is heard regularly on *Friday Night is Music Night* on Radio 2.

■ Most exciting moment of career: 'Appearing before members of the Royal Family and appearing in the BBC's winning entry in the 1974 Nordring Radio Prize, which won all the awards.' ■ Likes watching old movies and watching other performers. Dislikes learning words and script. ■ Married to Brian Offen, has one child and lives in Middlesex.

BRENDA SCOTT
'Writes jingles...'
BORN: 19th October 1940, in Thornaby-on-Tees, Cleveland. Father a welder in a steel company. EDUCATED: Robert Atkinson School, Thornaby. Some tuition in voice control as contralto. FIRST JOB: Window dressing in the daytime and singing with local orchestras at night. Made her first broadcast on *Roundabouts* on 19th September 1967. Has broadcast regularly with the BBC Midland Radio Orchestra, the Scottish Radio Orchestra, the Northern Dance Orchestra, The BBC Radio

Orchestra, the Johnny Patrick Orchestra and the Colin Crab Sextet. Is heard on many of Radio 2's music programmes including the *Jimmy Young Show, Charlie Chester Show*, the *John Dunn Show*, and *You and the Night and the Music*. Also writes lyrics and jingles for radio and television.

■ Most exciting moment of career: 'Doing "live" performances with Roger Moffatt on the *Late Show*.' [I hope everyone knows what you mean Brenda!] ■ Likes art, crochet, gardening in pots and cooking. Dislikes taped music in shops or anywhere. ■ Married to John Patrick, the conductor/composer/arranger and has two sons.

BETTY SMITH
'Melody Maker headline ... Betty Smith cracks U.S. charts...'
BORN: 6th July 1933, in Sileby, Nr; Leicester. Father a publican. EDUCATED: Stoneygate College, Leicester. Plays piano, tenor saxophone and clarinet. FIRST JOB: Singing and playing with Archie's Juvenile Band. Has sung and played with Billy Penrose Quartet, Freddie Randall Band, and fronts her own line-up, The Betty Smith Quintet. Made her first broadcast as a singer at the age of 15 and has made numerous broadcasts over the years with a variety of bands. Did a regular Saturday series featured with the Ted Heath Band and has been featured vocalist and instrumentalist with John Dankworth, Ken Macintosh and Sid Phillips. Did several American tours with Bill Haley. Programmes include *Saturday Club* as the resident Quintet, *Jazz Club, Workers Playtime, Mid-day Music Hall, Variety Band Box*, and *Radio 2 Ballroom*. As well as playing with her own Quintet she plays in The Best of British Jazz along with Jack Parnell, Kenny Baker, Don Lusher and Tony Lee. Also plays in a band fronted by her husband, bass player Jack Peberdy. Is heard regularly on Radio 2's *You and the Night and the Music, Music All the*

Way, Music While You Work and the *Early Show.*

■ Most exciting moment of career: 'Playing with Bobby Hackett on Dutch Television; and being told by Ted Heath that my record of *Bewitched, Bothered and Bewildered* had made the American charts, the first time an instrumental had made them for years. The headline in the "Melody Maker" that week read . . . "Betty Smith cracks American Charts!"' ■ A moment to remember: I was doing a *Workers Playtime* when Bill Gates was the producer and he always liked us to announce our own numbers. So after the first song, I say "Thank you very much ladies and gentlemen and now I'd like to play for you. . ." My mind went a complete blank – I tried again – "Now I'm going to play. . ." looking around frantically for help from some quarter. Bill Gates rushed on and said "I think she wants to play *Over the Rainbow*. On every broadcast after that I always wrote the titles of my songs on my hand in biro!' ■ Likes drinking. Dislikes smoking. ■ Married to Jack Peberdy and lives in London.

PETE SMITH
'Heaven forbid M.W.Y.W. should ever go "live" again. . .'

BORN: 28th July 1937, in London. Father an artist/designer. EDUCATED: Westminster City School. Royal College of Music, London. Plays trombone and piano. FIRST JOB: Trombonist with the Denny Boyce Orchestra at the Lyceum in 1958. Made his first broadcast in December 1958 on *Music While You Work*. Has played with Bill Collins, Johnnie Gray, Cyril Stapleton, Johnny Howard and the Nelson's Column Big Band. Is a freelance session musician who does a lot of writing and arranging especially for the BBC Radio Orchestra/Radio Big Band, Also fronts his own group Seminar which is heard regularly on Radio 2's *You and the Night and the Music, Night Owls* and *Music While You Work.*

■ Most exciting moment of career: 'Recording the *"Bones Galore"* album in 1969.' *'Music While You Work* has returned – heaven forbid it should ever go "live" again!'. ■ Likes playing football and squash. Dislikes bad pop groups (of which there are many). ■ Married to Eileen, has two children and lives in Kent.

ROSEMARY SQUIRES
'Singing with that delightful West Country burr. . .'

BORN: 7th December 1928, in Bristol. Father a Civil Servant. EDUCATED: St. Edmund's Girls School, Salisbury, Wiltshire. Took piano and guitar lessons. Her mother's family were all musicians or singers and early training in correct breathing technique came from here. FIRST JOB: Singing and dancing in a concert party after school that played army and airforce camps in the Salisbury area in 1941 at the age of 13. Worked as an assistant in an antique bookshop at 14; in an office at 15. Made her first broadcast in *Children's Hour* from Bristol at the age of 12. Sang with various American groups on army bases during the war and the Polish Military band 1946-48. Has also sung with the Blue Rockets, Tommy Sampson Ted Heath, Geraldo, Joe Loss, Cyril Stapleton, Eric Winstone, Eddie Thompson Trio, Alan Clare Trio, Max Harris and Kenny Baker. Broadcasts regularly with the BBC Radio Orchestra/Radio Big Band, and is heard on most of Radio 2's music programmes including *Big Band Special, You and the Night and the Music,* the *Late Show* and the daytime DJ shows. As Rosemary has been broadcasting regularly since the 40s, it would be well nigh impossible to list her radio credits. Sufficient to say she has had her own radio series on numerous occasions and has sung and worked with just about everybody who is anybody and is undoubtedly one of the most popular singers on radio, singing as she does with that delightful West Country burr which she has never lost.

■ Most exciting moment of career: 'Singing at the BBC Festival of Jazz at the Royal Albert Hall with the Alan Clare Trio. A tingling atmosphere as I stepped from a blacked-out rostrum into a white spotlight and a hushed audience. Then the magical sound of applause afterwards. (Not terrifically exciting but it's as I felt at the time.)' ■ A moment to remember: '*Workers Playtime* often produced the unexpected, because the factories chosen often lay off the beaten track. One in particular was a secret rocket base in Yorkshire. So secret in fact that all the road signs had been removed within the last five miles of the base! We had to ask local passers by the way. When we arrived the piano was out of tune, but the workers who were so isolated, gave us a super reception!' ■ Likes old films, psychic matters, reading, dancing, walking, Tibetan culture (she was secretary of Tibet Society of UK from 1972-75). Dislikes smoking, moral cowardice, over amplified pop noise, selfishness, rich foods and fog. ■ Lives in Kent.

DANNY STREET
'*One of the busiest singers...*'
BORN: 22nd April 1941, in Stirling, Scotland. Father a master butcher. EDUCATED: Stirling High School. As a tenor sang in Logie Church Choir. Studied Stage Craft and Singing for six years. FIRST JOB: Also his first broadcast, singing on *Come Thursday* on BBC Radio from Dundee. Sang with the Jack Carter Band in Castle Richmond for a year before moving to London in 1963. Spent the next seven years as vocalist with the Johnny Howard Band. Broadcasts regularly with the BBC Radio Orchestra/Radio Big Band and is one of the country's busiest session singers. Is heard on most of Radio 2's music programmes including *Big Band Special, String Sound, You and the Night and the Music,* the weekend *Late Shows,* the weekend *Early Shows* and the daytime DJ shows.

■ Most exciting moment of career: 'My own

half-hour show with the Scottish Radio Orchestra on BBC Television in Scotland. Also representing the BBC at the Nordring Radio Festival in Jersey in 1981.' ■ Likes golf and good wine. Dislikes beer. ■ Married to Helenor, has three children and three boxers and lives in London.

IAIN SUTHERLAND
'*Conducting the first public concert at the Barbican...*'
BORN: 1936 in Glasgow. Studied violin at the Royal Scottish Academy of Music, gaining his Performer's Diploma. During National Service he was Leader of the Grenadier Guards Orchestra. He then became an orchestral and session player with the major London Orchestras. He made his first broadcast with his own orchestra on *Morning Melody* in 1964. In 1966 was appointed conductor of the BBC Scottish Radio Orchestra. Moved to London as a freelance conductor in 1972 and regularly conducts the BBC Concert Orchestra. Has made many appearances at the Royal Festival Hall in the BBC International Festival of Light Music and also conducted the BBC's 60th Anniversary Concert there. Conducted the BBC Concert Orchestra in the first public concert at the new Barbican Centre. Is heard regularly on such Radio 2 programmes as *Friday Night is Music Night* and *Melodies for You,* and as a guest conductor on Radio 3. He is Vice President of the Television and Radio Industries Club; a Councillor of the British Academy of Songwriters, Composers and Authors; Patron of the Young Persons Concert Foundation and a member of the BBC Central Music Advisory Committee.

■ Most exciting moment of career: 'Conducting the BBC Concert Orchestra at the first public concert at the Barbican Centre; and making my debut with the Philharmonia Orchestra at the Royal Festival Hall.' ■ A moment to remember: 'While conducting the BBC Northern Ireland Orchestra during the early

70s, a freelance guitarist was booked for the afternoon recording session. Although his wife was expecting him home for supper, Billy and I went for a quick drink in the BBC Club. One drink led to another and we were the last to leave. Billy decided he would walk the fifteen minutes or so to his home and by way of a peace offering to his wife, bought a large bottle of vodka to take with him. I didn't hear about his hilarious if frightening trip until some time later. After leaving the club, guitar case clutched in one hand and the vodka in a brown paper bag in the other, he had hardly gone a hundred yards through Belfast's dark curfewed streets, before he found himself spreadeagled against a wall, in a blaze of light, stuttering out his explanation of what was in the brown paper bag to the security forces sergeant. Being of a generous disposition Billy was soon handing around his peace offering to the appreciative Tommies, who having warned him to waste no time in getting home, disappeared into the darkness. The mere idea of such a thing as a field telephone never crossed his mind until he had been stopped, questioned and joined in a kerbside toast no fewer than three times, when even his befuddled brain registered the fact that the patrols seemed a bit heavy that night. As might be expected, when he explained to his wife about the visiting conductor and how he'd been stopped three times by the army, the bottle of vodka was produced from it's bag—empty!' ■ Likes history, current affairs, sport (golf, soccer and rugby). Dislikes trendy philistines. ■ Married to Barbara and lives in Hertfordshire.

Fife and Drum Band. Studied theory of music at Sydney Conservatorium of Music and harmony with Australian composer Ray Hanson. Had private clarinet and saxophone lessons. Plays flutes, clarinet and alto and soprano saxophones. FIRST JOB: Playing with a trio for weddings and parties. Made his first broadcast for ABC in Sydney in 1960 on the *Spike Milligan Show*. His first broadcast in the UK was in 1964 when he played with the Johnnie Spence Band on the *Tommy Steele Show*. Has played with Nelson Riddle, Lalo Schifrin, Henry Mancini, Michel Le Grand, Count Basie, David Rose, Quincy Jones, Burt Bacharach, Jack Parnell, Don Sebesky, Duncan Lamont, Ted Heath, the London Symphony Orchestra and the Royal Philharmonic Orchestra. With his own group, Ray Swinfield's Argenta Ora, he is heard regularly on such programmes as *Sounds of Jazz, Night Owls, You and the Night and the Music* and Pete Murray's *Late Show*. Ray's own composition *The Sydney Suite* was broadcast on *Sounds of Jazz* and is included on a highly acclaimed album by the group called The Winged Cliff. They have made two LP's, the first, *Rain Curtain* was released in 1981.

■ Most exciting moment of career: 'Tomorrow!' ■ A moment to remember: 'On the *Spike Milligan Show*, which was my first broadcast in Sydney, Spike wasn't there when we were due to start rehearsing. He was discovered much later asleep under a loose carpet in a room adjacent to the studio. People had been walking through, but no notice had been taken of the lump under the carpet.'
■ Likes music, drinking and girls (Ret.). Dislikes vacuum cleaners and people who speak while eating apples. ■ Married to Rosemarie (Head of Make-up at RADA), has one daughter, Caroline, and lives in Surrey.

RAY SWINFIELD
'An Australian import who plays the best jazz flute around. . .'
BORN: 14th December 1939, in Sydney, Australia. Father a garage forecourt attendant. EDUCATED: Mortlake Primary School. Homebush Boys High School, Sydney. Started on fife at school and played in the Boys Club

GEOFF TAYLOR
'New Faces winner. . .'
BORN: 2nd March 1948 in Ilford Essex. Father a maintenance manager. EDUCATED: William

Morris Technical College. FIRST JOB: Lead singer with a vocal group at the age of 15. Made his first broadcast on the Joe Henderson Show in October 1974. In 1975 won television's *New Faces* and was given a recording contract. Has toured the world in cabaret appearing in Australia, South Africa and many European countries. Has also done several troop tours for BFBS. Has sung with Nat Temple, Chris Allen and Ray Davies. Is heard regularly on many of Radio 2's music programmes including the *Gloria Hunniford Show* and *You and the Night and the Music.*

■ Most exciting moment of career: 'My first broadcast'. ■ Likes walking in the country. ■ Lives in Essex.

BRYDEN THOMSON
'A moment of stunned embarrassment. . .'

Father a welder. EDUCATED: Ayr Academy. Royal Scottish Academy of Music. Mozarteum: Staatliche Hochschule fur Musik, Hamburg. Plays the piano and cello. FIRST JOB: Teaching music in schools. Has also taught at the McMaster University Ontario. Has been Assistant Conductor BBC Scottish Orchestra; Principal Conductor of the BBC Philharmonic when it was the BBC Northern Symphony Orchestra and Principal Conductor of the BBC Welsh Symphony Orchestra. Is now the Music Director of the Ulster Symphony Orchestra; the Chief Guest Conductor of the BBC Welsh Symphony Orchestra and the Conductor Elect of the RTE Symphony Orchestra.

■ Most exciting moment of career: 'When I had a hole in one playing golf!' ■ A moment to remember: 'The stunned embarrassment I showed when the cymbal player, at the climax of the *Sorcerer's Apprentice*, crashed in too soon. This was during a "live" performance and one of the first concerts I ever conducted.' ■ Likes golf and gardening. Dislikes the lack of honesty and integrity. ■ Lives in Eire.

MARIE TOLAND
'Forty pounds down the drain. . .'

BORN: Newcastle upon Tyne. EDUCATED: Kenton Comprehensive School. South East Northumberland Technical College. FIRST JOB: Singing with the Don Smith Band at the Oxford Galleries Newcastle upon Tyne. 'I had always wanted to be an actress and studied acting and drama from the age of 8. I also took a Drama Design course at college.' Has played at the People's Theatre Newcastle upon Tyne. Made her first broadcast on Metro Radio. Has fronted her own band Burlesque, and her own vocal groups, the Berkeley Squares and the Chickadees. Has sung with Tommy and Jack Hawkins, Ray McVay, Andy Ross, Ray Davies, Johnny Howard, The Greatest Swing Band in the World (on a Johnny Mathis tour), Stan Reynolds, Monty Babson and the Syd Lawrence Orchestra. Also spent twelve months as a backing vocalist with Freddie Starr ('what an experience!') Is heard regularly on many of Radio 2's music programmes including the *Gloria Hunniford Show* and *You and the Night and the Music,* singing with the Birmingham String Orchestra conducted by Ray Davies and also with the Art Walters Quintet.

■ Most exciting moment of career: 'Touring with Johnny Mathis with my vocal group the Chickadees and ending up with a week at the London Palladium, and appearing at the Royal Festival Hall with Syd Lawrence. Also hearing for the first time the great voices of Sassy, Ella, Sinatra, Bennett and Mark Murphy.'
■ A moment to remember: 'When I went for my audition with Syd Lawrence, I had spent £40 on having my hair permed. I was very nervous, but I thought I looked nice and sang well. When Syd came out of the sound box, his face was white and had a look of horror. He told me I had the job, but my hair was, to put it mildly, awful and I should go and get it straightened! Well, £40 down the drain, but I had a great job with a wonderful band. I never did get it straightened, I waited until it grew out, so I had my £40 worth. As for Syd, I often thought of wearing a shocking pink wig to work, just to

see the little "waster's face"!' ■ Likes cooking, the theatre, jazz, reading and travel. Dislikes prententious people, cold weather and greediness. ■ Lives in London.

coast. ■ Married to Anne, has two children and lives in London.

DICK WALTER
'D.W. Tentette Esq. . .'
BORN: 13th December 1946, in Beckenham, Kent. Father 'something in the City'. EDUCATED: Beckenham and Penge Grammar School. Nottingham University. Studied piano and clarinet as a child and later added saxophone and flute. Paid his dues in writing for big bands by running and writing for the University Jazz Orchestra FIRST JOB: Three hours of questionable activity in an undesirable Nottingham night club. Played lead alto with Maynard Ferguson in 1969, but from then on concentrated on writing and arranging. His first arrangement for the Radio Big Band was *The Fool on the Hill* and was broadcast in 1968. Since the early 70s he's been active mainly as a composer in TV commercials and films, but has always maintained a link with arranging through the Radio Orchestras and two singers in particular, Danny Street and Norma Winstone. His arrangements are heard on many of Radio 2's music programmes, particularly *Big Band Special*.

■ Most exciting moment of career: 'Still waiting.' ■ A moment to remember: 'For a couple of years in the 70s, I ran a band which did occasional broadcasts. As it had ten members and was run by me it was, not unreasonably called the Dick Walter Tentette. Like all such bands, it was made up of freelance stuido players and, if we were lucky, some marvellous jazz players like Kenny Wheeler and John Taylor. For years I'd been listening to records by somebody's sextet, somebody else's nonet and so the name of our band seemed self explanatory. It came as a bit of a surprise after a couple of months to receive an enquiry from a tax office addressed to: "D.W. Tentette Esq. . ."' ■ Likes playing the saxophone and the Suffolk

PAT WHITMORE
'I hear a bird. . .'
BORN: Wolverhampton. Father a steelworker. EDUCATED: St. Bartholomew's School, Penn. Municipal Grammar School, Wolverhampton. Took singing lessons in Wolverhampton and in London studied with Dorothy Robson. Also plays the piano. FIRST JOB: Dental nurse. Has also worked in accountancy. Made her first broadcast in February 1958 for BBC producer John Simmonds. Has sung with the Band of the Welsh Guards, BBC Concert Orchestra, The Royal Philharmonic Orchestra, Bill McGuffie Quartet, Cliff Adams Singers, Mike Sammes Singers, Ambrosian Singers and the Birmingham Symphony Orchestra. Programmes include literally hundreds of varying documentaries for Charles Chilton; *Roundabout, Sam Costa Show, A Year in Song, Grand Hotel, Joe Henderson Show.* Is heard regularly on Radio 2's *Friday Night is Music Night, Melodies for You, String Sound, Among Your Souvenirs,* and *You and the Night and the Music.*

■ Most exciting moment of career: 'Singing under the direction of Elmer Bernstein with the Royal Philharmonic Orchestra, closely followed by meeting Nat King Cole and also appearing in the Nordring Radio Festival in Norway in 1975.' ■ A moment to remember: 'On one occasion I was recording a programme for the army at Colchester. I was singing *How are Things in Glocca Morra,* or at least I was supposed to sing it. The orchestra played the introduction and I started to sing the first line, "I hear a bird", but I had started in the wrong key. I stopped. Intro again, "I hear a bird" wrong key again. A third time the intro and "I hear a bird" and from somewhere in the hall a voice came, "Why don't you ask it to give you the note"!' ■ Likes dressmaking, Brownie/Guiding (as a Guider), my family.

Dislikes violence in any form. ■ Married to John Newman, has two children and lives in Middlesex.

TOMMY WHITTLE
'An exchange with Gerry Mulligan. . .'

BORN: 13th October 1926, in Grangemouth, Stirlingshire. Father a river pilot on the River Forth. EDUCATED: St. Aloysius College, Glasgow. Taught himself to play the clarinet with a few initial lessons from Sammy McLean of Falkirk and, later in London, Aubrey Franks. When a friend loaned him his tenor saxophone, he decided to become a professional musician although his parents thought it would be much safer if he got an office job! Plays all the saxes, clarinets and flutes. FIRST JOB: Playing with the Claude Giddings Band at the Gillingham Pavillion, and the Norman Williams Band in Gillingham. Made his first broadcast with Lew Stone somewhere around 1943. Has played with Johnnie Claes, Lew Stone, Rex Owen, Carl Barriteau, Harry Hayes, Ted Heath, Geraldo, Cyril Stapleton Show Band, Jack Parnell, ATV Orchestra. Fronted his own band at the Dorchester Hotel, London for two and a half years. Was the featured soloist with the BBC Showband and was heard on the Ted Heath broadcasts and *Jazz Club*, the *Arthur Askey Show* and the *Kenneth Williams Show* with his wife Barbara Jay. Fronts his own Quartet and is heard regularly on many of Radio 2's music programmes including *You and the Night and the Music*. His most recent album release, *The Nearness of You*, featuring his Quartet with Barbara Jay.

■ Most exciting moment of career: 'In 1956 I travelled on the *Queen Mary* as a passenger with my Quartet, to New York to play there in an exchange with the Gerry Mulligan Quartet. We were well received and the whole trip was very exciting.' ■ A moment to remember: 'As featured sax soloist with the BBC Showband, Cyril Stapleton would usually have me playing a fast jazz number which he always wanted to

rehearse first, no matter where it came in the programme. Sometimes this would get me down as it would mean playing something frantic at maybe 9am, which I found a bit shattering to the nerves. Then one day my two children had found some keys and locked my tenor case without my knowing. As I never locked it, I never carried the keys with me so on arriving at the Paris Cinema for rehearsal I couldn't open my case and had to phone for the keys to be sent by taxi. But I enjoyed it when Cyril called out *"Lester Leaps In"* as first number – he was foiled and had to rehearse a string number instead!' ■ Likes playing tennis. Dislikes queues. ■ Married to vocalist Barbara Jay (qv), has two sons Martin and Sean and lives in Hertfordshire.

NORMA WINSTONE
'In a class of her own. . .'

BORN: 23rd September 1941, in London. Father a labourer. EDUCATED: Dagenham County High School. Studied piano and organ at the Trinity College of Music, London. FIRST JOB: Clerk in an insurance office. Was also a temporary transport manager for a time when the transport manager dropped dead and his assistant walked out! Made her first broadcast on *Jazz Club* in April 1967. Has sung with the Michael Garrick Sextet, Mike Westbrook Band, John Dankworth Orchestra, Mike Gibbs, Kenny Wheeler Big Band, and Azimuth (with husband John Taylor and Kenny Wheeler). Has recorded one album with the Kenny Wheeler Big Band and three albums with Azimuth. Programmes include *Jazz in Britain* (Radio 3), various co-productions with Dutch and German Radio on Radio 2. Sang on the Dutch entry for the Nordring Radio Festival in 1981 when they won. Broadcasts regularly with the BBC Radio Orchestra/Radio Big Band and is heard on many of Radio 2's music programmes including *Big Band Special* and *You and the Night and the Music*. Has established herself as one of the country's top jazz singers. Has also written the lyrics to many songs.

■A moment to remember: 'My very first broadcast went out at 1.30 on a Sunday morning, I remember I was singing Clifford Brown's *Joy Spring*. The next day my husband had to telephone Carmen McCrea who was in town for a few days, about a recording session. He just happened to mention that I admired her singing very much and wanted to meet her.

"Did you say Norma Winstone?" said Carmen McCrea, "I want to meet her, I heard her on the radio last night." Quite a coincidence that she should have been listening to her radio at 1.30am! It was a great thrill.' ■Likes reading and Indian food. Dislikes meat but isn't a strict vegetarian. ■Married to pianist John Taylor, has two sons and lives in London.

BBC WELSH SYMPHONY ORCHESTRA

The BBC Welsh Symphony Orchestra was founded in 1928 when its first concert was conducted by Sir Henry Wood. The orchestra performs locally, nationally and internationally on both radio and television and takes part in the Henry Wood Promenade Concerts from the Royal Albert Hall.

Chief Conductor: Erich Bergel   *Associate Conductor*: Owain Arwel Hughes

Leader: Desmond Bradley
Associate Leader: Barry Haskey

First Violins
Marion Mattison
Jane Oldham
Simon Weinmann
Sybil Olive
Paul Mann
Joy Kershaw
Gary Veale
Terry Porteus
Claire Carson

Second Violins
Maureen Doig
Richard Newington
Gillian Rutland
Francis Howard
Hilary Minto
Ann Rich
Gillian Weinmann
Elin Edwards
Vicki Ringguth

Violas
Geoffrey York
Jane Gillie
Naomi Gaffney
Martin Smith
Trevor Davies
Sarah Chapman
David McKelvay
Ania Leadbeater

Cellos
John Senter
David Haime
Terence Lonergan
Margaret Bune
John Howard
Jennifer Plenderleith
Jennifer Istance
Adrian Wright

Basses
Michael Wright
Norman Mason
John Bush
William Graham-Wright

Flutes
Douglas Townshend
Roger Armstrong

Oboes
David Cowley
Catherine Senter

Cor Anglais
John Macintyre

Clarinets
Martin Ronchetti
Eileen Newington

Bass Clarinet
Michael Saxton

Bassoons
Robert Codd
Martin Bowen

Contra Bassoon
David Buckland

Horns
Robert Cook
William Haskins
David Lloyd
William Davis
Robert Clayton

Trumpets
Robert Ferriman
Thomas Proctor
Andrew Cuff

Trombones
Daniel Hannaby
Andrew Russell

Bass Trombone
David Smith

Tuba
Nigel Seaman

Timpani
Steven Barnard

Percussion
David Bibby
Christopher Stock

Harp
Valerie Aldrich-Smith

BBC SCOTTISH SYMPHONY ORCHESTRA

The BBC Scottish Symphony Orchestra was founded in 1935, mainly due to the efforts of the BBC's Director of Music in Scotland at the time, Ian Whyte. Its first principal conductor was Guy Warrack, who was succeeded by Ian Whyte in 1946, a position he held until his death in 1960. Christopher Seaman has been the orchestra's principal conductor since 1971. The Orchestra gives many public concerts in Glasgow and appears regularly at the Henry Wood Promenade Concerts in London.

First Violins
Geoffrey Trabichoff (Leader)
Bernardus Buurman (Asst. Leader)
Bernard Docherty
Peter Isaac
peter Jones
Ella Miller
John Hounam

Second Violins
Christopher Latham (Asst. Prin.)
John Scullion
Georgina Mason
Rae Siddall
Caroline Ellis
Diane James
Elizabeth Wallace
Alistair Sorley

Violas
Carolyn Sparey (Principal)
Joy Watson (Asst. Principal)
Alistair Beattie
Charles Ketteringham
Mysie Ann Pelly
Gillian Reid
Patricia Field

Cellos
Anthony Sayer (Principal)
Katrin Eickhorst (Asst. Prin.)
Anthony Calverley (Sub-Principal)
Myra Chahin
Gerald Gifford
Robert Lay

Double Basses
Peter Moore (Principal)
Terence Darke (Asst. Prin.)
Alan Ferguson
Derek Hill

Flutes
Rosemary Eliot (Principal)
Joanne Boddington
George McIlwham

Piccolo
George McIlwham (Principal)

Oboes
Philip Hill (Principal)
Rodney Mount

Cor Anglais
Rodney Mount (Principal)

Clarinets
Geoffrey Haydock (Principal)
Duncan Nairn

Eb Clarinet
Geoffrey Haydock (Principal)

Bass Clarinet
Duncan Nairn (Principal)

Bassoons
Michael Norris (Principal)
Andrew Gordon

Horns
David Flack (Principal)
Shelagh Watson
Maurice Temple (Principal)
Ian Lambert

Trumpets
Nigel Boddice (Principal)
Eric Dunlea
Geoffrey Boult

Trombones
Peter Oram (Principal)
Philip Wheldon

Bass Trombone
Ian Murray (Principal)

Tuba
Anthony Swainson (Principal)

Timpani
Gordon Rigby (Principal)

Percussion
Heather Corbett (Principal)

BBC SYMPHONY ORCHESTRA

The BBC Symphony Orchestra was founded in 1930, with Sir Adrian Boult as the founder conductor. Sir John Pritchard was appointed Chief Conductor in October 1982. The orchestra regularly gives concerts at the Royal Festival Hall and throughout the UK as well as giving 'live' and recorded concerts in the BBC's studios. In addition, it undertakes an overseas tour each year and takes part in the Henry Wood Promenade Concerts at the Royal Albert Hall.

First Violins
Bela Dekany
Rodney Friend
Vivien Dixon
Maurice Brett
Anne Wills
Audrey Brett
Charles Renwick
Russell Dawson
Edwin Dodd
Claire Simpson
John Crawford
Jane Foottit
Ruth Ellis
Regan Crowley
Julian Trafford
Robert Pool
Andrew Price

Second Violins
Jeffrey Wakefield
Trevor Connah
Frances Barlow
Charles Barnes
Anthony Cleveland
Philip Lee
Gwendoline Hill
Anne Ashcroft
Avril MacLennan
Katherine Wilson
Mary Bird
Hanna Gmitruk
Mark Walton

Violas
John Coulling
Graeme Scott
Eric Sargon
Norman Kent
Michael Duffield
Amanda Denley
David Melliard
Barrie Townsend
Philip D'Arcy
Gerald Manning
Timothy Welch

Cellos
Ross Pople
Martin Elmitt
Graham Bradshaw
Richard Eade
Hilary Jones
Janice Brodie
Charles Martin
Peter Esswood
Peter Freyhan
Sara Gilford

Basses
Gerald Brinnen
Godfrey Herman
Juliet Cuningham
Peter Hodges
Patrick Lannigan

Flutes
David Butt
Christine Messiter
Richard Stagg
Patricia Morris

Oboes
John Anderson
David Thomas
Mark Howells
Jane Marshall

Clarinets
Colin Bradbury
Roger Fallows
Donald Watson
Anthony Jennings

Bassoons
Geoffrey Gambold
Graham Sheen
Susan Eastop
John Burness

Horns
Alan Civil
Derek Taylor
Michael Baines
James Handy
Christopher Larkin

Trumpets
William Houghton
Iaan Wilson
Norman Burgess
Andrew Hendrie

Trombones
Christopher Mowat
Anthony Parsons
Tom Winthrope
Richard Tyack

Tuba
James Gourlay

Timpani
John Chimes
David Stirling

Percussion
James Holland
Terence Emery
David Johnson
Kevin Nutty

Harps
John Marson
Elisabeth Fletcher

BBC CONCERT ORCHESTRA

Previously known as the BBC Theatre Orchestra and the BBC Opera Orchestra, the Concert Orchestra took that title in 1952 when its Principal Conductor was Gilbert Vinter. It now has two Principal Conductors, Ashley Lawrence and James Lockyer and is heard regularly on Radio 2's *Friday Night is Music Night* and *Melodies for You.*

First Violins
John Bradbury
Martin Loveday
Vivien Hind
Gwyneth Barkham
Michael Spencer
Robert Cooper
Michael Howson
Philip Gibson
Cynthia Bowes

Second Violins
William Rogers
Nigel Edwards
Clive Hobday
Jayne Ross
Vyvyan Brooks
Peter Lilley
Helen Cooper
Julia Rose

Violas
Stephen Broom
Elizabeth Driscoll
Brian Masters
Angela Bonetti
Cecily Rice
Penelope Thompson

Cellos
Nigel Blomiley
Shelley Gunning
Julia Bradshaw
Martin Bradshaw
Josephine Abbott
Mark Bethel

Double Basses
Clare Tyack
Roderick Dunk
Richard Watson
David Daly

Flutes
Jane Pickles
Robert Dawes

Oboes
Linden Harris
Michael Jeans

Clarinets
Michael Meyerowitz
Kenneth Martin

Bassoons
Gavin McNaughton

Horns
David Lee
Adrian Norris
David Cropper
Alison Orr-Hughes

Trumpets
Robert Nicholas

Trombones
David Thornett
Cliff Jones
Andrew Ross

Timpani & Percussion
Bernard Davis
John Cave

Harp
Andrew Knight

THE BBC PHILHARMONIC ORCHESTRA

During the 20s, in the very early days of the BBC, the Northern Wireless Ensemble was formed in Manchester. In 1934 it became the BBC Northern Orchestra and in 1982, the BBC Philharmonic Orchestra. Still based in Manchester, the orchestra, which broadcasts around 120 concerts a year, has done many foreign tours including a visit to Hong Kong in 1979. Edward Downes has been its Principal Conductor since 1980 and Günther Herbig its Chief Guest Conductor.

First Violins
Dennis Simons (Leader)
Andrew Orton (Asst. Leader)
Tom Bangbala (Principal)
John Resek
Pamela Whitworth
Glenn Janes
Pauline Doig
Janet Fuest
Gordon Gange
Rohi Gazder
Jennifer Ingham

Second Violin
Robert Chasey (Principal)
Cecily Holliday (Asst. Prin.)
Carol Box (Sub-Principal)
Brenda Cropper
David Beck
Julian Gregory
Nigel Jay
Stephen Muth
Glen Perry
Clare Smith
John Wade
Alyson Zuntz

Violas
Janet Fisher (Asst. Prin.)
John Walker-Jones
(Sub-Principal)
Joan Butler
David Brownlow
Vivienne Campbell
Susan Baker
Tricia Howitt
Ruth Parker
Michael Smith

Cellos
David Fletcher (Principal)
John Chillingworth (Asst. Prin.)
Stephen Threlfall (Sub-Prin.)
Timothy Ang
Marilyn Armour
Elizabeth Brierley
Kim Mackrell
Richard Park
Anna Swarbrick

Basses
Jeffrey Box (Principal)
Michael Escreet (Assistant Principal)
Peter Bailey (Sub-Principal)
Ivor Hodgson
Roy McGeoch
Richard Standley
Philip Venters
Peter Willmott

Flutes
Alan Lockwood (Principal)
Janet Bannerman
Anthony Walker

Piccolo
Anthony Walker

Oboes
David Powell (Principal)
Margaret Tindale
Bernard O'Keefe

Cornet
Ian Coull

Trombones
Paul Reynolds (Principal)
Peter Leary

Bass Trombone
Michael Payne

Tuba
Tom Atkinson (Principal)

Timpani
Raymond Lomax (Principal)

Percussion
Paul Patrick (Principal)
Geraint Daniel

Cor Anglais
Bernard O'Keefe

Clarinets
Paul Dintinger (Principal)
Mark Jordan
Keith Deacon

E Flat Clarinet
Mark Jordan

Bass Clarinet
Keith Deacon

Bassoons
David Chatwin (Principal)
Jonathan Holland
William Greenlees

Contra Bassoon
William Greenlees

Horns
Jonathan Goodall (Principal)
Kenneth Monks
Neil Grundy
Mark Brook
David Garbutt

Trumpets
Patrick Addinall (Principal)
Mark Mosley
Ian Coull

THE BBC RADIO ORCHESTRA

The *BBC Radio Orchestra* is the latest in a long line of BBC Light Orchestras that goes back to the London Radio Dance Band directed by Sidney Firman in the Savoy Hill Days. For many years it was known as the BBC Dance Orchestra with such famous MDs as Jack Payne, Henry Hall and Stanley Black. Then came the BBC Show Band with Cyril Stapleton, which was followed by further changes of name to the Variety Orchestra and the Revue Orchestra. The present name came into being in October 1964 and as well as playing as a complete line-up, the BBC Radio Orchestra divides into two halves, the strings and the Radio Big Band. It has no regular conductor as such, but uses a series of guest conductors.

Leader: Michael Tomalin)

Violins
Michael Tomalin (Leader)
Dennis McConnell (Asst. Ldr.)
Jackie Bower (Principal)
Max Teppich (Principal)
Margot Rusmanis
Joan Adams
Patrick Cornford
Robert Chew
Andrew Laing
Stephen Dudley
Michael Hall (Principal)
Sally Brooke-Pike (Principal)
Susan Voss
Ruth Ferguson
Caroline Rutherford
Mark Stratford
Catherine Smart
Stephen Merson
Donald Purnell
Phillippa Ballard

Violas
Dennis Wood (Principal)
Kenneth Hannington (Prin.)
Susan Taylor
Rebbecca Wing
Ian Scott
Ellen Jackson

Celli
Gwenda Milbourn (Principal)
Sylvia Mann (Principal)
June Thompson
Josephine Fitzgerald
Ruth East
Bernard Vocadlo

Basses
Bill Brown
Paul Morgan

Flutes
Tony Arnopp
Judith Havard

Oboe/Cor Anglais
Chris Hooker

Saxophones
Barry Robinson
Gordon Keates
Pete Warner
Nigel Nash
Derek Hyams

Trumpets
Nigel Carter
Brian Rankine
Paul Eshelby
John Thirkell

Trombones
Derrick Tinker
Brian Kershaw
Eddie Lorkin
Tom Cook

Piano

Guitars
Bob Moore
Graham Atha

Drums
Paul Brodie

Percussion
Tim Barry

Harp
Maureen Mulchinock

The author and publisher thank the following for supplying photographs:

Douglas Allen Photography
Dennis Austin
Barnaby's Studios Ltd
BBC News Stills
BBC Photography Library
Alistair A Beattie
Challis Bousfield
Neville Chadwick
Joseph Coomber
Ken Cotton
D B Studios
D C Photos
Paul Deaville Photography
The Decca Record Company Limited
Roger J Delany
Chris Edge
Ron Gazzard
Graham Forbes Gordon
'Great Occasions'
Wilfred Green Photography
Gretchen
Handford Photography
Jack Hickes Photographers Ltd
Humphrey-Saunders Studios Ltd
Jaymar Studios Ltd
Derek Johnston
Dafydd Jones, Sunday Express Magazine
Dennis King
Lloyd Photography
Eric G Lovat
Jo Lustig Ltd
Norman McCann Ltd

Dough McKenzie Photographic Services
Keith McMillan
Hamilton Marshall
Ron Massey
Brian Maynard
Tony Meech
Roger Morton
Tim Motion
Dave Muscroft Photography
Northamptonshire Newspapers
Norwyn Photographic Service
Avinash Patel
David Pearson Photography
Ryan Peregrin
Photo-Petrina
Radio Times
David Rose Studios
John Rose Associates
Raymond Sacks
Scope Features
Sheffield Newspapers
Peter Simpkin
Don Smith
South West Picture Agency Ltd
Pamela Sutton
Symbiosis Recording & Design
Syndication International
Norman Tozer
Universal Pictorial Press
Peter Ventham
Walkerprint
Dennis J Williams